STUDIES IN EVANGELICAL HISTORY AND THOUGHT

Wesley as a Pastoral Theologian

Theological Methodology in John Wesley's
Doctrine of Christian Perfection

STUDIES IN EVANGELICAL HISTORY AND THOUGHT

A full listing of all titles in this series
appears at the close of this book.

STUDIES IN EVANGELICAL HISTORY AND THOUGHT

Wesley as a Pastoral Theologian

Theological Methodology in John Wesley's Doctrine of Christian Perfection

David B. McEwan

Foreword by Herbert B. McGonigle

Copyright © David B. McEwan 2009

First published 2009 by Paternoster

Paternoster is an imprint of Authentic Media
PO Box 6326, Bletchley, Milton Keynes, MK1 9GG

authenticmedia.co.uk

The right of David B. McEwan to be identified as the Author of this Work
has been asserted by him in accordance with the Copyright, Designs
and Patents Act 1988.

All rights reserved. No part of this publication may be reproduced, stored in a retrieval system, or transmitted, in any form or by any means, electronic, mechanical, photocopying, recording or otherwise, without the prior permission of the publisher or a license permitting restricted copying. In the UK such licenses are issued by the Copyright Licensing Agency, Barnard's Inn, 86 Fetter Lane, London, EC4A 1EN

British Library Cataloguing in Publication Data
A catalogue record for this book is available from the British Library

ISBN 978-1-84227-621-1

Typeset by H.F. Griffiths
Printed and bound by Lightning Source

STUDIES IN EVANGELICAL HISTORY AND THOUGHT

Series Preface

The Evangelical movement has been marked by its union of four emphases: on the Bible, on the cross of Christ, on conversion as the entry to the Christian life and on the responsibility of the believer to be active. The present series is designed to publish scholarly studies of any aspect of this movement in Britain or overseas. Its volumes include social analysis as well as exploration of Evangelical ideas. The books in the series consider aspects of the movement shaped by the Evangelical Revival of the eighteenth century, when the impetus to mission began to turn the popular Protestantism of the British Isles and North America into a global phenomenon. The series aims to reap some of the rich harvest of academic research about those who, over the centuries, have believed that they had a gospel to tell to the nations.

STUDIES IN EVANGELICAL HISTORY AND THOUGHT

Series Editors

David Bebbington, Professor of History, University of Stirling, Stirling, Scotland, UK

John H.Y. Briggs, Senior Research Fellow in Ecclesiastical History and Director of the Centre for Baptist History and Heritage, Regent's Park College, Oxford, UK

Timothy Larsen, Professor of Theology, Wheaton College, Illinois, USA

Mark A. Noll, McAnaney Professor of History, University of Notre Dame, Notre Dame, Indiana, USA

Ian M. Randall, Director of Research, Spurgeon's College, London, UK, and Senior Research Fellow at the International Baptist Theological Seminary, Prague, Czech Republic

*To Christine, James and Shona, in grateful thanks
for their unfailing love, support and encouragement
during the research and writing of this book*

Contents

Foreword by Herbert B. McGonigle xiii

Acknowledgements xv

Abbreviations xvii

Chapter 1 – Introduction 1

Chapter 2 – John Wesley and the 'Quadrilateral': An Overview 5
   The Rediscovery of John Wesley as a Theologian 5
      The Work of Albert C. Outler 7
   John Wesley and the 'Quadrilateral' 10
      The Role of the United Methodist Church General Conferences 10
      The Elements of the 'Quadrilateral' 13
         Scripture 13
         Reason 15
         Tradition 16
         Experience 17
   The 'Wesleyan Quadrilateral': The Debate 21
   The 'Wesleyan Quadrilateral' as a Conceptual Model 22
   The Utility of the 'Wesleyan Quadrilateral' in Theologising 27
   Wesley's Understanding of the Role of Theology in the Christian Life 29
      Wesley as a Practising Theologian 32
      John Wesley's Place in the Methodist Movement 33
   Conclusion 35

Chapter 3 – Wesley and his Journey from Oxford 'Methodist' to the Founder of the Methodist Societies. 1725-1739 37

John Wesley in His Eighteenth-Century Setting 38
  The 'Long Eighteenth Century' 38
  The Rise of the Study of Religion... 40
  The Church of England 42
  The Wesley Family Home 44
  An Overview of John Wesley's Spiritual Journey, 1725-1739............... 46
The Rise of Methodism, 1725-1739 48
  Defining a "Good Christian": Wesley's Understanding of the Nature
    of God and Human Beings 50
  Becoming a "Good Christian": Wesley's Understanding of the God-
    Human Relationship 54
    "The Circumcision of the Heart," January 1, 1733................................... 58
    Contact with the Moravians in Georgia, 1735-1737................................. 61
    Contact with the Moravians in London, 1738-1739................................. 64
  Knowing you are a "Good Christian": Wesley's Understanding of
    Assurance 68
Wesley's Theological Methodology: Its Sources, Tools and their
Interrelationship... 74
  Wesley's Understanding Prior to Aldersgate, 1725-1737...................... 75
  Wesley's Theological Method 1725-1737: A Summary 79
  The Founder of the Methodist Societies, 1738-1739.............................. 80
    The Importance of His Aldersgate Experience (May 24, 1738) 80
    The Formation of the Methodist United Societies 84
Conclusion 85

**Chapter 4 – Wesley's Leadership of the Methodist Movement:
The Years of Critical Development, 1740-1769** 90
  Wesley's Spiritual Vision: His Understanding of the Nature of God,
  Human Beings and their Relationship 91
  Wesley's Theological Methodology: Its Sources, Tools and their
  Interrelationship.. 93
    "The true, the scriptural, experimental religion" of the Heart 94
    The Living Voice of God: The Work of the Holy Spirit...................... 101
    The Written Voice of God: The Scriptures... 104
    The Personal Encounter with God: Reason 109
    The Personal Encounter with God: Experience 111
      Doctrine: "Substance" and "Circumstance".. 114
    The Ethos of the Community 115
  The "Substance" of Christian Perfection: Wesley's Doctrinal
  Understanding... 118

> *"Love Excluding Sin"* 122
> *Receivable Now by Faith Alone* 124
> *Instantaneously* 127
> *The Witness of the Spirit to Christian Perfection* 128
>
> Dealing with the Challenges and Objections from His Critics 132
> > *The Nature of Christian Perfection* 133
> > *Is Christian Perfection Attainable in This Life or*
> > *Only at the Point of Death?* 135
>
> The "Circumstance" of Christian Perfection: Wesley's Pastoral
> Understanding 138
> > Seeking the Relationship of Perfect Love 141
> > Entering the Relationship of Perfect Love 144
> > The Assurance of Perfect Love 147
> > Maintaining the Relationship of Perfect Love 148
> > Cautions to Those Professing Christian Perfection 151
>
> Conclusion 155

Chapter 5 – Wesley as the Mature Leader of the Methodist Movement: The Years of Reflection and Consolidation, 1770-1791 160

> Wesley's Spiritual Vision: His Understanding of the Nature of God,
> Human Beings and their Relationship 161
> > The Divine-Human Synergy in Salvation 161
>
> Wesley's Theological Methodology: Its Sources, Tools and
> Their Interrelationship 163
> > "The true, the scriptural, experimental religion" of the heart 164
> > The Personal Encounter with God: The Holy Spirit and the
> > > Scriptures 167
> > The Personal Encounter with God: Reason and Experience 169
> > The Methodist Ethos 172
>
> The "Substance" of Christian Perfection: Wesley's Doctrinal
> Understanding 176
> > Objections Considered 177
> > The Nature of Entire Sanctification Clarified 178
> > The Nature of Christian Perfection Clarified 181
>
> The "Circumstance" of Christian Perfection: Wesley's Pastoral
> Understanding 184
> > The Role of the Methodist Societies 185
> > The Nature of Christian Perfection 191
> > > *The Relationship Between Sin and Infirmities* 193
> > The Experience of Christian Perfection 195

Seeking the Experience of Perfect Love 196
The Assurance of Perfect Love 199
Maintaining the Relationship of Perfect Love 201
Recovering the Relationship of Perfect Love 205
Conclusion 206

Chapter 6 – Conclusions 210
Wesley's Theological Perspective: God and Humans Characterised by Love and Relationships 210
"The true, the scriptural, experimental religions" of the Heart 211
Wesley's Theological Methodology: God and the Means of Grace 212
The Living Voice of God: The Work of the Holy Spirit 213
The Written Voice of God: The Scriptures 213
The Personal Encounter with God: Reason 214
The Ethos of the Faith Community 214
The Personal Encounter with God: Christian Experience 215
Wesley's Theological Methodology: Developing an Effective Model 215
The Wesleyan Quadrilateral as a Model: Its Conception and Utility 215
The Dynamic Neural Network as a Model: Its Conception and Utility 216
Wesley's Theological Method in Pastoral Practice 217
The "Substance" of Christian Perfection 217
The "Circumstance" of Christian Perfection 217
Conclusions 218

Bibliography 221
Primary Sources 221
Secondary Sources 222

General Index 241

Foreword

Starting with the pioneer work of Dr Albert Outler in the 1960s, when he began to investigate the sources behind John Wesley's theology, there has been a growing interest in how Wesley integrated his theological system. This has led to the emergence of what has become known as Wesley's quadrilateral, best represented as SCRIPTURE, tradition, reason and experience. Although this geometric figure has limitations in its usefulness, it does indicate that Wesley read and studied Scripture through the interpretative lens of the other three hermeneutic mediums. Now Dr David McEwan's book focuses attention on Wesley's theological method by analysing his explication of the doctrine of Christian holiness. The choice of this doctrine for examination is well made. Wesley himself declared it was 'the grand depositum' of Methodism and that the movement was raised up by God 'to reform the Church and the nation and to spread scriptural holiness over the land.' Some earlier studies of this doctrine have been landmark works in both biblical and theological analysis, particularly William Sangster's The *Path to Perfection* (1943), and Harald Lindstrom's *Wesley and Sanctification* (1946). Now Dr McEwan's study, working from what he calls 'the Methodist ethos,' looks at Wesley's sanctification teaching in terms of how he used it among his Methodist people.

Among other strengths this investigation has is the way it demonstrates so clearly that above all else, John Wesley was a pastoral, a practical theologian. He cared about how the Christian life was lived and in sixty years of ministry he never wavered in his deep conviction that Christians are both called of God and enabled by God to live lives of 'inner and outer holiness;' viz. holiness of heart and life. It was this conviction that led John Wesley to establish the Methodist Societies and encourage the people to join the class meetings, the band meetings, the love feasts, etc. This book is particularly well researched in the evidence it collects from Wesley's many publications that demonstrates his concern with encouraging the Methodists to live lives of daily holiness and usefulness.

Dr McEwan argues convincingly that John Wesley's pastoral concern for promoting scriptural holiness grew more emphatic as his ministry progressed. While this involved theological constructions and some particular distinctions and definitions that continue to raise serious questions, Wesley's concern was much more than merely advocating propositional arguments. Wesley preached, taught, published, promoted and defended an understanding of Christian holiness that always focussed on our Lord's Great Commandment. 'You shall love the Lord your God with all your heart …and your neighbour as yourself.' I warmly commend Dr McEwan's study for its biblical and theological emphases but particularly for the significant contribution it makes to the current interest in John Wesley's pastoral and practical theology.

Herbert B. McGonigle
Senior Lecturer in Historical Theology and Wesley Studies
Nazarene Theological College
Manchester
England
July 2008

Acknowledgements

I wish to express my thanks and gratitude to a number of people who were instrumental in helping me to research and write this book. My deepest appreciation goes to Professor Philip C. Almond, my thesis supervisor at the University of Queensland. His advice, insight and encouragement have been greatly valued, as he has helped me to think through the research question and explore avenues of investigation that I would otherwise have neglected. Dr. Ed Conrad was the one who first suggested to me that I pursue my doctoral studies at the University of Queensland and has offered me helpful support along the way. My interest in Wesley and Wesley studies really began when I was pastoring the Stockton-on-Tees Church of the Nazarene and Arthur Johnstone, one of the lay members of the congregation, gave me a set of Wesley's *Works* as a gift. Later I was encouraged by several faculty members at Nazarene Theological Seminary in Kansas City, USA and in the years since they have continued to offer support and good advice. In particular, I would like to mention Dr. Paul Bassett, Dr. Alex Deasley and Dr. Rob Staples. My research program was initially shaped by Dr. Randy Maddox (now at Duke University, USA) and then a number of the faculty at Ridley College, Melbourne. In the latter stages I am grateful for the help given by Dr. William J. Abraham (Southern Methodist University, USA), particularly for the personal papers that he made available to me during an important phase of my studies. I wish to acknowledge the help of the librarians at the Sugden Collection, Queen's College, University of Melbourne, the Nazarene Theological College library and the John Rylands library at the University of Manchester in England. The faculty, staff and students of Nazarene Theological College-Brisbane have faithfully offered encouragement during those long days when it all seemed to be more than I could handle. Special thanks are due to Heather Griffiths our college librarian, for she spent many hours tracking down sources for me and prepared the manuscript for submission to the publisher. My thanks also to Rev. Dr. Anthony Cross for his editorial work. I am deeply grateful to Dr. Herbert McGonigle for writing the Foreword to this work.

As ever, the greatest thanks must go to my own family, who have suffered long and patiently during this whole process. I could not possibly have got to this point without the constant love, support and assistance of my wife, Chris.

She has endured many long and lonely hours for my sake, gladly allowing me to spend many weeks overseas, in libraries, and at the office in pursuit of my studies and writing. Our two children, James and Shona, have been equally understanding and supportive. Both of our parents have also contributed greatly by their love and encouragement over the years.

Nazarene Theological College
Brisbane
August 2008

Abbreviations

Letters (Telford)   *The Letters of the Rev. John Wesley.* 8 vols., ed. John Telford. London: Epworth Press, 1931.

Notes (NT)   John Wesley, *Explanatory Notes upon the New Testament.* London: Wesleyan Methodist Book Room, n.d.

Works (Jackson)   *The Works of John Wesley.* 14 vols., 3rd ed., ed. Thomas Jackson. London: Wesleyan Methodist Book Room, 1872. Reprint, Kansas City, MO: Beacon Hill Press of Kansas City, 1979.

Works   *The Bicentennial Edition of the Works of John Wesley.* 35 vols. Projected, ed.-in-Chief, Frank Baker. Nashville, TN: Abingdon Press, 1984-. Vols. 7, 11, 25 and 26 of this edition originally appeared as the *Oxford Edition of the Works of John Wesley.* [Oxford: Clarendon, 1975-1983].

Vols. 1-4: *Sermons I, II, III, and IV,* ed. Albert C. Outler, 1984-1987.

Vol. 7: *A Collection of Hymns for the Use of the People Called Methodists*, eds. Franz Hildebrandt & Oliver Beckerlegge, 1983.

Vol. 9: *The Methodist Societies: History, Nature, and Design*, ed. Rupert E. Davies, 1989.

Vol. 11: *The Appeals to Men of Reason and Religion and Certain Related Open Letters*, ed. Gerald R. Cragg, 1989.

Vol. 18: *Journals and Diaries I, 1735-38*, eds. W. Reginald Ward & Richard P. Heitzenrater, 1988.

Vol. 19: *Journals and Diaries II, 1738-43*, eds. W. Reginald Ward & Richard P. Heitzenrater, 1990.

Vol. 20: *Journals and Diaries III, 1743-54*, eds. W. Reginald Ward & Richard P. Heitzenrater, 1991.

Vol. 21: *Journals and Diaries IV, 1755-65,* eds. W. Reginald Ward & Richard P. Heitzenrater, 1992.

Vol. 22: *Journals and Diaries V, 1765-75,* eds. W. Reginald Ward & Richard P. Heitzenrater, 1993.

Vol. 23: *Journals and Diaries VI, 1776-86,* eds. W. Reginald Ward & Richard P. Heitzenrater, 1995.

Vol. 24: *Journals and Diaries VII, 1787-91,* eds. W. Reginald Ward & Richard P. Heitzenrater, 2003.

Vol. 25: *Letters I, 1729-39,* ed. Frank Baker, 1980.

Vol. 26: *Letters II, 1740-55,* ed. Frank Baker, 1982.

WTJ *Wesleyan Theological Journal*

CHAPTER 1

Introduction

John Wesley (1703-91) was the major founder and leader of the Methodist United Societies in Britain, guiding the movement organisationally, spiritually and theologically. After his death, it became a major Protestant denomination in many parts of the world. Over the years there was very little positive evaluation of Wesley as a theologian by scholars within Methodism itself, let alone those in other church traditions. This began to change in the 1960's and since then many scholars have written about Wesley as a theologian, with a key area of interest being his theological method. The scholar who played a critical role in the resurgence of Wesley studies was Albert C. Outler, who describes Wesley as a folk theologian in order to emphasise that his theology was always focused on aiding the life and ministry of his people. Wesley was a man of action, for whom thinking and living were inseparable – a feature that many characterise as a key element in postmodern theologising. Outler asserts that Wesley had added experience to the Anglican authorities of Scripture, tradition and reason, and the resulting "Wesleyan quadrilateral" was both distinctive and quite possibly unique. If Outler is correct in his evaluation, then Wesley's theological method can make a positive contribution to the current approaches to theologising and is, therefore, worthy of scrutiny. Many Methodist documents and scholarly works (particularly in North America) have claimed that Wesleyans do have a distinctive approach to theologising, even if the exact nature of this distinctiveness is contested. Others claim that Outler's whole enterprise was misguided and should now be relegated to an item of historical interest as it makes no vital theological contribution today.

There are two definite but interrelated issues here: (1) does Wesley have a distinct theological method that has value for today; (2) what then are the constituent elements of this method and how do they interrelate? I hope to demonstrate that his theological method is more highly developed and coherent than has been generally recognised. The focus of much recent investigation has been on the sources individually and they are often studied in isolation from each other and the larger setting of Wesley's pastoral ministry. I believe that the tendency to examine his sources individually, or to treat them apart from Wesley's actual ministry, fails to uncover the way that they are actually utilised in pastoral practice. Furthermore, this failure stems from the tendency to begin with an analysis of the components rather than seeking to understand the theological framework holistically. The aim of this investigation is to discover whether John Wesley had an identifiable, holistic, and distinctive approach to theologising that can be captured by a more appropriate model than the quadrilateral. The initial assumption is that Wesley does have a distinctive theological method, with its utilisation of Scripture, reason, tradition and experience. There is a general agreement amongst many Wesley scholars that the elements identified by Outler are to be found in Wesley's own writings, even if the conception and utility of the model is contested. What is more, the term is still commonly used to refer to the sources in Wesley's theological method and there are many scholars who refer to the four elements in conjunction with each other but do not use the actual term. However, having identified the components still leaves the key issue of how they are interrelated in pastoral practice. Outler stated that no one has been wholly successful in reproducing Wesley's methodology in a contemporary form and using it to address the issues facing the church today.[1] Given that there is a general agreement amongst many Wesley scholars that the elements identified by Outler are to be found in Wesley's own writings, the problem seems to lie with the model that has been developed and/or the way that it is applied. The critical question is whether there is anything in Wesley's writings that might provide a unifying principle for developing a better model than the quadrilateral? This investigation proposes that such a master principle may be found in Wesley's vision of the essential nature of God, human beings and their interrelationship. The implications of this holistic picture may then be seen in his theological methodology, allowing a new model to emerge for consideration. The conceptual value and utility of this new model can then be tested, and it is proposed to do so by examining Wesley's pastoral approach to the doctrine of Christian perfection. Wesley's understanding of Christian perfection makes an excellent case study because it was his most controversial doctrine and very easily misunderstood, both from within and outside his Methodist movement. There will be no attempt to critically examine his doctrinal beliefs as such, because the intention is to use them only for illustrative purposes.

This exploration seeks to reflect a postmodern approach, with its emphasis on personal knowledge and interaction with the community. It is situated primarily in the area of the history of Christian thought and is located in the area of modern Enlightenment Studies. Wesley's personal and ministry context determines much of the shape of his argument and the utilisation of his sources; consequently some attention must be paid to the influences on theology in the eighteenth century (particularly within Wesley's Church of England and Methodist setting) but this is not the focus of the research. The more limited aim is to look at Wesley's actual use of, and interaction between, his theological sources in pastoral ministry, rather than the derivation and nature of

---

[1] Albert C. Outler, "The Wesleyan Quadrilateral-in John Wesley," *WTJ* 20, no. 1 (Spring 1985).

the sources. It is important, therefore, to be aware of the various ways the Wesley materials have been used in the past, both by his supporters and his critics; in many cases his writings have been dealt with in isolation from their original context and this distorts the inferences to be drawn. There is always a danger of imposing a modern systematic grid on Wesley and then abstracting his doctrine from its context, thereby ceasing to examine the life setting as an essential part of seeking to understand his theological method in its pastoral setting. He wrote extensively for almost seventy years and utilised a rich variety of genres for his theological communication. Particular attention will be paid to seeking to identify the key elements in the early, developing and mature stages of his ministry, and noting any significant changes. The majority of the research is centred on Wesley's own writings, with an examination of the relevant and significant secondary sources where they contribute to understanding his pastoral practice. However, many of Wesley's own materials are still not available in a scholarly edition, with less than half of the projected volumes in the Bicentennial Edition of his *Works* published. This means there are critical gaps in the letters, doctrinal and pastoral writings, which has placed limitations on my research and the conclusions drawn.

There is no doubt that the vast majority of Wesley's theological writings are occasional pieces, written in response to questions and criticisms arising from both friends and detractors of the Methodist movement, as well as from his own spiritual journey. This means that on the surface Wesley will often appear to be inconsistent, but is there is a deeper consistency beneath the apparently random nature of his responses? The range of material will be noted and a comparison will be made of his methodology in the sermons, the letters, the journals and diaries, seeking to identify any master principle(s) guiding his work. This includes an assessment of his utilisation of the Methodist society meetings, the preacher's conferences, the liturgy, and his pastoral advice to see if there are any significant developments impacting his methodology. It will be especially important to note the way he uses his sources in the light of the particular people or situations being addressed, trying to discover any variations in approach that would be theologically significant in the development, articulation, and defence of the doctrine of Christian perfection.

Chapter 2 begins with a review of the secondary literature to establish Wesley's credentials as a pastoral theologian and the role of theology in his understanding of Christian life and ministry. Outler's evaluation of Wesley's theological methodology and his suggested conceptual model, the 'Wesleyan Quadrilateral', is investigated (particularly its adoption by Wesleyan theologians in North America), before briefly examining the subsequent debates. It concludes with an analysis of the findings and their implications for this investigation. We then turn in Chapter 3 to a brief overview of Wesley's historical setting in the eighteenth century that will provide the foundation for studying Wesley's life and ministry from 1725 until 1739. The focus of these years is his own spiritual journey and they are identified as the critical foundation years for his pastoral leadership of the Methodist movement from 1740 until his death in 1791. The first step is to examine his understanding of the nature of God, human beings and their interrelationship (his spiritual vision). This sets the framework for an examination of his own spiritual journey and the influence this has on his theological method during this time; the impact of his spiritual experience at Aldersgate in May 1738 is particularly important here. The theoretical framework for the doctrine of Christian perfection is clearly established by the close of this period. Chapter 4 deals with the period from 1740 to 1769 and the critical development years of Wesley's leadership of the Methodist movement. It is apparent that his spiritual vision remains remarkably constant during this time. Wesley's conviction about the central importance of 'heart religion' and its influence on his theological methodology is examined in detail. The sources and tools that he utilises can now be identified more clearly and their interrelationship explored. In this period Wesley distinguished between the 'substance' of a doctrine (its theological definition) and its 'circumstance' (how it is to be experienced in life) and this is critical in his pastoral approach. This material is analysed to identify how in practice he selected and utilised his theological sources in the development, articulation, and defence of the doctrine of Christian perfection. This same approach is followed in Chapter 5 dealing with his mature leadership of his people (1770-91), seeking to uncover any significant variations in his method in these final years. Chapter 6 contains the points for discussion raised by the research and the final conclusions.

I hope to demonstrate that Wesley is best understood as a pastoral theologian, whose concern is with the spiritual formation of his people. His vision of the nature God, human beings and their interrelationship is remarkably consistent over his whole ministry and is centred in love, trust and relationships, rather than the intellectual comprehension of propositional truth about God, humans and the process of salvation. This makes the heart and transforming relationship central to his theologising, rather than logical systems and precise doctrinal statements. The four critical elements (Scripture, reason, tradition and Christian experience) of his theological methodology have been correctly identified by many scholars but not enough attention has been given to the role of the Holy Spirit in the whole process. Wesley believes that it is God himself who is the only source and authority for theologising and he communicates with us through the ministry of the Holy Spirit, who utilises the means given above. The element of mystery is important here, as love and relationships are not reducible to mechanical systems that are purely intellectually comprehended. This demonstrates why the quadrilateral as a model is inadequate due to its static, mechanical and hierarchical nature. There is a need to offer a dynamic model that takes full account of the ever-present ministry of the Holy Spirit within the Church and that is the aim of this exploration.

CHAPTER 2

John Wesley and the 'Quadrilateral': An Overview

In order to examine John Wesley's theological methodology in pastoral practice, two critical points need to be established: that there is a distinctive Wesleyan theological method to be examined, and that his understanding of the role of theology in the life of the Christian community impacts his pastoral use of this method. This chapter is intended to show that there is widespread agreement amongst current Wesleyan scholars, particularly in North America, that Wesley is to be understood primarily as a pastoral theologian and that he did employ a characteristic theological method. Albert Outler's claims regarding Wesley's theological method have received extensive support and there is a broad consensus that he did make use of Scripture, tradition, reason and experience in his theologising. There is much less agreement concerning the nature and interrelationship of the elements, the value of the quadrilateral as a model, its value as a Methodist distinctive and its utility for current theologising.

The chapter begins by briefly reviewing the literature that deals with the rediscovery of John Wesley as a theologian. The major portion of the chapter is centred on Outler's development of the 'Wesleyan Quadrilateral' (Scripture, Reason, Tradition and Experience) as a conceptual scheme to explain Wesley's methodology and how it was subsequently widely adopted by theologians within the United Methodist Church (UMC) in North America. This is followed by a brief examination of the debates that have since arisen over the quadrilateral as a conceptual model and its utility for current practise. Attention is then paid to Wesley as a pastoral theologian, whose primary interest was in the practicalities of the Christian life rather than academic speculation and formal systematic theology. Finally, there is a review of Wesley's place in the modern Methodist movement, before concluding with an evaluation of Outler's position and the implications of these findings for understanding Wesley's theological practice. This sets the stage for my utilisation of Wesley's doctrine of Christian perfection to illustrate the central focus of my research.

The Rediscovery of John Wesley as a Theologian

After John Wesley's death, the Methodist movement became increasingly diverse and fragmented as each new generation faced the challenges of the nineteenth and twentieth centuries and responded to them in varying ways. Randy Maddox describes the move by many Methodist theologians in the nineteenth century towards developing systematic theologies in which they came to rely less and less on Wesley himself since, in their opinion, he failed to address many of the issues required in this type of work. In the early to mid-twentieth century Wesley was usually quoted to support particular theological and mission agendas, with the result that he came to be seen less and less as a real theologian.[1] This negative judgement remained relatively unchanged until the 1960s.[2] However, as early as 1946 there were signs that this evaluation was about to change with the publication of works by William R. Cannon and Harald Lindström.[3] While Cannon admits Wesley was no "systematic theologian," he was not "inconsistent or contradictory in his theological opinions."[4] Maddox judges the 1960 publication of *John Wesley's Theology Today* by Colin Williams as a critical turning point in Methodism's attitude towards Wesley.[5] Further evidence of this change is seen by the agreement to

---

[1] Randy L. Maddox, "Reclaiming an Inheritance: Wesley as Theologian in the History of Methodist Theology," in *Rethinking Wesley's Theology for Contemporary Methodism*, ed. Randy L. Maddox (Nashville, TN: Abingdon Press, 1998), 217-23. For some typical negative evaluations, see V. H. H. Green, *The Young Mr. Wesley: A Study of John Wesley and Oxford* (London: Wyvern Books, 1963), 19; V. H. H. Green, *John Wesley* (London: Thomas Nelson & Sons, 1964), 154-55. See also Ronald A. Knox, *Enthusiasm: A Chapter in the History of Religion with Special Reference to the XVII and XVIII Centuries* (Oxford: Clarendon Press, 1950), 447.

[2] See Maddox, "Reclaiming an Inheritance," 213-16; Thomas A. Langford, "Introduction: A Wesleyan/ Methodist Theological Tradition," in *Doctrine and Theology in the United Methodist Church*, ed. Thomas A. Langford (Nashville, TN: Kingswood Books, 1991), 14; John Chongnahm Cho, "Adam's Fall and God's Grace: John Wesley's Theological Anthropology," *Evangelical Review of Theology* 10, no. 3 (1986): 202; Henry D. Rack, "John Wesley as Theologian," *Epworth Review* 27, no. 1 (2000): 43.

[3] William R. Cannon, *The Theology of John Wesley, with Special Reference to the Doctrine of Justification* (New York: Abingdon Press, 1946); Harald Lindström, *Wesley and Sanctification: A Study in the Doctrine of Salvation* (Wilmore, KY: Francis Asbury Press, 1980; reprint, New York: Abingdon Press, 1946). Other important early works are George Croft Cell, *The Rediscovery of John Wesley* (New York: Henry Holt & Company, 1935; reprint, Lanham, MD: University Press of America, 1983); John L. Peters, *Christian Perfection & American Methodism* (Pierce & Washabaugh, 1956; reprint, Francis Asbury Press, 1985); Maximin Piette, *John Wesley in the Evolution of Protestantism*, trans. J. B. Howard (London: Sheed & Ward, 1937).

[4] Cannon, *Theology of John Wesley*, 7-8.

[5] Maddox, "Reclaiming an Inheritance," 223. Williams identifies the doctrine of sanctification as the key by which to interpret Wesley as a theologian; see Colin W. Williams, *John Wesley's Theology Today: A Study of the Wesleyan Tradition in the Light of Current Theological Dialogue* (Nashville, TN: Abingdon Press, 1960), particularly 5-9 and 201-06.

produce a critical edition of Wesley's writings under the editorship of Frank Baker,[6] as well as the inclusion of a volume on Wesley, written by Albert C. Outler, in the Library of Protestant Thought.[7] Outler was to play a vital role in establishing Wesley as an important theologian for the whole Christian church.[8]

The Work of Albert C. Outler

In the preface to *John Wesley* Outler identifies the common evaluation of Wesley as an "evangelist-reformer" and how this is inadequate.[9] "For Wesley...evangelizing and theologizing were two functions of his single chief endeavor: the effective communication of the gospel."[10] Outler believes Wesley's "chief intellectual interest, and achievement, was in what one could call a folk theology: the Christian message in its fullness and integrity, in 'plain words for plain people.'"[11] This emphasised that "theology, for Wesley, was always to be vindicated in its service to the Christian life."[12] Outler offers this summary of Wesley as a theologian:

---

[6] Frank Baker, ed.-in-Chief, *The Bicentennial Edition of the Works of John Wesley*, 35 vols projected. (Nashville, TN: Abingdon, 1984ff. Volumes 7, 11, 25, and 26 originally appeared as the *Oxford Edition of The Works of John Wesley*. Oxford: Clarendon, 1975-83). Hereafter cited as *Works*.

[7] Albert C. Outler, ed., *John Wesley* (New York: Oxford University Press, 1964). While acknowledging the valuable work of Outler and the significance of this volume, William J. Abraham is one leading Methodist theologian who argues that Wesley is not, in fact, primarily a theologian but a "spiritual father"; see William J. Abraham, "The End of Wesleyan Theology," *WTJ* 40, no. 1 (Spring, 2005): 22-25.

[8] Albert C. Outler, "John Wesley as Theologian-Then and Now," *Methodist History* 12, no. 4 (1974): 65. See also Albert C. Outler, "The Place of Wesley in the Christian Tradition," in *The Place of Wesley in the Christian Tradition: Essays Delivered at Drew University in Celebration of the Commencement of the Publication of the Oxford Edition of the Works of John Wesley*, ed. Kenneth E. Rowe (Metuchen, NJ: Scarecrow Press, 1976), 14; Albert C. Outler, *Theology in the Wesleyan Spirit* (Nashville, TN: Discipleship Resources, 1975); Albert C. Outler, "Towards a Re-Appraisal of John Wesley as a Theologian," in *The Wesleyan Theological Heritage: Essays of Albert C. Outler*, ed. Thomas C. Oden and Leicester R. Longden (Grand Rapids, MI: Zondervan, 1991), 39-54; Outler, ed., *John Wesley*, 119.

[9] William Abraham refers to John Wesley as one of several who "are dismissed summarily from the canon of serious theology simply because they are construed as revivalists or evangelists and therefore necessarily as lightweight scholars." See William J. Abraham, *The Logic of Evangelism* (Grand Rapids, MI: Wm. B. Eerdmans, 1989), 7.

[10] Outler, ed., *John Wesley*, iii.

[11] Ibid. See also Albert C. Outler, "John Wesley's Interests in the Early Fathers of the Church," *Wesleyan Theological Heritage*, 98-100; Albert C. Outler, "John Wesley: Folk Theologian," *Wesleyan Theological Heritage*, 111-24.

[12] Outler, ed., *John Wesley*, iv.

He seems never to have felt the impulse to produce anything resembling a comprehensive exposition of his theological ideas. ... Short doctrinal summaries are scattered throughout his writings, and these give ample evidence that his thought was consciously organized around a stable core of basic coordinated motifs. But there is no extended development of his system, and for the simple reason that there never seemed to be a *practical need* for such a thing.[13]

It is this lack of a systematic presentation that has been the chief cause of other scholars disparaging Wesley as a serious theologian.[14] However, there are many books, articles and dissertations that focus on Wesley's importance in such areas as pastoral theology, spiritual formation, discipleship, holy living, the ecumenical movement, and theological methodology.[15]

In a pioneering article written for the 1972 General Conference of The United Methodist Church, Outler assessed the role of John Wesley as a theologian.[16] He states that Wesley provided much theological and ethical instruction to guide the Methodist movement but he never seemed to have toyed with the idea of a *summa theologiae* or even a catechism. The doctrinal standards of Methodism were to be found in *The Doctrine of Justification according to the Church of England*, the dialogues between Wesley and his preachers (published as *Minutes of Conversations Between the Rev. Mr. Wesley and Others*, 1744 et seq.), and "The Model Deed" (1763). This latter document set the negative limits of Methodist doctrine in that his preachers were to preach nothing than that contained in Wesley's *Notes Upon the New Testament* and his four volumes of *Sermons*.[17] According to Outler,

---

[13] Ibid., 27.

[14] This must not be taken to mean that Wesley had no theological system. Barry Bryant notes that Wesley himself used the term "system of doctrines" several times in his writings: see Barry E. Bryant, "John Wesley's Doctrine of Sin" (PhD thesis, King's College, University of London, 1992), 11. Bryant also notes that theologians such as Cannon, Lindstrom, Cox, Borgen, Deschner, Collins, Clifford and Watson have worked with a similar model.

[15] Maddox, "Reclaiming an Inheritance," 224-26. For an excellent listing of the published work on Wesley as a theologian, see: the selected bibliography in Randy L. Maddox, *Responsible Grace: John Wesley's Practical Theology* (Nashville, TN: Kingswood Books, 1994).; Kenneth J. Collins, *Wesley Bibliography*(Asbury Theological Seminary, 2005, accessed October 7 2005); available from http://www.ats.wilmore.ky.us/news/wesley.htm.

[16] The article first became available to the wider world of scholarship in Albert C. Outler, "The Wesleyan Quadrilateral-in John Wesley," *WTJ* 20, no. 1 (Spring 1985): 7-18. It was reprinted in Albert C. Outler, "The Wesleyan Quadrilateral-in John Wesley," *Doctrine and Theology*, 75-88.

[17] Outler, "The Wesleyan Quadrilateral-in John Wesley," 8. There are either 43 or 44 sermons in the collection depending on how you classify "Wandering Thoughts"; it was not in the first edition of 1760 but was found in subsequent editions issued before 1763.

This provided his people with a doctrinal canon that was stable enough and yet also flexible. In it, the Holy Scriptures stand first and foremost, and yet subject to interpretations that are informed by 'Christian Antiquity', critical reason *and* an existential appeal to the 'Christian experience' of grace, so firmly stressed in the *Explanatory Notes*.[18]

Outler judges that this shows Wesley to be a man clearly interested in a coherent doctrinal standard without being tied down to narrow definitions or too juridical a form. His working concepts of doctrinal authority were complex and dynamically balanced, showing every evidence of being carefully worked out.[19]

... we can see in Wesley a distinctive theological *method*, with Scripture as its pre-eminent norm but interfaced with tradition, reason and Christian experience as dynamic and interactive aids in the interpretation of the Word of God in Scripture. Such a method takes it for granted that faith is human *re*-action to an antecedent action of the Holy Spirit's prevenience, aimed at convicting our consciences and opening our eyes and ears to God's address to us in Scripture. This means that our 'knowledge of God and of the things of God' is more nearly a response of trusting faith in God in Christ as Grace Incarnate than it is a mental assent to dogmatic formulations however true. This helps explain Wesley's studied deprecations of "orthodoxy," "theological opinions," "speculative divinity" and the like. ... And it justified Wesley's willingness, given honest consensus on essential Christian doctrine, to allow for wide variations in theological formulation and thus for Christians "to think and let think." This was less a mood of doctrinal compromise than it was a constructive alternative to the barren extremes of "dogmatism," on the one side, and "indifferentism" on the other.[20]

Outler postulates that Wesley had added "experience" to the Anglican authorities of "Scripture, tradition and reason," bringing about the move from a theoretical faith to an existential one.[21] He concludes that it is this "Wesleyan quadrilateral" which placed the whole question of religious authority into a new context, relating it more closely to the individual's conscience, small-group consensus and linking it practically to the ideal of "accountable discipleship," thus making every Methodist a theologian.[22] He was convinced that Wesley's

---

[18] Ibid.

[19] Ibid.

[20] Ibid., 9.

[21] For the development of the Anglican authorities, see Nigel Atkinson, *Richard Hooker and the Authority of Scripture, Tradition and Reason: Reformed Theologian of the Church of England?* (Carlisle: Paternoster Press, 1997). See also William J. Abraham, "The Wesleyan Quadrilateral," in *Wesleyan Theology Today: A Bicentennial Theological Consultation*, ed. Theodore H. Runyon (Nashville, TN: Kingswood Books, 1985), 120.

[22] Outler, "The Wesleyan Quadrilateral-in John Wesley," 10-11.

theological method was distinctive and quite possibly unique, for he could not identify any of his disciples who adopted it as a whole or in his theological spirit.[23]

John Wesley and the 'Quadrilateral'

As part of the discussions on the merger of the Evangelical United Brethren and the Methodist Church in 1968, a study commission was formed with Outler as Chair to harmonise the differing strands of theological tradition in the two groups and to bring a report to the 1972 General Conference. The report is the first document to refer to the "quadrilateral" (due to Outler's input[24]) and was included in the denomination's 1972 *Book of Discipline*; it is in this context that the debate over the value and utility of the quadrilateral initially arose.[25]

The Role of the United Methodist Church General Conferences

In his introduction to the report Outler dealt with the danger of their doctrinal standards being diminished or lost and he felt confident that they had put in place an adequate safeguard against this:

> We have not altered these standards, as such, but we have proposed *a genuinely new principle for doctrinal self-understanding* in The United Methodist Church. Thus, we have tried to reaffirm our share in the Christian tradition, as a whole, even as we have also tried to accent, once again, *the distinctive Wesleyan guidelines* (Scripture, tradition, experience, reason); and it is these guidelines that we propose to you as our best safeguard against doctrinal indifferentism (emphasis mine)![26]

Outler is sure that this represents a critical development and Ted Campbell verifies that "this fourfold locus of religious authority gained remarkable acceptance as a tool for theological analysis and as a starting point for the recovery of the Wesleyan theological tradition in a modern context."[27] Campbell confirms that Outler was successful in demonstrating that Wesley did

---

[23] Ibid., 11-17.
[24] See Ted A. Campbell, "The 'Wesleyan Quadrilateral': The Story of a Modern Methodist Myth," *Doctrine and Theology*, 155-60; William J. Abraham, *Waking from Doctrinal Amnesia: The Healing of Doctrine in the United Methodist Church* (Nashville, TN: Abingdon Press, 1995), 57-58; Maddox, *Responsible Grace*, 36; Don Thorsen, "*Sola Scriptura* and the Wesleyan Quadrilateral," *WTJ* 41, no. 2 (Fall, 2006): 18-19.
[25] Langford, *Doctrine and Theology*, 19. See also Abraham, *Doctrinal Amnesia*, 31-49.
[26] Albert C. Outler, "Introduction to the Report of the 1968-72 Theological Study Commission," *Doctrine and Theology*, 24.
[27] Campbell, 154.

use these sources "and perhaps even more critically, Outler showed that there are in Wesley certain indications of conceptual patterns which link various ones of these four elements together, and from which a fourfold pattern might be inferred."[28] At the time William J. Abraham went further:

> I have no doubt however that Wesley was committed to the quadrilateral. A careful reading of the standard sermons reveals that Wesley characteristically appealed to Scripture, tradition, reason and experience when he wanted to support or defend his theology. To be sure, Wesley did this in an informal manner, but this is the way he generally works, given the constraints that the sermon form imposed upon him as a writer.[29]

Thomas Langford saw the quadrilateral as being "commonly and enthusiastically endorsed" by the United Methodist Church so that it now becomes a strategic element in the denomination's identity. It was widely agreed that even though the term is not found in Wesley's own writings, it "is generally true to Wesley's intention and mode of theological work."[30]

During the following years a great deal of debate emerged and in 1984 the General Conference established another theological commission to study the theological statements in the *Discipline* and report back at the following Conference in 1988. During these four years the process of analysis and reflection on the quadrilateral intensified, with an increasing number becoming dissatisfied with the formulation in its individual components and overall conception, as well as its actual usability in practice.[31] The end result was that

---

[28] Ibid., 159. Outler had linked the titles of Wesley's two documents to obtain the fourfold pattern: *The Doctrine of Original Sin* (1756) and the preface to his *Works* (1771).

[29] Abraham, "The Wesleyan Quadrilateral," 120. See also William J. Abraham, "On How to Dismantle the Wesleyan Quadrilateral: A Study in the Thought of Albert C. Knudson," *WTJ* 20, no. 1 (Spring, 1985): 35, 42-43 especially; William J. Abraham, "Response: The Perils of a Wesleyan Systematic Theologian," *WTJ* 17, no. 1 (Spring, 1982). This positive evaluation was to change later—see below.

[30] Thomas A. Langford, "The United Methodist Quadrilateral: A Theological Task," *Doctrine and Theology*, 232.

[31] Some of the critical works which reject various aspects or the whole of the quadrilateral are: Abraham, "The Wesleyan Quadrilateral"; Scott J. Jones, *John Wesley's Conception and Use of Scripture* (Nashville, TN: Kingswood Books, 1995); Ted A. Campbell, *John Wesley and Christian Antiquity: Religious Vision and Cultural Change* (Nashville, TN: Kingswood Books, 1991); Schubert M. Ogden, "Doctrinal Standards in the United Methodist Church," *Doctrine and Theology*; Joel B. Green, "Scripture in the Church: Reconstructing the Authority of Scripture for Christian Formation and Mission," in *The Wesleyan Tradition: A Paradigm for Renewal*, ed. Paul W. Chilcote (Nashville, TN: Abingdon Press, 2002); Leroy T. Howe, "United Methodism in Search of Theology," *Doctrine and Theology*; Abraham, "The End of Wesleyan Theology."; Abraham, *Doctrinal Amnesia;* William J. Abraham, "What's

the term itself was dropped from the 1988 *Book of Discipline* and the references where it occurred modified to refer to "theological guidelines."[32] In the eyes of many this did nothing to address their concerns and the debate has continued vigorously to the present day. However, the idea of the quadrilateral remains deeply entrenched within an influential section of UMC theologians and historians, so that its basic formulation continues in the current doctrinal standards.[33] For example, the present *Book of Discipline* states as part of its section on "Our Doctrinal History" that its founders believed that there is a core of Christian truth that can be identified and must be preserved in the midst of religious toleration and theological diversity. "This living core, as they believed, stands revealed in Scripture, illumined by tradition, vivified in personal and corporate experience, and confirmed by reason."[34] In a subsequent section on "Theological Guidelines: Sources and Criteria" the reference to the four elements is linked directly to Wesley and goes on to say:

> The interaction of these sources and criteria in Wesley's own theology furnishes a guide for our continuing theological task as United Methodists. In that task Scripture, as the constitutive witness to the wellsprings of our faith, occupies a place of primary authority among these theological sources.
>
> In practice, theological reflection may also find its point of departure in tradition, experience, or rational analysis. What matters most is that all four guidelines be brought to bear in faithful, serious, theological consideration. Insights arising from serious study of the Scriptures and tradition enrich contemporary experience. Imagination and critical thought enables us to understand better the Bible and our common Christian history.[35]

Right and What's Wrong with the Quadrilateral?" (Unpublished private paper from personal correspondence with Dr. Abraham, n.d.).

[32] Campbell, "The Wesleyan Quadrilateral," 155-58.

[33] A compelling outline of the debate can be seen in various articles written by William J. Abraham and appropriate reference will be made to these in the following section of the chapter. See also n. 73 in Randy L. Maddox, "Respected Founder/Neglected Guide: The Role of Wesley in American Methodist Theology," *Methodist History* 37, no. 2 (1999): 87-88.

[34] United Methodist Church, *The Book of Discipline of the United Methodist Church – 2000* (United Methodist Communications, 2004, accessed), http://umc.org/interior.asp?ptid=1&mid=519.

[35] Ibid. (accessed). See also Ted A. Campbell, *Methodist Doctrine: The Essentials* (Nashville, TN: Abingdon Press, 1999), 35-40; Thomas C. Oden, *Doctrinal Standards in the Wesleyan Tradition* (Grand Rapids, MI: Francis Asbury Press, 1988); Russell E. Richey, Dennis M. Campbell and William B. Lawrence, *Marks of Methodism: Theology in Ecclesial Practice* (Nashville, TN: Abingdon Press, 2005): 13-15; World Methodist Council, "Wesleyan Essentials of Christian Faith," (World Methodist Council, 1996, accessed), http://www.worldmethodistcouncil.org/index.php?option=com_content&task=view&id=22&Itemid=9.

The four sources are then listed and developed separately, with each one containing references to the other three. The closing section under "Reason" summarises their understanding of the process of theological reflection:

> In theological reflection, the resources of tradition, experience, and reason are integral to our study of Scripture without displacing Scripture's primacy for faith and practice. These four sources – each making distinctive contributions, yet all finally working together – guide our quest as United Methodists for a vital and appropriate Christian witness.[36]

The Elements of the 'Quadrilateral'

In a recent article Don Thorsen draws our attention to a point of critical importance to remember when investigating the nature of the quadrilateral:

> Wesley knew that all authority comes from God and that religious authorities with which we function are somehow derivative of God's ultimate authority. Even Scripture only represents a derived or secondary religious authority. Thus, while the focus of so much of this study is on Scripture, tradition, reason, and experience, we must not forget that Christians ultimately look to God alone as their source of religious authority.[37]

Bearing this in mind, we now turn to a brief examination of each of the elements (Scripture, reason, tradition and experience) before considering the continuing debate over the quadrilateral as a conceptual model and its value for theologising today.

SCRIPTURE

There is little dispute that in Wesley's own writings, the Scriptures play a primary role in his theological methodology; this placement was not simply a matter of convenience, but a matter of intense conviction. Scott Jones has given one of the most thorough examinations of Wesley's conception and use of Scripture and he demonstrates Wesley's commitment to the primary authority of Scripture and his consistent use of it as the source and norm for Christian teaching and practice.[38] One of the critical conclusions from his analysis was

---

[36] Church, *2000 Discipline* (accessed). It is of interest that the section on "The Wesleyan 'Standards' in Great Britain" makes no reference to these four "guidelines"; see Church, *2000 Discipline* (accessed).

[37] Thorsen, "*Sola Scriptura*," 20. Thorsen does not develop this point in the article, but it is a salutary reminder of Wesley's emphasis on the essence of Christianity being a personal relationship with God, as we shall see later.

[38] Jones, *Wesley's Use of Scripture*, 32-33, 160. For a list of Wesley's writings that Jones examined, see pp. 224-25. A similar evaluation of Wesley's use of Scripture is given by Donald A. Thorsen, *The Wesleyan Quadrilateral: Scripture, Tradition, Reason*

that Wesley's favourite passages are soteriological – especially those that point to Christian perfection and holiness.[39] Jones shows that Wesley was aware that Scripture cannot be applied simplistically and that in salvation history there is progressive revelation from the Old Testament to the New Testament.[40] Furthermore, this soteriological focus is Wesley's key hermeneutical principle for reading the text.[41] Chuck Gutenson argues that Wesley's life-long immersion in Scripture gave him a perspective that grasped the fundamental nature of the *missio dei*. His focus on "the general tenor of Scripture" emphasised the overarching themes of the biblical narrative (particularly the soteriological ones) and enabled the person to interpret any particular text more faithfully, especially if they were themselves pursuing a holy life and were open to the guidance of the Spirit.[42] However, this was not a simplistic biblicism, for Wesley never limited his theological sources to the Bible alone. Outler tells us that Wesley always interpreted the *solus* in *sola fide* and *sola scriptura* to mean "primarily" rather than "solely" or "exclusively."[43] Schmidt

---

& Experience as a Model of Evangelical Theology (Grand Rapids, MI: Francis Asbury Press, 1990), 72-74; Chuck Gutenson, "Theological Method for a Man of One Book," *Asbury Theological Journal* 59:1 & 2 (Spring/Fall, 2004): 49-61; Outler, ed., *John Wesley*, 28; Abraham, "The Wesleyan Quadrilateral," 120; Richard A. Miller, "Scriptural Authority and Christian Perfection: John Wesley and the Anglican Tradition" (PhD thesis, Drew University, 1991), 182-86; Maddox, *Responsible Grace*, 36-37; Thorsen, "*Sola Scriptura*." All of them make the point that Scripture has a primary but not an exclusive authority for Wesley.

[39] Jones, *Wesley's Use of Scripture*, 155-57. Wesley believed that the Scriptures were "sufficient" in matters of faith and practice—see also R. Larry Shelton, "John Wesley's Approach to Scripture in Historical Perspective," *WTJ* 16, no. 1 (Spring 1981): 38-39; A. Skevington Wood, *The Burning Heart: John Wesley, Evangelist* (London: Paternoster Press, 1967), 210; Williams, *Wesley's Theology Today*, 23-25; Martin Schmidt, *John Wesley: A Theological Biography*, trans. Dennis Inman, vol. II.2: *John Wesley's Life Mission* (London: Epworth Press, 1973), 67; Duncan S. Ferguson, "John Wesley on Scripture: The Hermeneutics of Pietism," *Methodist History* 22, no. 4 (1984): 239-40; Robert W. Burtner and Robert E. Chiles, eds., *A Compend of Wesley's Theology* (New York: Abingdon Press, 1954), 17.

[40] This is of special importance for the doctrine of Christian perfection because many objections were raised against it using Old Testament examples; see Jones, *Wesley's Use of Scripture*, 150-58.

[41] See Shelton, "Wesley's Approach to Scripture," 38-39; Wood, *The Burning Heart*, 210; Williams, *Wesley's Theology Today*, 23-25; Schmidt, *Wesley's Life Mission 2*, 67; Ferguson, "Wesley on Scripture," 239-40; Burtner and Chiles, eds., *A Compend of Wesley's Theology*, 17.

[42] Gutenson, "Theological Method for a Man of One Book," 60-61.

[43] Outler, ed., *John Wesley*, 28. See also Jones, *Wesley's Use of Scripture*, 32-33; Thorsen, *The Wesleyan Quadrilateral*, 72-74; Martin Schmidt, *John Wesley: A Theological Biography*, trans. Norman P. Goldhawk, vol. II.1: John Wesley's Life

verifies Outler's understanding:

> [Wesley] was quite clear about two things: first, that the biblical message could not be isolated or applied to the present situation merely by private and personal study of the printed word; and second, that it required a dialogue with the cultural consciousness of the time to become living, ... He would not tolerate a primitive, mechanical biblicism. Consequently he strongly opposed the high-sounding claim that a man might be exclusively concerned with the study of the Bible; he recognized this as rank enthusiasm.[44]

REASON

The Enlightenment saw an increasing confidence in the powers of human reason as a source of knowledge.[45] Many of the scholarly debates of the eighteenth century were over the relationship between revelation and reason and Wesley shared this essential concern. Rebekah Miles maintains that Wesley had to tread a fine line between undervaluing or overvaluing reason; the former led to charges of enthusiasm and the latter undercut the primacy of Scripture.[46] Her analysis of Wesley's material leads her to conclude that he rejected reason as an independent source of knowledge in favour of all knowledge coming from experience that reason then processes. Unlike Scripture, tradition and experience which are all sources from which to draw data, reason is a tool that processes this data.[47] Even as a tool it is always liable to distortion and deceit due to sin. An individual's reasoning must always be subject to dialogue with

---

Mission (New York: Abingdon Press, 1972), 111; Miller, "Scriptural Authority," 182-86; Maddox, *Responsible Grace*, 36-37; Thorsen, "*Sola Scriptura*".

[44] Schmidt, *Wesley's Life Mission 1*, 111. See also Thorsen, *The Wesleyan Quadrilateral*, 127-45; Langford, "United Methodist Quadrilateral," 239-43; David H. Tripp, "'Observe the Gradation!' John Wesley's Notes on the New Testament," *Quarterly Review* 10, no. 2 (1990).

[45] See for example: Anthony Armstrong, *The Church of England, the Methodists and Society 1700-1850* (London: University of London Press, 1973); Gordon Rupp, *Religion in England, 1688-1791* (Oxford: Clarendon Press, 1986); J. C. D. Clark, *English Society, 1660-1832: Religion, Ideology and Politics During the Ancien Regime*, 2nd ed. (Cambridge: Cambridge University Press, 2000); Roy Porter, *The Creation of the Modern World: The Untold Story of the British Enlightenment* (New York: W. W. Norton & Company, 2000).

[46] Rebekah L. Miles, "The Instrumental Role of Reason," in *Wesley and the Quadrilateral: Renewing the Conversation*, ed. W. Stephen Gunter et al. (Nashville, TN: Abingdon Press, 1997), 79-81. See also Maddox, *Responsible Grace*, 40; Miller, "Scriptural Authority," 182.

[47] Miles, "The Instrumental Role of Reason," 77-85. See also Isabel Rivers, *Reason, Grace, and Sentiment: A Study of the Language of Religion and Ethics in England 1660-1780*, vol. 1, *Whichcote to Wesley* (Cambridge: Cambridge University Press, 1991), 233; Miller, "Scriptural Authority," 186-209; Williams, *Wesley's Theology Today*, 32.

other Christians in conference, since its claims have to be publicly defensible.[48] Miles claims that while Wesley clearly employs the Aristotelian position that was dominant at Oxford, he was also open to some of the influences of Cambridge Platonism. This is seen particularly in his understanding of "spiritual senses" that complement our "natural senses" and make us aware of spiritual realities. This comes very close to the Platonic view of innate ideas and it had the potential to leave Wesley open to charges of enthusiasm.[49] He was careful to ensure that his readers understood that his confidence was not in natural human reason alone – the ministry of the Holy Spirit to assist and enlighten it was essential. That is why he had such a strong insistence on the primary authority of Scripture by which these "inward impressions" must be tested.[50] "Wesley is claiming an epistemological privilege for the Christian. Both Scripture and the Holy Spirit, as sources of correct information about spiritual things, can enlighten the mind so that it can reason correctly in these areas."[51] Jones concludes that Wesley usually couples "Scripture and reason"; it is far more common than Scripture with either tradition or experience.[52] Furthermore, "reason served as a reliable mediating force between Scripture and tradition and as a creative force in addressing issues neither commanded nor forbidden by Scripture and tradition. Therefore reason contributed to matters that could be decided in the church by the mutual agreement of the members."[53]

TRADITION

Laurence Wood proposes that Wesley was willing to give a place in his theological methodology to historical tradition at a time when many scholars were regarding it with increasing scepticism. They regarded the tradition of the church as lacking in any authority for the present age and held that truth had to be established by reason alone.[54] The landmark work by Campbell verifies that studies of early Christianity (especially the church of the first three centuries) were very important in the late seventeenth and early eighteenth centuries,

---

[48] Miles, "The Instrumental Role of Reason," 94-103. See also Miller, "Scriptural Authority," 209; Jones, *Wesley's Use of Scripture*, 66-67.

[49] Miles, "The Instrumental Role of Reason," 88-91. See also Maddox, *Responsible Grace*, 27. Maddox notes the importance of John Locke's *Essay on Human Understanding* and Peter Browne's *The Procedure, Extent, and Limits of Human Understanding* for Wesley. On the "spiritual senses," see W. Stephen Gunter, "Personal and Spiritual Knowledge: Kindred Spirits in Polanyian and Wesleyan Epistemology," *WTJ* 35, no. 1 (Spring, 2000).

[50] See Maddox, *Responsible Grace*, 31-32.

[51] Jones, *Wesley's Use of Scripture*, 169. See also Maddox, Responsible Grace, 40-41.

[52] Jones, *Wesley's Use of Scripture*, 164-67.

[53] Thorsen, *The Wesleyan Quadrilateral*, 124. See also Jones, *Wesley's Use of Scripture*, 77-78; Laurence W. Wood, "Wesley's Epistemology," *WTJ* 10, no. 1 (Spring 1975): 54.

[54] Wood, "Wesley's Epistemology," 49.

particularly at Oxford University where Wesley was both a student and a teacher. Like Wood, Campbell judges that the attitude to these studies varied widely, nevertheless, amongst many Anglicans the early church was seen as a model to be re-instituted, renewed or revived in terms of polity, doctrine, liturgy and personal piety.[55] The use of the term 'tradition' in relation to Wesley has come under attack in the studies by Campbell and Jones who concluded that Wesley did not refer to tradition as a theological source because of the way it was defined by Roman Catholicism.[56] No one seems to dispute that Wesley focused on the early Church and the Elizabethan Church of England, nor did he use tradition in the Roman Catholic sense; nevertheless, he did draw examples and models from the whole history of the Church. Many scholars seem willing to concede the technical point raised by Campbell and Jones, but argue that Wesley's wide-ranging appeal to the history of the Church still makes tradition the best term to identify this aspect of his theological method.[57] Campbell believes that Wesley's appeal to tradition centred around: finding patterns for customs, beliefs and virtues to be restored; a lesser interest in using it to refute practices or beliefs he opposed; and defending the practices and beliefs of the Church of England.[58] Maddox concurs that tradition was a more restricted norm than either Scripture or reason for Wesley. While he does refer to the early Church for some doctrinal positions, the majority of the references are to models of Christian living that he was trying to recover.[59]

EXPERIENCE

This religious source is the one that is "the most elusive and complex of the authorities in his methodology."[60] Thorsen has shown that experience was a part of the Anglican theological method prior to Wesley and it was common in sermonic and devotional literature, being used to confirm and elaborate

---

[55] Campbell, *Wesley and Antiquity*, 9-21.

[56] Ibid. While the critical study is Campbell's, his conclusions are supported by Jones, *Wesley's Use of Scripture*. See also the articles by them in Gunter et al, *Wesley and the Quadrilateral*. They prefer to use the terms "Christian antiquity" and the "Church of England" when identifying Wesley's use of the Church's past as a source for theologising. See also Ted A. Campbell, "Scripture and Tradition in the Wesleyan Tradition," in *Orthodox and Wesleyan Scriptural Understanding and Practice*. ed. S.T. Kimbrough, Jr. (Crestwood, NY: St Vladimir's Seminary Press, 2005), 159-69.

[57] For example, see Thorsen, *The Wesleyan Quadrilateral;* Maddox, *Responsible Grace*. Campbell admits that Wesley had a concern for the whole of the Christian tradition; see Ted A. Campbell, "The Interpretative Role of Tradition," in *Wesley and the Quadrilateral*.

[58] Campbell, *Wesley and Antiquity*, 104-07. See also Maddox, *Responsible Grace*, 43; Thorsen, *The Wesleyan Quadrilateral*, 126-27.

[59] Maddox, *Responsible Grace*, 42-43. See also Jones, *Wesley's Use of Scripture*, 169-71; Campbell, *Wesley and Antiquity*, 111.

[60] Miller, "Scriptural Authority," 211.

Christian truth established by Scripture, tradition and reason.[61] He states that Wesley gave it an explicit and practical expression, making it more central to the task of theologising and Maddox concurs that this is his significant contribution.[62] From the literature two key issues are raised by Wesley's use of experience as a theological source: what was the nature of experience (private or community) and what was its purpose (to formulate or to confirm doctrine derived from Scripture)?[63]

Regarding the nature of experience, the danger is to reduce it to the single category of an individual's private perspective (enthusiasm in Wesley's day). Isabel Rivers writes that Wesley continually struggled to avoid a private, subjective understanding dominating his Methodist societies, while maintaining the worth of experience and struggling to give it objective definition.[64] Miller emphasises that Wesley's conception of faith is very important in relation to experience. For Wesley, faith was always in God himself and not in our experience of God. This allowed our subjective experience of God to become objective knowledge of God and of our salvation: "Faith accesses the spiritual senses subjectively to apprehend the data while objectively, the Spirit of God accesses these same senses to supply that data."[65] Winfield H. Bevins draws particular attention to the role of the Spirit in Wesley's theological method and is convinced that this aspect has not been adequately studied by scholars engaged in the debate over methodology. He explicitly links the presence of the Spirit with each of the four sources in order to give emphasis to the importance of specifically Christian experience.[66] Clive Marsh advances the argument by suggesting that Wesley distinguished between "Christian experience" and "life experience," though the two do interact. Christian experience (as a direct result of the presence of the Spirit) and theological thinking actually forms and shapes people's general life experience. Such experience is crucial in Methodism due

---

[61] Donald A. Thorsen, "Experimental Method in the Practical Theology of John Wesley," *WTJ* 24 (1989): 120-22. See also Miller, "Scriptural Authority," 227; Jones, *Wesley's Use of Scripture*, 95.

[62] Maddox, *Responsible Grace*, 31-44. See also Thorsen, *The Wesleyan Quadrilateral*, 201; Winfield H. Bevins, "Pneumatology in John Wesley's Theological Method," *Asbury Theological Journal* 58, no. 2 (Fall, 2003); Miller, "Scriptural Authority", 225; Thorsen, "*Sola Scriptura*."

[63] Randy L. Maddox, "The Enriching Role of Experience," *Wesley and the Quadrilateral*, 108-12.

[64] Rivers, *Reason, Grace, and Sentiment*, 241-42.

[65] Miller, "Scriptural Authority," 219-20.;

[66] Bevins, "Pneumatology in John Wesley's Theological Method," 101-07, 10. See also Albert C. Outler, "A Focus on the Holy Spirit: Spirit and Spirituality in John Wesley," *Quarterly Review* 8, no. 2 (1988); Lycurgus M. Starkey, Jr., *The Work of the Holy Spirit: A Study in Wesleyan Theology* (Nashville, TN: Abingdon Press, 1962), 15-22, 140-45; Jason E. Vickers, "Charles Wesley's Doctrine of the Holy Spirit: A Vital Resource for the Renewal of Methodism Today," *Asbury Theological Journal* 61, no. 1 (Spring 2006).

to its emphasis on a religion of the heart, lived faith (not doctrinal comprehension) and practical Christianity.[67]

> By insisting on the objectivity of the agency of the Spirit and of the Scriptures as normative for personal experience, Wesley could emphasize subjective experience as the means of the believer realizing all God willed for them without becoming mired in the errors of "enthusiasim" [sic].[68]

Maddox believes Wesley taught that experience is both a "direct inward awareness" (impacting a person's spiritual senses) and a "corporate experience" (conference), with the latter guarding against the enthusiasm of private individual experience. Of special value to Wesley was "corporate long-term experience" that included both the living and the dead saints of the church. This was why he emphasised the role of spiritual biography in providing models of Christian living for his own people to emulate.[69] Rivers concurs that Wesley was interested in gathering large numbers of examples of Christian experience and then publishing them so that others might learn from and be inspired by them.[70] Thus experience can be communicated, provide evidence second-hand and be held up as a model for others to follow. It was the quality of the life of the believer that enabled you to distinguish a true experience of God from false enthusiasm.[71]

One of the central tasks of theology is to gather and share this type of experience as a way of providing public evidence of central Christian teachings – the second issue to be considered. Thorsen states that Wesley saw it as important for addressing doctrinal issues not clearly dealt with in Scripture or tradition, and here it plays a more substantial role than in other settings.[72] Maddox is in agreement that Wesley's "most frequent appeals to experience were on issues where his distinctive interpretation of Scripture was being challenged,"[73] and he identifies three clear issues where this is evident: is assurance essential to justification; do believers continue to struggle with an inclination to sin; is entire sanctification instantaneous or gradual?[74] Wesley

---

[67] Clive Marsh, "Appealing to 'Experience': What Does It Mean?," in *Unmasking Methodist Theology*, ed. Clive Marsh, Brian Beck, Angela Shier-Jones and Helen Wareing (London: Continuum, 2004), 118-24.

[68] Miller, "Scriptural Authority," 220-21.

[69] Maddox, "The Enriching Role of Experience," 118-19. See also Rivers, *Reason, Grace, and Sentiment*, 241-42.

[70] Rivers, *Reason, Grace, and Sentiment*, 214-20. See also Miller, "Scriptural Authority", 212-13, 33-34.

[71] Rivers, *Reason, Grace, and Sentiment*, 243.

[72] See Thorsen, "Experimental Method," 129. See also John R. Renshaw, "The Atonement in the Theology of John and Charles Wesley" (ThD thesis, Boston University, 1965), 67-69.

[73] Maddox, *Responsible Grace*, 46.

[74] Ibid. See also Bryant, "John Wesley's Doctrine of Sin", 41-50.

believed that Scripture was silent on these issues and so experience (by default) settled it. As Francis McConnell points out, "Wesley believed that professed experiences of revelation should be submitted to all available tests,"[75] and this includes the personal and corporate experiences of the Christian community. Monk affirms this viewpoint and demonstrates why experience must not be isolated from Wesley's other authorities:

> This emphasis upon the experimental nature of religion, particularly the stress upon the personal, inner relationship with God, carries with it the danger of undercutting the authority of external form, practice, or tradition. Wesley recognized this danger, and with the insistence upon experiencing religion went the insistence that there be checks and balances which test the authority of the experience itself. The truths about God taught in Scripture, the well-tried doctrines formulated through tradition, the form of the Christian life as exemplified in other believers, all stand along with experience as authoritative criteria for the Christian faith. These authoritative elements in fact become a believer's own, through experience, since it keeps them from being only irrelevant externals.[76]

Genuine spiritual experience can be distinguished from false enthusiasm because it has manifest fruits, so that it can be validated not only by the individual's appeal to his own experience, but by an observer's judgement based on Scripture and reason.[77] Maddox insists that Wesley was convinced it was essential to consider the long-term practical effects of each doctrinal alternative in the life of the Christian community. This helps to explain why he strongly supported the role of conferencing in order to minimise selectivity in data.[78] Wesley was clearly open to the experience of the people of God across all boundaries of class, education and generations.[79] This fits with the model of the early church where doctrinal reflection emerged out of the daily life so that the corporate life (experience) of the church was both the stimulus and goal of doctrinal reflection.[80]

Maddox maintains that Wesley's focus on experience as an individual subjective consciousness is confined to the role of empowering Christian living (assurance) and sometimes to confirm doctrine – but never to derive it.[81] The

---

[75] Francis J. McConnell, *John Wesley* (New York: Abingdon Press, 1939), 151.

[76] Robert C. Monk, *John Wesley: His Puritan Heritage* (Nashville, TN: Abingdon Press, 1966), 72. Experience as the appropriation of the authority of the Scriptures and tradition, and not the source of it is also supported by Williams, *Wesley's Theology Today*, 32-33.

[77] Rivers, *Reason, Grace, and Sentiment*, 243. See also Thorsen, "Experimental Method," 125.

[78] Maddox, "The Enriching Role of Experience," 124.

[79] Ibid., 125.

[80] Ibid.

[81] Ibid., 122-23.

nearest Wesley came to formulating a doctrine from experience is in *The Doctrine of Original Sin*, written to refute a deistic understanding, but he still interprets this from a biblical viewpoint.[82] Jones verifies that for Wesley it is Scripture that teaches the Christian what should be expected and experience then confirms it was actually accomplished.[83]

> For years he had based his preaching on the doctrine of perfection on the clarity of key Scripture passages. Experience functioned to show that his interpretation was correct, because people did actually experience what the Scripture had promised. But here Wesley suggests that if such confirmation had not taken place, his original exegesis might be thrown into question – he might have 'mistaken the meaning of those scriptures'.[84]

The evidence of personal experience is used to support the scriptural claim, but if no one in the history of the Church ever testified to the experience, then Wesley believed his interpretation of Scripture must be wrong.[85]

The 'Wesleyan Quadrilateral': The Debate

Colin Williams is particularly significant in the development of the concept of the quadrilateral, as was the first Methodist theologian to explicitly identify the four elements of Scripture, tradition, experience and reason as sources of authority in theologising.[86] These four elements are also mentioned in articles published in 1960 by Gerald Anderson, Frank Baker and Reginald Kissack.[87] Lycurgus Starkey refers to the four elements in his book in 1962, as do Bernard Jones, H. E. Lacy and Ernest Stoeffler in their articles for the *London Quarterly and Holborn Review* in 1964.[88] John R. Renshaw's doctoral thesis from Boston University in 1965, under the section on "Theological Criteria," explicitly lists

---

[82] Maddox, *Responsible Grace*, 45.

[83] Jones, *Wesley's Use of Scripture*, 96-100.

[84] Ibid., 101.

[85] Ibid., 178.

[86] Williams, *Wesley's Theology Today*. See also Campbell, "Doctrine and Theology," 155-58.

[87] Reginald Kissack, "John Wesley's Concept of the Church," *Asbury Seminarian* 14, no. 2 (1960): 12-17; Frank Baker, "John Wesley's Churchmanship (II)," *London Quarterly and Holborn Review* 185 (October 1960): 269-72; Gerald H. Anderson, "The Challenge of the Ecumenical Movement to Methodism," *Asbury Seminarian* 14, no. 2 (1960): 25.

[88] Starkey, The Work of the Holy Spirit, 142-45; F. Ernest Stoeffler, "The Wesleyan Concept of Religious Certainty: Its Pre-History and Significance," *London Quarterly and Holborn Review* 189 (April 1964): 135; Bernard E. Jones, "Reason and Religion Joined: The Place of Reason in Wesley's Thought," *London Quarterly and Holborn Review* 189 (April 1964): 111-13; H. Edward Lacy, "Authority in John Wesley," *London Quarterly and Holborn Review* 189 (April 1964): 116-18.

Scripture, reason, tradition and experience, with no reference to the work of Outler in his bibliography.[89] A similar listing of the four elements was given by Charles Rogers in his doctoral thesis from Duke University in 1967.[90]

The 'Wesleyan Quadrilateral' as a Conceptual Model

None of the sources examined for this thesis deny that Wesley made use of Scripture, reason, tradition and experience in his theologising and so in that limited sense the identification of the four elements of the quadrilateral is true to Wesley himself. However, this consensus breaks down the moment one tries to find agreement on the nature, interrelationship and use of these elements in practical theologising, or even if four is the correct number. For example, Langford would like to see "praxis" and "wisdom" added to the guidelines;[91] Scott Jones would differentiate between "Christian antiquity" and the "Church of England" to make it five;[92] Howard Snyder would add "the created order" to make it five;[93] Kenneth Howcroft would like to add "context";[94] Barry E. Bryant and John A. Newton would seek to reduce the guidelines to three – Scripture, reason and experience,[95] while Robert E. Cushman would prefer Scripture, tradition and experience.[96]

No one has seriously argued that Wesley did not make use of Scripture and most are willing to concede that it was central in his theologising. It is the articulation of this centrality that is subject to much debate. Langford suggests that to affirm the primacy of Scripture does not conclude an argument but is to begin a process, as there is no clear view on how it functions authoritatively or serves as a criterion for theological statements.[97] All agree that Wesley made

---

[89] Renshaw, "Atonement in Wesley," 59-67.
[90] Charles A. Rogers, "The Concept of Prevenient Grace in the Theology of John Wesley" (PhD thesis, Duke University, 1967), 17-24.
[91] Langford, "United Methodist Quadrilateral," 238-39.
[92] Jones, *Wesley's Use of Scripture*, 62-103. For the distinction between antiquity and the Church of England see also Campbell, *Wesley and Antiquity*, 108-13 especially.
[93] Howard A. Snyder, "The Babylonian Captivity of Wesleyan Theology," *WTJ* 39, no. 1 (Spring, 2004).
[94] Kenneth G. Howcroft, "Reason, Interpretation and Postmodernism: Is There a Methodist Way of Reading the Bible?," *Epworth Review* 25, no. 3 (1998): 38.
[95] John Anthony Newton, "The Ecumenical Wesley," *Ecumenical Review* 24 (1972): 172; Bryant, "John Wesley's Doctrine of Sin," 8, 12.
[96] Robert E. Cushman, *John Wesley's Experimental Divinity: Studies in Methodist Doctrinal Standards* (Nashville, TN: Abingdon Press, 1989), 11.
[97] Langford, "United Methodist Quadrilateral," 233-35. On Wesleyan hermeneutics, see: Barry L. Callen and Richard P. Thompson, eds., *Reading the Bible in Wesleyan Ways: Some Constructive Proposals* (Kansas City, MO: Beacon Hill Press of Kansas City, 2004). This book contains eleven essays, mainly from the *Wesleyan Theological Journal*. See also Joel B. Green, "Contribute or Capitulate? Wesleyans, Pentecostals and

use of reason, but disagree over the impact and influence of the Enlightenment on his understanding and use of it. Claiming that Wesley made use of tradition has created a number of issues. Though it is generally agreed that it sets "theological activity in specific historical contexts and social location,"[98] the actual definition of 'tradition' remains problematic and imprecise.[99] No one seems to question that Wesley made use of experience but the meaning of the term remains problematic, as well as the relationship between the objective and subjective, general human experience and specifically Christian experience.[100] Jones comments that Wesley was often too uncritical in accepting the testimony of others; he was too trusting that their experience was objective and he certainly had no understanding of the "plurality of perspectives."[101]

In reading the relevant literature, it is apparent that the claim of the quadrilateral to represent the theological method of both Wesley and Methodism is fraught with problems. William J. Abraham is one of the most trenchant critics of the whole concept and he has written extensively on it from the beginning. Even with his initial favourable evaluation he had reservations and noted that there is no official reference to it in British Methodist theology from 1850 to 1950, and there is very little current interest amongst British scholars.[102] Stephen Dawes (a British Methodist) agrees that the term holds little appeal for British Methodists and where it does occur it is used informally, with only slight awareness of the complexity or acrimony of the American debates.[103] He draws attention to the fact that in British Methodism it is the Conference that is the "final authority" in all matters concerning the

---

Reading the Bible in a Post-Colonial Mode," *WTJ* 39, no. 1 (Spring, 2004); Donald A. Thorsen, "The Future of Biblical Studies in the Wesleyan Tradition: A Theological Perspective," *WTJ* 30, no. 2 (Fall, 1995); Dean Flemming, "The Third Horizon: A Wesleyan Contribution to the Contextualization Debate," *WTJ* 30, no. 2 (Fall, 1995); Bryan P. Stone, "Wesleyan Theology, Scriptural Authority, and Homosexuality," *WTJ* 30, no. 2 (Fall, 1995).

[98] Langford, "United Methodist Quadrilateral," 236. See also Thomas A. Langford, "Is There Such a Thing as Wesleyan Theology?," *Epworth Review* 15, no. 2 (1988): 67-68.

[99] As noted earlier, Campbell questions the identification of 'tradition' with 'Christian antiquity'. The key study is Campbell, *Wesley and Antiquity*. His conclusions are supported by Jones, *Wesley's Use of Scripture*. See also the articles by Campbell and Jones in Gunter et al, *Wesley and the Quadrilateral*.

[100] See for example Langford, "United Methodist Quadrilateral," 237.

[101] Jones, *Wesley's Use of Scripture*, 179.

[102] See Abraham, "The Wesleyan Quadrilateral," 119.

[103] see Stephen Dawes, "Revelation in Methodist Practice and Belief," in *Unmasking Methodist Theology*, 112; Stephen Dawes, "The Primacy of Scripture and the Methodist Quadrilateral," (The Methodist Sacramental Fellowship, January 1998). The informal use of the term occurs in a number of the articles contained in *Unmasking*, though references to the constituent elements of Scripture, reason, tradition and experience are more common; see in particular the articles by Barbara Glasson, Clive Marsh and Angela Shier-Jones.

interpretation of its doctrines, emphasising the work of God through community, mutuality and connexionalism.[104] Abraham's reservations about Outler's position were demonstrated by four critical questions he raised regarding their meaning, internal relations, justification (why only these four?), and practicality.[105] His questions became more persistent when his book *Doctrinal Amnesia* was published in 1995 and he relegated the quadrilateral to a debatable hypothesis by Outler and denied it was "constitutive of Wesley's theology." In Abraham's judgement, the critical problem with the quadrilateral is that at its heart it "involves a fatal running together of a reduced account of ecclesial canons with the norms of Enlightenment theories of knowledge."[106] These norms are empty of content since each of the four guidelines are in themselves highly debateable. He argues that you cannot put Scripture and tradition in the same category with reason and experience: the latter are "concepts of justification or rationality" in the field of epistemology, while the former deals with testimony, tradition, and conscience.[107] Thus Christians are in danger of becoming rational, autonomous agents for all of their beliefs based upon the evidence presented to them. Even gathering this evidence is problematic as it would be impossible to examine every single item of data from the four sources. The quadrilateral also fails to deal with the need for a critical understanding of revelation. Abraham believes the whole notion should now be scrapped.[108] If it is has any value at all, it is as a first (but not very

---

[104] Dawes, "Revelation in Methodist Practice and Belief," 114-16. See also Angela Shier-Jones, "Conferring as Theological Model," *Unmasking Methodist Theology*; Angela Shier-Jones, *A Work in Progress: Methodists Doing Theology* (Peterborough, ENG: Epworth Press, 2005), 44-49.

[105] Abraham, "The Wesleyan Quadrilateral," 120. See also Langford, "United Methodist Quadrilateral," 233-38; Howe, "Doctrine and Theology." Abraham believes that most UMC scholars who defend the quadrilateral have not yet adequately answered these questions—see Abraham, "What's Right and What's Wrong with the Quadrilateral?", 14 (see n. 36).

[106] Abraham, *Doctrinal Amnesia*, 61. See also William J. Abraham, *The Logic of Renewal* (Grand Rapids, MI: Wm. B. Eerdmans, 2003), 163-69.

[107] Abraham, *Doctrinal Amnesia*, 62. A similar point had been made earlier in Ogden, "Doctrinal Standards." See especially pp. 44-45.

[108] Abraham, *Doctrinal Amnesia*, 63-64. For a similar critique see also Abraham, "What's Right and What's Wrong with the Quadrilateral?" In this essay he critiques especially the work of Langford, Maddox, and Outler himself. He claims that Outler in his later years tried to distance himself from his formulation. See also Abraham, "The End of Wesleyan Theology."; William J. Abraham, "Keeping up with Jones on John Wesley's Conception and Use of Scripture," *WTJ* 33, no. 1 (Spring, 1998); William J. Abraham, "The Revitalization of United Methodist Doctrine and the Renewal of Evangelism," in *Theology and Evangelism in the Wesleyan Heritage*, ed. James C. Logan (Nashville, TN: Abingdon Press, 1994), 35-50.

adequate) attempt at an epistemology for the Wesleyan tradition.[109]

Like Abraham, Campbell questions whether the quadrilateral was a real conception for Wesley himself, arguing that you cannot simply link two Wesley documents together in order to extract this fourfold pattern. He argues that the quadrilateral is a modern tool,[110] and the two points of reference in Wesley that led to the coining of the term are not as clear as Outler and others claim.[111] Leroy T. Howe is another scholar who is unhappy with the notion of the quadrilateral. He avers that the only source of faith and understanding is God himself. As guidelines, the fourfold pattern ought to help discern those events of divine self-presentation from which alone faith and understanding originate. "Not even the guideline of Scripture, alleged to be primary, can be the source of faith. It *can* be a source of judgments made *about* faith, in the sense of a criterion by which such judgments constantly get scrutinized."[112] Howe criticises the notion of appealing to all four of the guidelines as stated in the UMC documents; even when acknowledging that the primacy of Scripture is part of the Methodist tradition, the other three elements can be the starting point for reflection. How do you adjudicate the relative weighting of the four in any situation and what happens if one or more of the three propose something not in Scripture? Do you then make Scripture exclusive rather than primary to avoid this problem?[113]

> It is difficult to conceive of even a single serious theological proposal which, upon application of the four guidelines, one could exclude unambiguously from consideration as beyond the range of permissible utterance within the Christian community. By arbitrarily defining the degree of force one or other guideline is to

---

[109] Abraham, *Doctrinal Amnesia*, 59-60. His recent writings have been even more critical; see for example Abraham, "What's Right and What's Wrong with the Quadrilateral?"; Abraham, *The Logic of Evangelism*, 146; Abraham, "The End of Wesleyan Theology." For a concise overview of his own understanding, see William J. Abraham, *Canon and Criterion in Christian Theology: From the Fathers to Feminism* (Oxford: Oxford University Press, 1998). Wesley's epistemology is also treated in Bryant, "John Wesley's Doctrine of Sin", 33-80; Wood, "Wesley's Epistemology"; Kevin Twain Lowery, *Salvaging Wesley's Agenda: A New Paradigm for Wesleyan Virtue Ethics* (Eugene, OR: Pickwick Publications, 2008).

[110] Campbell, "Doctrine and Theology," 159-61.

[111] Ibid., 160.

[112] Howe, "Doctrine and Theology," 55. A brief and undeveloped reference to God's authority as our "guide" is found in Campbell, *Methodist Doctrine: The Essentials*, 40; see also Thorsen, "Sola Scriptura," 20.

[113] Howe, "Doctrine and Theology," 56-58. For example, Stephen Dawes argues that reason and experience are foundational since they are necessary to interpret the Scripture in the first place; see Dawes, "The Primacy of Scripture and the Methodist Quadrilateral."

have in a particular discussion, one could establish almost any belief as Christian.[114]

Not all the evaluations of the quadrilateral have been so negative, even though almost no one now accepts Outler's formulation uncritically. Randy Maddox's examination of the evidence leads him to conclude that while the quadrilateral cannot be linked directly to Wesley, "a conjoined consideration of Scripture, reason, experience, and 'tradition'...as criteria in his theological judgements is not entirely inappropriate."[115] He summarises Wesley's

---

[114] Howe, "Doctrine and Theology," 56.

[115] Maddox, *Responsible Grace*, 36. A general agreement with this position may be found in Gregory S. Clapper, *John Wesley on Religious Affections: His Views on Experience and Emotion and Their Role in the Christian Life and Theology* (Metuchen, NJ: Scarecrow Press, 1989), 2, 20, 28, 45-46, 55-57; Heather Ann Ackley, "A Constructive Wesleyan Theological Proposal: Redemption and Sanctification of Human Gender and Sexuality," *Asbury Theological Journal* 59, no. 1 & 2 (Spring-Fall, 2004); Paul M. Bassett, "The Holiness Movement and the Protestant Principle," *WTJ* 18, no. 1 (Spring, 1983); Allan Coppedge, "John Wesley and the Issue of Authority in Theological Pluralism," *WTJ* 19, no. 2 (Fall, 1984); Leon O. Hynson, "The Wesleyan Quadrilateral in the American Holiness Tradition," *WTJ* 20, no. 1 (Spring, 1985); R. Larry Shelton, "The Trajectory of Wesleyan Theology," WTJ 21, no. 1 & 2 (Spring-Fall, 1986): 160-63; John E. Stanley, "A Theology of Urban Ministry, Supported by the Wesleyan Quadrilateral," *WTJ* 38, no. 1 (Spring, 2003); Charles Yrigoyen Jr., *John Wesley:Holiness of Heart and Life* (Nashville, TN: Abingdon Press, 1996); Thomas C. Oden, *John Wesley's Scriptural Christianity: A Plain Exposition of His Teaching on Christian Doctrine* (Grand Rapids, MI: Zondervan, 1994), 55-99; Ben Witherington III, "*Praeparatio Evangelii*: The Theological Roots of Wesley's View of Evangelism," in *Theology and Evangelism*, 51-80; Gunter et al, *Wesley and the Quadrilateral*, 129-42; Allan Coppedge, *John Wesley in Theological Debate* (Wilmore, KY: Wesley Heritage Press, 1987), 27-34; John B. Cobb, Jr., *Grace & Responsibility: A Wesleyan Theology for Today* (Nashville, TN: Abingdon Press, 1995), 155-76; Thomas C. Oden, *Systematic Theology: The Living God*, vol. 1 (San Francisco: HarperCollins, 1987), 330-51; H. Ray Dunning, *Grace, Faith, and Holiness: A Wesleyan Systematic Theology* (Kansas City, MO: Beacon Hill Press of Kansas City, 1988), 55-94; Lorna Lock-Nah Khoo, *Wesleyan Eucharistic Spirituality* (Adelaide: ATF Press, 2005), 109-64; Barry L. Callen, *Discerning the Divine: God in Christian Theology* (Louisville, KY: Westminster John Knox Press, 2004), 61-62, 105-06; Michael Lodahl, "Theology on the Rough Road to Emmaus: Questioning the Quadrilateral," in *It's All About Grace: Wesleyan Essays in Honor of Herbert L. Prince*, ed. Samuel M. Powell (San Diego, CA: Point Loma Press, 2004), 17-24; Leon O. Hynson, *Through Faith to Understanding: Wesleyan Essays on Vital Christianity* (Lexington, KY: Emeth Press, 2005): 42-43; Mark W. Stamm, *Let Every Soul Be Jesus' Guest: A Theology of the Open Table*, (Nashville, TN: Abingdon Press, 2006), x-xi, 8-9; Rogers, "Prevenient Grace," 17-24; Bevins, "Pneumatology in John Wesley's Theological Method"; Roger E. Olson, "The World Its Parish: Wesleyan Theology in the Postmodern Global Village," *Asbury Theological Journal* 59:1 & 2 (Spring/Fall, 2004): 23-24; Randy L. Maddox, "Responsible Grace: The Systematic

theological method by stating that the quadrilateral "of theological authorities could more adequately be described as a unilateral rule of Scripture within a trilateral hermeneutic of reason, tradition, and experience."[116] Jones agrees that while Scripture is clearly primary for Wesley, his sources are interdependent, forming a "single but complex locus of authority."[117]

> A correct understanding of Scripture is dependent on the other four. Reason and antiquity are needed for proper interpretation. The Church of England is the best transmitter of Scripture because it is, in Wesley's view, 'the most Scriptural national church' of his time. Experience proves the promises of Scripture to be true and can even correct one's interpretation at times. Conversely, the very definition of how the other four are properly used involve their fidelity to Scripture. Any position that denies the inspiration and authority of Scripture is irrational. Only those parts of antiquity and the Church of England that conform to Scripture are authoritative. Experience alone cannot prove or generate doctrine; it merely confirms or corrects what Scripture teaches.[118]

The Utility of the 'Wesleyan Quadrilateral' in Theologising

When the elements of the quadrilateral have been identified, it still leaves the key issue of how they are, in practice, interrelated in Wesley's theologising and

---

Nature of Wesley's Theology Reconsidered," *Quarterly Review* 6, no. 1 (1986): 24-34; Maddox, *Responsible Grace*, 26-36, 99; Jones, *Wesley's Use of Scripture*, 102; Thorsen, *The Wesleyan Quadrilateral*, 19-20; John Munsey Turner, "Methodism: An Apologia," *Epworth Review* 15, no. 2 (1988): 21-22; Richard Clutterbuck, "Our Doctrines," *Epworth Review* 24, no. 3 (1997): 29; Howcroft, "Reason and Interpretation," 38; Timothy L. Smith, "John Wesley and the Wholeness of Scripture," *Interpretation* 39, no. 3 (1985): 248; Thomas W. Ogletree, "In Quest of a Common Faith: The Theological Task of United Methodists," *Quarterly Review* 8, no. 1 (1988): 47; Charles Wood, "Wesleyan Constructive Theology," in *Wesleyan Theology Today*, 73; Jung Yang, "The Doctrine of God in the Theology of John Wesley" (PhD thesis, University of Aberdeen, 2003), 73; Ted A. Campbell, "Scripture as an Authority in Relation to Other Authorities: A Wesleyan Evangelical Perspective," *Quarterly Review* 11, no. 3 (1991): 34-35; Mark T. Kurowski, "The First Step toward Grace: John Wesley's Use of the Spiritual Homilies of Macarius the Great," *Methodist History* 36, no. 2 (1998); Thorsen, "*Sola Scriptura*."

[116] Maddox, *Responsible Grace*, 46. See also Lodahl, "Theology on the Road to Emmaus," 17-18. On p. 18 Lodahl uses the term '*perichoretic*' to picture the "ongoing dynamic of mutual indwelling, mutual enrichment, and mutual creation among the elements" of the quadrilateral.

[117] Jones, *Wesley's Use of Scripture*, 102. See also Langford, "United Methodist Quadrilateral," 233.

[118] Jones, *Wesley's Use of Scripture*, 102. Note Jones is actually working with five sources here, due to his separation of antiquity and the Church of England, but his basic position on the 'quadrilateral' is in line with Maddox.

whether this is a genuinely practical method that would continue to be relevant for the church today. Joel Green speaks for many when he asserts it is

> an artificial formulation that represents neither Wesley's position and practice nor the Wesleyan tradition. Not only can a theological emphasis on the conjunction of Scripture, Tradition, Reason, and Experience not be traced back to Wesley's own theological method, but also it has never been clear among modern-day Methodists how these four authorities might be correlated and especially whether or how differences among them on any given topic...might be adjudicated. And many of us believe that the ascent of Reason, Tradition, and Experience as theological benchmarks has resulted in the further marginalization of the Bible from the center of the church's struggle for faithfulness in belief and practice.[119]

Durwood Foster agrees that there are liabilities with the four guidelines, but still maintains that the "Wesleyan tradition would seem to have a special vocation in the attainment of a cohesive Christian hermeneutic integrating Scripture, tradition, reason, and experience."[120] Thorsen believes that while "the term is more of a shorthand reference to their interdependent relationship than to a well-developed or defined statement of Wesley's concept of theological method and religious authority. ... [it] serves as a helpful model or tool for investigating the complexity and dynamic of Wesley's approach to theology."[121] He says that Wesley did not articulate a precise hierarchical relationship between them because he did not expect them to contradict each other. In giving primacy to Scripture, he was free to introduce the other sources to organise, illumine and apply Scripture.[122] Thus they do not add to biblical truth, but confirm and apprehend it and the danger of a static and mechanical literalism in biblical interpretation is avoided, as well as irresponsible appeals to enthusiastic, mystical or other subjective experiences.[123]

> While *sola scriptura* valuably reminds us of the need for maintaining the primacy of scriptural authority, the quadrilateral provides a far better principle of religious authority because it embodies as well as advocates a complex dynamic of relevant

---

[119] Green, "Scripture in the Church" in *The Wesleyan Tradition*, 39. See also Campbell, "The Wesleyan Quadrilateral" in *Doctrine and Theology*, 155; Langford, "United Methodist Quadrilateral" in *Doctrine and Theology*, 232-43.

[120] Durwood Foster, "Wesleyan Theology: Heritage and Task," in *Wesleyan Theology Today*, 34. See also Barbara Glasson, "Stories and Storytelling: The Use of Narrative within Methodism," in *Unmasking Methodist Theology*, 101, 04-06; Dawes, "Revelation in Methodist Practice and Belief," 112-13.

[121] Thorsen, *The Wesleyan Quadrilateral*, 229.

[122] Ibid., 72-74. See also Thorsen, "*Sola Scriptura*," 26-27.

[123] Ibid., 74-99. See also Olson, "The World Its Parish: Wesleyan Theology in the Postmodern Global Village," 24.

authorities, which best contributes to meeting the challenges of postmodernism, contextualization, and globalization.[124]

Wesley's Understanding of the Role of Theology in the Christian Life

Almost every writer consulted on John Wesley and his theology agrees that his dominating concern was for practical Christianity.[125] Outler maintains that Wesley's theological genius lay in the area of practical theology, where "doctrinal opinions were to be valued for their service to vital faith."[126] He believes that Wesley always sought to avoid a split between belief and behaviour, while being careful to keep the distinction between "faith itself and all conceptualizations of faith."[127] He would allow for differing opinions on doctrinal formulations provided they did not undercut the life of faith. Maldwyn Hughes put it very finely when he wrote that for Wesley "the Christian life is born not of intellectual illumination, but of the heart-experience of Jesus Christ" and thus the starting point for his theology was faith.[128] Theology was to be done in the midst of society where the practical concerns of individuals seeking how to live the Christian life were paramount. Wesley was always open to new light being shed on his theological understanding of his relationship with God, and thus he actively sought the contributions of others to his theological development.[129] Conceding that Wesley was flexible in his theological understanding does not mean that he was a theological vagrant.

---

[124] Thorsen, "*Sola Scriptura*," 27. In fact, he strongly believes that "the quadrilateral provides the best principle of religious authority for representing God and God's kingdom in the world today."

[125] See for example Thomas A. Langford, *Practical Divinity: Theology in the Wesleyan Tradition* (Nashville, TN: Abingdon Press, 1983), 20; Frank Baker, "Practical Divinity-John Wesley's Doctrinal Agenda for Methodism," *WTJ* 22, no. 1 (Spring, 1987); Gregory S. Clapper, "Wesley's 'Main Doctrines' and Spiritual Formation and Teaching in the Wesleyan Tradition," *WTJ* 39, no. 2 (Fall, 2004): 104-21; Kenneth J. Collins, *The Theology of John Wesley: Holy Love and the Shape of Grace* (Nashville, TN: Abingdon Press, 2007): 1-5; Bryant, "John Wesley's Doctrine of Sin", 3-8; Langford, "United Methodist Quadrilateral" in *Doctrine and Theology*; Green, *Young Mr. Wesley*, 164; Renshaw, "Atonement in Wesley," 69-70; Clapper, *Wesley on Religious Affections*, 2; Monk, *Puritan Heritage*, 68-69; Piette, *Evolution of Protestantism*, 435; J. Ernest Rattenbury, *Wesley's Legacy to the World: Six Studies in the Permanent Values of the Evangelical Revival* (London: Epworth Press, 1928), 112-13; James S. Thomas, "How Theology Emerges from Polity," in *Wesleyan Theology Today*, 14-15.

[126] Outler, ed., *John Wesley*, iv.

[127] Ibid., 27.

[128] H. Maldwyn Hughes, *Wesley and Whitefield* (London: Charles H. Kelly, n.d.), 130. See also Schmidt, *Wesley's Life Mission 2*, 189; Monk, *Puritan Heritage*, 73.

[129] Edgar W. Thompson, *Wesley: Apostolic Man: Some Reflections on Wesley's Consecration of Dr. Thomas Coke* (London: Epworth Press, 1957), 14-15.

Wynkoop proposes that as one studies all the changes Wesley makes,

> ... it becomes obvious that he is discovering the difference between the "substance" of doctrine and the "circumstance" of it, a category of analysis which he considers of real importance. In other words, some truths are firm, and biblical study and experience continue to prove them firm. They are the "fundamentals," such as the truth that men may be saved from all sin in this life. The method, time, adaptation to imperfect humanity and a host of other questions having no direct scriptural word, yield their truth to us as to Wesley, only in experience. As important as these truths may be, they are not revealed truths, but historical and in that sense peripheral. Wesley did not consider any question relative to faith beneath his dignity or unworthy of his concern. But he did not fall into the trap of confusing the circumstance with the substance of Truth.[130]

This evaluation of Wesley coincided with an increasing questioning by many theologians of the centrality of systematic theology as the way to theologise, and an increasing openness to the worth of a practical and contextualised theology that focused on the communication of Christian truth within the Christian community as a whole, and not merely within an academic setting. Maddox observes that Anglicanism in Wesley's time was particularly focused on the first four centuries of the Church, where theology was a practical discipline to guide the character and practice of the Christian.[131] The discipline of study, instruction and pastoring was directed towards forming a thoroughly Christian worldview in the believer. The role of the theologian (who was normally a pastor) was to understand and then communicate the nature of the relationship between God and the human race, integrating reflection on anthropology and soteriology with that on the nature of God. This made theology a very practical concern that sought to communicate its truths primarily through catechisms, liturgies, commentaries and spiritual discipline manuals. Much of the theologising was in response to the needs and questions of the Christian community.[132] Maddox identifies Wesley as having this same

---

[130] Mildred Bangs Wynkoop, "A Hermeneutical Approach to John Wesley," *WTJ* 6, no. 1 (Spring 1971): 15-16. See also Rob L. Staples, "Sanctification and Selfhood: A Phenomenological Analysis of the Wesleyan Message," *WTJ* 7, no. 1 (Spring 1972): 4-7; A. Skevington Wood, "Lessons from Wesley's Experience," *Christianity Today* 7 (April 1963): 5-6. On 'substance' and 'circumstance', see also Mildred Bangs Wynkoop, *A Theology of Love: The Dynamic of Wesleyanism* (Kansas City, MO: Beacon Hill Press of Kansas City, 1972), 302-62.

[131] Randy L. Maddox, "John Wesley: Practical Theologian?," *WTJ* 23, no. 1-2 (Spring-Fall, 1988): 122-47. See also Thorsen, "Experimental Method," 117-41; Randy L. Maddox, "Wesleyan Resources for a Contemporary Theology of the Poor," *Asbury Theological Journal* 49, no. 1 (1994): 36-44.

[132] Maddox, "John Wesley: Practical Theologian?," 123. For many, this makes Wesley an outstanding pastoral theologian; see for example, Piette, *Evolution of Protestantism*,

set of concerns with his "praxis-related theology" that was developed from and communicated through a variety of forms: creeds (the Articles of Religion), liturgies (*Book of Common Prayer*), sermons (the Homilies and his own sermons), commentaries (*Explanatory Notes on the Old Testament* and the *New Testament*), hymns, conferences, occasional essays, catechetical materials, educational and devotional material (*Christian Library*), journals and letters. He concludes that Wesley clearly pursues serious theological activity in the forms common to his Anglican setting and appropriate to the early Christian model of practical theology.[133] A comparable judgement is made by Thomas Langford:

> Practical divinity, for Wesley, treats theology as intrinsically related to life; conversely, theological themes cannot be separated out and interpreted independently as an intellectual enterprise ... [it] is intentionally transformative, it underwrites proclamation and the nurturing of Christian life; ... [it] is neither a distanced reflection upon life nor an intellectual interpretation of life ... [it] is pragmatic in the sense that it operates on the conviction that knowledge is only gained through engagement; contrariwise, knowledge is not found through spectatorship as an abstract observer ... [it] holds text (biblical) and context (social and cultural) in tight tension; each requires the other for insight and interpretation. ... [it] never allows an ahistorical text or an independent social order to function as a matrix of interpretation.[134]

Furthermore, "Wesley's primary interest in the formation of Christian character shapes his discussion of theological issues and provides his theological emphases."[135] This perception of the role of theology (and the theologian) has profound implications for his theological methodology. For Wesley, doctrines were not ends in themselves but guidelines to help his people

---

417; Abraham, *The Logic of Evangelism*, 9, 143; Schmidt, *Theological Biography*, Vol 1, 115.

[133] Maddox, "John Wesley: Practical Theologian?," 130-33. See also Maddox, ""Respected Founder," 72; Randy L. Maddox, "Reading Wesley as a Theologian," *WTJ* 30, no. 1 (Spring, 1995).

[134] Langford, "Introduction," 10. See also Rivers, *Reason, Grace, and Sentiment*, 217-22; Kenneth J. Collins, "A Hermeneutical Model for the Wesleyan *Ordo Salutis*," *WTJ* 19, no. 2 (Fall, 1984); Ole E. Borgen, *John Wesley on the Sacraments: A Definitive Study of John Wesley's Theology of Worship* (Nashville, TN: Abingdon Press, 1972; reprint, Grand Rapids, MI: Zondervan, 1985), 36-37; Langford, "United Methodist Quadrilateral" in *Doctrine and Theology*, 239; Ole E. Borgen, "No End without the Means : John Wesley and the Sacraments," *Asbury Theological Journal* 46, no. 1 (1991); Patrick S. Franklin, "John Wesley in Conversation with the Emerging Church," *The Asbury Journal* 63, no. 1 (Spring 2008).

[135] Langford, "United Methodist Quadrilateral" in *Doctrine and Theology*, 239. It is why Wesley's *Christian Library* has more biography than any other genre of literature.

know how to tell the gospel story and live it with integrity.[136] The goal of the life of faith was holiness, with his understanding of Christian perfection as the "most distinctive single element."[137]

WESLEY AS A PRACTISING THEOLOGIAN

Mark Horst proposes that "any attempt to discern the method or logic of his [Wesley's] thought must begin with what he does rather than what he says about it. If his theologizing has a discernible method it seems to have been unsystematically determined by his life of religious reflection and concern, to have sprung from his understanding of the nature of Christian faith."[138] Horst states that faith has intellectual, dispositional and practical components; critically, "faith is a disposition of the heart when it fundamentally reshapes the believer's attitudes and emotions, thoughts and practices in relation to God, our neighbour, and ourselves."[139] He concludes that Wesley's conception of the dynamic relationship between the intellectual, affective and methodical aspects of faith emphasised Christianity as a way of life. Furthermore, "Both the content and form of Wesley's thought illustrates his continual refusal to separate a conceptual account of Christian truth from its application in the believer's life and binds his discussion of Christian teachings and practices to emotions and attitudes."[140] Theology cannot be done "just on paper," it is "the process of shaping lives according to the model of God's handiwork and therefore primarily a prescriptive rather than a descriptive exercise. It presupposes an obedience to God's will as concretely manifest in law and gospel and made known to us in Scripture, tradition, experience, and reason."[141] It is this process that reminds us that Wesley's own understanding and practice developed over the span of his own spiritual journey, both from his personal experience and that of his community.[142] Maddox advances the argument by

---

[136] Ibid.

[137] Outler, ed., *John Wesley*, 30. Outler continues to develop and nuance this understanding of Wesley; see the bibliographic listing of Outler's writings in Maddox, *Responsible Grace*, 396-97. One of the critical articles is Albert C. Outler, "A New Future for Wesley Studies: An Agenda for 'Phase III'," *The Future of the Methodist Theological Traditions*, 34-52. See also Frank Baker, *John Wesley and the Church of England* (London: Epworth Press, 1970), 117.

[138] Mark L. Horst, "Experimenting with Christian Wholeness: Method in Wesley's Theology," *Quarterly Review* 7, no. 2 (1987): 12.

[139] Ibid., 13-14.

[140] Ibid., 17.

[141] Ibid., 19-20. See also Cushman, *Wesley's Experimental Divinity*, 11, 19-36, 79-83.

[142] Maddox divides Wesley's life and ministry into three sections: early Wesley (1725-1738), middle Wesley (1739-65), late Wesley (1766-91); see Randy L. Maddox, "Continuing the Conversation," *Methodist History* 30, no. 4 (1992): 236-37. See also Frank Baker, "Unfolding John Wesley: A Survey of Twenty Years' Studies in Wesley's Thought," *Quarterly Review* 1, no. 1 (1980); Randy L. Maddox, "'Celebrating the

stating that when we do theology there is a tension between our preunderstanding and the new material that is presented for integration into, or transformation of, our current understanding. As Wesley faced each new challenge to his previously-held beliefs, he had to decide whether to retain, revise or reject the conviction at issue. Maddox deduces that the mature Wesley consciously sought to guide this by Scripture as enlightened by reason, experience and tradition.

> ...Wesley's use of the various resources for doctrinal reflection was ultimately *dialogical*. It was not a matter of simply using whichever resource seemed more helpful, or of playing one resource off against another, but of conferring among them until some consensus was found. His expectation of such consensus was based on the assumption that it is the same self-revealing God being encountered through Scripture, tradition and experience – when each of these is rightly and rationally utilized.[143]

"As such, if there was a process to Wesley's doctrinal reflection, it is best described as a 'hermeneutical spiral' of becoming aware of and testing pre-understandings."[144] This was rarely methodical, as he dealt with issues when they arose in his life or pastoral ministry. He dealt with these, and he usually only dealt with the specific aspect of the doctrine that was under challenge, by drawing on the sources and criteria most relevant to the particular situation or audience.[145]

JOHN WESLEY'S PLACE IN THE METHODIST MOVEMENT

Wesleyan theologian Mildred Bangs Wynkoop is one of many who has questioned where Wesley fits in the present church – is he Methodism's mentor or guru?[146] She noted the tendency by some to make him the authority that must still decide every facet of Methodist life and doctrine, while others see him more as a spiritual guide who is to be respected but not slavishly followed. A provocative analysis of the danger of labelling Wesley according to one's own theological position is given by William Abraham who observes how Wesley

---

Whole Wesley': A Legacy for Contemporary Wesleyans," *Methodist History* 43, no. 2 (January 2005); Stanley Banks, "Our Wesleyan Heritage: Christian Perfection," *Asbury Seminarian* 14, no. 2 (1960); Kenneth J. Collins, "A Reply to Randy Maddox," *Methodist History* 31, no. 1 (1992).

[143] Maddox, "The Enriching Role of Experience," 122. See also the conclusion in Gunter et al, *Wesley and the Quadrilateral*, 129-42.

[144] Maddox, *Responsible Grace*, 47.

[145] Ibid.

[146] Mildred Bangs Wynkoop, "John Wesley-Mentor or Guru?," *WTJ* 10 (Spring 1975). Her own conclusion was that he was to be regarded as a mentor.

has been shown to fit within a whole range of theological schools.[147] Abraham's own evaluation is:

> John Wesley is not some norm of truth; nor is he a folk theologian waiting to be organized into a systematic theologian; nor is he merely our brother in the faith; nor is he a doctor of the church; nor is he a prince of the church. He was and is a minister of the gospel who has birthed us indirectly in the faith. *He is a thinker and spiritual guide who* has gone on to Glory and whose work, with all its shortsightedness and shortcomings, *can still bring us to God and foster holiness of life and thought* (emphasis mine).[148]

Wesley himself clearly denounced any ideas of being regarded as a bishop or other hierarchical official;[149] it is the image of 'spiritual guide' that is

---

[147] Abraham, "The End of Wesleyan Theology," 13-14. He lists some of the options as: a Social Gospeller or Personalist, Fundamentalist or Modernist, Liberal or Conservative, Liberationist or Pietist, Radical or Moderate, Revisionist or Traditionalist, Marginalist or Centrist, Systematician or Occasionalist, Inclusivist or Exclusivist, Feminist or Patriarchialist, Holiness or Pentecostal, Conventionalist or Charismatic, Confessionalist or Pluralist. Even within the Evangelical camp, there are intense debates over the understanding of sanctification (Kenneth Collins and Randy Maddox), the place and significance of baptism in the Spirit (Donald Dayton and Lawrence Wood), whether we should see Wesley as a centrist or at the margins (Joerg Rieger and Scott Jones), how to read the significance of the affections in Wesley's theologizing (William Abraham and Gregory Clapper). See also Kenneth E. Rowe, ed., *The Place of Wesley in the Christian Tradition* (Metuchen, NJ: Scarecrow Press, 1976); Kenneth J. Collins, "The Promise of John Wesley's Theology for the 21st Century: A Dialogical Exchange," *Asbury Theological Journal* 59, no. 1 & 2 (Spring-Fall, 2004); H. O. Thomas, "Whenceforth Wesley: John Wesley's Theology from Then to Now," *Methodist History* 43, no. 4 (July, 2005); Jonathan Dean, "'Mystics and Pharisees': Methodist Identity in an Ecumenical Age," *Epworth Review* 34, n. 4 (October 2007); Langford, *Practical Divinity;* John Stacey, ed., *John Wesley: Contemporary Perspectives* (London: Epworth Press, 1988).

[148] Abraham, "The End of Wesleyan Theology," 13. It was reading this essay that first introduced me to the thought of Wesley as a "spiritual father" and some of the possible implications of that for my own study. See also Abraham, *The Logic of Renewal*, especially 153-72. On Wesleyan spirituality, see the excellent introduction by Frank Whaling in *John and Charles Wesley: Selected Writings and Hymns*, ed. Frank Whaling, The Classics of Western Spirituality (New York: Paulist Press, 1981), 1-64. See also Wesley D. Tracy, "John Wesley, Spiritual Director: Spiritual Guidance in John Wesley's Letters," *WTJ* 23, no. 1 & 2 (Spring-Fall, 1988); Steve Harper, "John Wesley: Spiritual Guide," *WTJ* 20, no. 2 (Fall, 1985).

[149] Note his vehement rejection of the title in dealing with North American Methodism and its use by Francis Asbury. See *Letters* (Telford), 7: 238-39; 8: 91. His own preferred title for those who would succeed him was superintendent. For a thorough examination of the issue of Wesley and authority, see Baker, *John Wesley and the Church of*

common, both in relation to his own ministry and that of his preachers.[150] In a letter to one of his preachers in 1767, Wesley wrote, "I will not attempt to guide those who will not be guided by me."[151] This underscored that during his lifetime it was a voluntary relationship and not one enforced by legal constraint. The image was further enriched in his letter to Francis Asbury in 1788, where he described himself being "under God the father of the whole [Methodist] family."[152] A 'spiritual guide' or 'spiritual father' is essentially about relationships based on love and community (persuasive authority), rather than obedience and hierarchical structure (coercive authority).[153] At the heart of this image there is a destination known and experienced by the guide, who then seeks to enable others to arrive at the same destination. It involves an effective sharing of actual experiences of the problems and pitfalls, while offering effective solutions and necessary encouragement. This has profound implications for Wesley's theology and theological method in pastoral practise.

Conclusion

This chapter has focused on a review of two key and inter-related elements in the thought of John Wesley: a consideration of Wesley as a theologian and an examination of the 'Wesleyan Quadrilateral' as a conceptual model for describing his theological method. The overview has established that there is a general consensus among scholars that Wesley was primarily a practical or pastoral theologian, for whom the starting point had to be the reality of the person's encounter with the living God in Jesus Christ rather than formal systems of doctrine. The argument by Abraham and others that Wesley should be understood as a spiritual guide and mentor for his people seems soundly

---

England; Adrian Burdon, *Authority and Order: John Wesley and his Preachers* (Aldershot, ENG: Ashgate Publishing, 2005).

[150] See for example *Works*, 20:201; 26:586. Note particularly his constant use of the term in his sermon "On Obedience to Pastors" (*Works*, 3: 374-83.); "An Address to the Clergy" (*Works* (Jackson) 10: 480-500), and his 'Letter to the Rev. Dr. Rutherforth' (*Works*, 9: 374-88.).

[151] *Letters* (Telford), 5: 64.

[152] *Letters* (Telford), 8: 91. This image of "spiritual father" also recurs elsewhere in his writings; see for example *Works* (Jackson), 10:357; *Letters* (Telford), 8:168. The description was also used by a visitor who met Wesley in 1769; see Richard P. Heitzenrater, *The Elusive Mr. Wesley: John Wesley as Seen by Contemporaries and Biographers*, vol. 2 (Nashville, TN: Abingdon Press, 1984), 87.

[153] Wesley could clearly be autocratic and require obedience, but it was within the framework of a voluntary relationship. In a letter of 1789 Wesley commented that fifty years earlier several young men "offered to serve me as sons in the gospel" on the terms that they served where Wesley appointed and this was still the practice; see *Letters* (Telford), 8:168. See also his comments on the free link with his preachers ("those who love *him*") to John Fletcher in *Letters* (Telford), 5:84.

based; consequently, it makes the role of Wesley's own spiritual experience an integral part of his pastoral ministry. In terms of his theological method, there is widespread agreement that Wesley did make reference to the four sources identified by Outler that form the quadrilateral (Scripture, reason, tradition and experience), though there is much less agreement about their nature and interrelationship. The use of 'tradition' is disputed, especially by Thorsen and Jones, but making explicit reference to antiquity and the Church of England does not materially alter the case put forward by Outler and others. Though a number of scholars make reference to the ministry of the Holy Spirit as a source of assistance in Wesley's theologising, it is not developed explicitly and the focus remains on the primacy of one of the elements – usually Scripture. It is Winfield Bevins who emphasises the role of the Spirit in Wesley's theological method as a significant contribution and links it explicitly with the quadrilateral, though this is not greatly expanded. In a similar vein, Thorsen and Howe point out that the role of God himself in theologising is too easily overlooked or minimised.

There is much greater debate over Outler's proposal that the concept of the quadrilateral is true to Wesley himself, and that it is a Methodist distinctive of value in theologising today. In support of Outler's basic contention, the United Methodist Church maintains a clear reference to the four elements (but no longer to the term itself) in its *Book of Discipline* and they are also utilised by some British Methodists without any formal recognition of the term 'quadrilateral'. The crucial question debated amongst scholars is whether Wesley's theological method is as clear, sophisticated and useful as Outler and a number of other scholars believe. In examining the recent literature on Wesley studies, it is apparent that the most common method of approaching Wesley as a theologian has been by dissection and analysis, looking at aspects and themes of his work in some detail before trying to organise the material around some integrating concept that would tie the diverse findings together. The focus on analysing the origins, nature and interrelationship of the four elements as an explanation of his method, rather than their actual use by Wesley in his pastoral work, is very much a feature of the Modernism that has dominated theological scholarship for so long. If we take the analogy of a jigsaw puzzle, there has been a tendency to examine in depth the piece(s) the scholar has identified as critical before they then try to complete the puzzle based upon a picture constructed from their own presuppositions. The accompanying reductionism must necessarily impact their perception of Wesley's own vision of the nature of Christian life and ministry. We now have a number of positions put forward by various scholars, but there seems little prospect of a new consensus emerging that would advance the current debate.

CHAPTER 3

Wesley and his Journey from Oxford 'Methodist' to the Founder of the Methodist Societies, 1725-1739

After examining the literature on Wesley as a pastoral theologian and the 'quadrilateral' as a conceptual model for theologising, a case has been established for investigating Wesley's theological method in pastoral practice. Wesley's own writings that give insight into his spiritual journey and pastoral role in Methodism span the years from 1725 to1791. For the purposes of this study his life and ministry has been considered in three stages: the foundational years from 1725-1739; the critical development years as leader of the Methodist movement 1740-1769; his mature leadership of the Methodists from 1770-1791.

The purpose of this chapter is to demonstrate that Wesley understands the essential nature of God as a God of love and the implications of this for God-human relationships was present from the earliest days of his public ministry. The doctrine of Christian perfection has been selected as the test case because it was a controversial doctrine both within Methodist circles and amongst their detractors. The foundation for his mature understanding of the doctrine of Christian perfection is laid during this period, though various aspects will be nuanced in the ensuing years. What is clearly in development is his theological method, even though references to Scripture, reason, antiquity and the Church of England are present from the beginning. The events surrounding his Aldersgate experience on May 24, 1738 are vital for his spiritual development and will profoundly impact his theological methodology. While he had exercised a pastoral role as an Anglican priest for many years, it is only with the formation of the Methodist societies that we can begin to explicitly trace his pastoral approach to issues revolving around the doctrine of Christian perfection.

We begin with a brief examination of the background needed to understand Wesley's setting in the eighteenth century. Attention is then paid to Wesley's own spiritual journey in the period 1725-1739; this covers his time at Oxford, as a missionary to Georgia and finally his role in forming and leading the Methodist United Societies. Utilising his own written materials, the study investigates his understanding of the nature of God, human beings and their mutual relationship during this period before examining his developing theological methodology. This is followed by an examination of Wesley's doctrinal understanding of Christian perfection and his emerging pastoral ministry to the people called Methodists.

John Wesley in His Eighteenth-Century Setting

We cannot avoid reading history and biography through the particular lens provided by our personal and community experiences. Over time, as communities and persons change, the readings also change, reflecting our choice of sources, evaluation of the evidence, determination of significance, and interpretation of the findings. John Wesley's life spanned almost the whole of the eighteenth century and to understand his life and work it is important to locate his life in its historical setting. This section is only intended to introduce some of the necessary critical features that need to be grasped, as an exhaustive examination of this period and Wesley's biography is beyond the scope of this book.[1]

The 'Long Eighteenth Century'

Earlier scholarship tended to identify this period as 'The Age of Reason' or 'The Enlightenment'[2] but current historians have increasingly preferred to call it 'the long eighteenth century' in order to indicate the wider continuities and changes beyond a narrow consideration of philosophy.[3] Recent scholarship also reflects a greater diversity of opinion about the changes that took place as the century unfolded.[4] Roy Porter continues to identify this period as the British

---

[1] For recent books on Wesley's life and the formation of Methodism, see Kenneth J. Collins, *A Real Christian: The Life of John Wesley* (Nashville, TN: Abingdon Press, 1999); Kenneth J. Collins, *John Wesley: A Theological Journey* (Nashville, TN: Abingdon Press, 2003); Henry D. Rack, *Reasonable Enthusiast: John Wesley and the Rise of Methodism*, 3rd ed. (London: Epworth Press, 2002); John Munsey Turner, *John Wesley: The Evangelical Revival and the Rise of Methodism in England* (London: Epworth Press, 2002); Richard P. Heitzenrater, *Mirror and Memory: Reflections in Early Methodism* (Nashville, TN: Kingswood Books, 1989); Richard P. Heitzenrater, *Wesley and the People Called Methodists* (Nashville, TN: Abingdon Press, 1995). For a brief but helpful overview of Wesley and his eighteenth century setting see Philip R. Meadows, "Wesleyan Theology in a Technological Culture," *WTJ* 41, no. 1 (Spring 2006): 29-33

[2] For a classical example of this, see Gerald R. Cragg, *The Church and the Age of Reason, 1648-1789* (Harmondsworth, ENG: Penguin Books, 1970).

[3] See particularly J. C. D. Clark, *English Society, 1660-1832: Religion, Ideology and Politics During the Ancien Regime*, 2nd ed. (Cambridge: Cambridge University Press, 2000). Clark's bibliography lists the works of many current specialist historians who have adopted this term, see especially n. 3 on p. x.

[4] For two diverse evaluations by current specialists, see Ibid. and Roy Porter, *The Creation of the Modern World: The Untold Story of the British Enlightenment* (New

Enlightenment, during which the secular value system that prevails in much of Western society today was formed.[5] In terms of religious life, Porter believes this period saw a fundamental change in the way people viewed God, themselves and their relationship due to the rise of rationalism; he sees the Enlightenment in Britain taking place within rather than against Protestantism. There was a more optimistic view of human beings and their abilities, having the reason and capacity to fulfil their duties to God (often identified impersonally as the "Supreme Being"), and humanity through their God-given faculties. Religion increasingly became identified with moral virtue; education and knowledge were then regarded as central to the achievement of personal and community happiness rather than "personal salvation."[6] It was neither an age of religious apathy, nor was it a time of "Christianity triumphant."[7]

> Enlightened minds ceased to equate religion with a body of commandments, graven in stone, dispensed through Scripture, accepted on faith and policed by the Church. Belief was becoming a matter of private judgement, for individual reason to adjudicate within the multi-religionism sanctioned by statutory toleration.... As religion became subjected to reason, Christianity ceased to be a 'given' and became a matter of analysis and choice.[8]

J. C. D. Clark judges scholars like Porter overestimate the changes of this period, as he believes much survived with an inner coherence into the nineteenth century.[9] In his opinion, what was lost at the end of the eighteenth century was "the hegemonic status and the integrity of a certain body of ideas, beliefs, customs, and practices."[10] What remained was a broadly-shared and deeply-held set of beliefs (especially religious beliefs) that bound most of the people together from which, admittedly, they drew differing conclusions. While it was a period of transition, he denies that you can label this as "secularisation." He suggests that the authority of "tradition" remained, particularly in religious matters, where it was a route to clarity (the "pristine church") rather than obscurantism.[11] Clark's evaluation of the religious atmosphere of the period is also radically different to Porter's, though he concurs that the Enlightenment found a home *within* the Christian churches.

York: W. W. Norton & Company, 2000). Both agree that there is no single picture to be obtained. For an evaluation of the general evangelical position in this period, see D. W. Bebbington, *Evangelicalism in Modern Britain: A History from the 1730s to the 1980s* (London: Unwin Hyman, 1989), 20-74.

[5] Porter, *Modern World*, xxii, 5-22, 476-84.
[6] Ibid., 100-02.
[7] Ibid., 96-99.
[8] Ibid., 99.
[9] Clark, *English Society*, 9-16.
[10] Ibid., 16.
[11] Ibid., 9-16.

Clark claims that most historians now reject the idea of the church acquiring a secular outlook in this period, or that religion was reduced to moral decency.[12] He reminds us that "religious affiliation was commonly assumed to be natural, not voluntary" for the Church of England and Nonconformity.[13] Both church and university harboured a variety of intellectual positions which they protected or resisted, but not to the point of damaging the establishment of the church or royal supremacy in its government. He judges that the antithesis between science and religion was almost unknown and very few scientists were atheists.[14] Today we usually see religion as a private matter, contrasting with the secular society, but "from the Reformation to the nineteenth century ... Christianity was characterised by a drive to engage with and work through the material realm in a way which implied no essential difference of kind between the two. Whether the emphasis was on faith or works, practical engagement was the result."[15] In spite of a widespread abandonment of belief in miracles, a belief in Providence was left largely intact.[16] Clark sees the growth in this period in Dissent, not in atheism; the main challenge to established religion and its social consequences came from heterodox theology. Legally, England remained a confessional state, with space created for Nonconformity to exist.[17] He believes that Evangelicalism in general, and Methodism in particular, became powerful phenomena in this period because they arose from within Established Church practice and drew on its wide diffusion and latent strength.

The Rise of the Study of Religion

In the light of the above survey, particular attention must be paid to recent discussions on the invention of "religion" as a subject for scientific study in the seventeenth and eighteenth centuries. According to Wilfred Cantwell Smith the ability to understand human discourse is the ability to understand the people and the community whose discourse it is. Some symbols, forms and doctrines are exceptionally durable, but what they mean they always mean to some person or persons at some time and place.[18] Peter Harrison believes the critical

---

[12] Ibid., 28. See particularly n. 25 and 26.
[13] Ibid., 26.
[14] Ibid., 29. Additional support for Clark's view is given by Alister E. McGrath, *The Foundations of Dialogue in Science and Religion* (Oxford: Blackwell Publishers, 1998).
[15] Clark, *English Society*, 29.
[16] There was a discrediting of the whole supernatural realm, including witchcraft, magic, ghosts, good and evil spirits. See Porter, *Modern World*, 219.
[17] Clark, *English Society*, 29-31. See also William J. Abraham, *Saving Souls in the Twenty First Century: A Missiological Midrash on John Wesley* (Sheffield, ENG: Cliff College Publishing, 2003), 4-8.
[18] Wilfred Cantwell Smith, *Belief and History* (Charlottesville: University Press of Virginia, 1977), 16-19. For an extended discussion of the meaning and relationship between faith and belief see also Wilfred Cantwell Smith, *Faith and Belief* (Princeton:

change in the meaning of religion occurred in seventeenth century England when many Protestant scholars began to use it to refer to a system of ideas and their observable outworking and practices.[19] It shifted from a dynamic of the heart to an impersonal doctrinal system, from the singular (religion) to the plural (religions), from a personal to a propositional conception of truth. You could now write of the Christian religion over against other religions, of one system of Christian belief over against other systems of Christian belief.[20]

In Harrison's opinion, the dominant Protestant theology of the period sharply distinguished between revelation and nature as the two sources of religious truth. From this emerged the study of "natural religion" and "revealed religion."[21] What is now revealed is an "objective religion" with propositions to be believed in order for salvation to be attained–it was no longer a revelation of God himself. By the close of the seventeenth century, reason had come to be a criterion of revelation.[22] This changed the focus to rational knowledge and understanding (propositional truth), and away from trust and love (relational truth). A major concern was to accumulate evidence for or against the religion being studied.[23] This was reinforced, according to Smith, by a change in the meaning of belief. It altered from a reference to a relationship in which the note of trust is prominent to an acceptance of propositional truth based on argument or proof that is persuasive, but without certain knowledge.[24] Smith contends that you could not believe in God in classical Christian usage without a personal encounter with him.[25] The Christian first came to God through a

---

Princeton University Press, 1979), 69-127; Wilfred Cantwell Smith, *The Meaning and End of Religion* (New York: The New American Library, 1964).

[19] Peter Harrison, *The Bible, Protestantism, and the Rise of Natural Science* (Cambridge: Cambridge University Press, 1998), 92-107. The Reformers attempted to work with "literal meanings" accessible to any individual scholar without reference to Church authorities. Gradually the Protestant and Catholic "religions" were reduced to "abstracted, depersonalised systems which were intended to represent in propositional terms the sum total of the religious lives" of the people; see Peter Harrison, *'Religion' and the Religions in the English Enlightenment* (Cambridge: Cambridge University Press, 1990), 1-3; Harrison, *Bible and Protestantism*, 1.

[20] Smith, *Meaning and End*, 37-39.

[21] Harrison, *'Religion' and the Religions*, 2, 19.

[22] Ibid., 6-7.

[23] Ibid., 20-26. See also Smith, *Meaning and End*, 39-44.

[24] Smith, *Belief and History*, 41-49. English has no verbal form for the word faith (although Hebrew and Greek do) and so in English "to believe" is used to represent this "act of faith." In the *Authorised Version* of the Bible (1611), "belief" only occurs once, but "faith" occurs 233 times. The critical change came with the writings of John Locke (1632-1704). He used the word "faith" for assent to any proposition upon the credit of the proposer.

[25] Ibid., 80-87. In the Bible faith is clearly associated with persons (God and neighbours), so faith in Christ involves first a recognition of who he is and then a total

personal encounter and then believed in him. Faith is therefore prior to belief and theology is the conceptualisation for one's own day of that prior faith; faith is thus the insight to "see."[26] Furthermore, "faith is recognition plus response"; it is never mere knowledge but always involves "acknowledge." The increasingly rationalist approach led to a reaction by men like Richard Baxter and Henry Scougal, who sought the deeper piety of the tradition and a return to "true religion."[27] Smith particularly notes that "so far as corporate religious life is concerned, the movement of return to a re-emphasis on a richer and more personal and more moral attitude is to be seen in the work of the German pietists and of John Wesley."[28] In such a setting, Wesley's emphasis on the experiential dimension (both personal and corporate) of the Christian faith would stand in contrast to the emerging objectification of the faith amongst many of his scholarly contemporaries.[29]

The Church of England

V. H. H. Green identifies the late seventeenth and early eighteenth century as a crucial period in the history of the Church of England because it witnessed the start of the first genuinely critical attitude to Christian theology.[30] Men like John Tillotson (1630-94) and Thomas Tenison (1636-1715) held that reason itself could provide all that was needed in the way of divine truth; the role of Scripture was simply to confirm the findings of reason. This led to less emphasis on biblical doctrines and more emphasis on the "truths of natural religion" and the ethics which spring from obedience to conscience.[31] During the same period, the authority of tradition was increasingly questioned by many due to the focus on the new age of scientific experiment, and the stigma attached to the word because of its associations with Roman Catholicism and the High Church Tories' denigration of patristic authority. This was balanced in

---

dedication to him. See his extensive analysis of the use of *pistis* and its cognates in Scripture, where the overwhelming reference is to God or Christ as persons.

[26] Ibid., 79.

[27] Smith, *Meaning and End*, 44. See also n. 143 and other examples given in notes 119-20 on p. 41. Scougal's *The Life of God in the Soul of Man* (1677) had a great impact on Wesley and an abridged edition of it was published by him in 1744.

[28] Ibid.

[29] Smith, *Belief and History*, 61-68.

[30] V.H.H. Green, *The Young Mr. Wesley: A Study of John Wesley and Oxford* (London: Wyvern Books, 1963), 9.

[31] Rupert E. Davies, *Methodism* (London: Penguin, 1963), 32. See also Richard A. Miller, "Scriptural Authority and Christian Perfection: John Wesley and the Anglican Tradition" (PhD thesis, Drew University, 1991), 145; A. Skevington Wood, "The Eighteenth Century Methodist Revival Reconsidered," *Evangelical Quarterly* 53, no. 3 (1981); Anthony Armstrong, *The Church of England, the Methodists and Society 1700-1850* (London: University of London Press, 1973).

the late seventeenth century by a revival of interest in Christian antiquity by men like William Beveridge (1637-1708) and Robert Nelson (1656-1715), both of whom had a profound impact on John Wesley.[32] The scientific revolution of the seventeenth century led to a thorough questioning of the existence of miracles, the relationship of revelation and reason and a concern over the fate of those who had never heard of Christianity.[33]

> Theology ceased to be the subject which instigated the methods of thought and defined the limits of their operations and became rather the object of thought to which the methods of an emancipated philosophy were applied and concerning which a critical examination was undertaken. In other words, men no longer started with the premises of revealed religion, but they began at the point of their own discoveries and on the basis of those discoveries called into question the primary assumptions of the faith.[34]

This had a far-reaching impact on Christianity and reduced it to little more than a correct set of opinions formulated on the basis of natural reason.

Henry Rack's recent biography of John Wesley contains a concise review of the religious life and the spectrum of theological traditions in eighteenth century England.[35] The two main parties in the Church of England were the Latitudinarians and the High Churchmen. The former emphasised what they saw as the essentials and were open to the benefits of science and reason, with "doctrinal authority...found in a balance of scripture, reason and the Fathers."[36] As the eighteenth century progressed they came increasingly to stress reason as the touchstone of Christian truth, with morality as its content. Rack verifies Harrison and Smith's assertion that faith became "a firm assent of the mind" rather than "personal trust" and salvation was primarily through a sincere attempt to obey God's law; the work of Christ was to make up what was lacking in their own efforts.[37] The High Churchmen tended to stress ascetic piety, relatively frequent communion and a special focus on the teaching and practice of the early church of the first five centuries (more so by the Nonjurors); their views were most common among the lower clergy, with Samuel Wesley and all his sons being of this persuasion.[38] Rack notes that most

---

[32] Miller, "Scriptural Authority," 145-46.

[33] Armstrong, *Methodists and Society*.

[34] William R. Cannon, *The Theology of John Wesley, with Special Reference to the Doctrine of Justification* (New York: Abingdon Press, 1946), 16.

[35] Rack, *Reasonable Enthusiast*. Rack's documentation is quite thorough and nearly all the other sources consulted agreed in general terms with his summary. See also Frank Baker, *John Wesley and the Church of England* (London: Epworth Press, 1970).

[36] Rack, *Reasonable Enthusiast*, 24.

[37] Ibid., 24-25.

[38] See *Letters*, (Telford), 6:156, 61. Here Wesley declares himself to be a High Churchman and the son of a High Churchman.

of the clergy were concerned to promote a reasonable faith and to uphold moral duty. This led to a desire for certainty in religious knowledge and personal salvation, which was expressed by the natural, the reasonable and the moral.[39]

The Wesley Family Home

On one of the many occasions that John Wesley wrote about the danger of separation from the Church of England, we find the following testimony written in 1789:

> *From a child* [emphasis mine] I was taught to love and reverence the Scripture, the oracles of God; and next to these, to esteem the primitive Fathers, the writers of the three first centuries. Next after the primitive church, I esteemed our own, the Church of England, as the most scriptural national Church in the world.[40]

His initial Christian experience and theological understanding were clearly formed by his upbringing in the Epworth parsonage.[41] The evidence contained in the extant writings of Samuel and Susanna Wesley shows quite clearly the influences of both their Puritan and Established Church heritage, as well as the intellectual developments of their day.[42] In both parents there was an

---

[39] Rack, *Reasonable Enthusiast*, 26-34.

[40] John Wesley, *The Works of John Wesley*, ed. Thomas Jackson, 3rd ed., 14 vols. (London: Wesleyan Methodist Book Room, 1872; reprint, Kansas City, MO: Beacon Hill Press of Kansas City, 1979), 13:272. (hereafter cited as *Works* (Jackson))

[41] The main works consulted in preparing this section were: Susanna Wesley, *Susanna Wesley: The Complete Writings*, ed. Charles Wallace Jr. (New York: Oxford University Press, 1997); Franklin Wilder, *Father of the Wesleys* (New York: Exposition Press, 1971); Frank Baker, "Susanna Wesley: Puritan, Parent, Pastor, Protagonist, Pattern," in *Dig or Die*, ed. James S. Udy and Eric G. Clancy (Sydney: World Methodist Historical Society Australasian Section, 1981); Robert C. Monk, *John Wesley: His Puritan Heritage* (Nashville, TN: Abingdon Press, 1966); Adam Clarke, *Memoirs of the Wesley Family: Collected Principally from Original Documents*, 2 vols., vol. II (London: William Tegg, 1860); George J. Stevenson, *Memorials of the Wesley Family* (London: Partridge & Co., 1876); Samuel Wesley, *The Pious Communicant Rightly Prepared; or, a Discourse Concerning the Blessed Sacrament: . . . To Which Is Added, a Short Discourse of Baptism: With a Letter Concerning the Religious Societies* (London: Charles Harper, 1700); Luke Tyerman, *The Life and Times of the Rev. Samuel Wesley, M.A.* (London: Simpkin, Marshall & Co., 1866); Rack, *Reasonable Enthusiast;* John A. Newton, *Susanna Wesley and the Puritan Tradition in Methodism* (London: Epworth Press, 1968); Claire Wolfteich, "A Difficult Love: Mother as Spiritual Guide in the Writing of Susanna Wesley," *Methodist History* 38, no. 1 (1999); G. Stringer Rowe, "Mrs. Wesley's Conference with Her Daughter. An Original Essay by Mrs. Susannah Wesley," *Proceedings of the Wesley Historical Society* 1, no. 3 (1896-97).

[42] For further background information see Frank Baker, "Wesley's Puritan Ancestry," *London Quarterly and Holborn Review* 187 (July 1962).

unconscious mixing of the two theological traditions to produce a particular synthesis that would have a lasting impact on John. An important factor in the Wesley home was Samuel's interest in the emerging science of his day. Gilbert McEwen's study of the *Athenian Mercury,* for which Samuel wrote many articles on the relationship of revelation and reason, has demonstrated that there was openness to the developing sciences and experimental learning.[43] They reflect a conservative position in which reason (regarded as imperfect due to the Fall) was seen to help in reducing the seeming contradictions between the emerging science and revelation.[44] Susanna seems to have placed more emphasis than Samuel on the role of reason in the Christian life, and even when some mystical tendencies emerged in her writings they were not divorced from reason. Her high estimate of the abilities of reason are seen when she specifically located most errors in the depravity of the will, rather than a defect of understanding.[45]

In both parents the goal of the Christian life was quite clearly holy living.[46] The predominant influence in the home is usually given to Susanna, with Samuel playing a lesser role;[47] it is Susanna's input that seems crucial to the development of their children's spiritual life. In Rack's judgement, in another age she would have made an "able devotional writer or practical theologian."[48] Susanna's letters stressed seeking Christian perfection, loving God and having pure motives.[49] Holiness was to be pursued diligently, and while sinning was inevitable in this present life, it was to be resisted with all one's efforts. They stressed the place of love in Christian experience (both for God and neighbour), though Susanna seemed to give it greater emphasis.[50] Nevertheless, one cannot escape the general impression that obedience and moral duty were the elements that a child would most likely remember, particularly in the light of the rational, methodical and disciplined approach to life and education in the home by Susanna.[51] The depravity of the will was highlighted, so that if the perverse will could be bridled (as she very evidently aimed to do in her method of child-rearing), a real change in one's spiritual condition through self-effort was

---

[43] Gilbert D. McEwen, *The Oracle of the Coffee House: John Dunton's Athenian Mercury* (San Marino, CA: The Huntington Library, 1972), 31, 114-15.
[44] Ibid., 135-37.
[45] See Wesley, *Susanna Wesley*; Stevenson, *Memorials*.
[46] See Wesley, *Pious Communicant*, 1; Stevenson, *Memorials*, 181.
[47] Rack, *Reasonable Enthusiast*, 58-60. See also Baker, "Susanna Wesley: Puritan, Parent, Pastor, Protagonist, Pattern," 77-88.
[48] Rack, *Reasonable Enthusiast*, 50. A view also supported by Wallace and most of her biographers.
[49] See especially Clarke, *Wesley Family Memoirs*, 38-85.
[50] See Stevenson, *Memorials*, 180; Wolfteich, "A Difficult Love," 57-62.
[51] See Newton, *Susanna Wesley & Puritan Tradition*, 53. She wrote many theological treatises for her children, gave weekly personal instruction in the faith to them all and maintained regular correspondence when they had left home.

possible. While she made it clear that it took the work of the Holy Spirit to actually become a Christian, the priority rested with a personal decision and commitment to obey the will of God.[52] This reflects a prominent stream in seventeenth century Puritanism that emphasised the prior preparation to be done by a sinner (to show sufficient contrition) before God will justify. The ground of assurance is then found in the quality of the preparation.[53] When this is coupled with an emphasis on very strict personal examination, the cultivation of a tender conscience and an emphasis on rigorous obedience to the will of God, the possibility of successful preparation is greatly diminished. The evidence of a life of faith was the performance of good works and without these, faith could not be genuine. Samuel seemed to have a doctrine of assurance but it was not well-developed; it was based on the performance of good works, a 'sensible' presence of Christ in the Communion service, and a direct witness of the Spirit.[54]

An Overview of John Wesley's Spiritual Journey, 1725-1739

Wesley's spiritual life was shaped by the blending of the Puritan and Established Church influences in the home, alongside his mother's deep interest in the continental and English pietists and mystics.[55] He was reared in the 'holy living' tradition, where the clear goal of the Christian life was the pursuit of personal holiness, though the attainment of it in this life was denied because of the presence of sin while in this mortal body. The normal way of entry into the Christian life was by infant baptism and thereafter a strong emphasis was placed on obedience, spiritual discipline and rigorous self-examination, with a stress on the centrality of love for God and neighbour demonstrated in works of piety and mercy. The only sense of assurance that one was accepted by God came from the evidence of a good life and a rigorous obedience to that which God had commanded in Scripture. Wesley was particularly aware of the place of method and discipline in the Christian life. He had been taught that most errors in Christian living came from a depravity of the will rather than a defect of understanding, therefore, personal choices and personal commitment were vital elements in the life of faith (both parents were Arminian in theological orientation). While there was a high regard for the powers of human reason, it

---

[52] See Stevenson, *Memorials*, 178-80.

[53] Alister E. McGrath, *Iustitia Dei: A History of the Christian Doctrine of Justification*, 2 vols., vol. II, *From 1500 to the Present Day* (Cambridge: Cambridge University Press, 1986), 117-18.

[54] See Wesley, *Pious Communicant*. John Wesley believed that his father did have an "inward witness" to his salvation in the months before his death; see the later evaluation of his father's spiritual life in *Works*, 26:288-89.

[55] For an examination of Wesley's spirituality, see Stephen Dawes, "The Spirituality of 'Scriptural Holiness'," *Epworth Review* 30, no. 2 (2003).

was not at the expense of the necessity of divine revelation. He had been taught to revere the traditions of the early church and his own Church of England, the place of Scripture and the role of reason in theological method.[56] He initially embraced the empirical philosophy of John Locke,[57] with its stress on experience as the source of all knowledge. Wesley shared in the rising confidence in the power of reason to understand the self, the world and God. He was well aware of the 'scientific method' of observation, measurement and experimentation to produce demonstrable results and he had a life-long interest in keeping current with the latest discoveries; his interest in the experimental method is obvious throughout his life. It was his intense conviction that genuine Christianity could be known by certain evidences, and in many ways the story of his personal spiritual pilgrimage is a search for such incontrovertible evidence.

Wesley's decision to prepare for ordination in January 1725 was the critical event that initiated his serious pursuit of holy living and it would shape his whole theological development. He began to read a number of important works that emphasised that holiness was essentially an inner reality, seated in the heart and that it impacted every aspect of a person's life.[58] In response to reading Jeremy Taylor's *Rule and Exercises of Holy Living* he noted the importance of purity of intention and began to keep a diary to promote personal piety and to enable his spiritual growth to be measured.[59] The diaries also reveal the gradual appearance of a like-minded group of people more or less associated with Wesley who sought to live the holy life by means of a methodical and communitarian approach.[60] It is from these years that we see a definite pastoral

---

[56] For further background on theological method in the Church of England that Wesley so clearly valued, see Nigel Atkinson, *Richard Hooker and the Authority of Scripture, Tradition and Reason: Reformed Theologian of the Church of England?* (Carlisle: Paternoster Press, 1997); Henry R. McAdoo, *The Spirit of Anglicanism: A Survey of Anglican Theological Method in the Seventeenth Century* (New York: Charles Scribner's Sons, 1965).

[57] Heitzenrater, *Mirror & Memory*, 109. See especially n. 9 where he details a number of works that emphasize and analyse this point. For a detailed discussion, see Richard E. Brantley, *Locke, Wesley, and the Method of English Romanticism* (Gainesville, FL: University of Florida, 1984).

[58] References to his reading are to be found in the letters, the diaries and in Green, *Young Mr. Wesley*. The family letters from this period are found in *Works*, 25:157-242. The critical works and their reading dates are: *The Imitation of Christ* by Thomas à Kempis (1726); William Law's *A Practical Treatise upon Christian Perfection* (1726) and *A Serious Call to a Devout and Holy Life* (1728). See *Works*, 18:243-45.

[59] See the editorial introduction to the diaries by Richard P. Heitzenrater, *Works*, 25:302ff. See also the available extracts in *Works*, 18, 19, 23 and 24. For further background information see Heitzenrater, *Mirror & Memory*.

[60] *Works*, 25:322-25. In November 1729 Wesley took up a position as a tutor at Lincoln College and became involved with his brother Charles and a small number of his friends

influence in his letters as he assumed the role of spiritual director for many friends and acquaintances. During this time his sermons became a public sounding board for his developing spiritual insights. His decision to go to Georgia in 1735 centred on his desire to meet his own spiritual needs and so be able to better meet the spiritual needs of others:[61] "My chief motive, to which all the rest are subordinate, is the hope of saving my own soul. I hope to learn the true sense of the gospel of Christ by preaching it to the heathens."[62] He believed his only hope lay in preaching the gospel to others, because their salvation would confirm his own state of grace.[63] The whole Georgia episode was largely a personal disappointment for him, but it did contribute in many ways to later Methodist structure and practice.[64] Most importantly, it brought him into personal contact with "living witnesses" to the experience of God that he so earnestly sought.[65] Wesley returned to England from Georgia expressing a deep desire to have the assurance that he was a Christian, to know that he had the faith so clearly defined in Scripture and in the Homilies, having a *constant* assurance that he was a child of God, freed from sin, fear and doubt.[66] During this period he struggled to reconcile the formal theological understanding of the process of salvation and its confirming marks learned from home, his studies and community life at Oxford, with his own experience. Critically, he needed to reconcile his intellectual understanding of Christianity and his actual spiritual experience, as these were intimately entwined and mutually informed each other.

The Rise of Methodism, 1725-1739

In an early letter written by his mother we find her expressing the hope that

---

who met on some sort of regular basis for Bible study, the reading of the Christian classics and mutual accountability. The important apologia for early Methodism is found in a letter (October 19, 1732) to Richard Morgan Sen. in Ibid., 335-44. A further brief outline of their practice is contained in a letter to his mother on August 17, 1732 in Ibid., 354-55. By the end of 1730, the group had established a pattern of living that was a corporate and public expression of a 'method' that had started with John in 1725; see Heitzenrater, *Mirror & Memory*, 69-73.

[61] See for example *Works*, 25:432-36.
[62] Ibid., 439.
[63] Ibid., 439-41.
[64] At Savannah and Frederica he began a small group ministry that was a forerunner of the later class and band meetings of Methodism; see *Works*, 18:157, 60. The influence of the Moravian community with its singing was also noted at this time.
[65] See *Works*, 4:371-88; 18:121-216; 25:444-529. The information on the *Journals* from the introduction is very helpful in understanding the background to Wesley's final published material; see *Works*, 18:37-91. For an evaluation of these years, see Rack, *Reasonable Enthusiast*, 107-36; Heitzenrater, *Mirror & Memory*, 58-73.
[66] *Works*, 18:243-44.

John was "a good Christian."[67] There were three key issues to be considered before he could give an adequate response: (1) the definition of a "good Christian," (2) how to become and then remain a good Christian, (3) how do you *know* you are a good Christian?[68] These had to be answered not only for his personal spiritual journey, but also for his pastoral ministry offered to others. His spiritual experience and pastoral ministry are intimately linked and have profound implications for his theological method. Defining a "good Christian" required Wesley to explore his understanding of the nature of God, the nature of human beings and the relationship between them, as well as a depiction of the qualities to be evidenced in the Christian's life and character in order to be called "good." He obviously started with a picture of such a person provided by his home and church upbringing and this was to be subsequently influenced by his personal and pastoral experiences for the rest of his life. Since personal piety and practical theology were intimately linked,[69] he was convinced that the effectiveness of his ministry fundamentally depended on his own spiritual progress. Ministry to others could only flow from his personal experience and not from mere book learning.

It is important to observe from the very outset that Wesley was strongly predisposed to eclecticism in theology (Puritanism, High Church, Pietism, Mysticism, Arminianism) because of the influences of home, where the focus was not a narrowly-conceived doctrinal correctness but holy living. This gave a great deal of freedom to mine the spiritual riches of the Church from its apostolic beginnings.[70] It also made theology a servant and not the master of the Christian life; doctrine was important, but not as important as Christian character and practice. As Wesley's theological methodology cannot be studied in isolation from his own spiritual pilgrimage, it is important to note where he considered himself to be at the start of this period. A "good Christian" was defined as one who had received salvation in baptism and was exhibiting a measure of freedom from sin (shown by an outward goodness and a willing

---

[67] *Works*, 25:194.

[68] Richard Heitzenrater raised these issues in the context of evaluating Wesley's Aldersgate experience in 1738; in my opinion they can also be applied to this early period. See *Mirror & Memory*, 108.

[69] See for example *Works*, 25:208. Wesley agreed with his mother's concern that "practical divinity" would be the heart of his studies at Oxford; this had to do with the essentials of the faith, rather than speculative matters not essential for salvation; see Ibid., 160. His father gave quite detailed information that Wesley later published in 1735 as *Advice to a Young Clergyman*; see Ibid., 157-59.

[70] An overview of the historical development of the doctrine of Christian Perfection can be found in Paul M. Bassett and William M. Greathouse, *Exploring Christian Holiness: The Historical Development*, Exploring Christian Holiness, vol. 2 (Kansas City, MO: Beacon Hill Press of Kansas City, 1985); Paul M. Bassett, ed., *Holiness Teaching-New Testament Times to Wesley*, ed. A. F. Harper, Great Holiness Classics, vol. 1 (Kansas City, MO: Beacon Hill Press of Kansas City, 1997).

repentance when failure occurred). He was relying on outward evidences for his salvation and this salvation was maintained by a balance of faith and good works (obeying the commands of Scripture and using the means of grace), "But all that was said to me of inward obedience or holiness I neither understood nor remembered."[71]

Defining a "Good Christian": Wesley's Understanding of the Nature of God and Human Beings

The extant material does not display anything in Wesley's conception of the Trinitarian nature of God that was novel or outside of orthodox belief.[72] God was not an absentee or indifferent Being, but rather one who ruled over his Creation through his divine Providence, and this clearly favoured those who made a positive response to his commands.[73] In the sermon "On Guardian Angels" we find the first explicit reference to the fact that God is love and that he favours those who are most like him.[74] Wesley believed that another essential divine quality is happiness and this was to be shared by his creatures.[75] During these years a central theme in his writings had to do with the scriptural assertion that human beings are created in the "image of God." While this was a theological commonplace, it became central to his conception of salvation, and especially his understanding of Christian perfection. The first university sermon discussed what it meant for the human race to be created in the image of God.[76] He painted a very high picture of Adamic perfection,[77] but it was love that was central:

> His [Adam's] affections were rational, even, and regular–if we may be allowed to say 'affections', for properly speaking he had but one: *man was what God is, Love.* [emphasis mine] Love filled the whole expansion of his soul; it possessed

---

[71] *Works*, 18:243. The editors note Wesley's custom of writing memoranda on important events and this is clearly one such, prepared at the time and then incorporated into his published *Journal* two years later (possibly with some revision); see n.30, p. 242.

[72] For a recent theological discussion on Wesley, Wesleyanism and the Trinity, see M. Douglas Meeks, ed., *Trinity, Community, and Power: Mapping Trajectories in Wesleyan Theology* (Nashville, TN: Kingswood Books, 2000); Kenneth J. Collins, "A Reconfiguration of Power: The Basic Trajectory in John Wesley's Practical Theology," *WTJ* 33, no. 1 (Spring, 1998).

[73] He strongly upheld God's positive care for us on our earthly pilgrimage; see for example "Seek First the Kingdom," in *Works*, 4:220.

[74] *Works*, 4:232. Love is the core quality that is at the heart of what it means to be created in God's image; see Ibid., 217-73, 94.

[75] Ibid., 310.

[76] Ibid., 354. See also *Works*, 3:533.

[77] *Works*, 4:293-95. Wesley explicitly stated his appeal was to the Biblical account and to reason.

him without a rival. Every movement of his heart was love: it knew no other fervour.[78]

Love is a relational quality and God is a Triune Being who is in relationship with the other persons of the Godhead as well as the persons that he created; it is the relationship of holy love that is defines their personhood rather than some ontological substance.[79] Wesley was adamant that love (and happiness) can only truly exist where there is liberty and the power of contrary choice. He believed that all persons desired to be happy and were capable of virtue through personal choice, for "where there is no choice, there can be no virtue." [80] Human freedom required obedience to be tested,[81] and we failed the test by freely choosing to violate God's clear command, resulting in sin entering the world. The impact of this on humanity was that "sin hath now effaced the image of God. He is no longer nearly allied to angels. He has sunk lower than the very beasts of the field. His soul is not only earthly and sensual, but devilish."[82] In describing the effects of disobedience, Wesley distinguished between "certainties" based on Scripture and "probabilities" based on observation.[83] The doctrine of original sin was, therefore, one of the "fundamental" truths of religion and its sure evidence was the fact of death.[84] It impacted not only the body, but also the very nature of each person:

> But these chains of darkness ... are within us, too; they enter into our soul; ... Our nature is distempered, as well as enslaved; ... Our body, soul, and spirit, are infected, overspread, consumed, with the most fatal leprosy. We are all over, within and without, in the eye of God, full of diseases, and wounds, and putrifying sores.[85]

His language here is of sin as a disease that has infected the human race and that needs to be "cured." This therapeutic language stands in marked contrast to the forensic terminology that had dominated so much of Protestant theology, with its stress on guilt and forgiveness.[86]

---

[78] Ibid., 294.

[79] See Ibid., 225-35, 348-50.

[80] Ibid., 228. This desire for happiness was the prime motivation for all of our thoughts and actions; see Ibid., 209, 38-39.

[81] Ibid., 295.

[82] Ibid., 354.

[83] Ibid., 296. In describing the effects of the Fall, Wesley took note of the latest findings in physiology and medicine, but he believed that Christianity offered the only explanation for the realities of human existences; see pp. 296-99.

[84] Ibid., 302-03.

[85] Ibid., 354.

[86] For a fuller discussion on this point and its implications, see Randy L. Maddox, *Responsible Grace: John Wesley's Practical Theology* (Nashville, TN: Kingswood Books, 1994), especially 73-83. Wesley did use forensic language in other settings, just

Wesley believed that God intended the human race to regain all that had been lost due to the wrong choice exercised in Eden. This was to be accomplished as a result of re-establishing a right relationship with God. Even at this stage of his spiritual journey, Wesley had rejected the notion that human beings were basically good and could work out their salvation by their own efforts. Likewise, he had dismissed the Calvinist ideas of predestination and election as impugning God's justice and mercy. However, like the Calvinists, he was sure that the "natural man" (all persons apart from the influence of God's grace) was not open to be taught of God and unable to earn his favour.[87] This left him with a problem that took many years to solve, though there are hints of his final answer through the role of prevenient grace even in this period. Wesley stressed the need for knowledge of our own sinfulness, because this was the foundation of all true religion: "Because if man be not naturally corrupt, then all religion, Jewish and Christian, is vain, seeing it is all built on this–all method[s] of cure presupposing the disease."[88] The only answer to our plight was to be found in Jesus Christ, for in him we are restored to "such a measure of present happiness as is a fit introduction to that which flows at God's right hand for evermore."[89] In Wesley's judgement the need to "recover our first estate, from which we are thus fallen, is the one thing now needful–to re-exchange the image of Satan for the image of God, bondage for freedom, sickness for health."[90] All of God's providential dealings with us and the direct workings of the Holy Spirit are directed toward this end,[91] and it was envisaged in terms of perfect love:

> For to this end was man created, to love God; and to this end alone, even to love the Lord his God with all his heart, and soul, and mind, and strength. But love is the very image of God: it is the brightness of his glory. By love man is not only made like God, but in some sense one with him... Love is perfect freedom ... Love is the health of the soul, the full exertion of all its powers, the perfection of all its faculties.[92]

While Wesley clearly had established the nature of perfection as love from the beginning of this period, it remained largely an intellectual comprehension and there was no clear sense of how it was to be attained. He initially held a far more pessimistic view about the possibility of virtuous living while on earth than would be true in later years. Wesley believed that the will must yield to

---

as he also referred to sin in substantial terms and not simply relational ones. See also *Works*, 3:533.

[87] *Works*, 1:401-02.
[88] *Works*, 4:302.
[89] Ibid., 301.
[90] Ibid., 355.
[91] Ibid., 356-57.
[92] Ibid., 355-56.

any truth clearly known: "A distinct perception commands our assent, and the will is under a moral necessity of yielding to it."[93] Consequently, perfection was only possible in heaven, where a new incorruptible body would perfectly express the intentions of the will. This emphasis on truth is related to his understanding of the role of reason in the Christian life and it helps to explain why his scruples on doctrinal matters were so important to him at this point. The implications of this understanding of the relationship of intellect and will also impacted the way that his search for personal holiness and assurance unfolded. It raised critical questions on the possibility of certainty in the Christian life, and what happens when all we have to work with is probability. Pastorally, all these issues would be important when it came to judging the spiritual state of others: he did not seem to grasp that the same problem existed in trying to arrive at the truth of his own spiritual state. His time in Georgia (1735-1737) did not add significantly to Wesley's understanding of the nature of God and human beings beyond that exhibited at Oxford.[94] Love remained at the heart of his perception of the nature of God and humanity:

> Now, that the recovery of the image of God, ... is the one thing needful upon earth, ... For to this end was man created, to love God; and to this end alone, even to love the Lord his God with all his heart, and soul, and mind, and strength. But love is the very image of God: it is the brightness of his glory. By love man is not only made like God, but in some sense one with him. ... Love is perfect freedom. ... Love is the health of the soul, the full exertion of all its powers, the perfection of all its faculties.[95]

On Wesley's return to London at the beginning of 1738 his earlier comprehension of God as love and humanity created in his image (also defined in terms of love) remained as strong as ever. Its importance was seen in his developing dispute with the Calvinists over the process of salvation.[96] The dispute centred on whether salvation required a human response (a measure of free will) or was irresistible (predestination). Wesley's main reason for rejecting predestination ("a doctrine full of blasphemy") was because of the picture of Christ it portrayed: a Saviour who invited all to come but elected only a few effectively destroyed the justice, mercy and truth of the Father.[97] Wesley firmly believed that "the grace or love of God, whence cometh our

---

[93] *Works*, 25:174.

[94] See for example *Works*, 4:354; 25:502.

[95] *Works*, 4:355. See also Ibid., 383.

[96] The developments in the dispute can be read in the correspondence of the period. Note especially the early developments as outlined in a letter to James Hutton and the Fetter Lane society in *Works*, 25:637-41. It became apparent with the personal break between Wesley and George Whitefield in 1739 on the issue of predestination, but was made explicit by the publication of Wesley's sermon, "Free Grace"; see *Works*, 3:542-43.

[97] *Works*, 3:554-56.

salvation, is free in all, and free for all."[98] If it was not, then no real relationship was possible, since it would be based on coercion (election) rather than liberty and the power of contrary choice. For Wesley the critical factor was that "no Scripture can mean that God is not love, or that his mercy is not over all his works."[99] Love was a relational quality, and the rest of his developing theological picture of salvation had to harmonise with this essential understanding.

Becoming a "Good Christian":
Wesley's Understanding of the God-Human Relationship

Wesley was in the Arminian wing of the Church of England and this is seen in his strong emphasis on humanity's freedom of choice and moral agency in the process of the recovery of the image of God. For him, sin was always a result of choice; otherwise it impugned God's justice and goodness and denied the reality of love. Wesley did not stand with those who held to a narrow understanding of the *sola fide* and *sola gratia* of strict Calvinism; he was certain that God freely allowed humans the power of choice and this was not contrary to any of his divine attributes.[100] While the grace of salvation was bestowed at baptism, it was up to the individual to cooperate with that grace in the ongoing life of holiness. The major change in his awareness of how to become and then remain "a good Christian" began with reading two key works during 1725. The first was Jeremy Taylor's *Rules and Exercises of Holy Living and Rules and Exercises of Holy Dying* and the second was the *Imitatio Christi* by Thomas à Kempis.[101] It was primarily from these two authors that he slowly came to realise that a Christian was one who possessed an inward holiness and not merely one who achieved an outward standard of behaviour. A Christian was one who possessed inner virtues defined in terms of a pure intention, a proper inclination of the soul, and having the mind of Christ. An increasing personal dissatisfaction drove his search for a personal experience of God that was more than an intellectual affirmation of propositional truth found in Scripture, the Articles, the Homilies, or conformity to the outward exercises of devotion within formal church life. The significance of this shift in understanding lay in the fact that it personalised Christianity; it was not simply something to be believed and obeyed, but it was a relationship (based on love and trust) to be enjoyed. However, it would take many years before this became clear to him as an experiential reality.

This realisation of the interior aspect of being a Christian also made him

---

[98] Ibid., 544.
[99] Ibid., 556. He then gave a whole series of texts on God's invitation to all and the role of human choice in our eternal destiny; see p. 558-63.
[100] *Works*, 4:285.
[101] *Works*, 25:162-64.

begin to search for accounts of the holy life that were more than descriptions of behaviour, adherence to standards or intellectual assent to propositional truth (though a sermon preached in January 1727 showed no trace of an evangelical understanding of the faith).[102] The overwhelming picture from the early sermons of this period is of a relationship between God and the Christian dominated by notions of duty and self-discipline.[103] The Christian was a pilgrim and a "stoic" who bore with patience, endurance and resignation the suffering and evil that came their way; no state of "perfect happiness" was possible in this life and so our focus must be on heaven.[104] The role of the Holy Spirit was to assist us in the process of becoming righteous, but there was no clear understanding of how this would be achieved.[105] There were several brief references to the central importance of the two great commandments to love God and neighbour, but his descriptions were cast in moralistic terms.[106] He was sure that the place to begin to form a right relationship with God was by correcting the understanding through clearing the mind of all wrong belief.[107] However, mere knowledge by itself was insufficient in establishing a genuine and lasting relationship with God; our affections must also be regulated: "Indeed without doing this the other can't be done throughly [sic]–he that would well enlighten the head must cleanse the heart. Otherwise the disorder of the will again disorders the understanding, and perverseness of affection will again cause an equal perverseness of judgment."[108] A genuine Christian experience involved both the "head" and the "heart" and it was the latter that was crucial. He believed this was supported by the Bible:

> God everywhere declares: ... (2). That as good prayers without good works attending them are no better than a solemn mockery of God, so are good works themselves without those tempers of heart, from their subserviency to which they derive their whole value. (3). That those tempers which alone are acceptable to God, and to procure acceptance for which our Redeemer lived and died, are, ... Faith, ... Hope, ... Love of God, and our neighbour for his sake ... [109]

The implications of all this for Christian faith and practice are still not fully comprehended, but it will become a major element in his mature

---

[102] *Works*, 4:236-43.
[103] Ibid., 215-43.
[104] Ibid., 206, 12-14, 40. Letters from the period reflect the same stance; see for example *Works*, 25:209-11, 28-29.
[105] *Works*, 4:219.
[106] Ibid., 220. See n. 11 on our duty to neighbour, which is outward or social holiness.
[107] Ibid., 311-12.
[108] Ibid., 313.
[109] *Works*, 25:382.

understanding.¹¹⁰ At this early stage in his life, this goal of heart purity was to be achieved essentially by self-discipline and human effort, aided by God's grace. The references to the heart confirm that Wesley was beginning to see that Christianity had to do with an inner transformation and not merely outward conformity to rules and regulations.¹¹¹ The correlation between holiness, happiness and the centrality of love as the means to both would become explicit in his later sermons and correspondence. The way to actually experience this for himself was still under intense scrutiny and he made use of his wide circle of friends, as well as his reading, to further his search.

> My present sense is this. I was made to be happy; to be happy I must love God; in proportion to my love of whom my happiness must increase. To love God I must be like him, holy as he is holy; which implies both the being pure from vicious and foolish passions and the being confirmed in those virtues and rational affections which God comprises in the word charity. In order to root those out of my soul and plant these in their stead I must use, (1), such means as are ordered by God, (2), such as are recommended by experience and reason.¹¹²

For Wesley, a Christian could not be too happy or therefore too holy. This meant that he used the instituted means of grace (those ordered by God) as often as possible and with as great exactness as possible (focused on the practices of the primitive church, particularly as interpreted by the Nonjurors). As to "things indifferent in themselves," they were not indifferent to Wesley if they hindered or aided his pursuit of holiness and so "prudential means" (those recommended by experience and reason) were very important.¹¹³ Wesley came

---

¹¹⁰ For an examination of Wesley's moral psychology and its importance in understanding his conception of salvation see: Gregory S. Clapper, *John Wesley on Religious Affections: His Views on Experience and Emotion and Their Role in the Christian Life and Theology* (Metuchen, NJ: Scarecrow Press, 1989); Maddox, *Responsible Grace*, 69-70; Gregory S. Clapper, "'True Religion' and the Affections: A Study of John Wesley's Abridgement of Jonathan Edwards' Treatise on Religious Affections," *WTJ* 19:2 (Fall 1984).

¹¹¹ In a letter to his brother, Samuel, he passed on the following advice: "You are to labour with all your might to convince them that Christianity is not a negation, or an external thing, but a new heart, a mind conformed to that of Christ, 'faith working by love'." See *Works*, 25:444.

¹¹² Ibid., 293-94.

¹¹³ Ibid., 294. See also *Works*, 4:319-28. For an examination of the means of grace in Wesley's thought and practice, see Henry H. Knight III, *The Presence of God in the Christian Life: John Wesley and the Means of Grace* (Lanham, MD: Scarecrow Press, 1992); Rebekah L. Miles, "'the Arts of Holy Living': Holiness and the Means of Grace," *Quarterly Review* 25, no. 2 (Summer, 2005); Dean G. Blevins, "The Means of Grace: Toward a Wesleyan Praxis of Spiritual Formation," *WTJ* 32, no. 1 (Spring, 1997); Ole E. Borgen, *John Wesley on the Sacraments: A Definitive Study of John Wesley's*

to see that the whole of Christian duty could be summed up as Christ living in us; this fulfilled the Law and made us "perfect."[114] This was a decisive move from the Reformation stress on righteousness in terms of law, to righteousness as a right relationship made possible by a transformation of character through the indwelling Christ. This was confirmed by the first University sermon (November 1730), which dealt with the notion of salvation as a restoration of the image of God through Jesus Christ.[115]

Since love and relationship were now at the heart of his understanding of salvation, he was beginning to distinguish between perfect intention and perfect performance. The latter was the concern of those who upheld the centrality of perfect obedience to God's law; the former was related to the essential nature of a relationship based on love.[116] In a relationship of love, there can be pure intention (a matter of the heart) but flawed performance (due to a corruptible mind and body). Because of intention, the essential nature of sin was seen as a deliberate and wilful choice to harm the relationship; thus its 'voluntariness' was a crucial part of his definition of terms.

> Perfect, indeed, he [Apostle Paul] was from sin, strictly speaking, *which is a voluntary breach of a known law* [emphasis mine], at least from habits of such sin. As to single acts he 'knew whom he had believed'. He knew who had promised to forgive these, not seven times but seventy times seven.[117]

The nuances and implications of this understanding are still some time in the future and it will become one of the most disputed points in his theological understanding, as it lies at the heart of the theological disagreements between the Calvinist and Arminian wings of the evangelical revival in the eighteenth century. Holiness of heart as the centre of true religion heightened after 1732 as he read the writings of the mystics, especially the works of Bourignon, Guyon, Fénelon, Poiret, de Renty and Law (who by 1732 was strongly under the influence of Böhemist mysticism). They almost convinced him outward works

---

Theology of Worship (Nashville, TN: Abingdon Press, 1972; reprint, Grand Rapids, MI: Zondervan, 1985).

[114] Heitzenrater, *Mirror & Memory*, 30.

[115] *Works*, 4:293-303.

[116] Wesley had first grappled with this distinction as a result of his scruples over the damnatory clauses in the Athanasian Creed. In correspondence from his father, Samuel wrote that there was a distinction between what is wilful and what may be in some measure involuntary; he believed the clauses were directed at the former. See Ibid., 25:182.

[117] Ibid., 318. This was a letter to Ann Granville (October 3, 1731); he had written earlier to Mary Pendarves (June 19, 1731): "because, *all sin being a voluntary breach of a known law* [emphasis mine], none but he who seeth the heart, and consequently how far this breach of his law is voluntary in each particular person, can possibly know which infidel shall perish, and which be received to mercy." See Ibid., 287-89.

were useless in the pursuit of inner holiness, defined now as the "union of the soul with God." The focus of the mystical approach was love and so the love of God was seen as the "one thing needful."[118] The centre of such a faith was the heart, where the life of God redirected the affections, purified intentions, restored virtues and brought about a life of love. This was all clearly in place by the time of his landmark sermon, "The Circumcision of the Heart", written at the end of 1732 for delivery at St. Mary's, Oxford on January 1, 1733.[119]

"THE CIRCUMCISION OF THE HEART," JANUARY 1, 1733

Wesley affirmed that the essential definition of being "a good Christian" was one who had experienced an inner change and not simply one who conformed to external standards; "... the distinguishing mark of a true follower of Christ, of one who is in a state of acceptance with God, is not either outward circumcision or baptism, or any other outward form, but a right state of soul – a mind and spirit renewed after the image of him that created it...."[120] He then went on to define what he meant by the "circumcision of the heart" :

> ... it is that habitual disposition of soul which in the Sacred Writings is termed 'holiness', and which directly implies the being cleansed from sin, 'from all filthiness both of flesh and spirit', and by consequence the being endued with those virtues which were also in Christ Jesus, the being so 'renewed in the image of our mind' as to be 'perfect, as our Father in heaven is perfect'.[121]

It is important to note that this first explicit description of renewal and perfection was defined negatively as being cleansed from sin (prior), and only then positively as being infused with the virtues of Christ.[122] He clarified that

---

[118] *Works*, 4:329-45, 54-58, 74.

[119] *Works*, 1:401-14 and the introductory comments on pp. 398-400. Outler notes that here we find nearly all the basic elements of his mature understanding of soteriology and this is before his contact with the Moravians in Georgia or his Aldersgate experience in May 1738. For the background leading up to the writing of the sermon see *Works*, 25:335-44, 64-71. Such was its quality that Wesley regarded it as one of his most careful and complete statements of his understanding of holiness and he wrote in 1778 that he could not improve upon it. It was the only one of his early sermons to be included in *Sermons On Several Occasions*. We can see that Wesley's grasp of the essence of the doctrine of Christian perfection as a relationship of love is clearly established by the end of 1732.

[120] *Works*, 1:402.

[121] Ibid., 402-03.

[122] Ibid., 403. The centrality of love is also seen in another sermon from 1733 entitled "The Love of God." The sermon focused almost exclusively on the first great commandment to the neglect of love of neighbour. Later he would always link the love of God (prior) and the love of neighbour. See *Works*, 4:332. The centrality of love is further emphasised in the preface to his *A Collection of Forms of Prayer, For Every Day in the Week* in *Works* (Jackson), 11:203-08.

we cannot achieve this through our own efforts:

> ... we are convinced that we are not sufficient of ourselves to help ourselves; that *without the Spirit of God we can do nothing* but add sin to sin; that it is *he alone* 'who worketh in us' by his almighty power, either 'to will or do' that which is good–it being as impossible for us even to think a good thought *without the supernatural assistance of his Spirit* as to create ourselves, or to renew our whole souls in righteousness and true holiness (emphasis mine).[123]

The exact way in which the Spirit worked with each person was still not clear to Wesley himself, but he was certain that it required God's grace assisting us in some way. This grace was available only through faith:[124] "that faith which is not only an unshaken assent to all that God hath revealed in Scripture ... 'Jesus Christ came into the world to save sinners'; he 'bare our sins in his own body on the tree'; 'he is the propitiation for our sins; and not for ours only, but also for the sins of the whole world'; ..."[125] Wesley was still seeing faith largely in terms of assent to propositional truth and the dimension of personal trust was missing.[126] This is made even clearer when we read his later editorial addition (it immediately followed the final semi-colon that ended the previous quotation) when the sermon was published in 1748:

> ...but likewise the revelation of Christ in our hearts: a divine evidence or conviction of his love, his free, unmerited love to me a sinner; a sure confidence in his pardoning mercy, wrought in us by the Holy Ghost–a confidence whereby every true believer is enabled to bear witness, 'I know that my Redeemer liveth'; that *I* 'have an advocate with the Father', that 'Jesus Christ the righteous is' *my* Lord, and 'the propitiation for *my* sins.' I know he 'hath loved *me*, and given himself for *me*'. He 'hath reconciled *me*, even *me* to God'; and *I* 'have redemption through his blood, even the forgiveness of sins'.[127]

This demonstrates that the vital missing element in his theological understanding of salvation during this period was understanding faith as trust. The missing dimension in his own life was a personal, inward experience of God and this could not occur until he saw the dimension of trust and relationship as an integral part of a full-orbed definition of faith. The limiting of

---

[123] *Works*, 1:403-04.
[124] Ibid., 404.
[125] Ibid., 405.
[126] For an examination of Wesley's changing understanding from faith as assent to propositional truth to trusting confidence and spiritual experience, see Rex D. Matthews, "'With the Eyes of Faith': Spiritual Experience and the Knowledge of God in the Theology of John Wesley," *Wesleyan Theology Today*, 406-15; Mark L. Horst, "Experimenting with Christian Wholeness: Method in Wesley's Theology," *Quarterly Review* 7, no. 2 (1987): 11-23.
[127] *Works*, 1:405.

faith to assent in effect left him with no other option but to exercise rigorous self-discipline in cultivating his relationship with God, seeking to put into practice what his intellectual discoveries were showing him.[128] That all this was finally unsatisfactory is amply demonstrated in the next few years, even though his theological grasp of the way of salvation is remarkably clear.

A crucial element in this sermon was his explicit reference to perfection, making it central to his whole conception of what it meant to be a Christian:

> Yet lackest thou one thing, whosoever thou art, that to a deep humility and a steadfast faith hast joined a lively hope, and thereby in a good measure cleansed thy heart from its inbred pollution. If thou wilt be perfect, add to all these charity: add love, and thou hast the 'circumcision of the heart'. 'Love is the fulfilling of the law,' 'the end of the commandment'. Very excellent things are spoken of love; it is the essence, the spirit, the life of all virtue. It is not only the first and great command, but it is all the commandments in one. Whatsoever things are just, whatsoever things are pure, whatsoever things are amiable or honourable; if there be any virtue, if there be any praise, they are all comprised in this one word – love. In this is perfection and glory and happiness.[129]

This upheld an essentially relational understanding of Christianity even though, as we saw earlier, it would not become an experiential reality for him for several years. The entire sermon was a very carefully thought-out exposition of what would become his most distinctive doctrine: Christian perfection understood as perfect love of God and neighbour, anchored in faith in Christ's revelation of that love and its power.[130] It was all the more remarkable for describing an experience of grace that Wesley himself did not possess. It helps us to understand why he would not settle for anything less as his own experience and why he was willing to try so many avenues of church tradition to find it.

In sharp contrast to this message, the impact of mysticism was to be seen in a number of sermons in 1733 and 1734, with a strong imbalance on the side of the love of God separated from the love of neighbour.[131] Wesley preached to the university again in 1735 and his sermon exhibited a common view of the 'art of dying' that was so popular with preachers of the period. He returned to his therapeutic language for salvation, but did so in quite negative terms: "But as perfect holiness is not found on earth, so neither is perfect happiness: some remains of our disease will ever be felt, and some physic be necessary to heal

---

[128] See Ibid., 412-14.

[129] Ibid., 407. Wesley was sure that loving God with all our being was not to deny the legitimate love of other things that God provided for us to enjoy; see *Works*, 1:408; 4:310-12.

[130] *Works*, 1:398-99.

[131] See for example *Works*, 4:331-45. A brief reference to loving the neighbour is found in *Works*, 25:398.

it."[132] The sermon was permeated by a strong note of Christian stoicism, with only death and heaven providing deliverance from the sin and miseries of life on earth.[133] In his preface to *The Christian's Pattern* published in 1735 Wesley had re-focused on Christian perfection as love, but defined in terms of a "union of our will with God's" that enables us to be made a "partaker of the divine nature." It is the union of our will with the divine that is "the highest degree of Christian perfection." In order to attain this, a person had to pass through several stages till the soul be fully purged from "all wilful, habitual sin" and is enlightened by the knowledge and practice of virtue. The book then gives "in the most experimental manner" how we may conform our will to the divine using the means of grace.[134]

CONTACT WITH THE MORAVIANS IN GEORGIA, 1735-1737

Wesley's contact with the Moravians in Georgia convinced him that the essence of religion lay in a personal transformation brought about by the living presence of the Holy Spirit in the person's life. In a letter he wrote: "I entirely agree with you that religion is love and peace and joy in the Holy Ghost; that as it is the happiest, so it is the cheerfullest thing in the world."[135] He then referred to the other triad that was becoming commonplace in his writings–faith, hope and love; he longed to experience these for himself and then "with the power of the Holy Ghost preventing, accompanying, and following me, I know that I (that is, the grace of God which is in me) shall save both myself and those that hear me."[136] This need for an inward change was underscored in another letter: "that whatsoever we do, and whatsoever we suffer, if we are not renewed in the spirit of our mind by the love of God shed abroad in our hearts by the Holy Ghost given unto us, we cannot enter into life eternal."[137] This is a new development in his spiritual quest, for now he frequently and explicitly writes of the ministry of the Holy Spirit to the individual Christian in the language of personal experience. At this moment, it still remains an intellectual affirmation outside his personal spiritual reality. Initially, Wesley was convinced that such spirituality could only be attained in the same conditions that faced the apostolic church. Holiness, love and simplicity went together, and the personal experience of them he believed was largely a matter of the right external conditions similar to those of the apostolic church.[138] His stress on self-denial (confirmed by the closing paragraphs of the letter) pointed to an understanding of salvation that still retained an emphasis on the necessity of works and the

---

[132] *Works*, 3:533-34.
[133] Ibid., 535-41.
[134] *Works* (Jackson), 14:202-07.
[135] *Works*, 25:500.
[136] Ibid., 501.
[137] *Works*, 4:385-86.
[138] Ibid., 25:441.

means of grace.[139] He continued to stress the notion of pure intention as the essence of holy living, seeking to please God in all things so that he would grow in holiness, the love of God and neighbour:[140]

> Let your one end be to please and love God! ... Seek nothing else! ... His Holy Spirit shall dwell in you, and shine more and more upon your souls unto the perfect day. He shall purify your hearts by faith from every earthly thought, every unholy affection. ... He shall fill you with peace, and joy, and love! Love, the brightness of his glory, the express image of his person! Love which never rests, never faileth, but still spreads its flame, still goeth on conquering and to conquer, till what was but now a weak, foolish, wavering, sinful creature, be filled with all the fullness of God![141]

It was the experience of the love of God that enabled us to be happy, and to be comfortable in death.[142] He mentioned the experience of several Christians to amplify this point. In connection with the death of his own father, he wrote: "But as his love was not perfect so neither was his comfort. He had intervals of anger or fretfulness, and therein of misery, giving by both an incontestable proof that as love can sweeten both life and death, so when that is either absent from, or obscured in, the soul, there is no peace or comfort there."[143] This was contrasted with the recent death of Henry Lascelles (one of the settlers in Frederica): "Here, we may observe, was no mixture of any passion or temper contrary to charity. Therefore was there no misery, perfect love casting out whatever might have occasioned torment. And whosoever thou art who hast the like measure of love, thy last end shall be like his!"[144] Here Wesley associated perfect love with approaching death, and not with an earlier stage of the Christian life. He observed that some of his people were growing in peace and holiness, and having a hope of enduring to the end: "Not that this hope has any resemblance to enthusiasm, which is a hope to attain the end without the means. This they know is impossible, and therefore ground their hope on a constant, careful use of all the means."[145] Notice that Wesley specifically mentioned hope

---

[139] Ibid., 442.

[140] *Works*, 4:371-74. A theme learned from à Kempis, Scougal, Taylor and Law; see also *Works*, 25:503.

[141] *Works*, 4:377.

[142] Ibid., 386-87.

[143] Ibid., 387.

[144] Ibid., 388.

[145] *Works*, 25:504. Enthusiasm is commonly defined in this period as blatant subjectivity, where a person's impulses, impressions, visions, dreams and even conduct are assumed to be the result of direct communication with the Holy Spirit. The person's own subjective impressions are then confused with the activity of God. For Wesley's own definition, see *Works*, 19:31-32. On 'enthusiasm' in connection with Wesley, see W. Stephen Gunter, *The Limits of 'Love Divine': John Wesley's Response to Antinomianism and Enthusiasm* (Nashville, TN: Kingswood Books, 1989); Ronald A. Knox,

and not assurance, and it was based on "means" and not the "witness of the Spirit." It still left the issue of performance based upon the practices of the apostolic church as central and Wesley never seemed confident that he could ever do these well enough, as the *Journal* reflections at the end of the period in Georgia demonstrate. He estimated "by the most infallible of proofs, inward feeling,"[146] that at the time he was not a Christian at all.[147] A later reflection led him to confess again that he was not a Christian, though it is very important to note that in the errata of the 1774 edition he said he was not sure of this. He was still trusting in good works, attendance at the means of grace, personal discipline and self-denial, and faith still defined as "a rational conviction of all the truths of Christianity."[148] However, due to his time in Georgia he was now more aware of that which was lacking:

> The faith I want is, 'a sure trust and confidence in God, that, through the merits of Christ, my sins are forgiven, and I reconciled to the favour of God.' I want that faith which St. Paul recommends to all the world ... which enables every one that hath it to cry out, 'I live not; but Christ liveth in me; and the life which I now live, I live by faith in the Son of God, who loved me, and gave himself for me.' I want that faith which none can have without knowing that he hath it; (though many *imagine* they have it, who have it not). For whosoever hath it, is 'freed from sin'; 'the whole body of sin is destroyed' in him. He is freed from fear, 'having peace with God through Christ, and rejoicing in hope of the glory of God'. And he is freed from doubt, 'having the love of God shed abroad in his heart, through the Holy Ghost which is given unto him'; which 'Spirit itself beareth witness with his spirit, that he is a child of God'.[149]

Wesley had now discovered experientially that his earlier definition of faith as assent was inadequate. Since the faith Wesley was seeking was clearly defined in the Homilies and these were a part of his studies from the very beginning, the problem was not access to an adequate theological definition of faith, but an experiential conviction that such a faith was both necessary and available to him. He had to come to the place of intense desire for the

---

Enthusiasm: A Chapter in the History of Religion with Special Reference to the XVII and XVIII Centuries (Oxford: Clarendon Press, 1950), 422-548; Lowell O. Ferrel, "John Wesley and the Enthusiasts," *WTJ* 23, no. 1 & 2 (Spring-Fall, 1988).

[146] *Works*, 18:208.

[147] Ibid., 207. Nearing Land's End, he wrote: "I went to America, to convert the Indians; but Oh! who shall convert me? Who, what is he that will deliver me from this evil heart of unbelief?'" See Ibid., 211 and n. 95.

[148] Ibid., 214-15. In the errata of the 1774 edition, Wesley doubted his totally negative evaluation here; he had even then the "faith of a *servant*, though not that of a *son*." This distinction and its implications is explored further in Laura Bartels Felleman, "John Wesley and the 'Servant of God'," *WTJ* 41, no. 2 (Fall, 2006).

[149] Ibid., 215-16. The definition of the faith he was seeking is from the *Homilies*, 'Of Salvation', Pt. III and it was to remain his most frequent definition. See especially n. 19.

experience of a personal relationship with God based on trust, rather than an intellectual comprehension of the Gospel based on assent.

CONTACT WITH THE MORAVIANS IN LONDON, 1738-1739

The critical developments in the brief period between his return to London and the founding of the first Methodist Societies centre around the events bordering Wesley's spiritual experience at a religious society meeting in Aldersgate Street on May 24, 1738.[150] During this period the most important change in his understanding of becoming a "good Christian" had to do with his new experiential understanding of faith as trust.

> ... I was on Sunday the 5th [March 1738] clearly convinced of unbelief, of the want of 'that faith whereby alone we are saved', with the full, Christian salvation.
> Immediately it struck into my mind, 'Leave off preaching. How can you preach to others, who have not faith yourself?' I asked Böhler whether he thought I should leave it off or not. He answered, ... 'Preach faith till you have it, and then, because you have it, you will preach faith.'
> Accordingly, Monday 6, I began preaching this *new* doctrine, though my soul started back from the work. The *first* person to whom I offered salvation by faith alone was a prisoner under sentence of death (emphasis mine).[151]

Wesley plainly admitted that he did not yet have the faith he sought, the faith that was essential to being a good Christian. He referred to this as a "new doctrine" and identified it as "salvation by faith alone." It was surely inconceivable that Wesley had not learned this from the Moravians in Georgia with whom he had conversed so often, so why was it new? In the light of Wesley's continued stress on personal discipline and religious resolutions, it appears he still believed in the necessity of faith and good works *prior to*

---

[150] The nature of Wesley's experience at Aldersgate is much debated and a thorough examination of it is beyond the scope of this book. See Randy L. Maddox, ed., *Aldersgate Reconsidered* (Nashville, TN: Kingswood Books, 1990). The select bibliography is particularly helpful. See also Albert C. Outler, "A Focus on the Holy Spirit: Spirit and Spirituality in John Wesley," *Quarterly Review* 8, no. 2 (1988); J. Ernest Rattenbury, *The Conversion of the Wesleys: A Case Study* (London: Epworth Press, 1938); Dale W. Brown, "The Wesleyan Revival from a Pietist Perspective," *WTJ* 24 (1989); Kenneth J. Collins, "Twentieth-Century Interpretations of John Wesley's Aldersgate Experience: Coherence or Confusion?," *WTJ* 24 (1989); David L. Cubie, "Placing Aldersgate in John Wesley's Order of Salvation," *WTJ* 24 (1989); A. Harold Wood, *The Aldersgate Experience of John Wesley* (Melbourne: Uniting Church Press, 1988); Kenneth J. Collins, *A Faithful Witness: John Wesley's Homiletical Theology* (Wilmore, KY: Wesley Heritage Press, 1993), 149-61; Dawes, "The Spirituality of 'Scriptural Holiness'," 52-53.

[151] *Works*, 18:228. Peter Böhler was a Lutheran minister who had subsequently been ordained into the Moravian ministry; he was a key leader in the Moravian community in London during these years.

justification and so the notion of "faith alone" for justification had not been accepted by him up till this point.[152] The other issue would seem to be the fact that Böhler was stressing an instantaneous conversion, and Wesley saw it as a gradual change wrought by obedience to the will of God. It was Böhler who explained to him that

> ... this faith was the gift, the free gift of God, and that he would surely bestow it upon every soul who earnestly and perseveringly sought it. I was now thoroughly convinced. And, by the grace of God, I resolved to seek it unto the end, (1) by absolutely renouncing all dependence, in whole or in part, upon my own works or righteousness, on which I had really grounded my hope of salvation, though I knew it not, from my youth up; (2) by adding to 'the constant use of all the' other 'means of grace', continual prayer for this very thing, justifying, saving faith, a full reliance on the blood of Christ shed for me; a trust in him as my Christ, as my sole justification, sanctification, and redemption.[153]

Böhler also showed him that true faith brought both dominion over sin and a constant assurance of forgiveness.[154] This contrasted sharply with his own experience prior to Aldersgate:

> In this vile, abject state of bondage to sin I was indeed fighting continually, but not conquering. ... During this whole struggle between nature and grace (which had now continued above ten years) I had many remarkable returns to prayer, especially when I was in trouble; I had many sensible comforts, which are indeed no other than short anticipations of the life of faith. But I was still 'under the law', not 'under grace' ... ; for I was only 'striving with', not 'freed from sin'. Neither had I 'the witness of the Spirit with my spirit'. And indeed could not; for I 'sought it not by faith, but (as it were) by the works of the law'.[155]

Wesley was not a heathen before Aldersgate, for he did experience times of victory over sin and the joy that came with it. Wesley had a relationship with God, but it was not the relationship he desired and was sure he needed. What was lacking was a sustained assurance of being accepted by God and having the power to always conquer sin. It was the insistence on constant assurance that was to prove troublesome for Wesley and was later, when he had come to a clearer theological understanding of the relationship between faith and assurance, to lead to a re-thinking of his evaluation of this stage of his life. Immediately after Aldersgate he was certain that faith was "not barely a

---

[152] Wesley admitted in a later reflection on this stage of his life that he had been essentially a "papist" for ten years because of his understanding of works; that had now changed with his views on justification by faith alone. See *Works*, 19:89-92.

[153] *Works*, 18:248-49.

[154] Ibid., 247-48. Wesley would later see this emphasis on "constant assurance" as an error.

[155] Ibid., 247. See also *Works*, 19:92-93.

speculative, rational thing, a cold, lifeless assent, a train of ideas in the head; but also a disposition of the heart."[156]

> Christian faith is then not only an assent to the whole gospel of Christ, but also a full reliance on the blood of Christ, a trust in the merits of his life, death, and resurrection; a recumbency upon him as our atonement and our life, as *given for us*, and *living in us*. It is a sure confidence which a man hath in God, that through the merits of Christ *his* sins are forgiven, and *he* reconciled to the favour of God;...[157]

Moreover, there was an immediate victory over the power of sin available to the new Christian. Following a long series of quotations from I John on being saved from sin, he wrote:

> He that is by faith born of God sinneth not, (1), by any habitual sin, for all habitual sin is sin reigning; but sin cannot reign in any that believeth. Nor, (2), by any wilful sin; for his will, while he abideth in the faith, is utterly set against all sin, ... Nor, (3), by any sinful desire; for he continually desireth the holy and perfect will of God; ... Nor, (4), doth he sin by infirmities, whether in act, word, or thought; for his infirmities have no concurrence of his will; and without this they are not properly sins. Thus, 'He that is born of God doth not commit sin.' And though he cannot say he *hath not sinned*, yet now '*he sinneth not*'.
> This then is the salvation which is through faith, even in the present world: a salvation from sin and the consequences of sin, both often expressed in the word 'justification', ... So that he who is thus justified or saved by faith is indeed 'born again'. He is 'born again of the Spirit' unto a new 'life which is hid with Christ in God'.[158]

Christians were saved from the fear, but not the possibility, of falling away from the grace of God, and to this salvation the Holy Spirit bore witness.[159]

Wesley was convinced that this salvation was for everyone and not simply a chosen few, due to the reality of God's love for the whole race.[160] This commitment meant he had to explain how choice was possible given his belief in original sin and its consequences. As an Arminian, he believed the solution was found in the concept of "free grace." In his sermon, "Salvation by Faith," he showed that "grace is the source, faith the condition, of salvation" and it was given to all.[161] All of salvation from the human perspective was purely by grace

---

[156] *Works*, 1:120.
[157] Ibid., 121. See also *Works* (Jackson), 13:499. Wesley affirmed there was a role for assent, but denied it was sufficient for salvation.
[158] *Works*, 1:124. This was too strong a statement and he would alter his opinion in the next phase of his ministry, as we shall see.
[159] Ibid., 122-23.
[160] Ibid., 122.
[161] Ibid., 118.

alone; there was nothing of any merit in human beings since the fall.[162] Such grace

> ... does not depend on any power or merit in man; no, not in any degree, neither in whole, nor in part. It does not in any wise depend either on the good works or righteousness of the receiver; not on anything he has done, or anything he is. ... for all these flow from the free grace of God. ... They are the fruits of free grace, and not the root. ... Whatsoever good is in man, or is done by man, God is the author and doer of it. Thus is his grace free in all, that is, no way depending on any power or merit in man, but on God alone, who freely gave us his own Son, ...[163]

Grace was free for all to whom it was given; otherwise it would undermine preaching by making the gospel unnecessary and destroy holiness by removing the motives of hope of heaven and fear of hell.[164]

Grace and faith did not, however, mean that people had no role to play in their salvation and Wesley denied that people had to be entirely passive while waiting for its bestowal. He rejected the 'stillness' doctrine of the Fetter Lane Moravians due to its impact on a person's life, producing doubt and a loss of faith.[165] The Moravian view was "that till they had true faith, they ought to be *still*, that is ... 'to abstain from "the means of grace", as they are called–the Lord's Supper *in particular*'; (2) 'that *the ordinances are not means of grace*, there being no other means than Christ'."[166] Wesley's response in his *Journal* is to then give an account of a woman who found faith through the Lord's Supper.

> What to be inferred from this undeniable matter of fact–*one that had not faith received it in the Lord's Supper?* Why, (1) that there are 'means of grace', i.e., outward ordinances, whereby the inward grace of God is ordinarily conveyed to man, whereby the faith that brings salvation is conveyed to them who before had it not; (2) that *one of these means is the Lord's Supper*; and (3) that *he who has not this faith ought to wait for it in the use both of this and of the other means which God hath ordained.*[167]

Wesley agreed that people should wait for true faith but he defined this in an active sense through making use of the means of grace. He believed they were a "means of grace" because they "do ordinarily convey God's grace to unbelievers." He was certain that you could use them without trusting in them.[168] This was a vital statement, for it emphasised that it was essential to

---

[162] Ibid., 117-18.
[163] *Works*, 3:545.
[164] Ibid., 545-57.
[165] See for example *Works*, 19:119-20.
[166] Ibid.
[167] Ibid., 121.
[168] Ibid., 131-34.

trust in God alone for salvation, while using (but not relying upon) the means that he had supplied. He was equally sure that scriptural faith must result in good works and holiness or it was not true faith.[169]

> That salvation, ... the Scripture teaches is only by or through faith; and the Church of England expressly teaches the same thing, viz. that the cause of our salvation is, only the righteousness and blood of Christ; and the condition of it, only faith, faith without works, faith exclusive of all works whatsoever ... but necessarily productive of all holiness and good works if we continue rooted and grounded therein.[170]

Wesley saw the role of the Christian community in a person's salvation as vitally important. "'Holy solitaries' is a phrase no more consistent with the gospel than holy adulterers. The gospel of Christ knows of no religion, but social; no holiness but social holiness. 'Faith working by love' is the length and breadth and height of Christian perfection."[171] This would now become a commonplace in his ministry, so sure was he of its significance for spiritual health.

Knowing you are a "Good Christian": Wesley's Understanding of Assurance

While at Oxford, Wesley had understood the early part of Jeremy Taylor's book on *Holy Living* to teach that we can never know if we have been forgiven by God, and this seemed to clash with what was taught later about grace being conferred in the Lord's Supper.[172]

> Now surely these graces are not of so little force as that we can't perceive whether we have 'em or not; and if we dwell in Christ and Christ in us, which he will not do till we are regenerate, certainly we must be sensible of it. ... But if we can never have any certainty of our being in a state of salvation, good reason it is that every moment should be spent, not in joy, but fear and trembling...[173]

Up till now Wesley had apparently been satisfied with the general evidence of salvation learned from his parents: doing the works of a Christian, striving for an increase in Christian perfection, accompanied by some measure of happiness.[174] Here the test of experience was clearly applied: being a good

---

[169] Ibid., 125-27.
[170] *Works*, 25:610. The reference is to the difference between the "faith of a servant" (pre-Aldersgate) and the "faith of a son" (post-Aldersgate) in his later reflections. See also *Works*, 19:103; *Works* (Jackson), 14: 320.
[171] *Works* (Jackson), 14: 321. He also quoted a series of texts on loving God and neighbour to illustrate this point; see p. 321-22 and *Works*, 19:122.
[172] *Works*, 25:167-70.
[173] Ibid., 169-70.
[174] Ibid., 160, 65-66.

Christian ought to involve a note of certainty and this was only possible by some form of inner evidence that would complement the outer evidence observed by others. Just what this inner evidence was and how it could be acquired would be the focus of his spiritual search leading up to his experience at Aldersgate in May 1738. Meanwhile, the only evidence he had to work with was sincerity: "to know that our hope is sincerity, not perfection, not to do well, but to do our best."[175] Wesley worked with the crucial distinction between intention and performance that we noted earlier. His formal understanding of the difference seems to have been derived from Robert Nelson's *The Great Duty of Frequenting the Christian Sacrifice*, which he had finally abridged in a sermon published in 1732.[176] Wesley noted that before the Fall the covenant of God with us was "do this and live"; a covenant demanding perfect obedience, which the human race was capable of giving at that time. After the Fall a new covenant was made; while the reward promised was the same, the condition had changed to "try to do this and live." In allowing for fallen human nature and its bodily consequences, God no longer required perfect obedience, but "earnest, hearty obedience"; keeping every law of God as far as it was now possible and doing the whole will of God in as full a manner as was in our power. Both covenants demand that we do all we can and performance is linked to ability; perfect performance was possible before the Fall, now we must do the best we can.[177]

Wesley hungered for evidence, and for a time considered virtues as solid evidence of the love that was the manifestation of faith; a tension then developed between his understanding of the importance of discipline and its disparagement by the mystics.[178] He was aware that an obsession with good works as the only viable measure of Christian faith tended to make what was supposed to be the result of acceptance with God the source of that acceptance. As his understanding of faith was tied to assent with no sensible evidence, every doubt put faith in jeopardy and so robbed him of assurance.[179] Nevertheless, even in 1733 he could write of the vital importance of assurance for our Christian walk:

> This is the next thing which the 'circumcision of the heart' implies–even the testimony of their own spirit with the Spirit which witnesses in their hearts, that they are the children of God. ... By this anchor a Christian is kept steady in the midst of the waves of this troublesome world, and preserved from striking upon either of those fatal rocks, presumption or despair.[180]

---

[175] Ibid., 318.
[176] *Works*, 4:526-28.
[177] Ibid., 527-28.
[178] See *Works*, 4:332; 18:213.
[179] *Works*, 4:367.
[180] *Works*, 1:406.

The sermon effectively urged his hearers to remain confident in God's promises and be disciplined, while rejecting works of darkness and everything contrary to God's law.[181] Wesley's *description* of the witness of the Spirit and assurance was fundamentally correct theologically and would not change much over the succeeding decades, but it remained an intellectual concept and not an experiential reality for him during these years.

It is clear that Wesley went to Georgia a convinced high churchman with very strong leanings towards the essentialist Nonjurors, with a continued stress on pure intention, attending the means of grace, self-discipline and performance. He viewed the writings of the primitive church as normative for all ages and situations. He was convinced that only in conditions similar to those faced by the apostolic church could the power and purity of that church be seen again. The motivation to go to Georgia clearly arose out of his disappointment with his own Christian experience and he hoped to find the assurance of personal salvation that he lacked in England; the assurance would come from the fruits of his pastoral ministry which would confirm that his presentation of the gospel was apostolic. On the voyage to Georgia the ship went through a number of storms and Wesley found that he was afraid to die. This contrasted sharply with the calm demeanour of the Moravians on board who testified to their relationship with God and its benefits.[182] He was deeply impressed with the spiritual quality of their lives and for the first time he now had living witnesses to the depth of spiritual experience and its accompanying assurance that he was so desperately seeking for himself. At his first meeting with August Spangenberg, the Moravian pastor in Georgia, Wesley was made aware of his own lack of personal assurance when Spangenberg asked:

'My brother, I must first ask you one or two questions. Have you the witness within yourself? Does the Spirit of God bear witness with your spirit that you are a child of God?' I was surprised, and knew not what to answer. He observed it, and asked, 'Do you know Jesus Christ?' I paused and said, 'I know he is the Saviour of the world.' 'True', replied he, 'but do you know he has saved you?' I answered, 'I hope he has died to save me.' He only added, 'Do you know yourself?' I said, 'I do.' But I fear they were vain words.[183]

Wesley had written of the witness of the Spirit in earlier years and would continue to do so while in Georgia but, as this exchange confirms, it was not an experiential reality for him. It was the example of the Moravians in particular that showed Wesley it was possible to have a personal, inward assurance. He

---

[181] Ibid., 407. The witness of the Spirit did not do away with the need to fulfil the terms of God's covenant, and God gave abounding grace with which to comply. See Ibid., 412, especially n. 111.

[182] Ibid., 140-43. Wesley noted that "this was the most glorious day which I have hitherto seen"; see p. 143.

[183] Ibid., 146.

spent a lot of time with them and interviewing the people (and others he met in Georgia) about their spiritual experience. He was a keen observer, wanting to put everything to the practical test–does it work as it is claimed to work? He had now met people who testified to a personal assurance that he lacked and, moreover, had demonstrated by their lives that their claims were valid. He was not going to settle for anything less in his own experience.

Given Wesley's conviction that the essence of Christianity was a relationship of love, the question immediately raised was: can you come into contact with love and not know it? If a freely-chosen relationship based on love was central to his understanding of salvation, then assurance could not be merely a matter of intellectual comprehension or behavioural performance, since both of these encompass only a part of what it meant to experience love. Wesley no longer defined faith primarily as assent to truth but as trust in relationship and he was certain that the presence of God must be known experientially, holistically and not simply rationally and intellectually– somehow it must be felt.[184] He had returned to England expressing a deep desire to have a felt assurance that he was a Christian and the decisive experience came at a society meeting in Aldersgate Street, London on May 24, 1738:

> In the evening I went very unwillingly to a society in Aldersgate Street, where one was reading Luther's *Preface to the Epistle to the Romans*. About a quarter before nine, while he was describing the change which God works in the heart through faith in Christ, I felt my heart strangely warmed. I felt I did trust in Christ, Christ alone for salvation, and an assurance was given me that he had taken away *my* sins, even *mine*, and saved *me* from the law of sin and death.[185]

Note here his own stress on the felt assurance that he received that night. In a letter to Henry Stebbing (July 1739), who had criticised him for the stress on feelings in his preaching, Wesley pointed out that the gospel is all about a real, inward change of heart and mind. From faith came the love of God shed abroad in the heart, the peace of God, and joy in the Holy Spirit; these ministrations of the Spirit must be "felt," by "feeling it in your soul," not simply by the more outward and distant effects.[186] He admitted that "whatever is spoke of the

---

[184] See for example *Works*, 3:549.

[185] *Works*, 18:249-50. Wesley says of his searching for faith in this period that it was "with strange indifference, dullness, and coldness, and unusually frequent relapses into sin." It is the last phrase that is of interest, signifying that this was not his usual pattern and thus confirming that Wesley had a measure of faith before Aldersgate.

[186] *Works*, 25:669-72. At one stage he commented on his own spiritual journey: "I *feel* [emphasis mine] no more love to him [God] than to one I had never heard of"; see *Works*, 19:18. Stebbing was an Anglican clergyman who wrote extensively to defend what he believed to be Anglican orthodoxy. Helpful biographical information on Wesley's correspondents and contacts can be found in Samuel J. Rogal, *A Biographical*

religion of the heart and of the inward workings of the Spirit of God *must* appear enthusiasm to those who have not felt them. ..."[187] This was further reinforced by his common description of the Methodists as a people who "have been made partakers of an inward, vital religion, even 'righteousness, and peace and joy in the Holy Ghost'."[188] Wesley believed that the witness of the Spirit was attested to by both Scripture and experience; particularly the reality of changed lives which were his "living arguments for what I assert."[189]

Wesley himself was soon tempted to doubt the reality of his experience at Aldersgate due to a lack of joy, but was comforted when told that peace and victory were the essential marks of faith but God gave "transports of joy" as it seemed good to him. The vital difference between his former and present state was that previously "I was striving, yea fighting with all my might under the law, as well as under grace. But then I was sometimes, if not often, conquered; now, I was always conqueror."[190] His spiritual struggles were to continue, especially when his new-found assurance was attacked and he was regarded as "an enthusiast, a seducer, and a setter-forth of new doctrines."[191] He struggled over the next days and weeks with the nature of this new faith–could it exist in varying degrees?[192] This drove him to search the Scriptures, where from I Cor. 3:1-3, 9, and 16 he concluded, "surely, then these men had some degree of faith, though it is plain their faith was but weak."[193] This led him to follow up an earlier resolve to go to the Moravian community in Germany where he "hoped the conversing with those holy men who were themselves living witnesses of the full power of faith, and yet able to bear with those that are

---

Dictionary of 18th Century Methodism. 10 vols. Lampeter: Edwin Mellon Press, 1997-1999.

[187] *Works*, 19:121-22.

[188] Ibid., 3. For further examples, see Ibid., 12, 23-26, 32, 36, 49-55.

[189] *Works*, 25:622-23. See also his refutation of the stance taken by Bishop Bull against the witness of the Spirit in Ibid., 599-600.

[190] *Works*, 18:250. This again illustrates that prior to Aldersgate, he knew a measure of grace and a degree of victory over sin

[191] Ibid., 252. The area of concern to his friends was his insistence on the fact that he had only truly become a Christian at Aldersgate and that unless they too had this same faith, they were not Christians. See n. 90 for a full account. See also Scott Kisker, "Justified but Unregenerate? The Relationship of Assurance to Justification and Regeneration in the Thought of John Wesley," *WTJ* 28, no. 1 & 2 (Spring-Fall, 1993); David Lowes Watson, "The 'Much-Controverted Point of Justification by Faith' and the Shaping of Wesley's Evangelistic Message," *WTJ* 21, no. 1 & 2 (Spring-Fall, 1986).

[192] Ibid., 253. See also *Works*, 19:30-31.

[193] *Works*, 18:254. Wesley clearly saw himself as one of the weak in the faith and continued to do so even after visiting the Moravian communities; see for example his letter to his brother Samuel, *Works*, 25:575-78. Here he still claims to be an "imperfect Christian" waiting for the witness of the Spirit. Other examples are found at Ibid., 582-85. These are further evidence that Aldersgate was not the consummation of his search for mature faith and assurance.

weak, would be a means, under God, of so stablishing my soul, that I might 'go on from faith to faith, and from strength to strength'."[194] Here at last he saw the kind of Christianity he believed was a reflection of New Testament times: "here I continually met with what I sought for, viz., living proofs of the power of faith: persons 'saved from *inward as well as outward sin*' and from all doubt and fear by the 'abiding witness of the Holy Ghost given unto them.'"[195] He then wrote a glowing account of his experiences to Charles:

> Young and old, they breathe nothing but faith and love, at all times and in all places. I do not therefore concern myself with smaller points, that touch not the essence of Christianity, but endeavour (God being my helper) to grow up in these, after the glorious examples set before me; having already seen with my own eyes more than one hundred witnesses of that everlasting truth, 'Everyone that believeth hath peace with God, and is freed from sin, and is in Christ a new creature.'[196]

The man who was to make possibly the greatest impact on Wesley was Christian David, with whom he spoke at great length, particularly on the subject of those who are "weak in faith" which caused Wesley such perplexity. He found comfort from the fact that David distinguished between the moment of justification and the assurance of it.[197] In David's account a clear distinction is made between justification (as forgiveness) and the "full assurance of faith," which he identified as the new birth; in the former situation, sin remained but did not reign, in the latter (presumably) there was no remaining sin.[198] What emerges from these accounts is a very real confusion in the Moravians' theological understanding of the process of salvation and the nature of assurance; the struggle for Wesley was to reconcile these views with his own Anglican heritage and personal experience.[199]

---

[194] *Works*, 18:254.

[195] Ibid., 260.

[196] *Works*, 25:557.

[197] *Works*, 18:270-72. Christian David was one of the key Moravian leaders and a close associate of Count Zinzendorf, the founder of the community at Herrnhut. Wesley then gave an account of conversations he had with several of the brethren about their experience; see Ibid., 273-97. Wesley records ten conversations and in later years he was to add some dissenting comments to these testimonies but at the time no adverse comment appeared; see Ibid., 281, 83, 88, 93. The longest testimony recorded is that of Christian David, presumably because it is the one with which Wesley most identified.

[198] *Works*, 18:274. David also mentions that assurance is given at justification, but "by degrees."

[199] See *Works*, 19:96-97, 106. In later years he was to claim that the Methodist doctrine of assurance was one of its major contributions to the Church at large. On Anglican and pietistic influences on his soteriology, see William H. Shontz, "Anglican Influence on John Wesley's Soteriology," *WTJ* 32, no. 1 (Spring, 1997); Kenneth J. Collins, "John Wesley's Critical Appropriation of Early German Pietism," *WTJ* 27, no. 1 & 2 (Spring-

His association with the Moravian community in London and Germany has both positive and negative features that shape his own theological development and the formation of the first Methodist societies. It is in the material from these years that we first begin to see clear evidence of a formal theological understanding of the process of salvation emerging in his writings intimately linked with its experiential reality, both in his own life and those who would follow his leadership. The *Journal* for the close of 1738 showed that all was not yet settled as far as his own spiritual pilgrimage was concerned, for he did not yet possess the "full assurance of faith" as described by the Moravians, though he was confident he had a measure of faith and was accepted in Christ.[200] He was positive about some of the marks of "a new creature" in Christ as he understood them from Scripture and the teaching of the Moravians, but he was concerned that he still lacked a settled love, joy, and peace.[201] This quality of an established and constant witness the Moravians saw as essential, and Wesley had not yet arrived at the place of theological and pastoral insight to evaluate if the Moravians were, in fact, correct. Later he came to believe that the Moravian position was not theologically or experientially sound; a Christian could experience an intermittent and weak assurance.

Wesley's Theological Methodology:
Its Sources, Tools and their Interrelationship

The Church of England clearly upheld the Scriptures as the primary theological source for all matters necessary to salvation (both doctrine and practice), and Wesley was in full agreement with this stance.[202] However, acknowledging the primacy of the Bible still left the matter of its interpretation and application to be faced. Wesley, his supporters and detractors within Protestant evangelicalism all appealed to the primacy of Scripture, but clearly arrived at differing interpretations and nowhere was this more obvious than with his doctrine of

---

Fall, 1992); J. Steven O'Malley, "Pietistic Influence on John Wesley: Wesley and Gerhard Tersteegen," *WTJ* 31, no. 2 (Fall, 1996).

[200] *Works*, 19:16-19. See also the letter to Samuel Wesley, dated October 30, 1738, *Works*, 25:575-78. Doubts of his state of salvation continue throughout this period; see for example *Works*, 19:20, 22, 27-31.

[201] *Works*, 19:16-19.

[202] See Wesley's use of the Anglican Article of Faith in John Wesley, *John Wesley's Sunday Service of the Methodists in North America with Other Occasional Services* (London: 1784; reprint, With an Introduction by James F. White, The United Methodist Publishing House and the United Methodist Board of Higher Education and Ministry, 1984), 307. Heitzenrater affirms that it is the Bible that "serves as the basic source of his vocabulary, imagery, and even illustration . . . it represents the matrix for his careful interweaving of material from other sources." See Richard P. Heitzenrater, "John Wesley's Principles and Practice of Preaching," *Methodist History* 37, no. 2 (1999). See also Wesley's own statements in *Works*, 19:32, 65-68, 72-73, 78, 116-18, 24.

Christian perfection.[203] In seeking to uncover Wesley's theological method, we must begin with the various communities in which he was located over these years as they were the ones who supplied the hermeneutical framework within which his reading of Scripture took place.

Wesley's Understanding Prior to Aldersgate, 1725-1737

One of the critical concerns during Wesley's early years at Oxford was the relationship of revelation and reason. Initially he seemed to value reason over revelation: "Whatever virtues are *recommended to us by reason, especially as assisted by revelation* [emphasis mine]."[204] This made reasonableness the judge of Scripture and methodologically it remained the practical authority for a number of years. He believed that divine truth was reasonable truth; faith being no more than giving assent to these reasonable truths.[205] In a letter to his mother on questions of predestination and assurance he wrote:

> Faith is a species of belief, and belief is defined, an assent to a proposition upon rational grounds. Without rational grounds there is therefore no belief, and consequently no faith. ...
> As I understand faith to be an assent to any truth upon rational grounds, I don't think it possible, without perjury, to swear I believe anything unless I have rational grounds for my persuasion.[206]

At this stage, faith was little more than assent to a proposition upon rational grounds, based on reasonable evidence. It was by reason alone that he believed the doctrine of assurance and rejected the Calvinist doctrine of final perseverance; the former was expressed in the Scriptures (his reasonable evidence), but not the latter. The question was not the authority**Error! Bookmark not defined.** of the Scriptures or revelation as such, but whether it was reasonable. Wesley thought the doctrine of predestination was inconsistent with divine justice and mercy and therefore to be rejected; persons must be free agents or else we make God the author of sin and injustice.[207] Lest he be accused of being a mere rationalist, he sought to uphold the place of divine revelation:

> I call faith an assent upon rational grounds because I hold divine testimony to be the most reasonable of all evidence whatever. Faith must necessarily at length be

---

[203] Wesley was well aware that Scripture could be quoted to support any theological position; see *Works*, 4:247-49.

[204] Ibid., 219. See also Ibid., 208, especially n. 12.

[205] *Works*, 25:175-76.

[206] Ibid., 175. This is in agreement with the emerging Enlightenment definition of faith as outlined by Harrison and Smith earlier.

[207] Ibid. See also Ibid., 180.

resolved into reason. God is true, therefore what he says is true. ... When anyone can bring me more reasonable propositions than these, I am ready to assent to them. Till then it will be highly unreasonable to change my opinion.[208]

Susanna took him to task over his understanding and recommended that he read Bishop John Pearson on faith.[209] She urged him to distinguish between reason and revelation and made it plain that revelation was to be believed because it was God's revelation, not because it was reasonable from a human standpoint.[210] Through his correspondence with his mother and reading the books that she recommended, he came to agree with her understanding.

An assent grounded both on testimony and reason takes in science as well as faith, which is allowed on all hands to be distinct from it. I am therefore at length come over entirely to your opinion, that saving faith (including practice) is an assent to what God has revealed, because he has revealed it, and not because the truth of it may be evinced by reason.[211]

Note that the stress is still on faith as assent to propositional truth. It is important to observe that the matter was not settled by a simple appeal to Scripture and the quoting of one or more proof texts, however, he believed his new understanding was not contrary to Scripture. Towards the end of his time at Oxford he was concerned to counter the increasing claims of rationalism in University circles while not denying the benefits of reason itself in the area of religious studies. He affirmed that within its appointed sphere, reason was both a delightful and useful inclination.[212] Nevertheless, there were some areas where reason could not help, and so its limits had to be clearly identified.[213] In terms of his theological method, Wesley continued to make full use of reason to support his points, while seeking to uphold the primacy of Scripture in good Anglican fashion.[214] It is notable that during this period the Bible was not read and expounded primarily for doctrine, but for the method to be followed in holy living. He stressed the need to take the words of Scripture literally, unless by so doing the sense of them was absurd. A consistent biblical hermeneutic was beginning to emerge that would centre on the plain meaning of the text in its context and in the light of the message of the whole of Scripture (the "analogy

---

[208] Ibid., 175-76.
[209] Ibid., 178-79. Pearson had been Bishop of Chester and had written the classical work, *An Exposition of the Creed* (1656); he was to become one of Wesley's favourite authors.
[210] He was not easily convinced of his mother's position; see *Works*, 4:215-23. Note especially p. 219.
[211] Ibid., 188. She also recommended he read the *Exposition of the Thirty-Nine Articles* (1710) by Bishop William Beveridge; see *Works*, 25:183-85.
[212] *Works*, 4:281, 337.
[213] Ibid., 283, 85-89. See also Ibid., 279-80.
[214] Ibid., 337.

of faith").²¹⁵ Wesley sought to base his arguments on what Scripture actually said, rather than on what it did not say. In dealing with matters that were not explicitly mentioned in Scripture, he would seek input from the heritage of the Church and the practical wisdom of the community of faith.²¹⁶

It was during his second term at Oxford that Wesley wrestled with the nature and relationship of evidence and certainty.²¹⁷ The empirical method that was so apparent in the emerging science of his day, with its confidence that firm and demonstrable evidence provided the solid foundation for a certain knowledge of the truth, was to form a core element in his own developing theological method.²¹⁸ Peter Browne had written that the senses are the only source of those ideas upon which all our knowledge is founded. However, sensible evidence was the ground of knowledge but not faith. Evangelical faith was an act of the will beyond assent to evidential religious propositions and was based to some extent upon things that are immediately comprehended, "the 'evidence of things not seen' [Heb. 11:1] or the assent of the understanding to the truth and existence of things inconceivable, upon certain and evident proof of their reality in their symbols and representatives." ²¹⁹ In abridgment, Wesley referred to evidence that was peculiar to a different sort of knowledge than that of matters merely human, without qualifying it further. This would later develop into a reference to the "spiritual senses" to complement our physical ones, and so provide an empirical base for spiritual knowledge, including assurance. At this point he still believed that there was no sensible perception of God or his truth that would give us certainty (thus his early fascination with mysticism and an intuitive experience of the presence of God).²²⁰ A strong emphasis on experience would become one of the major sources of his developing theological methodology and it undoubtedly arose from his own personal spiritual journey. This will have a shaping effect on his theologising, keeping it more intensely relational and practical, rather than intellectual and abstract. The evidence from this period points to his theologising beginning with practice rather than theory, with the final goal (be holy) rather than the present situation, and it was to work with models (examples, illustrations, lives) rather than

---

²¹⁵ Ibid., 273. See also *Works*, 245-51, 337; 25:380; Heitzenrater, *Mirror & Memory*, 89-92.

²¹⁶ See for example *Works*, 4:306-17.

²¹⁷ See *Works*, 25:244-46.

²¹⁸ On empiricism and the scientific method, see Porter, *Modern World*, 130-83; John W. Haas, Jr., "John Wesley's Views on Science and Christianity: An Examination of the Charge of Antiscience," *Church History* 63, no. 2 (1994).

²¹⁹ Peter Browne, *The Procedure, Extent, and Limits of Human Understanding* (London: Innys, 1729), 250. Cited in Heitzenrater, *Mirror & Memory*, 114. Wesley published an abridgment of Browne in 1730. Heb. 11: 1 would become Wesley's own favourite scriptural definition of faith. See also John C. English, "John Wesley's Indebtedness to John Norris," *Church History* 60, no. 1 (1991).

²²⁰ See *Works*, 4:284-87, 94.

doctrines.

Wesley's memorandum on his spiritual state made upon his return to England gives an intriguing insight into how his theological method developed while he was in Georgia. He noted the various views of salvation given by the sources that he had consulted over the years: the Scripture, the Roman Catholics, Lutherans, Calvinists, English Divines, Essentialist Nonjurors, and Mystics.[221] Wesley agreed that the Scriptures taught him the fundamental truth that he was to keep the commandments. Essentially, these had to do with believing, hoping and loving; he was to follow after these tempers until they were fully attained by complying with all the outward works and means appointed by God for this purpose, and by walking as Christ walked. Exactly how this fitted into the Christian life he learned from the communities mentioned, both positively and negatively. The critical test that was applied to his discoveries was whether the views were consistent with both "reason and Scripture." It was from the Essentialist Nonjurors that he found the "sure rule" to interpreting the Scriptures–the ancient consensus of the Church (what has always been believed by everyone, everywhere). Under their influence he leaned too far for a time by making antiquity a co-ordinate rather than subordinate rule with Scripture.[222] Finally, he was attracted to the Mystic writers with their focus on a union with God and an internal religion that made everything else appear flat and insipid. However, by overemphasising "love alone," rejecting the place of good works altogether, dispensing with keeping the commandments and neglecting the means of grace, he concluded that their religion was nothing like that taught by Christ and the apostles. How he was delivered from their position was not clear to him, but he was sure they taught the most dangerous errors of all.[223]

While this recital covers more than just the Georgia years, it reflects the theological confusion that dominated his time in the colony. His letters and journal entries reveal a fascination with the apostolic church and the value of antiquity as a critical (if not, at times, dominant) component of his theological method. The listing of these Christian communities as well as the Scriptures indicates yet again that reading the Bible in isolation was insufficient to guide him into the spiritual experience that he sought. Even though Protestantism claimed it was the only sufficient rule for faith and practice, it still required

---

[221] See n. 95, *Works*, 18:212-13.

[222] In September 1736 he noted reading Bishop Beveridge's *Pandectae canonum conciliorum*; this convinced him that church councils could and did err so that "things ordained by them as necessary to salvation have neither strength nor authority unless they be taken out of Holy Scripture." See Ibid., 171.

[223] Ibid., 212-13. Note his later comments to his brother, Samuel: "I think the rock on which I had the nearest made shipwreck of the faith was in the writings of the mystics under which term I comprehend all, and only those, who slight the means of grace." See *Works*, 25:487.

interpretation and application and this was strongly influenced by the various reading communities given above. These communities were essential to an understanding and application of its message, even though they did not always agree amongst themselves as to the essential elements or application of that message. In this period we are made aware of the importance of the early church as a reading community for Wesley, though it was filtered through the Anglicanism inherited from his parents and education at Oxford.

Wesley's Theological Method 1725-1737: A Summary

Heitzenrater reminds us that there is a complex relationship between the biblical text and its interpretation, both personally and corporately. In these early years much of this seems to be simply taken for granted by Wesley and not examined in any considered way. The diary and letters show it was from his reading of non-biblical material, particularly the early church Fathers, à Kempis, Taylor and Law, that made him aware of the inadequacy of defining Christianity as an intellectual pursuit or a moral endeavour; genuine spirituality must involve the whole person.[224] The early Fathers, in the face of theological bickering and division, stressed a need to return to a simple religion based on the love of God, emphasising a unity in essentials of belief and a toleration of differences in the more subtle theological distinctions. Christianity was not a matter for argument but for practice–and this was decisive for Methodism and Wesleyan theology.[225] Heitzenrater believes this aided Wesley to sort through the confusing and conflicting suggestions provided by the English pietists and others who had helped start him on the path of holy living. Importantly, he came to see the value of consensus and this he believed was most purely exhibited in the writings of the Fathers of the first three centuries.[226]

It was not simply Wesley's reading that brought about this shift; the subsequent debates over matters of interpretation and value with others in his circle were equally significant. His correspondence shows that he would always submit his private reasoning to the judgement of others within the community (family, friends, other scholars and churchmen), even if he would not always accept their verdict.[227] From the beginning, Wesley saw the task of theologising as a community task and not one to be undertaken in isolation. It is in this sense that he refers to the value of experience as a descriptive tool and a testimony to various interpretations of doctrine and practice. This is clearly general life experience to which reference is being made, even though people may utilise

---

[224] See *Works*, 25:352.

[225] Heitzenrater, *Mirror & Memory*, 101. See also Albert C. Outler, "John Wesley's Interests in the Early Fathers of the Church," *Wesleyan Theological Heritage*, 97-110.

[226] Ibid., 71-77. See also *Works*, 25:391-93.

[227] For example, see the correspondence with his father over the Athanasian Creed and the Articles in *Works*, 25:181-82.

the words of Scripture and theological terminology in describing it. In working with the writings of various Christians (as well as the text of Scripture), Wesley had to utilise his own powers of reasoning. The value and use of reason in theologising came initially from his parents and then from the debates within the scholarly community at Oxford, particularly those over the relationship of reason, revelation, and faith. He recorded in his diaries and letters how he sought to resolve the tensions and work out the practical implications of the ideas he found in Scripture and his other reading. Heitzenrater believes there was no single, static method during this period, but an approach to holy living that continued to develop and change as he adopted, adapted, refined and often discarded suggestions met in the books and the community discussions that followed.[228]

The Founder of the Methodist Societies, 1738-1739

The months leading up to the society meeting at Aldersgate were filled with conversations concerning his spiritual state, particularly with Peter Böhler and other members of the Moravian community.[229] As he shared what he was learning with his friends and through his pulpit ministry, he began to meet with opposition, which acted as a further incentive for theological reflection.[230]

THE IMPORTANCE OF HIS ALDERSGATE EXPERIENCE (MAY 24, 1738)

It was the conversations in early 1738 with Böhler that were crucial and set in motion the events leading directly to his Aldersgate experience: "All this time I conversed much with Peter Böhler, but I understood him not; and least of all when he said, ... My brother, my brother, that philosophy of yours must be purged away.[231] Böhler himself wrote:

---

[228] The test applied was: "Does it work?" If not, then it must be modified or rejected. Wesley's question about working always related to advancing in holy living and this advance had to be evidenced not only in his personal life but also in the lives of others following the same method. See Heitzenrater, *Mirror & Memory*, 67.

[229] See for example *Works*, 18:223-28. For fuller accounts of the Moravian Church in this period and the inter-relationship with John Wesley, see: Allan Coppedge, *John Wesley in Theological Debate* (Wilmore, KY: Wesley Heritage Press, 1987); Heitzenrater, *People Called Methodists;* Herbert Boyd McGonigle, *John Wesley and the Moravians* (Ilkeston: The Wesley Fellowship, 1993); Maddox, ed., *Aldersgate Reconsidered;* Clifford W. Towlson, *Moravian and Methodist: Relationships and Influences in the Eighteenth Century* (London: Epworth Press, 1957); Colin Podmore, *The Moravian Church in England, 1728-1760* (Oxford: Clarendon Press, 1998).

[230] See for example *Works*, 18:223-27; 25:538-39.

[231] *Works*, 18:226. In a letter Böhler comments that John did not "properly believe on the Saviour, and was willing to be taught." See n. 25, p. 225.

> I took a walk with the elder Wesley, and asked him about his spiritual state. He told me that he sometimes felt certain of his salvation, but sometimes he had many doubts; that he could only say this, 'If what stands in the Bible be true, then I am saved.' Thereupon I spoke with him very fully; and earnestly besought him to go to the opened fountain, and not to mar the efficacy of free grace by his unbelief.[232]

If Böhler was correct in this estimation, the problem lay with Wesley's attempts to reason his way through to a relationship with God. This was due to his continued practical understanding of faith as assent, even though he had intellectually come to see it primarily as trust. The critical phrase here is Wesley's reliance on the propositional truth of Scripture as comprehended by the intellect, rather than a personal experience of God in the heart. Wesley, by his own confession, had a very limited personal experience of God prior to Aldersgate and all of his theologising up till this period was largely an intellectual affair.[233] After a further conversation with Böhler, he reported:

> I met Peter Böhler again, who now amazed me more and more, by the account he gave of the fruits of living faith–the holiness and happiness which he affirmed to attend it. The next morning I began the Greek Testament again, resolving to abide by 'the law and the testimony', and *being confident that God would hereby show me* [emphasis mine] 'whether' this 'doctrine was of God'.[234]

The role of personal testimony had been very important in these months and Wesley himself was impressed by Böhler's testimony. He was desperate for the experience Böhler described, but at this critical juncture he explicitly returned to the "testimony" of Scripture. It is of paramount importance to notice however, that it was not simply the written text to which he appealed, but the direct testimony of God himself through the written text. In a way that he had not yet clearly articulated, Wesley had come to realise the inadequacy of an intellectual comprehension of the text alone, and the vital importance of a direct spiritual encounter with God in and through the text, as well as in and through personal testimonies. If an experience was not scriptural in this sense, Wesley

---

[232] J. P. Lockwood, *Memorials of the Life of Peter Böhler* (London: 1868), 73-74, in Ibid., 228, n.49.

[233] Clive Marsh reminds us that there is a difference between "life experience" and "Christian experience"; the former may contain intellectual apprehension of God but only the latter can involve a direct awareness of God as a Person in a personal relationship with the individual or community. see Clive Marsh, "Appealing to 'Experience': What Does It Mean?," in *Unmasking Methodist Theology*. See also Jones, *Wesley's Use of Scripture*, 94-96; Jerry L. Mercer, "Toward a Wesleyan Understanding of Christian Experience," *WTJ* 20, no. 1 (Spring, 1985).

[234] *Works*, 18:232.

wanted none of it.[235] For example, a sticking point in his acceptance of Böhler's testimony was whether salvation was experienced gradually or instantaneously:

> But I could not comprehend what he spoke of an instantaneous work. I could not understand how this faith should be given in a moment; ... I searched the Scriptures again touching this very thing, particularly the Acts of the Apostles: but to my utter astonishment found scarce any instances there of other than instantaneous conversions–scarce any other so slow as that of St. Paul, who was three days in the pangs of the new birth. I had but one retreat left, viz., 'Thus, I grant, God wrought in the first ages of Christianity; but the times are changed. What reasons have I to believe he works in the same manner now?'
>
> But on Sunday 23, I was beat out of this retreat too, by the concurring evidence of several living witnesses, who testified God had thus wrought in themselves; giving them in a moment such a faith in the blood of his Son as translated them out of darkness into light, out of sin and fear into holiness and happiness. Here ended my disputing. I could now only cry out, 'Lord, help thou my unbelief!'[236]

Wesley was now convinced from his reading of Scripture that Böhler was right in his understanding of the nature of faith and the consequences of it in the Christian life; namely, forgiveness of sins, reconciliation with God, assurance from the witness of the Spirit and the new birth.[237] He had struggled with the notion of it being an instantaneous work till convinced by Scripture that this was the experience of the apostolic church. It must be observed that he would have read these passages many times in earlier years and not arrived at this conclusion–so what has changed? Given his reference to a direct experience of God shortly before, it must surely be the new theological perspective with which he now read these passages. This is confirmed by his next meeting with Böhler:

> When I met Peter Böhler again, he readily consented to put the dispute upon the issue which I desired, viz., *Scripture and experience*. [emphasis mine] I first consulted the Scripture. But when I set aside the glosses of men, and simply considered the words of God, comparing them together and endeavouring to illustrate the obscure by the plainer passages, I found they all made against me, and was forced to retreat to my last hold, that experience would never agree with

---

[235] Ibid., 233. Wesley summarised his own experience at this time by saying, "I see the promise. But it is afar off."
[236] Ibid., 234. The *Diary* entry for the day says Wesley was "convinced that faith c[onverts] at once;" see p. 576.
[237] See the earlier part of the *Journal* entry quoted above, Ibid., 233-234.

the literal interpretation of those Scriptures. Nor could I therefore allow it to be true till I found some living witnesses of it.[238]

This is the first time that the phrase "Scripture and experience" appears in Wesley's writings and it is very rarely used thereafter.[239] It is closely linked with his reference to the direct experience of God mentioned earlier, and would seem to indicate the vital importance of this new element in his theological method. Böhler had now intellectually convinced Wesley that the faith he sought was attainable in an instant as God's free gift; he had supported this from Scripture and had produced several witnesses who could clearly testify to the experience. The greatest stumbling block for Wesley remained the notion of instantaneousness and it was this that produced the greatest opposition from family, friends and those who heard him preach.[240] The meaning of the text was obviously not self-evident and it required the input of a direct personal experience of God and the witness of the community before his understanding changed. His new understanding had then to be tested against the text by reason, his own experience and the wisdom of the wider community–in Wesley's case this was the writings of the early Fathers as read through his Church of England upbringing and education. His assertion that God no longer worked this way was effectively ended by Böhler producing living witnesses to the same Christian experience that Wesley read about in the Book of Acts.[241] Once again, we must note that the testimony of these people would not have convinced him if he had not seen the same evidence of God's workings in Scripture itself. The New Testament, especially Acts, recorded many things that happened in the early church, but to Wesley that did not mean it always had to happen that way; there were areas of Scripture that reflected God's providential

---

[238] *Works*, 18:248. As a result of meeting and talking with "living witnesses," Wesley now believed that "this faith was the gift, the free gift of God, and that he would surely bestow it upon every soul who earnestly and perseveringly sought it. I was now thoroughly convinced." See Ibid., 248-49.

[239] John Wesley, *The Works of John Wesley: The Bicentennial Edition* [CD] (Abingdon Press, 2005, accessed). The search engine for the phrase only found 2 examples of it in the whole Wesley corpus, though there are many more references to the words individually.

[240] See Charles Wesley, *The Journal of the Rev. Charles Wesley, M.A.*, ed. Thomas Jackson, 2 vols., vol. 1 (London: John Mason, 1849; reprint, Kansas City: Beacon Hill Press of Kansas City, 1980), 1:84-85.

[241] *Works*, 18:235. He interviewed Mr. Hutchins and Mrs. Fox, who were "two living witnesses that God can (at least, if he does not always) give that faith whereof cometh salvation in a moment, as lightning falling from heaven." Wesley showed intense frustration in his letters to his old friend, William Law, that he had not been told about this experience by him; see *Works*, 25:540-50. On the relationship between Law and Wesley, see John R. Tyson, "John Wesley and William Law: A Reappraisal," *WTJ* 17, no. 2 (Fall, 1982).

dealings with the human race (description) that were not necessarily binding on future generations (prescription). The evening of May 1 saw the beginning of the Fetter Lane Society, and Böhler played a large role in setting this up and formulating its rules. It is from this society that both the Moravian society (later the Moravian Church) and the Methodist United Societies immediately sprang, placing the developing ministry of Wesley in the context of community.[242] His doubts continued after the experience at Aldersgate Street and he sought for further evidence on which to rest his hope. Once more, his assurance lay with living witnesses (the Moravian community in Germany) and not simply the written text of Scripture. The text was not, in itself, sufficient to answer the deep heart-issues with which he was wrestling, nor was the small evangelical community in England.

THE FORMATION OF THE METHODIST UNITED SOCIETIES

Aldersgate did not give Wesley the spiritual experience he was seeking, as he did not yet have *constant* assurance and its accompanying evidences. The relationship with Peter Böhler had shaped his expectations in a Moravian framework and though he was willing to allow that he now had "weak faith," the journey to Herrnhut was for the purpose of gaining "the full power of faith" by conversing with living examples of it.[243] On arrival at Herrnhut Wesley had opportunity to observe the community in their daily life, questioning them at length about their beliefs and experiences.[244] It is important to observe that Wesley did not simply accept their testimonies at face value, but examined their claims through intense questioning. This aspect of his methodology must not be overlooked and his favourable reception of personal and community witness was rarely a naive acceptance. The struggle for Wesley in the months ahead was recorded in his *Journal* as he sought to reconcile their theological perception with his Anglican heritage, the Scriptures and his own personal experience.[245] This led him to a gradual break with the Moravians because his final appeal was always to "the Law and the Testimony."[246] As we saw earlier,

---

[242] *Works*, 18:235-36.
[243] *Works*, 25:553. He was particularly impressed by testimonies of those "full of faith and love" and it was this that he was seeking for himself. See also *Works*, 18:260; 25:556-62, 71-74. He referred to them as "the Christians that love one another." However, not all his evaluations were as positive; see for example *Works*, 25:566-67.
[244] *Works*, 18:267-68. See also *Works*, 18:274, 79-81; 25:560-62.
[245] *Works*, 19:21. In January 25, 1739 he still talked about the new birth in Moravian terms; see Ibid., 32. For a more Anglican definition of the new birth see the notes in *Journal* (Curnock), 2: 256, 61, 74-75, 93 and his letter to Dr. Henry Stebbing on July 25, 1739 in *Works*, 25:669-72. Wesley published an account of his adherence to Church of England doctrine in September 1739; see *Works*, 19:96-97.
[246] *Works*, 19:116-18. The appeal to Scripture is also seen in a letter defending his position: "I allow no other rule, whether of faith or practice, than the Holy Scriptures." See *Works*, 25:615.

the critical issue was the adoption of the doctrine of "stillness" and the rejection of the means of grace in the Fetter Lane society because of Moravian influence.[247] Wesley's response was to quote "living witnesses" who had found faith while using the means of grace.[248] He became increasingly aware that the Moravian community did not hold to a single theological understanding of the *ordo salutis* and their personal testimonies bore witness to that confusion. While testimonies to assurance were common among them, Wesley noticed that the actual state of grace to which they were referring varied significantly. Even though he was not yet clear about the theological articulation of the way of salvation, he was certain about the transformed life that should be evident as a consequence of faith in Christ. It explains his growing opposition to the Moravian position as it was the practical results in the lives of Christians that led to his condemnation of it. Wesley strongly appealed to Scripture to support his case; once more, it was the experiences recounted in Scripture rather than the doctrinal passages that were most important in settling the issues. Wesley upheld his understanding of the message of Scripture as judged by its practical implications in the life of the person and the Christian community, its impact on missions and evangelism, and if it fostered holiness of heart and life. Inevitably there came a parting of the ways between the two groups, though the first actual Methodist society was founded in Bristol by Wesley on July 11, 1739. The first London Methodist society met at the Foundery in December 1739 and was further augmented when Wesley and a number of his supporters broke from the Fetter Lane society in July 1740 because of the impact of the stillness doctrine.[249]

Conclusion

Richard Heitzenrater reminds us that it is always important to examine carefully Wesley's own expectations at any given moment, his immediate reactions and then his later reflections. There is a clear distinction between Wesley's spiritual experiences and his theological development. In his opinion, Wesley was much better at describing his experiences than he was at analysing them theologically. The process of theological reflection takes many years, involving an integration of scriptural concepts, church teachings, life experiences, spiritual inspiration and rational reflection. All "experiential

---

[247] *Works*, 19:119-20. See also *Works*, 25:585-88, 90-93.
[248] *Works*, 19:121. See also Ibid., 93-94.
[249] For details of the founding of the Methodist United Societies, see Heitzenrater, *People Called Methodists*, 97-124; Rack, *Reasonable Enthusiast*, 183-250. Further background information on the importance of religious societies in England can be found in Scott Thomas Kisker, *Foundation for Revival: Anthony Horneck, the Religious Societies, and the Construction of an Anglican Pietism*, (Lanham, MD: Scarecrow Press, 2008).

descriptions" have to be read in the light of his later reflections, which incorporate hindsight that comes with increasing spiritual maturation.[250]

John Wesley, in the early stages of his preparation for ministry, displayed many of the characteristics to be found among his peers as the eighteenth century progressed. Initially we see a student keen to engage with the new scientific and philosophical developments of his time and who was embracing the changes brought about in the move from a pre-modern to a modern worldview. Wesley comes to Oxford already valuing reason and the empirical scientific method. He is sure that genuine Christianity can be known by certain evidence, and his life will be spent in pursuit of that evidence. Wesley's preparation for ministry is successfully channelled into the realm of practical divinity and he consistently maintains his determination to focus on matters essential to salvation and avoid speculative theology. Accordingly, his concept of true Christianity is not patterned on a system of theology but on the lives of people that he considers to have epitomised the Christlike life. His early writings bear witness to the central conviction that God's own nature is best understood as love. People are created in God's image and this too is essentially defined in terms of love. Consequently, the central focus of salvation is a relationship of love and not a scholarly command of doctrine. As a result of this shift, Wesley returns to the pre-modern understanding of faith primarily as trust (a relational quality) and not assent (an intellectual quality). Accompanying this is a return to understanding religion as a dynamic of the heart rather than a system of ideas; belief is once more a personal encounter with God rather than an acceptance of propositional truth based on persuasive argument or proof.

From the beginning there is a focus on holy living and the pursuit of Christian perfection. Wesley unequivocally identifies holiness with happiness, with love, with Christian perfection; they are one and the same thing considered under different heads. In the ground-breaking sermon, "The Circumcision of the Heart," perfection is not defined in terms of an ability to conform to the smallest detail of the Law, but set within the context of a whole-hearted relationship of love. Being restored to the image of God is basic to the whole process through an inward transformation of intentions, attitudes, will and understanding; good actions then flow from this. In harmony with this understanding, Wesley defined the essential nature of sin in relational terms. He was convinced that for love to be real, humanity had to exercise the power of choice to enter and maintain a relationship with God; he is convinced that a coerced relationship (the Calvinist doctrine of predestination) is a contradiction in terms. He believes that God has replaced the original covenant of works prior to the fall (do this and live) with a covenant of grace after the fall

---

[250] Richard P. Heitzenrater, "Great Expectations: Aldersgate and the Evidences of Genuine Christianity," in *Aldersgate Reconsidered*, ed. Randy L. Maddox (Nashville, TN: Abingdon Press, 1990). See especially pp. 50-51.

(believe/trust this and live) in order to suit the realities of the human condition as it is now experienced. A critical development that hinges, at least in part, on his developing understanding of the centrality of love, is the distinction he makes between intention and performance. The will may have a perfect intention, but the performance may be marred. If God sees the intention, then is the person condemned simply because of faulty execution? Wesley defines sin ("properly so-called") as a voluntary breach of a known law of God and this is based on his conviction that there must be personal culpability before we can be held accountable. Sin has to do with choices made where the consequences are known. The crucial question to be decided regarding whether an act, word or thought is sin has to do with its intention – is it intended to break or harm the relationship? If it is not, then the person is not culpable, and thus not guilty of sin. While breaches of the relationship may occur without the concurrence of the will, they are strictly speaking an infirmity. This is the crucial definition on which his whole claim to Christian perfection as a reality in this life stands or falls; it will occupy his pastoral attention for the rest of his life. In this early period, Wesley sees the experience of perfection in love requiring a cleansing from sin before an infilling of love can occur – the vessel must be pure before it can be filled with God's love. This sets perfection within a negative context of purging or purifying before a positive experience of the infilling of love is possible.

In many important ways it is his desire for an experiential confirmation of salvation that drives his theologising in these years, due to his personal lack of certainty that he is a "good Christian." Viewing Christianity as a relationship of love must involve the affective side of human nature. Assurance must then include more than behaviour, will and intention. The critical events leading up to and following Aldersgate demonstrate his concern for a personal experience of God and the impact this has on his ministry and theology. It was the example of the Moravians that showed Wesley it was possible to have a direct assurance of being in a right relationship with God. The evidence that he hungers for is not satisfied by submitting his conscience and behaviour to the standards provided by the Bible or the Church. Assurance prior to Aldersgate seems to rest on an outward, objective measurement of his life with that described in Scripture and it was on this basis he declared himself to be a Christian; what he lacked was an inward, subjective confirmation of his standing with God. Did this latter evidence require a new faith or a greater degree of faith? Without the latter evidence, was one not a Christian at all? Wesley clearly struggles at this point and his theological confusion is evident. It is immediately clear that Wesley was not satisfied with his spiritual state after Aldersgate and so it is wrong to see May 24, 1738 as the end of his search for "holiness and happiness."

You cannot separate Wesley's theological method from his intense concern for practical Christian living and his own life is clearly the laboratory in which the experimentation takes place. By the time of his return from Georgia, he has clearly worked with Scripture, reason, the early Church, his own Anglican inheritance and some materials from other times and traditions in his theological reflection. The most important breakthrough is the emergence of an explicit role for experience in his theological method. Aldersgate was a major step forward in his personal experience, but it would take many more years before Wesley himself would give his last evaluation as to what had actually happened then. He has now come to understand that there is a critical and major difference between the intellectual comprehension of doctrine in the context of general life experience and the experiential reality of a personal relationship with God through the presence of the Holy Spirit. Wesley obviously had access to the text of Scripture, the writings of the Fathers and the formularies of the Church of England from the very beginning. The issue was not his intellectual capacity to read and reason with these texts, but the perspective with which he approached his reading and his openness to various interpretations and applications. While it is possible to intellectually comprehend the nature of love in terms of description and application, this is a poor substitute for an actual personal experience. Once love has actually been experienced, it modifies shapes, enriches, colours and alters the focus and emphases of every aspect of life. Theory is helpful, but it always lacks many dimensions of actual lived experience. When Wesley is convinced that Christianity is more about the 'heart' than the 'head', about a lived relationship than an intellectual comprehension, his own intense desire to experience this reality for himself and those to whom he ministers motivates the remainder of his ministry. Intellectual assent to propositional truths about God, humanity and their interrelationship has a place since there are objective realities about God as a Person to be known–his nature, character and purposes. However, Wesley is convinced that these are not central to a relationship of love and must always be subordinate to heart experience, even if this cannot always be easily articulated. This can be pictured by the difference between a male nurse explaining breastfeeding to a new mother and the explanation given by a female nurse who has herself breastfed an infant; the male may have all the technical information at his disposal but it is a poor substitute for actual lived experience. As a spiritual guide and mentor, Wesley started out in the same position as the male nurse; it was the events around his Aldersgate experience that forever changed his perspective and understanding. Wesley now begins to write specifically about the need for a personal experience of the Holy Spirit in life and he is convinced that there must be a direct witness of the Spirit that the person is a Christian. As Clive Marsh reminds us, this brings to the fore the role of an explicitly Christian experience and not simply general life experience. Wesley now believes that a personal encounter with God is necessary before a truly Christian theology can be articulated. By the close of this period he is clearly emphasising the personal and corporate experience of Christian faith in contrast to the emerging objectification of it by many of his contemporaries. There is a settled focus on observing and interviewing people about their spiritual experience as he wants to put everything to the practical test–does it work as it is claimed to work?

The emphasis on a personal experience of God brought into focus the critical question of the role of Scripture. Wesley is thoroughly Protestant in upholding the Scriptures as the final authority in matters of faith and practice, giving frequent testimony to this fact from 1725 onwards. He maintains his conviction that all things had to be judged by Scripture but he was equally sure that the text needed interpretation and application; thus his concern that people use the whole counsel of God and avoid selectiveness in the texts. Wesley participates in the religious debates that emerged in the eighteenth century and he is initially disposed to value reason over revelation, propositional truth over relational truth, with its accompanying study of doctrinal systems and logic. Appeals to include reason, Christian antiquity or life experience did not settle the arguments as his detractors made similar pleas and arrived at very differing conclusions. Wesley is confident that God is a living Person and is therefore objectively real and can be known through the spiritual senses. Furthermore, he is convinced that God communicates with people directly through the work of the Holy Spirit and not simply through a written document (Scripture or the written records of other Christians), rationality or common life experience. This could make Scripture, reason and tradition secondary to the lived experience of the Spirit and open the door to charges of enthusiasm. On the other hand, to settle for a purely human reading and interpretation of a document (no matter how exalted the claims for its authorship may be) is to leave its interpretation open to the results of intellectual argument, logic, and the number and quality of various witnesses (both oral and written). To appeal to the Scripture in itself is fruitless, since the text must always be interpreted and applied by the reader on some basis other then the actual written words themselves. Wesley is beginning to realise that it is the direct work of the Spirit in a Christian's life and the community of faith that holds the answer to the dilemma and this is a critical challenge for the next phase in his life and ministry.

CHAPTER 4

Wesley's Leadership of the Methodist Movement: The Years of Critical Development, 1740 – 1769

The relationship between Wesley's initial understanding of the experience he sought, the actual experience he found and the description of it in formal theological language was complex. Furthermore, it was a dynamic process, as each stage of Wesley's spiritual journey required further theological reflection and this was then used to re-interpret past experiences as well as shape his expectation of future ones. By the close of 1739 Wesley emerges as the leader of the people called Methodists and his ministry begins to take a defining form that will mark the rest of his days. His core theological commitments and methodology are now in place. While the earlier material was predominantly concerned with his own spiritual journey, what now comes to the fore is Wesley's pastoral concern for his own people.

This chapter is intended to demonstrate the impact of Christian experience on Wesley's theological methodology as he offers pastoral guidance to the Methodists. Making use of this development, a new model of Wesley's theological method will be proposed. During these years there is much debate regarding his understanding of Christian perfection and in the process he identifies a vital difference between the substance and the circumstance of a doctrine. These two categories are critical for his theologising and in them we see a distinction emerge over the way he uses his sources. This chapter seeks to establish that this use is critical and it carries clear implications for his theological methodology.

The chapter begins with a brief overview of Wesley's spiritual vision–how he understood the nature of God, human beings and their relationship. It then moves on to a consideration of Wesley's theological methodology in this period. It examines his focus on Christianity as a religion of the heart and its implications, before going on to consider the work of the Holy Spirit in helping Christians understand God's teaching in their life and community. This leads into a study of the means that the Spirit uses; namely, Scripture, reason, Christian experience and the community ethos. With this as a background, we then explore Wesley's doctrinal understanding of Christian perfection in this period, before turning to his actual pastoral practice.

Wesley's Spiritual Vision: His Understanding of the Nature of God, Human Beings and Their Relationship

The theological foundation for Wesley's understanding of Christianity had been laid in the period 1725-1739. While this was to be further developed and nuanced in the following decades, the core soteriological beliefs that underpinned his understanding of Christian perfection had been established. Examining these in detail is beyond the scope of this book but a fine summary is found in his sermon, "The Scripture Way of Salvation" (1765), with its clear description of the whole *ordo salutis*.[1] In an earlier sermon ("Original Sin") he wrote

> Ye know that the great end of religion is to renew our hearts in the image of God, to repair that total loss of righteousness and true holiness which we sustained by the sin of our first parent. ... Keep to the plain, old 'faith, once delivered to the saints', and delivered by the Spirit of God to your hearts. Know your disease! Know your cure! ... By nature ye are wholly corrupted; by grace ye shall be wholly renewed.[2]

Salvation involves a reciprocal relationship of love, for God will only continue in a relationship in which we return the prior love he gives us. Failure to return the love is to experience God's gradual withdrawal, leading to an eventual fall into inward and then outward sin.[3] Wesley was convinced that a faithful relationship with God, grounded in grace, was possible from the very beginning. This was because its essential nature had to do with love and trust, not obedience and performance, though the latter elements would flow from the former ones and be defined by them.[4] In his sermon, "The Righteousness of Faith" (1746), Wesley clarified his previous understanding of the distinction between the "covenant of works" that applied in the original creation setting and the "covenant of grace" that applies now. Under the former nothing but absolute perfection and obedience would do in order to be accepted by God,

---

[1] *Works*, 2:155-69. See especially Outler's introduction, pp. 153-55. A full discussion of the nature and condition of justification, salvation and faith is found in his *A Farther Appeal to Men of Reason and Religion, Part I* in *Works*, 11:105-38. Other summaries of his position are found in *Works*, 1:181-82; 2:172-84, 91-93, 243-45; *Works* (Jackson), 8:275-98; 10:68; 14:323.

[2] *Works*, 2:185. See also *Works*, 11:106. On his understanding of original sin; see the introduction to the sermon on "Original Sin" in *Works*, 2:170-72. For an extended treatment, see *The Doctrine of Original Sin, According to Scripture, Reason, and Experience* in *Works* (Jackson), 9:191-464.

[3] *Works*, 1:442-43. See also Ibid., 250, 61-63.

[4] On the nature of justification and its relationship to the new birth (initial sanctification), see *Works*, 1:187, 431-32; 2:187, 98. The evidence of a justified life and what it means to be holy was explored in Wesley's series on the Sermon on the Mount; see Outler's introduction and the text of the thirteen sermons in *Works*, 1:466-698.

and this is impossible for all humans as they are now constituted.[5] Under the latter, we are accepted because "the free grace of God, through the merits of Christ, gives pardon to them that believe, that believe with such a faith as, working by love, *produces* [emphasis mine] all obedience and holiness."[6]

> And what is righteousness but the life of God in the soul, the mind which was in Christ Jesus, the image of God stamped upon the heart, now renewed after the likeness of him that created it? What is it but the love of God because he first loved us, and the love of all mankind for his sake?[7]

It is important to note that righteousness is not defined by Wesley in legal terms as obedience to law or conformity to an absolute standard, but as God's love expressed in a right relationship with himself and subsequently with all other persons. People were created in receipt of the fullness of God's love and with the ability to fully return that love to God and to other creatures.[8] This is summed up in terms of humans being both holy and happy through knowing, loving and enjoying God. Holiness is active love to God and neighbour based on God's prior love poured into the heart; happiness is the enjoyment and security in such a love.[9] It is the presence of these two qualities in a person's life that is "the strongest evidence" of the truth of Christianity.[10] Wesley believed this relationship of love with God was capable of increasing in depth and richness as the person maintained and developed their relationship of love with the neighbour.[11] The very nature of Christianity as a relationship involving the neighbour was underlined by the Sermon on the Mount, for you need other people to put its precepts into practice: "... Christianity is essentially a social religion, and that to turn it into a solitary religion is indeed to destroy it. ... When I say this is essentially a social religion, I mean not only that it cannot subsist so well, but that it cannot subsist at all without society, without living and conversing with other men."[12]

---

[5] See Outler's introduction in Ibid., 200-02. See also *Works*, 1:204; 2:27.
[6] *Works*, 2:27. See also *Works*, 1:203-6.
[7] *Works*, 1:481. See also Ibid., 495, 579.
[8] *Works*, 2:194. See also *Works* (Jackson), 9:292-93.
[9] See note 18, *Works*, 1:185. See also *Works*, 2:195; 11:125-28, 270; *Works* (Jackson), 10:75; 11:11; 14:212; *Letters* (Telford), 3:388. The Sermon on the Mount is described as an invitation to "true holiness, and happiness"; see *Notes (NT)*.
[10] *Works* (Jackson), 10:75-76. See also Ibid., 129-33.
[11] *Works*, 1:663.
[12] Ibid., 533-34. See also *Works*, 21:477-79. Wesley came to the conclusion that to preach in a place without forming a Society was to effectively condemn the new Christians to an eventual loss of faith; see Ibid., 424-25.

Wesley's Theological Methodology:
Its Sources, Tools and their Interrelationship

In the preface to the first published edition of his *Sermons on Several Occasions*, Wesley outlined its purpose:[13]

> I am a spirit come from God and returning to God; ... I want to know one thing, the way to heaven ... God himself has condescended to teach the way: ... He hath written it down in a book. O give me that book! At any price give me the Book of God! ... Let me be *homo unius libri*. Here then I am, ... I sit down alone: only God is here. In his presence I open, I read his Book; for this end, to find the way to heaven. Is there a doubt concerning the meaning of what I read? ... I then search after and consider parallel passages of Scripture, ... I meditate thereon, with all the attention and earnestness of which my mind is capable. If any doubt still remains, I consult those who are experienced in the things of God, and then the writings whereby, being dead, they yet speak. And what I thus learn, that I teach.
>
> I have accordingly set down in the following sermons what I find in the Bible concerning the way to heaven, with a view to distinguish this way of God from all those which are the inventions of men. I have endeavoured to describe the true, the scriptural, experimental religion, so as to omit nothing which is a real part thereof, and to add nothing thereto which is not. And herein it is more especially my desire, first, to guard those who are just setting their faces toward heaven ... from formality, from mere outside religion, which has almost driven heart-religion out of the world; and secondly, to warn those who know the religion of the heart, the faith which worketh by love, lest at any time they make void the law through faith, and so fall back into the snare of the devil.[14]

The purpose of the sermon corpus was to make available to ordinary people Wesley's understanding of the truths of Scripture, as well as what he has learned from the community of faith (past and present). The focus is clearly soteriology ("the way to heaven"[15]) and this in turn is set within a framework of a relationship with God, rather than intellectual knowledge and behaviour. The

---

[13] *Works*, 1:103. Outler states that Wesley described the intention of the entire project of his published sermons in the preface (written in 1746), and it remained unrevised in every edition from 1746-1787. See also Steve Harper, "Wesley's Sermons as Spiritual Formation Documents," *Methodist History* 26, no. 3 (1988); John R. Tyson, "Essential Doctrines and Real Religion: Theological Method in Wesley's *Sermons on Several Occasions*," *WTJ* 23, no. 1 & 2 (Spring-Fall, 1988).

[14] *Works*, 1:105-06.

[15] There are around 73 references to the phrase "the way to heaven" in Wesley's sermons, hymns and journals according to the search facility in John Wesley, *The Works of John Wesley: The Bicentennial Edition* [CD] (Abingdon Press, 2005, accessed). For Wesley's soteriological focus, see Kenneth J. Collins, "The Soteriological Orientation of John Wesley's Ministry to the Poor," *Asbury Theological Journal* 50, no. 1 (1995); Kenneth J. Collins, *The Scripture Way of Salvation: The Heart of John Wesley's Theology* (Nashville, TN: Abingdon Press, 1997).

preface implies that this relationship is currently estranged and its recovery is due only to God's initiative through Jesus Christ. Wesley believed that the whole purpose of the Incarnation was the restoration of the relationship between God and humans. To minimise subjectivity in interpretation, Wesley made it clear that understanding the message required consultation with other living witnesses and the written witness of those who had died in the faith (community experience). He did not substitute a book of written propositions accessible to our unaided intellectual comprehension for a conscious experience of a relationship with God (personally and communally), defined by love, and formed within the soteriological framework given in Scripture (to guard against enthusiasm and error).[16] A similar insight comes from the preface to his *Christian Library*, where the emphasis throughout was to be on "Practical Divinity," with the content representing the work of those noted for holding together the highest "piety" and "learning."[17] Wesley wrote, "the Christian Religion, according to the Scriptural account, is the plainest, clearest thing in the world: nothing stranger or harder to be understood than this, 'We love him, because he first loved us.'"[18] He sought to extract the "gold" through judicious editing (and translation) where necessary:

> I have endeavoured to extract such a collection of *English Divinity*, as (I believe) is all true, all agreeable to the oracles of God: and is all practical, unmixed with controversy of any kind; and all intelligible to plain men: such as is not superficial, but going down to the depth, and describing the height of Christianity. And yet not mystical, not obscure to any of those who are experienced in the ways of God.[19]

"The true, the scriptural, experimental religion" of the heart

As an Anglican, Wesley followed the non-dogmatic approach to Christianity that discouraged the endless formulation of creeds, confessions, and systematic treatises, while emphasising the centrality of the community at worship, united by a common liturgy. Building on the experiential and theological discoveries of the first part of his ministry, he continued to believe that love and

---

[16] He warns of Christians who had set their "private revelations" or "inward impressions" on the same footing with the Scripture; see *Works*, 19:166, 205, 79.

[17] John Wesley, ed., *A Christian Library Consisting of Extracts and Abridgments of the Choicest Pieces of Practical Divinity Which Have Been Published in the English Tongue*, 30 vols. (London: Thomas Cordeaux, 1819; reprint, First published in 1750 in 50 vols), 1:v-x.

[18] Ibid., viii.

[19] Ibid., ix. He affirmed in the opening of the sections on the early church fathers and the Puritan writers that the focus would be on practice, so that his Methodists could learn from the examples of their lives. See *Christian Library*, 2:3-4; 4:105-07.

relationship were crucial in terms of defining the essential nature of God and human beings.

> ... for in spite of all I can say they *will* represent one *circumstance* of my doctrine (so called) as the main *substance* of it. It nothing avails that I declare again and again, 'Love is the fulfilling of the law.' I believe this love is given in a moment. But about this I contend not. Have this love, and it is enough. For this I will contend till my spirit returns to God. Whether I am singular or no in thinking this love is instantaneously given, this is not my 'most beloved' opinion. ... Nay, I *love* (strictly speaking) *no opinion* at all ... I want, I value, I preach the love of God and man. These are my 'favourite tenets' ... 'more insisted' on by me ten times over, both in preaching and writing, than any or all other subjects that ever were in the world.[20]

The implication here is that salvation has to be understood within a framework of relationship between the Lover and the beloved (focusing on "the heart"), rather than a framework of laws between a Sovereign and a subject (focusing on an intellectual knowledge of their content and subsequent application). He could recount how many had come to faith but could give no "rational account of the plainest principles of religion. 'Tis plain God begins his work at the heart; then the inspiration of the Highest giveth understanding."[21] On the other hand, a person of eminent education knew very little of "heart religion, of scriptural Christianity, the religion of love, as a child three years old of algebra."[22]

---

[20] *Works*, 26:159-60. See also *Works*, 9:309; 26:203, 518; *Works* (Jackson), 10:347-48; *Letters* (Telford), 3:237; 4:34-35, 110-11, 134.

[21] *Works*, 20:274. See also *Works*, 11:477; 21:348; 26:362.

[22] *Works*, 21:20. Note the close correlation of heart religion with scriptural Christianity and love in *Works*, 1:161-64, 75; 11:269-70; 21:287; *Works* (Jackson), 10:72-75. On the language of the heart, its affections and theologising, see Gregory S. Clapper, *John Wesley on Religious Affections: His Views on Experience and Emotion and Their Role in the Christian Life and Theology* (Metuchen, NJ: Scarecrow Press, 1989); Philip R. Meadows, "'Candidates for Heaven': Wesleyan Resources for a Theology of Religions," *WTJ* 35, no. 1 (Spring, 2000): 110-12; Gregory S. Clapper, "Wesley's 'Main Doctrines' and Spiritual Formation and Teaching in the Wesleyan Tradition," *WTJ* 39, no. 2 (Fall, 2004). On the nature and importance of the affections and tempers, see Randy L. Maddox, "Holiness of Heart and Life: Lessons from North American Methodism," *Asbury Theological Journal* 50-51, no. 2-1 (1995-1996); Clapper, *Wesley on Religious Affections;* Gregory S. Clapper, "*Orthokardia* : The Practical Theology of John Wesley's Heart Religion," *Quarterly Review* 10, no. 1 (1990); Gregory S. Clapper, "John Wesley's "Heart Religion" and the Righteousness of Christ," *Methodist History* 35, no. 3 (1997); Gregory S. Clapper, "'True Religion' and the Affections: A Study of John Wesley's Abridgement of Jonathan Edwards' Treatise on Religious Affections," *WTJ* 19:2 (Fall 1984); Henry H. Knight III, "The Role of Faith and the Means of Grace in the Heart Religion of John Wesley," in *"Heart Religion" in the Methodist Tradition and Related Movements*, ed. Richard B. Steele (Lanham, MD: Scarecrow Press, 2001),

> I say of the *heart*. For neither does religion consist in *orthodoxy* or *right opinions*; ... A man may be orthodox in every point ... he may think justly concerning the incarnation of our Lord, concerning the ever blessed Trinity, and every other doctrine contained in the oracles of God. He may assent to all the three creeds–that called the Apostles', the Nicene, and the Athanasian–and yet 'tis possible he may have no religion at all, ... He may be almost as orthodox as the devil ... and may all the while be as great a stranger as he to the religion of the heart.[23]

In writing to the teachers at Oxford he said, "Do you continually remind those under your care that the one rational end of all our studies is to know, love, and serve 'the only true God, and Jesus Christ whom he hath sent'? ... that without love all learning is but splendid ignorance, pompous folly, vexation of spirit. Has all you teach an actual tendency to the love of God, and of all mankind for his sake?"[24] His concern was for "a religion worthy of the God that gave it. ... And this we conceive to be no other than love: the love of God and of all mankind; ... This love we believe to be the medicine of life, the never-failing remedy for all the evils of a disordered world, for all the miseries and vices of men."[25] With the focus on love, Wesley believed that God usually began his work in the heart: "Men usually feel *desires* to please God before they *know* how to please him. Their *heart* says, 'What must I do to be saved?' before they *understand* the way of salvation."[26] Doctrinal understanding may open up the possibility of a person entering an experience, it can challenge their experience or affirm it, but it cannot substitute for it. Even a knowledge of Scripture itself cannot substitute for a relationship of love.

> For how far is love, even with many wrong opinions, to be preferred before truth itself without love? We may die without the knowledge of many truths and yet be carried into Abraham's bosom. But if we die without love, what will knowledge avail?[27]

274-76; Richard B. Steele, "Introduction," in *"Heart Religion"*, xxx-xxxv; Richard B. Steele, *"Gracious Affection" and "True Virtue" According to Jonathan Edwards and John Wesley* (Metuchen, NJ: Scarecrow Press, 1994); Randy L. Maddox, "Reconnecting the Means to the End: A Wesleyan Prescription for the Holiness Movement," *WTJ* 33, no. 2 (Fall, 1998): 38-65.

[23] *Works*, 1:220-21. For a thorough discussion of Wesley's views on "opinions" and a list of references to his writings that mention them, see n. 65, p. 220. On "heart religion," see *Works*, 1:698; 11:272-74; 26:179; *Works* (Jackson), 11:11; *Letters* (Telford), 4:302-03.

[24] *Works*, 1:175-76. See also *Works*, 26:564-65.

[25] *Works*, 11:45. See also *Works*, 26:475; *Letters* (Telford), 3:203; 4:96-97.

[26] *Works*, 11:479.

[27] *Works*, 1:107. See also *Works*, 9:84-85; 26:223; *Works* (Jackson), 10:73. See his positive evaluation of the holy character of "heretics" like Montanus and Pelagius in *Works*, 2:555-56; *Letters* (Telford), 4:158.

The emphasis on "desire" and the concomitant downplaying of the understanding carries many implications for Wesley's theological methodology. Entering into and maintaining a loving relationship requires a far richer canvas than can be painted with a sterile series of propositions to be intellectually comprehended; it is far more the domain of the poet or artist, than that of the scientist. Little wonder that he did not expect unanimity on matters of opinion regarding doctrinal reflection on the experience of salvation.[28] Wesley now consistently affirmed the primacy of a relationship of love as the essence of Christianity and doctrinal affirmations were very much secondary (though not unimportant). Clapper argues that "heart religion" is Wesley's "orienting concern" theologically; that is, it "gives consistency to, and provides guidance for, the various particular theological activities that a thinker undertakes." This influences the selection, interpretation, relative emphasis and interweaving of theological affirmations and practices.[29] This is in harmony with the common observation amongst Wesleyan scholars that Wesley's whole theological enterprise can be identified as a 'theology of love'.[30]

While Wesley did not think that all Christians would agree with him theologically, either in methodology or doctrinal opinions, he did not think this necessitated a break in Christian fellowship.[31] He acknowledged that "although a difference in opinions or modes of worship may prevent an entire external union, yet need it prevent our union in affection? Though we can't think alike, may we not love alike? May we not be of one heart, though we are not of one opinion? Without all doubt we may."[32] Wesley noted that many problems arose because of misunderstandings rather than actual disagreements: "But if the difference be more in *opinion* than real *experience*, and more in *expression* than in *opinion*, how can it be that even the children of God should so vehemently

---

[28] See Outler's introduction to "Catholic Spirit", *Works*, 2:79-80. This desire to maintain fellowship in the face of differing opinions was a distinguishing mark of Methodism; see *Works*, 2:69-70; 9:32-42.

[29] Clapper, "Wesley's 'Main Doctrines' and Spiritual Formation and Teaching in the Wesleyan Tradition," 100. Clapper draws his material from Maddox, *Responsible Grace*, 18-19.

[30] Some of the best and most succinct accounts of this are to be found in David L. Cubie, "Wesley's Theology of Love," *WTJ* 20, no. 1 (Spring, 1985); W. Stanley Johnson, "Christian Perfection as Love for God," *WTJ* 18, no. 1 (Spring, 1983); Collins, *The Theology of John Wesley*; Wynkoop, *Theology of Love* .

[31] See *Works*, 19:152-53, 281; 26:419; *Letters* (Telford), 4:244; 5:98.

[32] *Works*, 2:82. See his plea for co-operation amongst evangelical clergy in *Works*, 7:736; 11:321; 21:444, 54-61. He believed that the "circumstantials" of public worship were a matter of indifference as they were in "no way determined by Scripture"; *Works* (Jackson), 10:502. See also *Works*, 7:733-37; 26:85-86, 128; *Letters* (Telford), 3:182-83; 4:216 and the preface in Wesley, ed., *Christian Library*, 15:4.

contend with each other on the point?"³³ He thought that you could differ in opinions and expressions and still exercise the same faith and experience the same love of God: "It is true believers may not all speak alike; they may not all use the same language. ... But a difference of expression does not necessarily imply a difference of sentiment. Different persons may use different expressions, and yet mean the same thing."³⁴ He concluded:

> But will anyone dare to affirm that all mystics ... , all Quakers, all Presbyterians or Independents, and all members of the Church of England, who are not clear in their opinions or expressions, are void of all Christian experience? That consequently they are all in a state of damnation, ... However confused their ideas may be, however improper their language, may there not be many of them whose heart is right toward God ... ?
>
> ... Let them use either this or such other expressions as they judge to be more exactly scriptural, provided their *heart* rests only on what Christ hath done and suffered for pardon, grace, and glory.³⁵

Wesley acknowledged the limits of language to describe a heart experience or to define it theologically. The language of love and relationship is far less precise than the language of science or mathematics, and the vagueness could be dangerous. This is where the ministry of the Holy Spirit in the community of faith acts as a dynamic system of checks and balances. His decision to break with Calvinistic Methodism was not initially over their "opinions" but over the divisions they caused in the societies (a clear demonstration of a lack of love). Wesley was content for both Arminians and Calvinists to be Methodists as long

---

[33] *Works*, 1:451-52. This was from "The Lord our Righteousness," written in 1765 to deal with the increasingly bitter disputes between the Calvinists and the Arminians over the nature and relationship of justification, imputed and imparted righteousness. Wesley admitted this was a critical issue which lay right at the heart of Christianity and all Christians surely ought to agree here—see pp. 450-51. See also *Letters* (Telford), 3:371-88. The public nature of the dispute *within* Methodism can be traced back as far as 1740; see *Works*, 19:174.

[34] *Works*, 1:454. See also *Works*, 11:73. On his positive approach to Roman Catholics, see *Works*, 20:200; *Works* (Jackson), 10:80-86. For further background on Wesley's approach to Roman Catholicism, see David Butler, *Methodists and Papists: John Wesley and the Catholic Church in the Eighteenth Century* (London: Darton, Longman and Todd, 1995); David M. Chapman, *In Search of the Catholic Spirit: Methodists and Roman Catholics in Dialogue* (Peterborough, ENG: Epworth Press, 2004), 6-43.

[35] *Works*, 1:461. His critical concern was for the possible outcome of a wrong opinion that led to antinomianism; see p. 462. Note his approval of the holy lives of Thomas à Kempis and Frances Sales in spite of their "great mistakes"; see *Works*, 9:85. Likewise, his support for William Law in *Works*, 11:172-73. Other examples may be found in *Works*, 11:278; *Letters* (Telford), 3:183; 4:271-72, 292, 94-96 and Wesley, ed., *Christian Library*, 15:4.

as they did not engage in bitter disputes that led to separation.[36] The same attitude was seen in his break with the Moravians in London who upheld the doctrine of stillness.[37] Wesley recognized that there would always be differing opinions due to various understandings that arise from people's limited knowledge of God and his ways. Therefore it was important to follow our own conscience on opinions and modes of worship: "everyone must follow the dictates of his own conscience in simplicity and godly sincerity. ... every man must judge for himself, as every man must give an account of himself to God. ... [otherwise] it entirely destroys the right of private judgment on which that whole Reformation stands."[38] The personal–community tension in salvation must finally be resolved in favour of the personal decision, as each one is ultimately responsible for and accountable to God for their salvation.

Wesley's "catholic spirit" was not, however, a "speculative latitudinarianism," an "indifference to all opinions," nor a "practical latitudinarianism," with its indifference to public worship and the manner of performing it.[39] Wesley insisted each person must be a faithful and committed member of a local congregation, while having an attitude of openness, love and encouragement to others.[40] There were a number of doctrines he deemed to be essential to being a Christian and were not a matter of "opinion."[41] Wesley was concerned with the rising popularity amongst Christians of the viewpoint that human beings were innately good, and in opposition to this view he staunchly

---

[36] See *Works*, 19:184-89, 231-32, 332-33; 20:66-68, 118, 30, 306, 18, 81-82, 456, 66; *Letters* (Telford), 5:90. See also his letters to John Newton in *Letters* (Telford), 4:297-300; 5:7-8. Later he would argue strongly against their theological position as, in his opinion, it did not encourage the formation of holy character. Further information on the Calvinistic controversy may be found in Rack, *Reasonable Enthusiast*, 450-61; Heitzenrater, *People Called Methodists*, 239-42, 67-68.

[37] See, for example, *Works*, 19:191.

[38] *Works*, 2:86. See also *Works*, 20:122. More information on Wesley's understanding and use of private judgement can be found in Leon O. Hynson, "The Right of Private Judgement," *Asbury Theological Journal* 60, no. 1 (Spring, 2005).

[39] *Works*, 2:87-92. See also *Works*, 11:477-79; *Letters* (Telford), 3:201-03.

[40] *Works*, 2:93-95.

[41] For an analysis of Wesley's varying lists of "essential doctrines" see Ted A. Campbell, "The Shape of Wesleyan Thought: The Question of John Wesley's 'Essential' Christian Doctrines," *Asbury Theological Journal* 59:1 & 2 (Spring/Fall 2004): 27-40. See also Jerry L. Walls, "What Is Theological Pluralism," *Quarterly Review* 5, no. 3 (1985); Randy L. Maddox, "Opinion, Religion and "Catholic Spirit": John Wesley on Theological Integrity," *Asbury Theological Journal* 47, no. 1 (1992); Howe Octavius Thomas, "John Wesley's Awareness and Application of the Method of Distinguishing between Theological Essentials and Theological Opinions," *Methodist History* 26, no. 2 (1988); Howe Octavius Thomas, "John Wesley's Understanding of Theological Distinction between 'Essentials' and 'Opinions'," *Methodist History* 33, no. 3 (1995).

upheld the doctrine of original sin.[42] Belief in original sin is "the first, grand, distinguishing point between heathenism and Christianity."[43]

> It is, *Christianity* or *heathenism*? For take away the scriptural doctrine of redemption or justification, and that of the new birth, the beginning of sanctification, or which amounts to the same, explain them as you do, suitably to your doctrine of original sin, and what is Christianity better than heathenism? ... Are *those things* that have been believed for many ages throughout the Christian world, real, solid *truths*, or *monkish dreams* and vain imaginations?[44]

The subsequent doctrines of justification and the new birth were equally "fundamental."[45] In "The Principles of a Methodist Farther Explained" (1746) he wrote: "Our main doctrines, which include all the rest, are three, that of repentance, of faith, and of holiness. The first of these we account, as it were, the porch of religion; the next, the door; the third is religion itself."[46] When defending his doctrinal position on justification, salvation, faith and the work of God in accomplishing them, he writes that he does "instil" into the people a few "favourite tenets ... as if the whole of Christianity depended upon them" and these are frequently summed up as: faith working by love, loving God and neighbour with one's whole being and doing all the good one can as a consequence. "For who can deny that all efforts toward a Christian life, without more than a bare belief, without a thorough *experience* and *practice* of these, are utterly vain and ineffectual?"[47] It is another reminder that his critical beliefs

---

[42] He published his lengthiest treatise against this understanding; see "The Doctrine of Original Sin: According to Scripture, Reason, and Experience," in *Works* (Jackson), 9:191-464. It was followed later by a sermonic abridgement ("Original Sin," 1759), which he regarded as a key doctrinal statement; see Outler's introduction to the sermon in *Works*, 2:170-72. The critical foundation for his belief in original sin and why he regarded it as an essential Christian doctrine was the clear teaching of the Scripture, confirmed by "daily experience"; see *Works*, 2:172-76; *Letters* (Telford), 4:67.

[43] *Works*, 2:182.

[44] *Works*, 21:205. Note Wesley's reference to that which has been believed "for many ages throughout the Christian world"; the greater the consensus here, the greater the certainty over correct doctrinal understanding.

[45] *Works*, 2:187. See also *Works*, 21:444, 56.

[46] *Works*, 9:227. In a letter to George Downing and to various clergymen he mentioned "three grand scriptural doctrines—Original Sin, Justification by Faith, and Holiness consequent thereon"; see *Letters* (Telford), 4:146, 237. A similar list is given in a letter to Lady Huntingdonin in John R. Tyson with Boyd S. Schlenther, *In the Midst of Early Methodism: Lady Huntingdon and Her Correspondence* (Lanham, MD: Scarecrow Press, 2006): 104-05. To the Earl of Dartmouth he mentioned "righteousness and peace and joy in the Holy Ghost . . . given only to those who are justified by faith"; see *Letters* (Telford), 4:147. To James Knox it is "Justification by Faith and Holiness" which is to be experienced and not just understood; see *Letters* (Telford), 4:303.

[47] *Works*, 11:128-29.

are tied to love and relationship and not simply doctrinal opinions, no matter how correct they may be.

The Living Voice of God: The Work of the Holy Spirit

If "true religion" is a matter of the heart and relationship, then the ministry of the Holy Spirit is absolutely vital to the initiation, development and consummation of the life of faith in both personal and community experience:[48] "In him are included all good things; all wisdom, peace, joy, love; the whole treasures of holiness and happiness; all that God hath prepared for them that love him."[49] Wesley's writings are now filled with references to the role of the Holy Spirit in the whole process of salvation: "And therefore every man, in order to believe unto salvation, must receive the Holy Ghost. This is essentially necessary to every Christian, not in order to his working miracles, but in order to faith, peace, joy, and love–the ordinary fruits of the Spirit."[50] The person who was impacted by the ministry of the Holy Spirit could not know this other than by personal experience: "It is confirmed by *your* experience and *mine*. The Spirit itself bore witness to my spirit that I was a child of God, gave me an *evidence* hereof, and I immediately cried, 'Abba, Father!'" This change is "directly witnessed to them by his Spirit ... [and they] cannot be satisfied with anything less than a direct testimony from his Spirit."[51] Furthermore, the work of the Spirit impacts the entire person, and not just the mind–our dispositions, tempers, affections, actions and intention.[52] Clapper reminds us that for Wesley

---

[48] For the vital importance of the ministry of the Spirit in Wesley's theologising, see Thomas A. Langford, "The United Methodist Quadrilateral: A Theological Task," *Doctrine and Theology*, 241; Rob L. Staples, "The Present Frontiers of Wesleyan Theology," *WTJ* 12 (Spring, 1977): 11-14; Rob L. Staples, "John Wesley's Doctrine of the Holy Spirit," *WTJ* 21, no. 1 & 2 (Spring-Fall, 1986); Rob L. Staples, "Wesleyan Perspectives on the Doctrine of the Holy Spirit," in *The Spirit and the New Age: An Inquiry into the Holy Spirit and Last Things from a Biblical Theological Perspective*, ed. Alex R. G. Deasley and R. Larry Shelton (Anderson, IN: Warner Press, 1986), 199-236; Lycurgus M. Starkey, Jr., *The Work of the Holy Spirit: A Study in Wesleyan Theology* (Nashville, TN: Abingdon Press, 1962); Jung Yang, "The Doctrine of God in the Theology of John Wesley" (PhD thesis, University of Aberdeen, 2003), 73; Winfield H. Bevins, "The Historical Development of Wesley's Doctrine of the Spirit." *WTJ* 41, no. 2 (Fall, 2006).

[49] *Works*, 1:660. See also *Works* (Jackson), 10:82.

[50] *Works*, 11:107-08. See also *Works*, 1:160, 309; 11:254; 26:431. This confirms Wesley's conviction since the events surrounding Aldersgate that you cannot believe in God (in the classical Christian sense) without a personal encounter with him through the Spirit; see Smith, *Belief and History*, 80-87.

[51] *Works*, 1:290-91. See also the correspondence with "John Smith" in *Works*, 26:178-83, 200-03, 31-33, 46-48.

[52] *Works*, 1:651. See also Randy L. Maddox, "'Celebrating the Whole Wesley': A Legacy for Contemporary Wesleyans," *Methodist History* 43, no. 2 (January 2005): 76.

the "tempers" are not simply feelings but "dispositions for all of life, master passions which shape all behaviour whether they are consciously felt or not."[53] Wesley wrote: "O when will you take knowledge that *our* whole concern, our constant labour, is to bring all the world to the religion which you feel, to solid, inward, vital religion!"[54] Wesley believed that while "no man on earth can explain the particular manner wherein the Spirit of God works on the soul, yet whosoever has these fruits cannot but know and *feel* that God has wrought them in his heart."[55] The Spirit may work more particularly on the understanding to open or enlighten it, discovering to us the things of God. Or he may work on the will and affections, withdrawing us from evil and inclining us to good. "But however it be expressed, it is certain all true faith, and the whole work of salvation, every good thought, word, and work, is altogether by the operation of the Spirit of God."[56] Clearly, in Wesley's understanding the Spirit impacts the cognitive, volitional and affectional elements of human life.

Critical to Wesley's view was the role of the "spiritual senses" which enabled the Christian to actually experience God's presence in their heart and life through the work of the Spirit.[57] The danger in this was, of course, that believers would so insist on the immediate work of the Spirit that they relied almost totally on spiritual intuition for their doctrine and practice. He was particularly concerned by beliefs that have all "the appearance of *enthusiasm*: overvaluing *feelings* and *inward impressions*; mistaking the mere work of *imagination* for the voice of the Spirit; expecting the end without the means; and undervaluing *reason, knowledge*, and *wisdom*, in general."[58] To limit this danger, Wesley realised the need for various safeguards and these had to be such that they did not deny or stifle the direct work of the Spirit in the heart. It is here that his concept of "the means of grace" becomes critical. While this phrase is normally used in connection with the sacraments and spiritual disciplines, Wesley also used it in connection with those sources that God uses

---

[53] Clapper, "Wesley's 'Main Doctrines' and Spiritual Formation and Teaching in the Wesleyan Tradition," 108.

[54] *Works*, 11:73.

[55] Ibid., 108. Note again that all our explanations fail to do justice to actual Christian experience.

[56] Ibid. See also *Works*, 11:171-72; 26:441.

[57] Wesley drew the comparison between the physical senses present in a child prior to birth with their actual use after birth, and the presence of "spiritual senses" in the person without God with their actual use after the "new birth" through the work of the Spirit; see *Works*, 2:160-61, 92-93. Wesley argued faith was to the spiritual world what our physical senses were to the natural world; see *Works*, 11:46-47, 56-57.

[58] *Works*, 21:396. The consequences of all this he outlines on pp. 396-97. For examples of its negative impact on the societies, see *Works*, 21:407, 15, 33, 38.

to instruct and guide people in their spiritual life.[59] "The chief of these means are prayer, whether in secret or with the great congregation; searching the Scriptures (which implies reading, hearing, and meditating thereon) ... and these we believe to be ordained of God as the ordinary channels of conveying his grace to the souls of men."[60] It is important to note that in both prayer and searching the Scriptures, Wesley implied that both personal and community reason and experience are vital elements. His theological method clearly utilises all of them, but he does not want to say that they are absolutely essential–this is properly limited to the work of the Holy Spirit.

> ... all outward means whatever, if separate from the Spirit of God, cannot profit at all, cannot conduce in any degree either to the knowledge or love of God. ... And all outward things, unless he work in them and by them, are mere weak and beggarly elements. Whosoever therefore imagines there is any intrinsic power in any means whatsoever does greatly err, not knowing the Scriptures, neither the power of God. We know that there is *no inherent power* in the words that are spoken in prayer, *in the letter of Scripture read, the sound thereof heard,* ... but that it is God alone who is the giver of every good gift, the author of all grace; that the whole power is of him, whereby through any of these there is any blessing conveyed to our soul. We know likewise that he is able to give the same grace, though there were no means on the face of the earth. ... *seeing he is equally able to work whatsoever pleaseth him by any or by none at all* (emphasis mine).[61]

It is imperative to understand that Wesley was arguing for the vital role of Christian experience (the presence of God himself in the person's life), and not merely general life experience, as the essential component in reading or hearing the Scriptures. The implication is that people devoid of the Spirit cannot comprehend the Scriptures as God intends. Furthermore, God can work directly in a person's life without utilising the Scriptures (or any other means) at all. Wesley has made it clear that it is the direct authority of the Spirit that is absolutely indispensable in theologising, making God himself the sole authority in matters of faith and practice. To maintain this stance was not easy and it has often been lost by his successors, who have frequently elevated Scripture (as a written document) to the place of primacy (or to a lesser extent, reason, experience or tradition), with only a casual link to the work of the Spirit.

---

[59] See Starkey, *The Work of the Holy Spirit*, 79-90; Knight, *Presence of God*. Knight writes about the "means" in the context of the presence of God and forming Christian identity, not as a key concept in Wesley's theological method.

[60] *Works*, 1:381.

[61] Ibid., 382. See also Starkey, *The Work of the Holy Spirit*, 142-45; On the centrality of God himself as the supreme authority in theological method and his use of Scripture, Tradition, Creeds, Word, Sacraments, and the consensus of faith, see Wilkinson, "Authority in Religion and Science."

The Written Voice of God: The Scriptures

Wesley was only too aware that his insistence on God as the sole authority in matters of faith and practice easily opened the door to mysticism and enthusiasm.[62] The written text was a guard against those who so insisted on the immediate work of the Spirit in the believer's life that they relied almost solely on spiritual intuition for their doctrine and practice. When confronted with the danger of false teaching in his societies, Wesley wrote:

> Hear with fervent and continual prayer *to him who alone teacheth man wisdom* (emphasis mine). And see that you bring whatever you hear 'to the law and to the testimony'. Receive nothing untried, nothing till it is weighed in 'the balance of the sanctuary'. Believe nothing they say unless it is clearly confirmed by plain passages of Holy Writ. Wholly reject whatsoever differs therefrom, whatever is not confirmed thereby.[63]

This underscores the critical role of God himself in the reading and comprehension of Scripture.[64] It confirms that the living word and the written word of God are intimately linked and mutually supportive, as the Bible was the word of God committed to writing.[65] In his debates with Calvinists over predestination Wesley makes reference in one of his shorter treatises to the fact that the issue will never be resolved simply by "reason" but by an appeal to Scripture: "Let the *living* [emphasis mine] oracles decide: And if these speak for us, we neither seek nor want farther witness."[66] It was an appeal not merely to words on a page to be rationally comprehended, but to the living presence of God who "speaks" through the printed words "today" just as he had done to those who originally wrote the Bible. He acknowledged that to refute their position the meaning of any one text or collection of texts must be interpreted in the light of "the whole scope and tenor both of the Old and New Testament."[67] The reading stance taken on any text or texts must derive from a basic conviction regarding God's essential nature displayed in the whole of Scripture. Against the Calvinists, Wesley argued that God's sovereignty cannot

---

[62] For a thorough examination of Wesley's interaction with mysticism, see Robert G. Tuttle Jr., *Mysticism in the Wesleyan Tradition* (Grand Rapids, MI: Zondervan, 1989). See also *Works*, 21:279, 442-43; 26:29, 56; *Letters* (Telford), 3:332-70; 4:106, 234.

[63] *Works*, 1:683-84. In his correspondence with "John Smith" Wesley totally rejected the idea proving doctrines by miracles or other signs as only the Scriptures were sufficient; see *Works*, 26:155.

[64] On the intimate link between the Spirit and the Word, see Staples, "John Wesley's Doctrine of the Holy Spirit," 94-101.

[65] See the preface to *Notes (NT)*.

[66] *Works* (Jackson), 10:285. Wesley appeals to the "plain meaning" of the text and warns of seeking to apply to individuals that which was meant to apply to the apostles, the Church or the Jewish community and nation; see pp. 285-95.

[67] *Works* (Jackson), 10:210-11.

be seen in isolation from his justice and mercy, and neither of these can be divorced from "the scriptural account of his love and goodness." Wesley noted that the Scripture expressly states that God is love and this love is toward all, not merely the "elect." On this basis, any particular text or texts that can be interpreted to support the application of predestination and election to the salvation of individuals must be wrong, as it contradicts God's nature as love, from which flows justice and mercy. These, in turn, cannot be inconsistent with God's sovereignty and God's gracious gift of human responsibility.[68] However, the main reason Wesley opposes the Calvinist interpretation of predestination, election and perseverance is because it diminishes a living relationship with God and "directly and naturally tends to hinder the inward work of God in every stage of it."[69]

There is a consistent and strong emphasis on the centrality of Scripture for both doctrine and practice throughout Wesley's writings from this period.[70] In replying to his critics, Wesley wrote: "... I trust it appears that these doctrines are no other than the doctrines of Jesus Christ; that they are all evidently contained in the Word of God, by which I alone desire to stand or fall; and that they are fundamentally the same with the doctrines of the Church of England."[71] When a critic suggested he make available the "ingredients" of Methodism in a public document he wrote that "the whole ingredients of Methodism (so called) have been discovered in print over and over; and they are enrolled in a public register, the Bible, from which we extracted them at first. ... We ought neither to add or diminish, nor alter whatever is written in that Book."[72] In advising Margaret Lewen, a Methodist laywoman, on her spiritual life, Wesley said: "All that you want to know of [God] is contained in one book, the Bible. Therefore your one point is to understand this. And all you

---

[68] *Works* (Jackson), 10:211-36, 42-55. See also his comments on Mk. 3:13 and 1 Jn. 4:8 in *Notes (NT)*.

[69] *Works* (Jackson), 10:256.

[70] *Works*, 4:393-94. See also *Works*, 1:384, 90; 9:34; 11:337, 40, 70, 75, 414; 19:162, 79; 20:439; 21:143, 59; 26:483, 521-23, 43-45; *Works* (Jackson), 13:510; *Letters* (Telford), 3:332-70; 4:111, 24, 31, 216, 334.

[71] *Works*, 11:172. Wesley believed that it was the hallmark of the Methodists that they were "Bible Christians"; see *Works*, 9:368-71. He strongly upheld the views of those "who make the written Word of God the whole standard of their faith"; see *Works*, 11:277; 26:10. His claim that he taught Scriptural doctrines which were in line with orthodox doctrines of the Church of England was much debated; for example the long correspondence with "John Smith" (apparently an Anglican clergyman of some standing). The first of these was written in May 1745 and the last August 21, 1747. See Baker's n. 18 in *Works*, 26:138-45. See also Wesley's letter to the Editor of *Lloyd's Evening Post* in *Letters* (Telford), 4:115-16. He reminded the Editor of the *London Magazine* that most of the content of his *Christian Library* was written by members of the Church of England; see *Letters* (Telford), 4:121.

[72] *Letters* (Telford), 4:131.

learn is to be referred to this, as either directly or remotely conducive to it."[73] He affirmed that every believer who "gives himself up to the guidance of God's Holy Spirit, may learn the foundation of his faith from the written word of God."[74] Wesley upheld the Protestant belief that every Christian was personally responsible before God for his or her reading of the text–the role of our own conscience guided by the Word of God.[75] This did not mean an individualistic approach, as the person was always set in a community of faith and the formation of the conscience was in a community setting and informed by its wisdom.[76] In this context, the Scriptures were to be read and understood soteriologically:

> No stress has been laid on anything as though it were necessary to salvation but what is undeniably contained in the Word of God. And of the things contained therein the stress laid on each has been in proportion to the nearness of its relation to what is there laid down as the sum of all–the love of God and neighbour.[77]

Wesley's hermeneutical key is not merely soteriology as a whole, but what he perceives to be the heart of it–the love of God and neighbour. This keeps the central interpretive focus on love and relationship, not doctrine or outward behaviour. The Bible is more akin to personal correspondence than an academic treatise, and was to be understood within this context. Critical to his understanding was the idea of the "analogy of faith", which in the *Notes (NT)* on Rom 12:6 he described as "the general tenor" of the whole of the Bible understood through a soteriological framework of original sin, justification by faith and present, inward salvation.[78] In the correspondence with 'John Smith' he agreed that it was important to work with "the general tenor of Scripture soberly studied and consistently interpreted" and "that the children of light walk by the joint light of reason, Scripture, and the Holy Ghost."[79] This affirms Wesley's conviction that for the Spirit-filled Christian, reason, Scripture and the living voice of the Spirit are not contradictory but in harmony. He reminded

---

[73] *Letters* (Telford), 4:247.
[74] *Works* (Jackson), 10:139.
[75] *Works*, 1:683-84.
[76] See *Works*, 11:453.
[77] Ibid., 277. Wesley perceives this as both scriptural and rational; see *Works*, 2:155-56.
[78] Rom. 12:6, *Notes (NT)*. See also *Works*, 1:183, 473; *Works* (Jackson), 10:490; *Letters* (Telford), 5:103-04.
[79] *Works*, 26:158. In terms of order, Wesley said, "We prove the doctrines we preach by Scripture and reason; and, if needed, by antiquity;" see *Works*, 11:310. See also *Works*, 2:293; 26:380, 475. 'John Smith' is clearly a pseudonym and there have been many attempts over the years to try and identify him. Outler believes that he was an Anglican clergyman, reasonably well-informed about Wesley and the Methodists, a good theologian, and a responsible churchman; see Albert C. Outler, ed., *John Wesley*. (New York: Oxford University Press, 1964), 3, n. 1.

Samuel Furly, an evangelical Anglican clergyman, that "the general rule of interpreting Scripture is this: the literal sense of every text is to be taken, if it be not contrary to some other texts. But in that case, the obscure text is to be interpreted by those which speak more plainly."[80]

Rather than supplying propositional truth for intellectual apprehension and doctrinal formulations, the Scriptures are used to define and illustrate the norms of the Christian life. This was not to deny the place of propositional truth nor its use in doctrinal formulation, but Wesley no longer saw this as primary or even finally essential, though such knowledge was not to be wilfully despised or neglected. Imperfect knowledge, ignorance and the subsequent mistakes arising from these impact our ability to understand the Scripture,

> especially with respect to those parts thereof which less immediately relate to practice. Hence even the children of God are not agreed as to the interpretation of many places in Holy Writ; nor is their difference of opinion any proof that they are not the children of God on either side. But it is a proof that we are no more to expect any living man to be infallible than to be omniscient.[81]

What he did consistently maintain was that in all essential matters relating to salvation, Scripture was clear thanks to the work of the Spirit in our lives.[82] For example, Wesley admitted a theological explanation of the "new birth" was beyond full human comprehension, "However, it suffices for every rational and Christian purpose that without descending into curious, critical inquiries, we can give a plain scriptural account of the nature of the new birth. This will satisfy every reasonable man who desires only the salvation of his soul."[83] Similarly, regarding the "marks" of the new birth, he gave them "just as I find them laid down in Scripture."[84] Another crucial hermeneutical rule that Wesley consistently applied was to see Law and Gospel going together as commands and promises.[85] He believed that God gave no command in Scripture apart from the promise of grace, and no promise without an implied moral responsibility: "We may yet farther observe that every command in Holy Writ is only a covered promise."[86] This was of particular importance in dealing with his

---

[80] *Works*, 26:557. See also *Letters* (Telford), 3:382.

[81] *Works*, 2:102. For example, on the transmission of original sin Wesley wrote, "The fact I know, both by Scripture and by experience. ... but *how* it is transmitted I neither know nor desire to know." See *Works*, 26:519.

[82] *Works*, 2:102.

[83] Ibid., 191. See also *Works*, 11:456.

[84] *Works*, 1:417. See also Ibid., 427.

[85] See Irv A. Brendlinger, "Transformative Dimensions within Wesley's Understanding of Christian Perfection," *Asbury Theological Journal* 59, no. 1 & 2 (Spring-Fall, 2004): 122-25.

[86] *Works*, 1:554-55. See especially n. 18. When defining what he meant by a Methodist in "The Character of a Methodist," he did so primarily by quoting from scripture. There

critics who denied the possibility of Christian perfection in this life.[87]

As far as possible, he wanted to utilise scriptural language and terminology in his preaching and public writing: "The Bible is my standard of language as well as sentiment. I endeavour not only to think but to speak as the oracles of God."[88] He would object when others sought to raise non-scriptural terms over those clearly from the text,[89] and his own written sermons are filled with scriptural language and allusions that he did not reference as quotations (as the footnotes to the *Bicentennial Edition* plainly demonstrates). Wesley's insistence on referring to "perfection" caused him endless difficulties with other Christians, but he was unwilling to drop it, or similar terms, as they were clearly scriptural: "But are they not found in the oracles of God? If so, by what authority can any messenger of God lay them aside, even if all men should be offended?"[90] A "perfect Christian" was simply defined as one who loved God with all their heart, soul, mind and strength on the basis of Scripture passages like Deut. 6:5; 30:6 and Ezek. 36:25-29.[91] The basic understanding of the nature of holiness likewise came directly from Scripture.[92] He frequently referred to the Sermon on the Mount and 1 Corinthians 13 when he wanted to describe and defend his teaching on holiness and Christian perfection[93] In responding to a charge of teaching "sinless perfection," Wesley quoted a brief excerpt from the Preface to his *Hymns and Sacred Poems* (1742) in which he utilises some 26 scripture passages to refute the charge.[94] It is of importance to note that his private correspondence, by contrast, contained very little direct quotation from Scripture, and Wesley rarely referred to a specific text to answer a particular need The letters more commonly contain material from Wesley's pastoral wisdom and experience, both directly from his own ministry and what he has read or heard from others.

In matters of practical discipleship Wesley also sought the authority of Scripture. When composing the General Rules of the United Societies he wrote: "These are the General Rules of our societies; all of which we are taught of God to observe, even in his written Word, the only rule, and the sufficient rule, both of our faith and practice. And all of these we know his Spirit writes on

---

are some 104 citations between pp. 35-42 in Works, 9:32-42. See also *Works*, 2:17-19; 9:34-35.

[87] See, for example, his letters to William Dodd in *Letters* (Telford), 3:157-58, 67-72.

[88] *Letters* (Telford), 5:8.

[89] *Works*, 19:136. His strong preference for scriptural language is seen in *Works*, 26:155-56; *Works* (Jackson), 10:312-15.

[90] *Works*, 2:99-100. He does admit that the terms do need to be explained; for example, does Paul contradict himself in both affirming and denying perfection in Phil. 2:12, 15?

[91] *Works* (Jackson), 8:279.

[92] *Works*, 2:194.

[93] Passages like these settled the question for him regarding the Scriptural base for his doctrinal position; see *Works*, 1:137, 499.

[94] *Works*, 11:339-40.

every truly awakened heart."[95] When rejecting the teaching of those who would reject the importance of self-denial he wrote, "How easily may we learn hence that they know neither the Scripture nor the power of God ... How totally ignorant are these men of an hundred particular texts, as well as of the general tenor of the whole oracles of God! And how entirely unacquainted must they be with true, genuine, Christian experience! Of the manner wherein the Holy Spirit ever did, and does at this day, work in the souls of men!"[96]

The Personal Encounter with God: Reason

> Tis true the children of God do not mistake as to the things essential to salvation. ... But in things unessential to salvation they do err, and that frequently. The best and wisest of men are frequently mistaken even with regard to facts ... circumstances ... actions ... the characters of men.[97]

Here Wesley acknowledged that the work of the Spirit in a believer's life was sufficient to enable the person to be certain about their salvation. However, this assurance did not extend to other matters of doctrinal and practical interest. In a "religion of the heart" there was a great danger of imagining yourself a Christian or that you were guided by the Spirit when neither was the case: "... how many impute things to him, or expect things from him, without any rational or scriptural ground!"[98] To help guard against this, "God has given us our own reason for a guide; though never excluding the 'secret assistance' of his Spirit."[99] In *An Earnest Appeal to Men of Reason and Religion* and *A Farther Appeal to Men of Reason and Religion*, Wesley sought to defend the place of reason in his theological understanding.[100] He wanted to demonstrate that reason, faith, love and Christianity belong together: "If therefore you allow that it is reasonable to love God, to love mankind, and to do good to all men, you cannot but allow that religion which we preach and live to be agreeable to the highest reason."[101] Wesley defined reason as "the eternal reason, or the nature of things: the nature of God and the nature of man, with the relations subsisting between them," as well as the "faculty of reasoning, of inferring one thing from another." It begins in knowing and then loving God, followed by loving all mankind, then serving and doing God's will. Such reason, Wesley

---

[95] *Works*, 9:73.

[96] *Works*, 2:248-49. Note again his stress on specifically Christian experience.

[97] Ibid., 101-02.

[98] Ibid., 54.

[99] Ibid. See also *Works*, 26:252, 402-04.

[100] For a detailed consideration of the background to these writings, see the introduction by Gerald R. Cragg in *Works*, 11:1-42.

[101] Ibid., 53. The argument is developed from p. 49 onwards. See also *Works*, 1:472; 19:201; 21:76; 26:149; *Works* (Jackson), 8:513.

believed, was used by the Lord and all his disciples.[102] He is certain, however, that reason must be soundly based and this requires the awakening of the spiritual senses by the Spirit of God through faith.[103] Without this, one cannot reason truly any more than you can reason about colours if you have no natural sight.[104] Reason and logic were essential to first understand and then apply scriptural doctrines to people's lives.[105] On the other hand, false doctrine was that which was "unsupported by reason, Scripture or authority."[106] Wesley was sure that the doctrine of Christian perfection was entirely reasonable and scriptural. He emphasised that the term itself was scriptural: "All the difficulty is to fix the meaning of it according to the Word of God."[107] He often demonstrated from passages like Rom. 6:1-2; 1 Pet. 4:1-2; 1 Jn. 3:8-9; 5:18 that the Bible clearly taught that the Christian can live without committing sin.[108]

In the area of practical concerns, reason was equally important. Generally, in order to know the will of God, a person was to consult the Scriptures, but in matters indifferent or undetermined "the Scripture itself gives you a general rule, applicable to all particular cases: 'The will of God is our sanctification.' ... In order therefore to know what is the will of God in a particular case we have only to apply this general rule."[109] In order to apply the rule, the Christian was to consider the outcome in their life and "this is to be determined partly by reason and partly by experience. Experience tells him what advantages he has in his present state, either for being or doing good; and reason is to show what he certainly or probably will have in the state proposed. ... Meantime the assistance of his Spirit is supposed during the whole process of the inquiry. ... This is the plain, scriptural, rational way to know what is the will of God in a particular case."[110] Wesley closed with this advice:

---

[102] *Works*, 11:55-56.

[103] Wesley agreed that faith itself included "a rational assent to the truth of the Bible," but it was primarily a "Christian grace" and "an immediate gift of God"; see *Works*, 26:157-59.

[104] *Works*, 11:56-58.

[105] In a letter to Miss March in 1768 he wrote, "We are reasonable creatures and undoubtedly reason is the candle of the Lord. By enlightening our reason to see the meaning of the Scriptures, the Holy Spirit makes our way plain before us"; see *Letters* (Telford), 5:96. He very commonly linked scripture and reason together; see for example *Works*, 26:567. For a thorough examination of this conjunction, see Jones, *Wesley's Use of Scripture*, 65-80; Thorsen, *Wesleyan Quadrilateral*, 169-200.

[106] *Works*, 11:175-76.

[107] Ibid., 65-66. The key texts used in this section are Gal. 2:20; Acts 15:9; 16:31; 2 Cor. 10:5; 1 Pet. 1:15

[108] Ibid., 65. Note that Wesley does not qualify his reference to sin here by the addition of 'wilful' or 'deliberate'.

[109] *Works*, 2:54-55. See also "A Plain Account of the People Called Methodists" (1749) in *Works*, 9:254-68.

[110] *Works*, 2:55.

> God can give the end without any means at all; but you have no reason to think he will. Therefore constantly and carefully use all these means which he has appointed to be the ordinary channels of his grace. Use every means which either reason or Scripture recommends as conducive ... either to the obtaining or increasing any of the gifts of God.[111]

The Personal Encounter with God: Experience

Throughout this period there is a constant reference to the experiential dimension of the Christian life (both personal and community). There is a genuine human need for certainty in a relationship with God, and not merely an intellectual affirmation.

> If the Bible be true, then none is a Christian who has not the marks of [a] Christian there laid down. One of these is, the love of God, *which must be felt*, if it is in the soul, as much as fire upon the body. Another is, the witness of God's Spirit with my spirit that I am a child of God.
>
> Till I have these marks I am not a Christian. And no power can give me these but that which made the world. It is God alone who worketh in me, both to will and to do of his good pleasure. *Faith is seeing God; love is feeling God* (emphasis mine).[112]

Wesley was aware of the twin dangers of a merely formal religion or enthusiasm and wrote that there was a need to guard against both errors "by a scriptural and rational illustration and confirmation of this momentous truth" of the witness of the Spirit. He believed little had been written on this except by those in error with their "crude, unscriptural, irrational explications."[113] Wesley believed that one of the things God had raised up the Methodists for was to teach and defend the reality of the witness of the Spirit to every Christian:

> It more clearly concerns the Methodists, so called, clearly to understand, explain, and defend this doctrine, because it is one grand part of the testimony which God has given them to bear to all mankind. It is by his peculiar blessing upon them in searching the Scriptures, *confirmed by the experience of his children* [emphasis mine], that this great evangelical truth has been recovered, which had been for many years wellnigh lost and forgotten.[114]

His theory of religious knowledge was intuitionist but it was not a one-sided subjectivism, "for I resolve none of my notions into immediate inspiration. ... I am ready to give up every opinion which I cannot by calm, clear, reason

---

[111] Ibid., 60.
[112] *Works*, 26:107-08.
[113] *Works*, 1:285.
[114] Ibid., 285-86. See especially n. 4, p. 286. See also *Works*, 26:181-83.

defend."[115] He believed his understanding of the Scriptures was correct regarding the inward witness of the Spirit, and he appealed to experience to confirm it:

> And here properly comes in, to confirm this scriptural doctrine, the experience of the children of God–the experience not of two or three, not of a few, but of a great multitude ... It has been confirmed, both in this and in all ages, by 'a cloud of' living and dying 'witnesses'. It is confirmed by *your* experience and *mine*. The Spirit itself bore witness to my spirit that I was a child of God, gave me an *evidence* hereof, and I immediately cried, 'Abba, Father!' And this I did (and so did you) before I reflected on, or was conscious of, any fruit of the Spirit. It was from this testimony received that love, joy, peace, and the whole fruit of the Spirit flowed. ...
>
> But this is confirmed, not only by the experience of the children of God–thousands of whom can declare that they never did know themselves to be in the favour of God till it was directly witnessed to them by his Spirit–but by all those who are convinced of sin, who feel the wrath of God abiding on them. These cannot be satisfied with anything less than a direct testimony from his Spirit ...[116]

Note that the reference to Christian experience is not merely to an individual's experience but to that of the community of faith in many times and places. Wesley emphasised that an objective experience of God was prior to our subjective experience and the evidence of a transformed life. The Spirit's prior objective work and witness was certainly to be known by spiritual intuition, but it was confirmed by the outward evidence of a changed life.[117] He agreed that experience was not sufficient to "prove a doctrine which is not founded on Scripture," but since this doctrine is founded on Scripture "experience is properly alleged to confirm it."[118] He was sure that there was also a place for an "indirect witness" through a good conscience, after reasoning and reflection on the person's spiritual life:

> Strictly speaking, it is a conclusion drawn partly from the Word of God, and partly from our own experience. The Word of God says everyone who has the fruit of the Spirit is a child of God. Experience, or inward consciousness, tells me that I have the fruit of the Spirit. And hence I rationally conclude: therefore I am a child of God.[119]

---

[115] *Letters* (Telford), 4:333. See also *Works*, 9:361.
[116] *Works*, 1:290-91.
[117] See "The Witness of the Spirit, Discourse 1" (1746), especially the introduction and n. 46 in Works, 1:267-69, 76-77. See also *Works* (Jackson), 10:266-84.
[118] *Works*, 1:296-97. In the Conference of 1747 he recorded in relation to assurance of justification that "It is dangerous to ground general doctrine on a few particular experiments." See *Works* (Jackson), 8:293.
[119] *Works*, 1:288.

Experience was not always a positive thing, however, and so Wesley constantly emphasised the need to question and examine the claims being made. In the debates with the Calvinists over predestination, he admitted "how easily then may a believer infer, from what he hath experienced in his own soul, that the true grace of God always works irresistibly in every believer! that God will finish wherever he has begun this work, so that it is impossible for any believer to fall from grace!"[120] In the early days of Methodism there were few clear testimonies to being "saved from all sin" and of those that were given, he always interviewed them closely about their experience.[121] "The question is not concerning the heart, but the life. And the general tenor of this I do not say cannot be *known*, but cannot be *hid* without a miracle."[122] As the revival continued, his *Journals* record an increasing number of people clearly testifying to being "saved from sin."[123] Wesley commented: "*Constant communion* with God the Father and Son fills their hearts with *humble love*. Now this is what I always did and do now mean by 'perfection'. And this I believe many have attained, on the same evidence that I believe many are justified."[124] These testimonies helped him to formulate doctrinal beliefs and explanations of the Scriptural teaching on the nature and extent of salvation. In his debates with the Moravians over the nature of justification and remaining sin, Wesley used the experience of several in his society to defend his doctrinal position.[125] A similar appeal was made regarding the nature of the Lord's Supper, both as a converting and a confirming ordinance.[126] It was experience that taught him that initial sanctification and entire sanctification were not given at the same moment: "But we do not know of a single instance, in any place, of a person's receiving, in one and the same moment, remission of sins, the abiding witness of the Spirit, and a new, clean heart."[127] He turned to experience and Scripture to show that perfection and its associated terms did

---

[120] *Works* (Jackson), 10:205.

[121] See for example *Works*, 20:44.

[122] Ibid., 162-63.

[123] *Works*, 21:239-43. See particularly the preface and the conclusion in Ibid., 258, 392. This refers to the great growth in the numbers of those professing Christian perfection between 1760 and 1762 and this section of the *Journal* is filled with their testimonies and Wesley's references to their testimonies. For some examples see *Works*, 21:244-45, 93-95, 308-09, 11-13, 25-33, 38-44, 82-85, 98, 401, 07, 14-17, 39, 48-49, 61-62, 74, 89-90, 503. Wesley was particularly impressed by the revival that broke out in Ireland, since it avoided the excesses of the London scene; see *Works*, 21:360-81. Another review of the work of God from April 1758 till November 1763 is given in Ibid., 439. See his retrospective account of the revival given in his *Short History of the People Called Methodists* in *Works*, 9:473-86.

[124] *Works*, 21:245. See also Ibid., 93, 96, 133, 221, 47.

[125] *Works*, 19:192, 95.

[126] Ibid., 158-59. See also *Works*, 21:244.

[127] Preface to the *Hymns and Sacred Poems* (1740) in *Works* (Jackson) 14:326.

not refer to perfect knowledge, judgement and behaviour.[128] Wesley was sure that God had raised up the Methodists to preach perfection but his critics raised the issue of what he would do if none had ever attained what he claimed the scriptures promised. "If I were convinced that none in England had attained what has been so clearly and strongly preached by such a number of Preachers in so many places, and for so long a time, I should be clearly convinced that we had all mistaken the meaning of those scriptures; and therefore, for the time to come, I too must teach that 'sin will remain till death.'"[129] This statement is a critical one as it affirms that Christian experience can verify one's understanding of the Bible, but if it does not, then the interpretation is incorrect. Christian experience is not self-authenticating and it needs guidelines or criteria for evaluation, and this is where Scripture is essential. Nevertheless, Wesley was confident that on many matters of practical Christian living "experience ... is so full, strong, and undeniable, that it makes all other arguments needless. Appeal we therefore to fact."[130]

DOCTRINE: "SUBSTANCE" AND "CIRCUMSTANCE"

An important development in this period is Wesley's distinction between the substance of a doctrine and its circumstance. This first appears in his own writings in connection with the nature of initial sanctification; Wesley said " ... I cannot conceive [it] to be other than instantaneous–whether I consider experience, or the Word of God, or the very nature of the thing. However, I contend not for the *circumstance*, but the *substance*; if you can attain it another way, do (emphasis mine)."[131] In connection with advice on promoting the work of God, we find these words:

> Strongly and explicitly exhort all believers to "go on to perfection." ... Shall we defend this Perfection, or give it up? You all agree to defend it, *meaning thereby*, (as we did from the beginning,) *salvation from all sin, by the love of God and man filling our heart.* ... *You are all agreed, we may be saved from all sin before death. The substance then is settled*; but, *as to the circumstance, is the change gradual or instantaneous?* It is both the one and the other (emphasis mine).[132]

The substance is clearly what is essential theologically whereas the

---

[128] *Works*, 2:100-01.
[129] *Works* (Jackson), 11:405-06.
[130] *Works*, 1:625.
[131] *A Farther Appeal to Men of Reason and Religion, Part 1*; see *Works*, 11:107. This same point is made in a letter to Mr. Downes in *Works*, 9:360. Wesley said, "We are concerned for the *substance* of the work, not the *circumstance*." He took a similar approach to the witness of the Spirit, arguing for the "substance" of it and not "the particular manner of explication" in *Works*, 26:291.
[132] Quoted from "The Large Minutes" in *Works* (Jackson), 8:328-29. See also Wynkoop, *Theology of Love*, 306-08.

circumstance has to do with how a believer may experience this reality in their own life. In dealing with objections to the ordering of his societies and the duties of its leaders, Wesley noted:

> There is much scripture for it, even all those texts which enjoin the *substance* of those various duties whereof this is only an indifferent *circumstance*, to be determined by reason and experience. ... You seem not to have observed, that the Scripture, in most points, gives only general rules; and leaves the particular *circumstances* to be adjusted by the common sense of mankind (emphasis mine).[133]

The substance was clearly defined by Scripture, but the circumstance was to be derived by reason and experience. The former was universally true and was prescriptive, whereas the latter concerned the actual experience or practical application and was descriptive. The Church as a whole would confess the former, but each Christian community might express the latter very differently. A case will be made that Wesley, when dealing with his critics, was most concerned to argue and defend the substance of Christian perfection and was willing to live and let live concerning the circumstance. Pastorally, for his own people, he gave much attention to the circumstance of Christian perfection because he wanted them to experience and maintain this relationship of love.

The Ethos of the Community

Wesley has unmistakably made reference to both antiquity and the Church of England as critical reading communities for his understanding and application of Scripture. There are also references to a number of individuals, groups and documents that are not located in either of these communities.[134] It appears that Campbell and Jones are correct in identifying a problem with the use of the term 'tradition' to label these communities and people due to its technical use by the Roman Catholic community.[135] Thomas Langford has proposed the term "ethos" as a better way to describe Wesley's references to the role of the community of faith.[136] This can be defined as its characteristic nature, attitudes and values; its way of viewing and living in the world. The emphasis is then on its dynamic, relational qualities rather than a static, formally-defined belief system. It was in this sense that Wesley strongly treasured the heritage of the early Church (especially of the first three centuries), the Church of England

---

[133] *Works*, 9:263.

[134] For Outler's examination of Wesley's sources as they are used in his sermons, see *Works*, 1:74-88.

[135] See Wesley's refutation of the primacy of tradition in the Roman Catholic sense in *Works* (Jackson), 10:86-128. See also *Works*, 9:34.

[136] See Langford, "Introduction," *Doctrine and Theology*, 11-13.

(particularly of the sixteenth and seventeenth centuries),[137] and his own emerging Methodist movement.[138] This latter point is critical and often ignored in any analysis of Wesley's use of tradition.[139] It is in these decades that a distinct Methodist ethos arises shaped by its Anglican roots but with conspicuously Wesleyan features: the sermons, hymns, liturgy, testimonies, society rules and accountability structures, conferences, letters, the growing corpus of Methodist writings and edited works, all largely bearing the stamp or seal of approval of John Wesley himself. Angela Shier-Jones sees this as the most important factor in understanding Methodism and the way it theologises as a community.[140]

In one of his many accounts of the rise of Methodism, John Wesley wrote that while they desired to be true to the doctrines and disciplines of the Church of England

> ... they observed neither these nor anything else further than they conceived it was bound upon them by their one book, *the Bible*, it being their one desire and design to be downright *Bible Christians*–taking the Bible, as interpreted by the primitive Church and their own, for their whole and sole rule.[141]

Wesley admitted that while the Scripture was clear in all necessary points, it did need to be explained and enforced. Here he explicitly identified the role of the community in interpreting the Scriptures and emphasised the continuity between the early church and the Church of England.[142] This interpretation applied both to doctrine and to practice. He particularly valued the contributions of the early apostolic fathers because "we cannot therefore doubt but what they deliver to us is the pure doctrine of the gospel; what Christ and his apostles taught, and what these holy men had themselves received from their own mouths." Given their eminent piety, "we cannot, with any reason, doubt of what they deliver to us as the gospel of Christ: but ought to receive it,

---

[137] *Works*, 4:393-94. He regarded the Church of England as a "scriptural church" and valued its authority "only less than that of the oracles of God." See for example *Works*, 9:308; 11:117, 63-71, 85, 290; 26:49-50; 419, 26; *Letters* (Telford), 3:245.

[138] In a letter Wesley said, "This is the scriptural way, the *Methodist* way, the true way"; see *Works*, 26:489.

[139] Neither Campbell or Jones' in their analysis of Wesley's theological authorities makes reference to Methodism itself ; see Jones, *Wesley's Use of Scripture*, 169-76; Campbell, "The Interpretative Role of Tradition," *Wesley and the Quadrilateral*.

[140] Shier-Jones, *Work in Progress*, 3-11 especially. See also Shier-Jones, "Conferring as Theological Model," *Unmasking Methodist Theology*; Stephen Dawes, "Revelation in Methodist Practice and Belief," *Unmasking Methodist Theology*, 114-16.

[141] "A Short History of Methodism" in *Works*, 9:368. See also *Works*, 26:29, 156, 203, 55; *Works (Jackson)*, 10:14.

[142] For a clear example of this link, see his response to Dr. Horner in *Letters* (Telford), 4:172-76.

though not with equal veneration, yet with only little less regard than we do the sacred writings of those who were their masters and instructors."[143] He firmly believed that all the essential doctrines of Christianity had been settled by the early church and it was now simply a matter of recovering and restating them for the present age: "But whatever doctrine is *new* must be *wrong*; for the *old* religion is the only *true* one; and no doctrine can be right unless it is the very same 'which was from the beginning'."[144]

Wesley upheld the authority of the community above that of any individual, no matter how exalted: "And her [the Church of England] authority ought to weigh more than even that of Bishop Bull, or that of any single man whatever. Authority, be pleased to observe, I plead against authority, reason against reason."[145] This was why his own Methodist Conferences were so important– especially in helping to understand and teach Christian perfection:[146]

> ... the *perfection* I hold is so far from being contrary to the doctrine of our Church that it is exactly the same which every clergyman prays every Sunday: "Cleanse the thoughts of our hearts by the inspiration of thy Holy Spirit, that we may *perfectly love thee*, and *worthily magnify* thy holy name." I mean neither more nor less than this. In doctrine therefore I do not dissent from the Church of England.[147]

On other questions he would sometimes refer to the authority of the early Church before his own. For example, on the vexed question of whether sin remained in believers after justification/regeneration, Wesley settled the question by an appeal to the "primitive church" and then his own Church of England (the Ninth Article), as well as the Greek, Roman Catholic and Reformed churches.[148] He utilised the views of the primitive church to support his position that the ministry of the Spirit was to all Christians in every age, arguing that his critics' interpretation was wrong.[149] The contribution of the community to understanding what was involved in practical discipleship was very important. When discussing the danger of exalting fasting beyond "all Scripture and reason," he especially valued the experience of the saints in these

---

[143] Wesley, ed., *Christian Library*, 1:iii-iv. The key writings are those of Clement, Ignatius, Justin Martyr, Polycarp and Macarius. Wesley regarded these early fathers as "endued with the extraordinary assistance of the Holy Spirit" and so hardly capable of mistake; see p. v-vi.
[144] *Works*, 1:324.
[145] *Works*, 11:453.
[146] *Works*, 21:165.
[147] *Works*, 9:409. In his *Farther Appeal* Wesley sought to uphold his position on the disputed doctrines of justification and salvation from the Liturgy, Homilies and the Articles; see *Works*, 11:108-17. See also Ibid., 417, 23, 43-51, 54. A similar position is taken in "The Principles of a Methodist"; see *Works*, 9:49-53.
[148] *Works*, 1:317-18. See also *Works*, 9:98-100.
[149] *Works*, 11:154-63. See also *Works* (Jackson), 10:508.

communities to illuminate and provide clear examples of the teaching of the Scriptures.[150] On the other hand, he noted many innovations in doctrine and practice that found their origins in Roman Catholicism "without any warrant either from antiquity or Scripture."[151]

The "Substance" of Christian Perfection:
Wesley's Doctrinal Understanding

The focus of this study is on Wesley's doctrine of Christian perfection as an illustration of his theological method, and not an analysis of it by other scholars.[152] Wesley's own viewpoint is to be traced predominantly in his sermons and a smaller number of critical works specifically on Christian perfection. In 1741 Wesley wrote the sermon "Christian Perfection" and this was the first with perfection explicitly in the title. The common Christian understanding implied that the Christian could never be free from sin in this life; not only did sin remain in the believer, but it was of such force that no lasting measure of victory over its power was possible.[153] As we saw earlier, Wesley believed that only humans before the fall were bound by a covenant of works, requiring absolute obedience and perfect performance. All persons since then are now living under a covenant of grace in which love and relationship are at the core, and this requires trust and a devoted passion for God. Both covenants are suited to the capacities and abilities of their subjects, with a corresponding responsibility and accountability. This required Wesley to distinguish between "sin properly so called" and "involuntary transgressions." The former were wilfully chosen, therefore culpable and brought condemnation; the latter were not wilfully chosen and consequently not

---

[150] *Works*, 1:592-611. See also *Works*, 2:239.

[151] *Works*, 2:71. See also *Works* (Jackson), 10:133-40.

[152] For a theological examination of Wesley's doctrine of Christian perfection, see such works as: Leo George Cox, *John Wesley's Concept of Perfection* (Kansas City, MO: Beacon Hill Press of Kansas City, 1964); William M. Greathouse, *John Wesley's Theology of Christian Perfection*, Occasional Paper No. 4 of the Wesley Fellowship (Ilkeston: The Wesley Fellowship, 1989); A. Skevington Wood, *Love Excluding Sin: Wesley's Doctrine of Sanctification*, Wesley Fellowship Occasional Paper #1 (Derbys, England: Moorley's Bookshop, 1986); Theodore H. Runyon, *The New Creation: John Wesley's Theology Today* (Nashville, TN: Abingdon Press, 1998); Christopher T. Bounds, "What is the Range of Current Teaching on Sanctification and What Ought a Wesleyan to Believe on this Doctrine?" *The Asbury Journal* 62, no. 2 (Fall 2007); Harald Lindström, *Wesley and Sanctification*; Collins, *Scripture Way of Salvation*, 153-90; Collins, *The Theology of John Wesley*, especially p. 279-312; Wynkoop, *Theology of Love*.

[153] See Outler's introduction in *Works*, 2:97-99. Outler thinks Wesley remains consistent with the position outlined in his 1733 sermon on "The Circumcision of the Heart." See also Wesley's comments on Phil. 3:12, 15 in *Notes (NT)*.

culpable and did not bring condemnation.[154] The critical distinction between sins and infirmities is that the latter were not "of a moral nature," though they may well lead to issues of a moral nature since we cannot be free from temptation in this life, any more than Christ was free. Wesley believed that those in Christ did not continue in wilful sin as they continued to walk in the power of the Spirit and they were not under condemnation for the residue of sin as long as they did not yield to it.[155] To continue in sin, willingly or unwillingly, was to demonstrate you were not yet truly a child of God, for even "babes in Christ" were so far perfect as not to sin (or at least, commit outward sin) due to the presence of the Holy Spirit.[156] Wesley believed that 1 Jn. 1:5-6, 9; 3:7-10; 4:17 confirmed that Christians can experience "perfect love" in this life, not just at the moment of death.[157] "It remains, then, that Christians are saved in this world from all sin, from all unrighteousness; that they are now in such a sense perfect as not to commit sin, and to be freed from evil thoughts and evil tempers."[158] Accordingly, all the promises given in Deut. 30:6; Ps. 51:10; Ezek. 36:25f are fulfilled.[159]

Wesley sought to demonstrate from Scripture that there was no condemnation for "sins of infirmity" due to the realities of our human condition since the fall. He agreed that both sins and infirmities were deviations from the perfect will of God and so needed Christ's gracious atonement, but he was insistent that the latter brought no condemnation.[160] This was because he felt the Scriptures gave no grounds for believing God condemned us for either omissions beyond our power or actions and reactions arising from sudden

---

[154] In particular, see "On Sin in Believers" (1763) and "The Repentance of Believers" (1767), *Works*, 1:317-52. Note especially Outler's introduction to both sermons on p. 314-16. See also *Works*, 2:103; *Works* (Jackson), 9:281; 14:212.

[155] *Works*, 1:235-38. Note his extensive quotation of Scripture texts here. See also *Works*, 1:240; *Works* (Jackson), 14:276

[156] See *Works*, 1:264, 317-19; 19:153-59. Sins are seen as chains, wounds, diseases and debts but they no need longer control the life of the new Christian; see *Works*, 1:320, 586. Wesley rejected the common Reformed idea that Paul was describing the normal Christian state in Rom. 7:7ff; see his very strong comments in *Notes (NT)* and *Works*, 1:322, 32-33. For further evidence on Wesley's understanding, see *Works*, 1:226, 321, 23, 435-41, 556-60; 2:84. A critical development in his doctrinal understanding was his conviction that there were stages in the Christian life. This arose from his reading of 1 Jn. 2:12-14 where the author mentions little children, young men and fathers—with the latter being seen as "properly Christians"; see *Works* (Jackson), 11:378-81. After 1750 he amended this to read that they are "perfect Christians" (indicating his continued confusion in 1741).

[157] *Works*, 2:119-20.

[158] Ibid., 120. See also Ibid., 117-18. His case is supported by extensive Scripture quotation.

[159] Ibid., 120-21. See also *Works* (Jackson), 8:279.

[160] *Works*, 1:241. "There is no guilt, because there is no choice."; see p. 241 See also *Works* (Jackson), 11:394-397.

surprises. He believed that biblically, condemnation was experienced only to the degree that the will was involved.[161]

> Christian perfection therefore does not imply... an exemption either from ignorance or mistake, or infirmities or temptations. Indeed, it is only another term for holiness. ... Thus everyone that is perfect is holy, and everyone that is holy is, in the Scripture sense, perfect. Yet we may ... observe that neither in this respect is there any absolute perfection on earth. There is no 'perfection of degrees', as it is termed; none which does not admit of a continual increase. So that how much soever any man hath attained, or in how high a degree soever he is perfect, he hath still need to 'grow in grace', and daily to advance in the knowledge and love of God his Saviour.[162]

This led him to develop an understanding of the need for a "repentance of believers" while the work of grace was continuing.[163] He warned that "some have vehemently maintained; yea, have affirmed that none are perfected in love unless they are so far perfected in understanding that all wandering thoughts are done away; unless not only every affection and temper be holy, and just, and good, but every individual thought which arises in the mind be wise and regular.[164] Wesley said this was an unscriptural notion and then proceeded to show in what ways our thought life could or could not be compatible with Christian perfection. The decisive issue was whether our thoughts were "inconsistent with perfect love"–the product of our humanity but not sinful. We could reasonably expect that "those wherein the heart wanders from God; from all that are contrary to his will, or that leave us without God in the world, everyone that is perfected in love is unquestionably delivered. ... All that are perfected in love are delivered from these; else they were not saved from sin."[165]

There were dangers in his absolute statements in "Christian Perfection" if they were taken literally and this became evident during the London revival from about 1758 to 1763 when some claimed an experience of absolute perfection, believing sin was completely destroyed at the moment of justification/regeneration.[166] His "Farther Thoughts on Christian Perfection"

---

[161] *Works*, 1:242-43.
[162] *Works*, 2:104-05.
[163] *Works*, 1:245-47.
[164] From the sermon "Wandering Thoughts" (1762) in *Works*, 2:126. See Outler's introduction in Ibid., 125-26. He mentions the role of two later sermons in qualifying Wesley's views of perfection— "On Sin in Believers" (1763) and "The Repentance of Believers" (1767). See also Charles H. Goodwin, "Setting Perfection Too High: John Wesley's Changing Attitudes toward the "London Blessing"," *Methodist History* 36, no. 2 (1998).
[165] *Works*, 2:134-35.
[166] In a letter to Anne Dutton (a staunch high Calvinist and a prolific writer and author) in 1740, Wesley himself was still setting his understanding of perfection too high—

(1763) was written to safeguard his position from the views held by Thomas Maxfield and George Bell, in which they claimed the perfected Christian was totally without sin and in an angelic state.[167] However, Wesley did not reject all that they taught:

> I like your doctrine of *perfection*, or pure love–love excluding sin. Your insisting that it is merely by *faith*; that consequently it is *instantaneous* (though preceded and followed by a gradual work), and that it may be *now*, at this instant.[168]

It was in this context that he published his major work, *A Plain Account of Christian Perfection, as believed and taught by the Reverend Mr. John Wesley, from the year 1725, to the year 1777*.[169] Here he traced how he had come to embrace his present understanding of Christian perfection; both those elements that had not changed and those that had been further nuanced due to experience.[170] Wesley clearly maintained that "... Christian perfection is that love of God and neighbour, which implies deliverance from all sin ... [it] is received merely by faith ... it is given instantaneously, in one moment. ... [and]

---

being free from all fears, doubts, unevenness of affections; see *Works*, 26:15. Wesley now rejected this position "because it is contrary to the whole tenor of Scripture; . . . it is contrary to the experience of the children of God; . . . it is absolutely new, never heard of in the world till yesterday." See *Works*, 1:325. The remainder of the sermon was a refutation of the perfectionist position from Scripture; see p. 325-32. See also *Works*, 26:157, 443.

[167] *Works*, 21:345. Wesley laments that the cautions in this were not observed much earlier. Thomas Maxfield was one of Wesley's early lay preachers, was in charge of the Foundery Society at one point and later ordained by the Bishop of Derry. He separated from Wesley over the perfectionist issue and became an Independent minister. George Bell was an ex-soldier and close associate of Maxfield. For further information on the perfectionist controversy see n. 2 in *Works*. 20:406; n. 42 in *Works*, 21:346; Rack, *Reasonable Enthusiast*, 333-42; Charles H. Goodwin, "Methodist Pentecost: The Wesleyan/Holiness Revival of 1758-1763," *WTJ* 33, no. 1 (Spring, 1998); Charles H. Goodwin, *The Methodist Pentecost: The Wesleyan Holiness Revival 1758-1763*, Merlin Methodist Monograph Number 4 (Ilkeston: Moorley's Bookshop, 1996); Goodwin, "Setting Perfection Too High"; Heitzenrater, *People Called Methodists*, 209-11.

[168] *Works*, 21:394. Wesley emphasised that these were his consistent views for the past twenty years or so. See also *Letters* (Telford), 4:192-94, 206.

[169] *Works* (Jackson), 11:366-446. The title initially ended with "1765" and was published in 1766, but the date was extended as the years of publication passed up to 1777, but no further alterations were made in the later editions; see Frank Baker, ed., *A Union Catalogue of the Publications of John and Charles Wesley*, Photocopy ed. (Durham, NC: The Divinity School, Duke University, 1966), 125. See also the historical overview in the *Minutes* of the 1765 Conference found in John Wesley, *Minutes of Several Conversations, between the Rev. John Wesley, A.M. And the Preachers in Connection with Him. From the Year 1744* (Leeds: Edward Baines, 1803), 11.

[170] In particular he noted that the language in the preface to the 1741edition of his *Hymns* was too strong; see *Works* (Jackson), 11:378-81.

we are to expect it, not at death, but every moment; that now is the accepted time, now is the day of this salvation."[171] This brief statement summarises his mature understanding of the substance of Christian perfection; he believed that the Holy Spirit bore witness to this work of grace and that this was the common privilege of all who had received it.

"LOVE EXCLUDING SIN"

Wesley had now come to see the vital distinction between inward and outward holiness.[172] The latter was defined in terms of not doing evil, doing good, using the means of grace, holding orthodox opinions and possessing a zeal for the church. He was aware that you could do all these things, but they are nothing without love, which is the power of real Christianity.[173] Wesley urged his people not to build on orthodoxy, right opinions, having rational and scriptural notions, or even membership in the Church of England. All these may be "so many helps to holiness. But they are not holiness itself. And if they are separate from it they will profit me nothing."[174] The critical question was what lay behind our outward actions–did they spring from a love for God or not?[175] Christian perfection was "the loving God with all our heart, mind, soul, and strength. This implies, that no wrong temper, none contrary to love, remains in the soul; and that all the thoughts, words, and actions, are governed by pure love."[176]

> For there is no motive which so powerfully inclines us to love God as the sense of the love of God in Christ. ... And from this principle of grateful love to God arises love to our brother also. ... Now this love to man, grounded on faith and love to

---

[171] *Works* (Jackson), 11:393. See also the summary of his doctrinal understanding of Christian perfection in 1764 in Ibid., 441-42.

[172] He comments in his *Journal* for January 4, 1740 as he looked back over his correspondence for the past 16-18 years, "How few traces of inward religion are here!" See *Works*, 19:134.

[173] See, for example, *Works*, 1:131-37, 219, 21-24, 635; 4:398-400; 11:62-63; *Works* (Jackson), 10:192. On Wesley's understanding of the nature and importance of "real Christianity," see the debates between Collins and Maddox in: Kenneth J. Collins, "The Motif of Real Christianity in the Writings of John Wesley," *Asbury Theological Journal* 49, no. 1 (1994); Randy L. Maddox, "Prelude to a Dialogue: A Response to Kenneth Collins," *WTJ* 35, no. 1 (Spring, 2000); Kenneth J. Collins, "Recent Trends in Wesley Studies and Wesleyan/Holiness Scholarship," *WTJ* 35, no. 1 (Spring, 2000); Kenneth J. Collins, "Real Christianity as Integrating Theme in Wesley's Soteriology: The Critique of a Modern Myth," *Asbury Theological Journal* 51, no. 2 (1996).

[174] *Works*, 1:694. See also *Works*, 2:149-50.

[175] *Works*, 1:220. See also *Letters* (Telford), 5:101-03, 140-41. This allowed for the presence of infirmities, ignorance, mistakes in judgement and therefore occasional mistakes in practice. These were not "properly a sin" due to a lack of culpability but did need "the atoning blood"; see *Works* (Jackson), 11:394-97.

[176] *Works* (Jackson), 11:394. See also *Works* (Jackson), 11:401-02; 14:261.

> God, ... is ... 'the fulfilling of the' whole negative 'law'. ... Neither is love content with barely working no evil to our neighbour. It continually incites us to do good ... It is therefore the fulfilling of the positive, likewise, as well as of the negative law of God.
>
> Nor does faith fulfil either the negative or positive law as to the external part only; but it works inwardly by love to the purifying of the heart, the cleansing it from all vile affections. ... At the same time, if it have its perfect work, it fills him with all goodness, righteousness, and truth.[177]

The vital quality was a heart right toward God (a relationship), seeking only to love him, glorify him and enjoy him forever, through faith in Jesus Christ.[178] The emphasis is undoubtedly on the positive presence of love in the heart that leaves no room for anything contrary. In other words, it is the infilling of love that lies at the heart of the experience, not a negative image of prior cleansing or purification before love can enter. Wesley's preferred picture of the experience of Christian perfection began with the person's positive desire to be filled with love, rather than having sin cleansed away.[179] As we shall see later, he was not entirely consistent at this point due to his conviction that God could work as he pleased in peoples' lives. The understanding that cleansing was prior to the infilling of love was more useful in certain contexts–particularly when dealing with the issue of sin itself.[180]

Christian perfection (and salvation as a whole) at its core had to do with desire rather than rational knowledge and understanding. If the desire was quickened, then the relationship would be established, with rational knowledge and understanding being developed as a result of the relationship. It was the desire that led to knowing, obeying, serving, not vice versa; passion rather than performance was decisive.[181] However, a love-based relationship was not then the excuse to live disregarding the other commandments God had given; there was no place for antinomianism.

> The plain indisputable meaning of that text [1 Jn. 5:3] is: 'this is the' sign or proof of the 'love of God', of our keeping the first and great commandment–to keep the rest of his commandments. For true love, if it be once shed abroad in our heart, will constrain us so to do; since whosoever loves God with all his heart cannot but serve him with all his strength.
>
> A second fruit then of the love of God ... is universal obedience to him we love, and conformity to his will; obedience to all the commands of God, internal

---

[177] *Works*, 2:42. See also *Works*, 1:417-26. Maddox sees this as the crucial development in Wesley's mature understanding; see Maddox, "'Celebrating the Whole Wesley': A Legacy for Contemporary Wesleyans," 76.

[178] *Works*, 1:690-93.

[179] *Works* (Jackson), 8:284.

[180] See the sermon, "The Repentance of Believers" for a clear illustration of this; note particularly *Works*, 1:346, 49.

[181] *Works*, 11:118.

and external; obedience of the heart and of the life, in every temper and in all manner of conversation.[182]

This active obedience was possible only because of the prior reception of grace; the believer must then continue in grace-enabled obedience throughout their Christian journey.[183] Wesley went so far as to say "it is impossible that any should retain what they receive without improving it."[184] However, in seeking to improve their relationship with God, it was important that the believer did not denigrate that which God had already accomplished. Spiritual progress in the Christian life was often hindered when Christians allowed this to happen: "Now this is the grand device of Satan: to destroy the first work of God in the soul, or at least to hinder its increase by our expectation of that greater work.[185]

RECEIVABLE NOW BY FAITH ALONE

Wesley held to the understanding that God suited the conditions required for a relationship with him to the capacities and abilities of his creatures. As we have seen, a critical distinction was made between humanity prior to the fall and after it. God had made a "covenant of works" with human beings in paradise prior to the fall which "required an obedience perfect in all its parts, entire and wanting nothing, as the condition of his eternal continuance in the holiness and happiness wherein he was created."[186] After the fall, with all persons losing both the capacity and ability to perfectly maintain these requirements, God, in his unmerited love, now established a new covenant of grace.

> Now this covenant saith not to sinful man, 'Perform unsinning obedience and live.' ... It doth not require any impossibility to be done ... Indeed, strictly speaking, the covenant of grace doth not require us to do anything at all, as absolutely and indispensably necessary in order to our justification, ...
> What saith then the covenant of forgiveness, of unmerited love, of pardoning mercy? 'Believe in the Lord Jesus Christ, and thou shalt be saved. ...
> ... This condition of life is plain, easy, always at hand ... through the operation of the Spirit of God.[187]

Essential at this point was the role of faith: "Exactly as we are justified by faith, so are we sanctified by faith. Faith is the condition, and the only condition of sanctification, exactly as it is of justification. It is the condition: none is

---

[182] *Works*, 1:427. See also *Works*, 1:312-13, 695-96; 26:483; *Works* (Jackson), 14:240-41. See his comments on Matt. 12:7 in the light of Matt. 19:17 (as well as those on 1 Jn. 5:3) in *Notes (NT)*.
[183] See, for example, *Works*, 2:160; 21:415.
[184] *Works*, 21:499. See also *Works* (Jackson), 9:310.
[185] *Works*, 2:140.
[186] *Works*, 1:204.
[187] *Works*, 1:206-08. See also Ibid., 208-09, 13-14.

sanctified but he that believes; without faith no man is sanctified. And it is the only condition: this alone is sufficient for sanctification."[188] It was faith that enabled the heart to be purified "by the power of God who dwelleth therein."[189] The relationship could only begin by believing in God and this implied a clear element of personal trust and not merely intellectual assent.[190] However, faith was not an end in itself:

> ... [it] is only the handmaid of love ... it is not the end of the commandment. God hath given this honour to love alone. Love is the end of all the commandments of God. Love is the end, the sole end, of every dispensation of God, from the beginning of the world to the consummation of all things. And it will endure when heaven and earth flee away; for 'love' alone 'never faileth'. Faith will totally fail; it will be swallowed up in sight, in the everlasting vision of God.[191]

Faith was now "the grand means of restoring that holy love wherein man was originally created. It follows, that although faith is of no value in itself ... yet as it leads to that end–the establishing anew the law of love in our hearts–and as in the present state of things it is the only means under heaven for effecting it, it is on that account an unspeakable blessing to man, and of unspeakable value before God."[192]

The first step in establishing a relationship with God was to know yourself and your true state without God; Wesley identified this as repentance and said it was possible only by God's grace.[193] Then came faith as a free gift given to the sinner, simply on the basis of their cry for mercy: "No merit, no goodness in man, precedes the forgiving love of God. His pardoning mercy supposes nothing in us but a sense of more sin and misery."[194] Wesley was positive that the love of God personally and objectively experienced provided the basis for our loving response to God and that gave the confidence to respond: "... we are saved from our sins only by a confidence in the love of God. As soon as we 'behold what manner of love it is which the Father hath bestowed upon us', 'we love him ... because he first loved us'."[195] Without this objective experience of

---

[188] *Works*, 2:163-64. See also *Works*, 21:321. Wesley has clearly defined faith as a divine evidence and conviction of God's promises in the Holy Scripture, that what God has promised he is *able* to perform, that he is able and willing to do it *now*, and finally that he actually does it. See *Works*, 1:138-39, 94, 230, 418-19; 2:160-63, 67-69; 11:106-07; *Works* (Jackson), 14:276, 279. He now believed that faith itself could exist in degrees and that "weak faith" may still be genuine faith; see his exposition of this in *Works*, 19:153-55; 26:125; *Works* (Jackson), 8:287-90

[189] *Works*, 1:139.

[190] Ibid., 1:634.

[191] Ibid., 2:38. See also Ibid., 2:39-41 and his comments on 1 Cor. 13:13 in *Notes (NT)*.

[192] *Works*, 2:41.

[193] *Works*, 1:225-26. See n. 55, p. 225 for more such references in Wesley.

[194] *Works*, 11:48.

[195] Ibid., 67-68. See also Ibid., 132-33.

divine love, there could be no basis for re-establishing a relationship with God on our part. Thus faith arose in response to love experienced, it did not enable it–this was the role of grace.[196] Wesley admitted that many contemporary witnesses were against his interpretation of faith implying a trust and confidence in God, but the Homily on Salvation was clear regarding the Church of England's position, as was Scripture and personal experience.[197] His conclusion was, "A confidence then in a pardoning God is essential to true faith."[198]

While the experience was receivable by faith alone, he continued to reject the notion that all the person had to do was wait for God to do his work of grace in their heart. Wesley had already declared how believers were to deal with remaining sin in order to avoid living in defeat and being cast into despair. This involved a fresh examination of the nature of repentance, which he saw as an essential part of the whole spiritual journey and not merely justification; he believed that repentance in the Christian meant a "kind of self-knowledge." Many initially felt they were justified and entirely sanctified at the same moment due to the power of their feelings, "in spite of Scripture, reason, and experience" clearly teaching this was incorrect.[199] Wesley denied there was final victory over sin unless and until God worked a "second time" to bring about a full deliverance.

> Indeed this is so evident a truth that wellnigh all the children of God ... generally agree in this, that although we may 'by the Spirit mortify the deeds of the body', resist and conquer both outward and inward sin, although we may *weaken* our enemies day by day, yet we cannot *drive them out.* ... Most sure we cannot, till it shall please our Lord to speak to our hearts again, to 'speak the second time, "Be clean"'. And then only 'the leprosy is cleansed.' Then only the evil root, the carnal mind, is destroyed, and inbred sin subsists no more. But if there be no such second change, if there be no instantaneous deliverance after justification, if there be none but a gradual work of God (that there is a gradual work none denies) then we must be content, as well as we can, to remain full of sin till death.[200]

---

[196] Ibid., 67-68.

[197] Wesley notes the explicit opposition to this view by the Council of Trent, as well as the opposition of nominal Christians; see *Works*, 11:68-70. The Scriptures Wesley quoted were Job 19:25; Jn. 20:28-29; Gal. 2:20; Col. 1:12-14. See also *Works*, 9:53, 228.

[198] *Works*, 11:70.

[199] *Works*, 1:336. See also *Works*, 2:164-66.

[200] *Works*, 1:346. Note the emphasis here on "cleansing." Outler comments that this understanding forms the basis for the post-Wesley view of entire sanctification as a second and distinct work of grace; see n. 81. The language of secondness is rare in Wesley. There are only nine references altogether to "second blessing," "second change" or "second awakening" in the whole Wesley corpus; see Tom A. Noble, "Endnote: Reflections on Holiness" (Unpublished paper from the Guatemala Nazarene Theology Conference, April 2002). Noble believes that Wesley's real concern was to

He affirmed that deliverance must come instantaneously by a definite work of God's grace, or it will not come at all. It is in this context that the believer was to repent, "For till we are sensible of our disease it admits of no cure."[201] Christians need to come to the place of believing that God can save from all remaining sin in the heart, based on his promises in such Scriptures as Deut. 30:6; Ezek. 36:25, 27, 29; Ps. 130:8; Lk. 1:68-69, 72-75 and 2 Cor. 7:1, and that he was both willing and able to do this "today."[202] This deliverance was by faith alone and faith must continue from moment to moment, otherwise we slip back into sin.[203]

Wesley continued to stress the place of the means of grace in helping people to prepare their hearts for God to work and to form a deep relationship with him. He held that they had always been a part of the gospel as the usual channels of God's grace.[204] There was no intrinsic power in them, for God alone gave grace, but Wesley was clear that Scripture directed Christians to use them as they waited for God to work.[205]

> ... in using all means, seek God alone. In and through every outward thing look singly to the *power* of his Spirit and the *merits* of his Son. Beware you do not stick in the *work* itself; if you do, it is all lost labour. Nothing short of God can satisfy your soul. ... Remember also to use all means as *means*; as ordained, not for their own sake, but in order to the renewal of your soul in righteousness and true holiness. If therefore they actually tend to this, well; but if not, they are dung and dross.[206]

INSTANTANEOUSLY

Wesley contended that this gift of faith was usually given in a moment, as amply illustrated in the Book of Acts; however, the actual circumstance of it was a matter of indifference to him, for he was willing to let God work as he preferred.[207]

> 'But does God work this great work in the soul *gradually* or *instantaneously*?' Perhaps it may be gradually wrought in some. I mean in this sense–they do not advert to the particular moment wherein sin ceases to be. But it is infinitely

---

emphasise the instantaneous aspect of Christian perfection. See also Timothy L. Smith, "John Wesley and the Second Blessing," *WTJ* 21, no. 1 & 2 (Spring-Fall, 1986).

[201] *Works*, 1:347, 50-51.
[202] Ibid., 347-48.
[203] Ibid., 349. See also *Works*, 2:144.
[204] *Works*, 1:381. See also *Works*, 19:151, 158-59; 21:233.
[205] *Works*, 1:382-84. Wesley emphasised that the means of grace could not *produce* the love of God and mankind, and said his own early life bore witness to this; see especially *Works*, 11:121-22; *Works* (Jackson), 11;402-03.
[206] *Works*, 1:396-97. See also *Works*, 1:395, 572-73, 612-31; 21:240.
[207] *Works*, 11:70-71.

desirable, were it the will of God, that it should be done instantaneously; ... And by this token may you surely know whether you seek it by faith or by works. If by works, you want something to be done *first*, *before* you are sanctified. ... If you seek it by faith, you may expect it *as you are*: and if as you are, then expect it *now*. It is of importance to observe that there is an inseparable connection between these three points—expect it *by faith*, expect it *as you are*, and expect it *now*! To deny one of them is to deny them all: to allow one is to allow them all.[208]

When meeting with some members of the Society who wondered why there had been initially so little evidence of Christian perfection in their area, Wesley said it was because they had been seeking it by their works, never expecting to receive it in a moment by faith.[209] If the person did not expect an instantaneous change, then it was unlikely that they would ever experience Christian perfection before death. That did not mean that this moment was necessarily dramatic and obvious. He gave the illustration that a person may be dying for some time, but there is an instant of death. "In like manner, he may be dying to sin for some time; yet he is not dead to sin, till sin is separated from his soul; and in that instant he lives the full life of love."[210]

THE WITNESS OF THE SPIRIT TO CHRISTIAN PERFECTION

Wesley cautioned that it was not sufficient to simply feel all love and no sin, as several of his people had experienced this before full renewal. "None therefore ought to believe that the work is done, till there is added the testimony of the Spirit, witnessing his entire sanctification, as clearly as his justification."[211] Wesley was convinced that it was the common privilege of every Christian to experience the witness of the Holy Spirit to the reality of Christian perfection, just as it was to their new birth.

> That this 'testimony of the Spirit of God' must needs ... be antecedent to the 'testimony of our own spirit' may appear from this single consideration: we must be holy of heart and holy in life before we can be conscious that we are so, ... But we must love God before we can be holy at all; this being the root of all holiness. Now we cannot love God till we know he loves us. ... And we cannot know his pardoning love to us till his Spirit witnesses it to our spirit. Since therefore this 'testimony of his Spirit' must precede the love of God and all holiness, of consequence it must precede our inward consciousness thereof, or the 'testimony of our spirit' concerning them.[212]

---

[208] *Works*, 2:167-69.
[209] *Works*, 21:325.
[210] *Works* (Jackson), 11:402.
[211] Ibid., 401-02.
[212] *Works*, 1:274-75. See n. 34 for the importance of this change post-1738. The same point is made in *Works*, 1:274, 86, 90. See also *Works*, 1:310; Maddox, "'Celebrating the Whole Wesley': A Legacy for Contemporary Wesleyans," 76-77.

All Christians could have an assurance of their acceptance with God through the witness of the Spirit as a gift; this could be lost but also recovered.[213] The manner of how this witness is manifested to the heart, he said he cannot explain: "But the fact we know: namely, that the Spirit of God does give a believer such a testimony of his adoption that while it is present to the soul he can no more doubt the reality of his sonship than he can doubt of the shining of the sun while he stands in the full blaze of his beams."[214] Wesley confessed that words were inadequate to describe this witness and he could simply repeat that it was an inward impression on the soul.

Wesley firmly believed that any subjective experience on its own was insufficient due to the human capacity to be deceived, and thus his insistence on the objective guidelines provided by Scripture, reason and conduct. The subjective side of assurance was dealt with in "The Witness of Our Own Spirit" (1746). There it was connected with the critical role of the conscience, which must itself be formed and evaluated by the Scripture: "But what is the rule whereby men are to judge of right and wrong; whereby their conscience is to be directed? ... the Christian rule of right and wrong is the Word of God, the writings of the Old and New Testament ..."[215] The Christian can avoid a wrong presumption as "the Holy Scriptures abound with marks whereby the one may be distinguished from the other. They describe in the plainest manner the circumstances which go before, which accompany, and which follow, the true, genuine testimony of the Spirit of God with the spirit of a believer."[216] These marks were summarised as repentance, new birth and the fruits of the Spirit—that is, personal transformation.[217] As a direct result of this transformation the person now loved, delighted and rejoiced in God.[218] The Christian needed to keep in balance the evidence of the internal assurance and the outward change to minimise self-delusion.[219] Wesley had often examined members of the societies who testified to other manifestations ("feelings") of the presence of the Spirit. An early account (1742) gives a clear example of this:

---

[213] *Works*, 1:238-39. See also *Works*, 1:287; 19:164. In the early 1740s Wesley tended to see assurance as either all or nothing, before he allowed for degrees of assurance as the revival proceeded; see *Works*, 1:154. In n. 179 Outler indicates where this change may be traced. He also refers to a comment by Wesley made around 1789 that the notion of having a constant assurance or not being a Christian at all was a major error.

[214] *Works*, 1:276. Outler's critical footnote here (n. 46) gives a thorough treatment of Wesley's theory of religious knowledge with its notion of a "spiritual sensorium" analogous to our physical senses.

[215] Ibid., 302-03.

[216] Ibid., 277-78.

[217] See, for example, *Works*, 11:292-96, 310, 21, 50-51, 62.

[218] *Works*, 1:275-76. See also *Works*, 11:139-41; 21:351.

[219] *Works*, 1:278-83.

> ... I approved of their experience (because agreeable to the written Word) as to their *feeling* the working of the Spirit of God, in peace and joy and love. But as to what some of them said farther concerning ... [various other physical sensations] the utmost I could allow, without renouncing both Scripture and reason, was that *some* of these circumstances might be from God ... working in an unusual manner, no way essential either to justification or sanctification; but that all the rest I must believe to be the mere, empty dreams of an heated imagination.[220]

One danger in Wesley's understanding of assurance was "enthusiasm"–the imagining you were a Christian when in fact you were not. To deal with this he wrote two important sermons on "The Witness of the Spirit" (Sermon I, 1746 and Sermon 2, 1767, but always printed together) and the warnings contained in "The Nature of Enthusiasm" (1750).[221] Sermon I is a plea for a middle course between enthusiasm and denying the witness altogether. He allowed that Rom. 8:16 may refer to either the witness of our own spirit or God's Spirit, "But I contend not; seeing so many other texts, with the experience of all real Christians, sufficiently evince that there is in every believer both the testimony of God's Spirit, and the testimony of his own, that he is a child of God."[222] With regard to the latter:

> ... the foundation thereof is laid in those numerous texts of Scripture which describe the marks of the children of God; ... These are also collected together, and placed in the strongest light, by many both ancient and modern writers. If any need farther light he may receive it by attending on the ministry of God's Word, by meditating thereon before God in secret, and by conversing with those who have the knowledge of his ways. And by the reason or understanding that God has given him–which religion was designed not to extinguish, but to perfect ... Every man applying those scriptural marks to himself may know whether he is a child of God.[223]

Observe here the way that Wesley runs together his theological sources. He has appealed to the experience of all "real Christians" and this is a reference to those in whom the Spirit is at work. This is closely linked with the written text of Scripture, the writings of the Christian community, attending public worship, prayer, conference, reason. It is the whole complex of sources and tools that is necessary to avoid self-delusion or despair. We can know this for ourselves by "immediate consciousness" and the role of our conscience, alongside the display of good works through love in action.[224] Both the direct witness of the

---

[220] *Works*, 19:295-96. See also Ibid., 296-98, 308, 17.
[221] See *Works*, 1:267-98; 2:44-60.
[222] *Works*, 1:271. He comments in his second sermon written twenty years later that he had not changed his mind on this; see Ibid., 286-87.
[223] Ibid., 271-72. Wesley then gives a long series of quotations from 1 Jn. in support of this viewpoint.
[224] Ibid., 273.

Spirit and the fruit of the Spirit go together and are both the norm and essential in the life of all believers.[225]

A second danger arose from the fact that Wesley, as an Arminian, believed that it was possible to lose one's relationship with God and thus forfeit eternal salvation. This possibility made it easy to confuse religious depression ("heaviness" in Wesley) with an actual loss of faith and salvation. The danger was that the depression would lead to a loss of faith in God:

> ... if we let go our faith, our filial confidence in a loving, pardoning God, our peace is at an end, the very foundation on which it stood being overthrown. ... Consequently whatever strikes at this strikes at the very root of all holiness. For without this faith, without an abiding sense that Christ loved me and gave himself for me, ... it is impossible that I should love God. ... And unless we love God it is not possible that we should love our neighbour as ourselves; nor, consequently, that we should have any right affections either toward God or toward man. It evidently follows that whatever weakens our faith must in the same degree obstruct our holiness.[226]

Wesley wrote two sermons in 1760 to deal with this: "The Wilderness State" and "Heaviness through Manifold Temptations."[227] In the former sermon, the issue is a loss of faith resulting in a loss of the witness of the Spirit, love, joy, peace and power over sin ("spiritual darkness").[228] Wesley was certain this arose because believers had sinned by commission or (more commonly) omission due to human frailty, temptation, or ignorance of Scriptural teaching; as the cause varied greatly, so must the "cure."[229] The sensible presence of God may or may not return immediately; "When either ignorance or sin has caused darkness, one or the other may be removed, and yet the light which was obstructed thereby may not immediately return. As it is the free gift of God, he may restore it sooner or later, as it pleases him."[230] The second sermon dealt with "heaviness" (essentially defined as grief and sorrow) which Wesley clearly distinguished from "darkness"; the latter being caused by some sin, the former simply resulting from the frailties of being human and was common to all Christians.

> So that upon the whole their heaviness well consisted with faith, with hope, with love of God and man; with the peace of God, with joy in the Holy Ghost, with inward and outward holiness. It did no way impair, much less destroy, any part of the work of God in their hearts. It did not at all interfere with that 'sanctification

---

[225] Ibid., 297-98.
[226] *Works*, 2:144.
[227] See Ibid., 202-35.
[228] Ibid., 205-08.
[229] Ibid., 214.
[230] Ibid., 220.

of the Spirit' which is the root of all true 'obedience'; neither with the happiness which must needs result from 'grace and peace' reigning in the heart.[231]

A Christian could still be living in the reality of Christian perfection, while battling depression. Wesley agreed that no Christian need experience "darkness," but very few escape the realities of "heaviness."

Dealing with the Challenges and Objections from His Critics

Many of Wesley's detractors claimed that the whole foundation of his doctrine was unscriptural. This was the decisive point, for Wesley had based his whole life and ministry on Christian perfection being thoroughly biblical. His response to the criticisms of William Dodd (an Anglican clergyman and frequent correspondent who opposed Wesley's views) was typical:

> When I began to make the Scriptures my study [1729] ... , I began to see that Christians are called to *love God with all* their *heart* and to *serve Him with all* their *strength*; which is precisely what I apprehend to be meant by the Scriptural term Perfection. After weighing this for some years, I openly declared my sentiments before the University in the sermon on the Circumcision of the Heart, ... About six years after ... I published my coolest and latest thoughts in the sermon on that subject. I therein build on no authority, ancient or modern, but the Scripture. If this supports any doctrine, it will stand; if not, the sooner it falls the better. Neither the doctrine in question nor any other is anything to me, unless it be the doctrine of Christ and His Apostles. If, therefore, you will please to point out to me any passages in that sermon which are either contrary to Scripture or not supported by it, and to show that they are not, I shall be full as willing to oppose as ever I was to defend them. I search for truth, plain Bible truth, without any regard to the praise or dispraise of men.[232]

Scripture was clearly the foundation and final court of appeal for his understanding; if it was not scriptural then it was wrong. We need to remember, however, that Wesley had already stated that his hermeneutical method involved working with the plain text, the analogy of faith, reason informed by the Spirit, and the ethos of the community, informed by Christian experience,

---

[231] Ibid., 224.

[232] *Letters* (Telford), 3:157-58. The letter is dated February 5, 1756. A further letter was written as a response to Dodd in 1767, emphasising again his adherence to Scripture; see *Letters* (Telford), 5:42-44. He defended his position on perfection to John Newton in 1765 in *Letters* (Telford), 4:299-300. In a letter to Joseph Townsend he noted "[Methodists] do exhort believers to go on unto perfection; and so do you, if you speak as the oracles of God"; see *Letters* (Telford), 5:59. A pastoral letter to Mrs. Maitland said: "As to the word, it is scriptural; therefore neither you nor I can in conscience object against it, unless we would send the Holy Ghost to school and teach Him to speak who made the tongue"; see *Letters* (Telford), 4:212.

both personal and community. Dodd responded by refuting what he thought Wesley had used as a proof text for his sermon ("On Christian Perfection"), since it was not faithful to the Scripture text used in the title (Phil. 3:12). Wesley admitted that the text appended to the sermon was utilised simply because the word "perfection" appeared in it, "But that text is there used only as an occasion or introduction to the subject. I do not build any doctrine thereon, nor undertake critically to explain it." His central concern here was to show that the term itself was "scriptural"; what it actually meant was another question.[233]

THE NATURE OF CHRISTIAN PERFECTION

Wesley wrote "The Principles of a Methodist" (1742) to refute the attack of Josiah Tucker (who was to become the Dean of Gloucester and a well-published writer and critic of Methodism) on a number of Methodist doctrines, including Christian perfection. He contended that much of the rejection of the doctrine was due to misunderstanding its nature, equating it with a "sinless perfection."[234]

> We willingly allow, and continually declare, there is no such perfection in this life as implies either a dispensation from doing good and attending all the ordinances of God; or a freedom from ignorance, mistake, temptation, and a thousand infirmities necessarily connected with flesh and blood.[235]

His belief was based on what he understood the Scripture to unmistakably say regarding life in this present body and conditions. This was defined as being Christlike, particularly in terms of motivation, intention and living in love, with the works that flow from that.[236] By defining perfection in terms of loving God

---

[233] *Letters* (Telford), 3:167-68. Wesley argued that perfection is only another term for holiness or "the image of God in man" and this he clearly defines as loving and serving God wholeheartedly. Dodd argued that Wesley set aside the authority of the ancient and modern church in matters of doctrine. Wesley firmly rejected this, saying he upheld the authority of the early church and the Church of England "But I try every Church and every doctrine by the Bible"; see Ibid., 172.

[234] This was the most common accusation levelled against Wesley's teaching. See for example the criticisms of George Whitefield in *Works*, 26:32-33, 261; of Joseph Humphreys in Ibid., 57-58, 62-63; of "John Smith" in Ibid., 170-71, 85-87; of the Bishop of London in Ibid., 484; of Richard Tompson in Ibid., 567, 70-71. See also *Letters* (Telford), 5:90. Wesley did not necessarily object to the term itself, though he did not contend for it; see *Letters* (Telford), 4:187, 213. In a letter to Lady Huntingdon, a staunch Calvinist, he emphasised that 'perfection' was simply the establishment of her soul in love; see Tyson and Schlenther, 104.

[235] *Works*, 9:53. See also *Works* (Jackson) 14:329.

[236] Ibid., 9:54-55. The main scriptures given are: Phil. 2:5; 1 Jn. 1:5, 7; 2:6, 10; 3:9; ; Ps. 24:4; 2 Cor. 5:17; 7:1; Ezek. 36:25, 29; 1 Thess. 1:3; 5:23; Gal. 2:20; 1 Pet. 1:5; 2:10; Mk. 12:30; Eph. 2:10; 5:2; Matt. 5:44; 6:10; Jn. 8:19; 17:23; Col. 3:12, 17.

and neighbour, Wesley was confident that the one who "experiences this is scripturally perfect. And if you do not yet, you may experience it: you surely will, if you follow hard after it; for the Scripture cannot be broken."[237] As for the belief that sin remained in those who claimed perfection, Wesley stated: "I believe not; but, be that as it may, they feel none, no temper but pure love, while they rejoice, pray, and give thanks continually. And whether sin is suspended or extinguished, I will not dispute; it is enough that they feel nothing but love."[238] His fundamental conviction was that "If there be anything unscriptural in these words, anything wild or extravagant, anything contrary to the analogy of faith, or the experience of adult Christians, let them 'smite me friendly and reprove me'; let them impart to me of the clearer light God has given them."[239] Note once again that Wesley emphasised the analogy of faith, and not individual proof texts. He appealed to the direct work of God in the person's life through the text as a means of grace and not merely intellectual comprehension. Due to the clear testimony of the Scriptures, Wesley believed that even "babes in Christ" were so far "perfect" as not to sin:

> If any doubt of this privilege of the sons of God, the question is not to be decided by abstract reasonings, which may be drawn out into an endless length, and leave the point just as it was before. Neither is it to be determined by the experience of this or that particular person. Many may suppose they do not commit sin when they do, but this proves nothing either way. 'To the law and to the testimony' we appeal. ... By his Word will we abide, and that alone.[240]

He followed this up with a long series of Scripture passages in support of his position.[241] His conclusion was: "In conformity therefore both to the doctrine of St. John, and to the whole tenor of the New Testament, we fix this conclusion: 'A Christian is so far perfect as not to commit sin.'"[242] The awareness of remaining sin should not cause trouble but should incite us to turn more and more to Christ, so "that we may go on conquering and to conquer. And, therefore, when the sense of our sin most abounds, the sense of his love should much more abound."[243]

---

[237] *Letters* (Telford), 4:213.
[238] Ibid.
[239] *Works*, 9:55.
[240] *Works*, 2:105-06. Wesley quoted a series of texts from Rom. 6: 1-18 to illustrate his point. For later important qualifications read "On Sin in Believers" in *Works*, 1:314-34.
[241] *Works*, 2:106-14. He particularly refers to I Jn 3: 8-9, where he points out that John does not qualify the "freedom" by adding "wilfully" or "habitually." However, note his own later qualifications in "The Repentance of Believers", "The Marks of the New Birth", and "The Great Privileges of those that are Born of God"; see n. 68, p. 107.
[242] Ibid., 116.
[243] *Works* (Jackson), 8:298.

IS CHRISTIAN PERFECTION ATTAINABLE IN THIS LIFE OR
ONLY AT THE POINT OF DEATH?

The greatest challenge to Wesley's understanding of Christian perfection came from those in the Reformed theological tradition who denied that it was possible for any human being to perfectly conform to God's law in each and every particular. According to them, any lack of conformity to God's perfect law in word, thought or deed, by commission or omission was sin, and thus all lived in sin until released by death. This was a point that troubled many within Methodism itself and it was of critical importance to clearly distinguish between sin (for which Wesley believed the Christian was culpable) and infirmities (for which he believed the Christian was not culpable).[244] Wesley agreed with his critics that Adam as created was perfectly capable of meeting all of God's requirements since he had no defect in his body, understanding or affections; he was able to apprehend clearly, judge truly, reason justly and act perfectly in total conformity to God's demands. Thus a covenant of works for Adam was in full harmony with God's loving justice.

> Adam in Paradise was able to apprehend *all* things distinctly, and to *judge truly* concerning them; therefore it was his duty so to do. But no man living *is* now *able* to do this; therefore neither is it the duty of any man now living. Neither is there any man now in the body who does or can walk in this instance by that rule which was bound upon Adam. Can anything be more plain than this–that Adam *could*, that I *cannot* avoid mistaking? Can anything be plainer than this–if he *could* avoid it, he *ought*? or than this–If I *cannot*, I *ought not*? I mean it is not my duty: for the clear reason that no one can do the impossible. Nothing in the Sermon [on the Mount] or the Law contradicts this.[245]

Since the fall, the body is now corrupted and clogs the soul, hindering its operations. "But we may observe that, naturally speaking, the animal frame will affect more or less every power of the soul; seeing at present the soul can no more *love* than it can *think*, any otherwise than by the help of bodily organs. If, therefore, we either *think*, *speak*, or *love* aright, it must be by power from on high.[246] Wesley's conclusion was:

> (1) As long as we live our soul is connected with the body. (2) As long as it is thus connected, it cannot think but by the help of bodily organs. (3) As long as these organs are imperfect, we are liable to mistakes, both speculative and practical. (4) Yea, and a mistake may occasion my loving a good man less than I ought, which is defective, that is, a wrong temper. (5) For all these we need the atoning blood,

---

[244] For an insightful discussion of this issue, see Colin N. Peckham, *John Wesley's Understanding of Human Infirmities* (Ilkeston: The Wesley Fellowship, 1997); Lori Haynes Niles, "Toward a Wesleyan Theology of Failure," *WTJ* 43, no. 1(Spring, 2008).
[245] *Letters* (Telford), 4:98. See also Ibid., 155.
[246] *Letters* (Telford), 5:4.

as indeed for every defect or omission. Therefore, (6) all men have need to say daily, 'Forgive us our trespasses.'[247]

Were all therefore condemned to a life of endless sinning and defeat? Wesley strongly rejected this pessimistic conclusion. He argued that God had now established a covenant of grace with fallen humanity and all the requirements of the law were met fully in Christ who had now established the law of faith, so that the one who believed in him would be fully accepted by God.[248] The "law of faith" established by Christ was fulfilled by love: "Faith working or animated by love is all that God now requires of man. He *has* substituted (not sincerity, but) love, in the room of angelic perfection."[249] Wesley agreed that it was still possible to offend against this law, since mistakes may spring from a heart of love. He reminded his people that they have no "stock of holiness" that is their own, but must always depend every moment upon Christ and so they always needed his atonement, intercession and advocacy with the Father. He was careful to maintain that we never achieved a state of grace in which we no longer needed the priestly work of Christ:

> ... we should still need His Spirit, and consequently His intercession for the continuance of that love from moment to moment. Beside, we should still be encompassed with infirmities and liable to mistakes, from which words or actions might follow, even though the heart was all love, which were not exactly right. Therefore in all these respects we should still have need of Christ's priestly office.[250]

His opponents saw this as an admission that "sinless perfection" was therefore impossible. Wesley responded by reminding them that Christians no longer needed the atonement to reconcile them to God or to restore his favour but rather to continue it. He argued that to give up a continuing atonement was in effect to give up "perfection," but we need not do either.[251] Living in a corrupted body did mean that "mistakes" would arise, not from a defect of love, but a defect of knowledge. As long as there was "no concurrence of the will," there was no sin.[252] He was positive that a relationship with God centred in love could be unbroken if the Christian acknowledged the mistake and its

---

[247] *Works*, 21:337. He then reinforced this position by giving the testimonies of several who were "saved from sin" who agreed they had a constant need of the "atoning blood"; see p. 338. See also *Works*, 2:100-02; *Works* (Jackson), 14:328-29.

[248] *Works* (Jackson), 11:414-15.

[249] Ibid., 416. Wesley saw this as being described in I Cor. 13. See also *Letters* (Telford), 4:155.

[250] *Letters* (Telford), 3:380.

[251] *Works* (Jackson), 11:417-18.

[252] *Letters* (Telford), 3:168. See his argument that continuing in wilful sin indicates you are no longer a child of God on pp. 168-70.

consequences as soon as they were aware of it and sought the continuing benefit of the atonement immediately.[253]

Regarding the time when the experience may be received, Wesley said at the Conference of 1745 that "none who seeks it sincerely shall or can die without it; though possibly he may not attain it, till the very article of death."[254]

> By 'perfection' I mean 'perfect love', or the loving God with all our heart, so as to rejoice evermore, to pray without ceasing, and in everything to give thanks. I am convinced every believer may attain this; yet I do not say he is in a state of damnation or under the curse of God till he does attain. No, he is in a state of grace and in favour with God as long as he believes. Neither would I say, 'If you die without it, you will perish'.[255]

Nevertheless, we ought to expect it sooner, even though "the generality of believers whom we have hitherto known were not so sanctified till near death" and this was equally true of the time when Paul wrote his epistles. This did not, however, prove that we may not experience it today.[256] The essential element was to be faithful to the grace received and as long as this continued, the person was in no danger of perishing at the end. Two years later (at another Conference) it was reaffirmed that every believer must "be entirely sanctified in the article of death" and till then he or she "daily grows in grace, comes nearer and nearer to perfection." It was also agreed that "many of those who died in the faith, yea, the greater part of those we have known, were not sanctified throughout, not made perfect in love, till a little before death."[257] Wesley agreed that Paul and the other New Testament writers applied the term "sanctified" to all Christians and not merely to those saved from all sin, unless it was qualified by "wholly, entirely" or suchlike (and this was not common). He believed there were clear promises of full deliverance in Scriptures: Deut. 30:6; Ps. 130:8; Ezek. 36:25, 29; Rom. 8:3,4; 2 Cor. 7:1; Eph. 5:25, 27;.I Jn. 3:8. There are the Scripture prayers for it: Jn. 17:20, 21, 23; Eph. 3:14, 16-19 and I Thess. 5:23. There are the clear commands: Matt. 5:48; 22:37. He concluded, "if the love of God fill all the heart, there can be no sin there." That this should before death is in the nature of the command, since it was the living and not the dead who were to love God, as well as the truth expressed in texts such as Tit. 2:11-14; Lk. 1:69-75. Wesley saw actual examples of the wholly sanctified in the Apostle John and all he referred to in I Jn. 4:17.[258] He was confident that the foundation

---

[253] *Works* (Jackson), 11:419.

[254] *Works* (Jackson), 8:285.

[255] *Letters* (Telford), 4:10.See also Ibid., 157-58.

[256] *Works* (Jackson), 8:285 See also *Works* (Jackson), 11:423.

[257] *Works* (Jackson), 8:294.

[258] Ibid., 294-96. He thinks there may be so few examples because it was still a young church. His own published prayers often carried this same focus on love; see for example *Works* (Jackson), 11:237-59. See also *Works* (Jackson), 10:350; 11:446.

for all his claims was the Scripture itself, as understood within his hermeneutical circle. He strongly advised that sanctification should be preached "scarce at all to those who are not pressing forward. To those who are, always by way of promise; always drawing, rather than driving."[259] This underscores again the centrality of love in Wesley's understanding, since a relationship of love, by its very nature, cannot be coerced, only invited. The question still remained that if perfection was possible in theory, did it ever happen in practice? Regarding living examples, Wesley said few would publicly confess this, since it would make them a target for either abuse or idolisation. For those who did attain the experience, they should only speak about it to fellow believers and then only when there was a good reason. In any case, testimony to entire sanctification should not be given hastily.[260] He did write that he knew many who had this relationship with God: "this is a point of fact; and this is plain, sound, scriptural experience."[261]

The "Circumstance" of Christian Perfection:
Wesley's Pastoral Understanding

From the early 1740's Wesley was clear in his own mind that the pursuit and propagation of Christian perfection was the very reason that Methodism existed:

> By Methodists I mean a people who profess to pursue ... holiness of heart and life, inward and outward conformity in all things to the revealed will of God; who place religion in an uniform resemblance of the great Object of it; in steady imitation of him they worship in all his imitable perfections; more particularly in justice, mercy, and truth, or universal love filling the heart and governing the life.[262]

Central to the communication of this message to the people were his sermons: "For the notorious truth of this [inward and outward holiness] we appeal to the whole tenor of our sermons, printed and unprinted–in particular to those upon *Our Lord's Sermon on the Mount*, wherein every branch of gospel obedience is both asserted and proved to be indispensably necessary to eternal salvation."[263]

---

[259] *Works* (Jackson), 8:286.

[260] Ibid., 297.

[261] *Works* (Jackson), 11:418. See clear references to people clearly professing perfect love in *Letters* (Telford), 3:168; 4:71-2, 133, 167, 186; 5:20, 102. Many of them were noted in the period 1759-66 especially. See also *Works*, 9:473-86. and the relevant sections of the *Journals*.

[262] *Works*, 9:123-24. Note the exhortation on pp. 124-125, where the social nature of the "pursuit" is emphasised. See also *Works* (Jackson) 14:329.

[263] *Letters* (Telford), 4:330-31. He also makes reference to the importance of "The Circumcision of the Heart"; see *Works*, 9:358.

It was not merely the written word that he had in mind, for in the Conference *Minutes* of 1745 Wesley noted the importance of preaching the promise of Christian perfection as soon as people began their relationship with God, a point that he had not seen so clearly before.[264]

> The more I converse with the believers in Cornwall, the more I am convinced that they have sustained great loss for want of hearing the doctrine of Christian perfection clearly and strongly enforced. I see, wherever this is not done, the believers grow dead and cold. Nor can this be prevented but by keeping up in them an hourly expectation of being perfected in love. I say, an 'hourly expectation'; for to expect it at *death*, or *some time hence*, is much the same as not expecting it at all.[265]

The importance of preaching was further underscored in a series of letters between John and Charles Wesley as the holiness revival of 1760-63 proceeded.[266]

The claims of Maxfield and Bell to "sinless perfection" and a number of other spiritual phenomena sparked a variety of reactions amongst the Methodists and their critics, including a number of points of debate between the brothers concerning the nature, manner and the timing of Christian perfection. John defined the nature of perfection as "the humble, gentle, patient love of God and man ruling all the tempers, words, and actions, the whole heart and the whole life."[267]

> As to the manner, I believe this perfection is always wrought in the soul by faith, by a simple act of faith; consequently in an instant. But I believe a gradual work both preceding and following that instant. ... As to the time, I believe this instant generally is the instant of death, the moment before the soul leaves the body. But I believe it may be ten, twenty, or forty years before death. ... I believe it is usually

---

[264] *Works* (Jackson), 8:283-84. Methodist preaching was usually accompanied by the singing of hymns and these carried their teaching on Christian perfection as fully as the sermons and other doctrinal writings. An examination of the hymnody is beyond the scope of this book, but its importance must be noted. For further study, consult *Works*, 7; Teresa Berger, *Theology in Hymns?: A Study of the Relationship of Doxology and Theology According to* A Collection of Hymns for the Use of the People Called Methodists (1780), trans. Timothy E. Kimbrough (Nashville, TN: Kingswood Books, 1995); John R. Tyson, *Assist Me to Proclaim: The Life and Hymns of Charles Wesley* (Grand Rapids, MI: Wm. B. Eerdmans, 2007).

[265] *Works*, 21:389. See also *Letters* (Telford), 4:321; 5:166.

[266] For Wesley's own account of this revival, see *A Short History of the People Called Methodists* in *Works*, 9:426-503. The testimonies to Christian perfection are found concentrated between pp. 473-86. Further accounts can be found in Wesley's *Journals* for the same period.

[267] *Letters* (Telford), 4:187.

many years after justification, but that it may be within five years or five months after it. I know no conclusive argument to the contrary.[268]

John admitted that the reality for most Christians was that this experience came to them just before death, but all could know it now by faith, if only they had that expectation. The creation of the expectation was the task of Methodism, so in a private note to Charles later he emphasised the vital role of actually preaching the message: "O insist everywhere on *full* redemption, receivable by *faith alone*! Consequently to be looked for *now*. ... Press the *instantaneous* blessing: then I shall have more time for my peculiar calling, enforcing the *gradual* work."[269] He believed that Charles had set the standard of perfection too high and this would have the practical result of many people renouncing the teaching: "That perfection which I believe, I can boldly preach, because I think I see five hundred witnesses of it. Of that perfection which you preach, you do not even think you see any witness at all."[270] During the course of the correspondence, he became concerned that Charles may have altered his theological position:

> I still think to disbelieve *all the professors* amounts to a *denial of the thing*. For if there be no living witnesses of what we have preached for twenty years, I cannot, dare not preach it any longer. The whole comes to one point,–Is there or is there not any instantaneous sanctification between justification and death? I say, Yes; you (*often seem to*) say, No. What arguments brought you to think so? Perhaps they may convince me too. Nay, there is one question more, if you allow there is such a thing,–Can one who has attained it fall? Formerly I thought not; but *you* ... convinced me of my mistake.[271]

This underscored the importance of actual Christian experience and reasoning to confirm his understanding of Christian perfection. He later reported that the work of God was still progressing in London and the North of England where "so many are groaning after full redemption." Early in 1767 Wesley thought that preaching on perfection had been lost throughout most of the country, so he encouraged the preachers "to speak plainly and to press believers to the constant pursuit and earnest expectation of it."[272] At the

---

[268] Ibid. The letter was dated September 1762. See also the *Minutes* of 1744 in *Works* (Jackson), 8:285.

[269] *Letters* (Telford), 5:16.

[270] Ibid., 19-20. The debate was to continue over several years, with John making the same points as he had earlier; see two of the key letters written in 1767 in Ibid., 38-39 and 40-41.

[271] Ibid., 41.

[272] Ibid., 46-47. In preaching on perfection, Wesley advised: "But we must speak very tenderly on this head, for it is better to lead men than to drive. Study to recommend it rather as amiable and desirable than as necessary." See *Letters* (Telford), 3:213; *Works* (Jackson), 8:286.

upcoming 1768 Conference in London it was to be determined "whether all our preachers or none shall continually insist upon Christian perfection."[273]

> Shall we go on in asserting perfection against all the world? Or shall we quietly let it drop? We really must do one or the other; and, I apprehend, the sooner the better. What shall we jointly and explicitly maintain (and recommend to all our preachers) concerning the nature, the time (now or by-and-by), and the manner of it (instantaneous or not)? I am weary of intestine [sic] war, of preachers quoting one of us against the other."[274]

The debate between the brothers on these issues was mirrored in the correspondence between John, his supporters and his critics during these years. It is to these that we now turn as we seek to examine his theological method in pastoral practice.

Seeking the Relationship of Perfect Love

Pastorally, Wesley held that a Christian generally had to be certain that a relationship of perfect love was possible before they would begin to seek this experience. However, he felt that a belief in the possibility of a relationship of perfect love was not essential to actually experiencing it. He noted the example of a Calvinist who never believed it until she experienced it shortly before her death.[275] The question Wesley posed to his Methodists was: did it honour Christ more to make him a total or partial healer, offering full salvation or half-salvation? The fact that many people gave false testimony to justification or sanctification was not an objection to the truth of the doctrines themselves.[276] He reminded Alexander Coates: "To say Christ will not reign alone in our hearts in this life, will not enable us to give Him all our hearts–This in my judgement is making Him an half-Saviour. He can be no more, if He does not quite save us from our sins."[277] It was vital, therefore, that his people listened to preachers and read material that would encourage them in their search, as these would help them to form a firm doctrinal foundation and aid them in their understanding and application of scripture.[278] It was crucial not to listen to the

---

[273] *Letters* (Telford), 5:61. See also Ibid., 88.

[274] Ibid., 93.

[275] *Letters* (Telford), 4:10-11. Wesley affirmed that it was essential to experience it prior to death as there is no post-mortem cleansing.

[276] Ibid., 158-59. For example, he wrote to Charles: "I believe several in London have imagined themselves saved from sin 'upon the word of others'; and these are easily known. For that work does not stand. Such imaginations soon vanish away." See Ibid., 199.

[277] Ibid., 158. Coates was a Methodist itinerant preacher.

[278] *Letters* (Telford), 5:130. He advised his people to read helpful material such as a *Serious Call* or "Christian Perfection" in *Letters* (Telford), 3:207; "The Circumcision of

seemingly wise advice of those who would deny this work of grace: "we have an unction from the Holy One ready to teach us of all things. O let us attend to *this inward teaching*, which indeed is *always consonant with the word*. Then *the word, applied by the Spirit*, shall be a light in all our ways and a lamp in all our paths" (emphasis mine).[279] In offering guidance to Samuel Furly, who clearly struggled with the doctrine, he wrote

> ... none can doubt but all Jewish believers were perfected *before* they died. But that many of them were perfected *long before* they died I see no reason to think. The Holy Ghost was not *fully* given before Jesus was glorified. Therefore *the law* (unless in a very few exempt cases) *made nothing perfect*. It is certain the word 'perfect' in the Old Testament bears several senses. But we lay no stress upon the word at all. The thing is *pure love*. The promise of this was given by *Moses*, but not designed to be fulfilled till long after. See Deuteronomy XXX. 1-6. By the whole tenor of the words it appears it was *then*, when He had *gathered* the Jews *from all nations*, that God was to *circumcise their hearts*. However, this may be fulfilled in you and me. Let us hasten toward it.![280]

This hastening was certainly encouraged by a firm grasp of the Scriptures, though he strongly argued against adopting a proof-text approach. Wesley urged Elizabeth Hardy, a member of the Bristol Society, to hold fast to the promise of Deut. 30, while admitting that a number of other verses she referred to were not proof texts for perfection.[281]

> But not only abundance of particular texts, but the whole tenor of Scripture declares, Christ came to 'destroy the works of the devil, to save us from our sins'– all the works of the devil, all our sins, without any exception or limitation. Indeed, should we say we have no sin to be saved or cleansed from, we should make Him come in vain. But it is at least as much for His glory to cleanse us from them all before our death as after it.[282]

As his people sought to understand this scriptural teaching, Wesley emphasised that it was important not to get involved in disputes with the critics of Christian perfection, otherwise it would undermine their confidence in God's gracious ability to perform the work.[283] He advised Dorothy Furly (Samuel

---

the Heart," "Christian Perfection," Preface to the *Hymns and Sacred Poems* (1741, 1742), and the *Minutes* in *Letters* (Telford), 3:212; 4:163; *Notes* (*NT*), Vol 1 of the *Sermons* and the *Appeals* in *Letters* (Telford), 5:25; *Thoughts* and *Farther Thoughts on Christian Perfection* in *Letters* (Telford), 4:268; 5:24; *Cautions and Directions given to the Greatest Professors in the Methodist Societies* in *Works* (Jackson), 11:430.

[279] *Letters* (Telford), 3:218.
[280] *Letters* (Telford), 4:79.
[281] Ibid., 11-12.
[282] Ibid., 12.
[283] For example, see his advice to Dorothy Furly in Ibid., 97.

Furly's sister) to keep friendship with those who have a deep relationship with God and are seeking for more, while avoiding those propagating contrary beliefs.[284] Proper encouragement would help her to continue in her walk and receive strength to do God's work "in the same proportion with your sense of His love."[285]

As the Methodists sought this experience of perfect love they were to be mindful of the many other traps and hindrances that would result in their spiritual loss. It was important to understand that "by resolutely persisting, ... in all the works of piety and mercy, you are waiting on God in the old scriptural way."[286] They should wait for the fulfilling of the promise "in universal obedience; in keeping all the commandments; in denying ourselves, and taking up our cross daily. These are the general means which God hath ordained for our receiving his sanctifying grace. The particular are,–prayer, searching the Scripture, communicating, and fasting."[287] To Miss March, he emphasised: "Prayer is the grand means of drawing near to God; and all others are helpful to us only so far as they are mixed with or prepare us for this."[288] In the process one was to praise God for what he had already done and then continue to fight against sin: "Unless you yield, you cannot but conquer. It is true that you will first conquer little by little. ... But there is also an instantaneous conquest: in a moment sin shall be no more. You are gradually dying for a long time. But you will die in a moment. O hasten to that happy time! Pray, strive, hope for it![289] He warned them that this strength may be lost by committing sins of commission or omission.[290] During this period it was important to retain confidence in a God who would fill them with "pure love."[291] He cautioned his people that a conviction of spiritual need was not condemnation: "You are condemned for nothing, if you love God and continue to give Him your whole heart." They had to hold fast what God had already done and God would continue to enrich them.[292] As this attitude was maintained, God would give all they seek "because God is love." We are not condemned even for coming short of the law of love because of the prayerful intercession of Christ: "I believe it is impossible not to come short of it, through the unavoidable littleness of our

---

[284] He gave similar advice to John Fletcher: "I seldom find it profitable for me to converse with any who are not athirst for perfection and who are not big with earnest expectation of receiving it every moment." See *Letters* (Telford), 5:83.

[285] *Letters* (Telford), 3:214-15. See also *Letters* (Telford), 3:218; 4:90-1.

[286] *Letters* (Telford), 3:208.

[287] *Works* (Jackson), 8:286.

[288] *Letters* (Telford), 4:90. He told her that she could remain in peace and joy until "perfected in love." Miss J. C. March was one of Wesley's most frequent correspondents, though not much is known about her.

[289] Ibid., 46.

[290] *Letters* (Telford), 3:214-15. See also Ibid., 218.

[291] *Letters* (Telford), 4:85-6.

[292] Ibid., 109.

understanding. Yet the blood of the covenant is upon us, and therefore there is no condemnation." He saw the law of love fully marked out in 1 Cor. 13 and people were to follow this loving faith to the best of their understanding while depending totally on Christ for any shortcomings.[293] Here, once more, Wesley urged his people to realise that condemnation was linked with intention and culpability, not with infirmity due to their humanity. In the face of discouragement it was important to remember that because they had not received the blessing yet did not mean they would not in the future. The danger was the temptation to believe there was no such thing and to doubt the word of witnesses who had testified to it. It was vital to "keep close to your *rule*, the Word of God, and to your *guide*, the Spirit of God, and never be afraid of expecting too much" (emphasis mine).[294] To focus on "inbred sin" was to come under its bondage, so the believer must keep focused on Christ and what he could do.[295] In the midst of trials, it was important to give thanks for the continuing work of God: "And why is this but to improve every right temper; to free you from all that is irrational or unholy; to make you all that you were–yea, all that you should be; to restore you to the whole image of God?"[296] He encouraged Ann Bolton to be wholly devoted to God and focused on one thing– to be holy, "an whole burnt sacrifice of love."[297] "I do not advise you to reason whether you have faith or not, but simply to look up to Him that loves you for whatever you want."[298] Here is an early caution about the danger side of reason, even for one who was a Christian; this will become more prominent in his pastoral advice from now on.

Entering the Relationship of Perfect Love

The critical issue of pastoral concern here was the debate over whether Christian perfection was an instantaneous or a gradual work. Wesley admitted that God can work as he chooses and he may bring people into this experience very quickly and without any perceptible gradual work at all (there were plenty of witnesses to this).[299] He believed it would be a gradual work for most people, and he referred to over forty scriptural texts that supported this understanding. In the light of the variety of ways in which God worked "one may affirm the work as gradual, another, it is instantaneous, without any manner of

---

[293] Ibid., 124.

[294] Ibid., 157. Notice the intimate link between the written word and the living voice of the Spirit.

[295] Ibid., 70.

[296] Ibid., 88-89.

[297] *Letters* (Telford), 5:80. Ann was one of Wesley's favourite correspondents and a devoted Methodist; he often stayed at her brother's home, where she also lived as she was unmarried at this time.

[298] Ibid., 151.

[299] *Letters* (Telford), 4:321.

contradiction."[300] However, the actual work itself is always instantaneous: "A gradual growth in grace precedes, but the gift itself is always given instantaneously. I never knew or heard of any exception; and I believe there never was one."[301] In writing to Samuel Furly he could state: "What all our brethren think concerning that circumstance of entire sanctification–that it is instantaneous, although a gradual growth in grace both precede and follow it, you may see in the *Minutes* of the Conference, wherein it was freely debated."[302] And in correspondence with Miss March he could state:

> Every one, though born of God in an instant, yea and sanctified in an instant, yet undoubtedly grows by slow degrees, both after the former and the latter change. But it does not follow from thence that there must be a considerable tract of time between the one and the other. A year or a month is the same with God as a thousand: if He wills, to do is present with Him. Much less is there any necessity for much suffering: God can do His work by pleasure as well as by pain. It is therefore undoubtedly our duty to pray and look for full salvation every day, every hour, every moment, without waiting till we have either done or suffered more. Why should not this be the accepted time?[303]

He reminded Ann Foard that she was to look for God's fulfilment of his promises now, not at death. Wesley continued to urge her: "you have only to believe and enter into rest. ... Why should you not now be all love? All devoted to Him that loves you?"[304] He assured her that time meant nothing to God: "Consequently He can as well sanctify in a day after we are justified as an hundred years." He gave the example of Ann Hooley (twelve years old) who was sanctified nine days after justification, though he admitted that some time between them was more usual.[305] Vital to attaining this experience was her heart's desire: "Does He not now read your heart, and see if it pants for His pure love? If so, are not all things ready? May you not now find what you never did before? Ask Him that loves you, whose nature and whose name is Love!"[306] She must maintain a steady belief in the promises of God and to remember that all was of grace and love, not her own work.[307]

In a number of letters concerning the London revival, he commented that there was something peculiar about the experience of most of those who had

---

[300] *Works* (Jackson), 11:423.
[301] *Letters* (Telford), 3:213. See also *Letters* (Telford), 4:225.
[302] *Letters* (Telford), 4:163. See also Wesley, *Minutes (1803)*, 48-49.
[303] *Letters* (Telford), 4:100. He reminded her to keep accountable with others and engage in good Christian conversation; see Ibid., 190.
[304] *Letters* (Telford), 5:32. Ann Foard was another of Wesley's regular correspondents and a member of one of the London Societies.
[305] *Letters* (Telford), 4:268.
[306] *Letters* (Telford), 5:37.
[307] *Letters* (Telford), 3:217.

entered a relationship of perfect love during this time:

> One would expect that *a believer should first be filled with love, and thereby emptied of sin* [emphasis mine]; whereas these were emptied of sin first, and then filled with love. Perhaps it pleased God to work in this manner, to make his work more plain and undeniable; and to distinguish it more clearly from that overflowing love, which is often felt even in a justified state.[308]

While this clearly puzzled Wesley, Elizabeth Hardy had found their experience to be a stumbling block to her. He reminded her that "The great point in question is, Can we be saved from all sin or not? Now, it may please God to act in that *uncommon manner* [emphasis mine], purposely to clear this point–to satisfy those persons that they are saved from all sin before He goes on in His work."[309]

> God will do His own work in His own manner, and exceeding variously in different persons. It matters not whether it be wrought in a more pleasing or painful manner, so it is wrought . .... Therefore trouble not yourself about the experience of others: God knows you, and let Him do with you as He sees best.[310]

This highlights that at the heart of Wesley's whole conception of Christian perfection was a passion for God, and it was this passion that was to be the motivation for the whole of life and ministry. He believed that love was essentially attractive and this should be the emphasis in preaching and teaching, rather than on the negative aspect of cleansing or purification. As we have seen earlier, he did not deny these aspects, particularly when writing on the subject of sin or the sinful nature; however, they were not normally to be the Christian's focus.

Pastorally, it was also important to clarify the relationship of faith and works when seeking a relationship of perfect love. He wrote to Dorothy Furly: "You are hindered chiefly by not understanding the freeness of the gift of God. You are perpetually seeking for something in yourself to move Him to love and bless you. But it is not to be found therein; it is in Himself and in the Son of His love."[311]

> Hold fast, therefore, that whereunto you have attained, and in peace and joy wait for perfect love. *We know this is not of works, lest any man should boast*; and it is

---

[308] *Works* (Jackson), 11:424. He felt there was scriptural support for this from Ezek. 36:25, 26.
[309] *Letters* (Telford), 4:167-68.
[310] *Letters* (Telford), 3:230. See also *Letters* (Telford), 4:56.
[311] *Letters* (Telford), 4:5.

no more of sufferings than it is of works. Nothing is absolutely pre-required but a sense of our want; and this may be a calm, peaceful, yet joyful sense of it.[312]

This did not mean that the person was to simply wait quietly for God to do all the work: "All who expect to be sanctified at all expect to be sanctified by faith. But meantime they know that faith will not be given but to them that obey. Remotely, therefore, the blessing depends on our works, although immediately on simple faith."[313] A hindrance to obtaining this blessing was a lack of "simple faith" because she allowed unprofitable theological reasoning to dominate her thoughts. Wesley thought this was largely due to listening to Calvinist preachers who, while they were "godly people," tended to lead believers "into unprofitable reasonings, which would probably end in your giving up all hope of a full salvation from sin in this life." His advice was to check doctrinal curiosity in this area.[314] He gave similar advice to John Fletcher: "I seldom find it profitable for me to converse with any who are not athirst for perfection and who are not big with earnest expectation of receiving it every moment."[315]

The Assurance of Perfect Love

Wesley believed that the Holy Spirit witnessed to the grace of Christian perfection as fully as he did to that of justification.[316] He was certain that this witness was scriptural and it was confirmed by many Methodists throughout Britain, Ireland, Holland, Germany and America, as well as by many who had no contact with Methodism (even Roman Catholics).[317] Writing to Peggy Dale, he said

> I hope you now again find the inward witness that you are saved from sin. There is a danger in being content without it, into which you may easily reason yourself. ... The witness of sanctification as well as of justification is the privilege of God's children. And you may have the one always clear as well as the other if you walk humbly and closely with God.[318]

---

[312] Ibid., 71.

[313] Ibid. See also *Letters* (Telford), 5:112-13.

[314] *Letters* (Telford), 5:60. See also Ibid., 56.

[315] Ibid., 83. John Fletcher was the vicar of Madeley, an outstanding pastor, preacher and theological writer. Wesley hoped he would succeed him as leader of the Methodist movement but Fletcher declined. Perhaps his greatest contribution to the Methodist movement was his *Checks to Antinomianism*, defending the Arminian position during the Calvinist controversy that re-emerged in 1770.

[316] He said that the view that there is no direct or immediate witness of sanctification was a "new position" and he denied it was true; see *Letters* (Telford), 5:6, 8.

[317] *Letters* (Telford), 5:21-22. See also *Letters* (Telford), 3:213.

[318] *Letters* (Telford), 5:50. Peggy Dale was another of Wesley's favourite correspondents; she lived in Newcastle.

He was convinced that the assurance of a "direct witness" was to be found in 1 Cor. 2:12; Rom. 8:16 and I Jn. 5:19.[319] He was equally sure that it was given instantly: "I never knew any one receive the abiding witness gradually; therefore I incline to think this also is given in a moment. But there will be still after this abundant room for a gradual growth in grace."[320] This witness was both direct and indirect (the "fruit of the Spirit"), but it was not always clear and not always the same intensity. He wrote again to Peggy Dale:

> It is a certain truth that the witness of sanctification is a privilege which every one that is sanctified *may claim*. Yet it is not true that every one that is sanctified *does enjoy* this. Many who are really sanctified (that is, *wholly devoted* to God) do not enjoy it as soon as that work is wrought; and many who receive it do not retain it, or at least not constantly. Indeed, they cannot retain it in two cases: either if they do not continue steadily watching unto prayer; or, secondly, if they give way to reasoning, if they let go any parts of 'love's divine simplicity.'[321]

Some received the witness in a "higher degree," but even they could still grieve the Spirit and backslide.[322] He was sure, however, that both the witness and the fruit go together and without the latter, the person was mistaken if they claimed perfection in love.[323] It was also important not to lose confidence in times of depression, such as that experienced by Mrs. Elizabeth Bennis. He referred her to his *Thoughts* and *Farther Thoughts on Perfection* for evidence to encourage her that she has "the genuine experience of the adult children of God. Oppose that authority to the authority of any that contradict (if reason and Scripture are disregarded), and look daily for a deeper and fuller communion with God."[324]

Maintaining the Relationship of Perfect Love

Wesley was confident that this experience of Christian perfection could be lost, as testimony, observation and the Scriptures confirmed (in particular, Heb. 10:29; 1 Jn. 2:15; 1 Thess. 5:16f; Eph. 4:30).[325] In writing to Mrs. Bennis, he pointed out that

---

[319] *Works* (Jackson), 11:420-21.
[320] *Letters* (Telford), 4:170.
[321] *Letters* (Telford), 5:78. See also *Letters* (Telford), 4:170; 5:142.
[322] *Works* (Jackson), 11:424.
[323] Ibid., 424-26.
[324] *Letters* (Telford), 5:24. Elizabeth Bennis was a key member of the Methodist Society in Limerick and a frequent correspondent with Wesley.
[325] *Works* (Jackson), 11:420-22, 426-27. See also *Letters* (Telford), 4:187; 5:26. He had written to Elizabeth Hardy indicating that some of the expressions in the hymns were too strong, since there is no state mentioned in Scripture from which we cannot fall; see *Letters* (Telford), 4:167; 5:41.

> ... it is very possible to cast away the gift of God, or to lose it little and little; though I trust this is not the case with you: and yet you may frequently be in heaviness, and may find your love to God not near so warm at some times as it is at others. Many wanderings likewise, and many deficiencies, are consistent with pure love . ...[326]

This often made it difficult for the person to be sure of their present experience or caused them to doubt the reality of their prior experience. For example, in writing to Miss March he noted:

> From what not only you but many others likewise have experienced, we find there is very frequently a kind of wilderness state not only after justification, but even after deliverance from sin; ... But the most frequent cause of this second darkness or distress, I believe, is *evil reasoning* [emphasis mine]: by this, three in four of those who cast away their confidence are gradually induced to do so.[327]

He highlighted in this letter what he believed to be the single greatest cause of the loss of a relationship of perfect love; it was "evil reasoning" and the associated loss of simple trust in Christ each moment.[328] While the nature of this reasoning is not explicitly identified by Wesley, it is often juxtaposed with "simple faith" and would seem to indicate a destructive intellectual analysis of the experience, rather than maintaining trust in the relationship. Writing to Jenny Lee (a member of the Limerick Society), Wesley rejoiced that she was now delivered from sin, purified in heart, and set free in Christ. She needed to stand fast by faith, looking to Jesus and trusting him alone: "Do not reason one moment what to call it, whether perfection or anything else. You have faith: hold it fast. You have love: let it not go. Above all, you have Christ! Christ is yours! He is your Lord, your love, your all! Let Him be your portion in time and in eternity!"[329] He reminded her, "You have but *one rule, the oracles of God. His Spirit will always guide you*, according to His Word" (emphasis mine).[330] Ann Foard was one who had now lost this state of grace,[331] and in writing to encourage her Wesley said: "When you believed you had the pure love of God, you was not deceived: you really had a degree of it, and see that you let it not go; hold the beginning of your confidence steadfast till the end!"[332] He advised her to read his *Thoughts* and *Farther Thoughts upon Perfection* because the experience of Christian perfection can be recovered at

---

[326] *Letters* (Telford), 4:221. See also *Letters* (Telford), 3:212.

[327] *Letters* (Telford), 4:270.

[328] See, for example, *Letters* (Telford), 5:171. See also *Letters* (Telford), 4:321; 5:7, 94, 100-01.

[329] *Letters* (Telford), 4:183. See also Ibid., 184, 97.

[330] Ibid., 213. For this emphasis on the intimate link between Spirit and Scripture, see also Ibid., 157.

[331] Ibid., 265-66.

[332] Ibid., 214.

any moment by faith.

> Some years since, I was inclined to think that one who had once enjoyed and lost the pure love of God must never look to enjoy it again till they were just stepping into eternity. But experience has taught us better things. We have now numerous instances of those who had cast away that unspeakable blessing and now enjoy it in a larger measure than ever.[333]

Nor was it necessary for her to suffer for a period of time before reclaiming the blessing as it came by "simple faith" in a moment. It was dangerous to try to fashion her own experience after that of another in the society.[334] He urged her to hold to God's word and not human reasoning and to keep her confidence in God's promises.[335]

As with his pastoral advice on the earlier stages of the spiritual journey, Wesley warned his people not to associate with those who would now deny the truth of perfection or have set it too high.[336] It was important to receive encouragement from like-minded believers within the society. Writing to Jane Hilton on her marriage plans regarding her future husband: "Is he clear with regard to the doctrine of Perfection? Is he athirst for it?" If not, he would be a hindrance to her and she would be in danger of losing her love for God.[337] Writing to Mrs. Emma Moon (a member of the society at Yarm) he stated that "opposition from their brethren has been one cause why so many who were set free have not retained their liberty. But perhaps there was another more general cause: they had not proper help. One just saved from sin is like a new-born child, and needs as careful nursing." Since this was lacking so often, many lost their experience of grace.[338] He advised his people to testify of the experience to those seeking after it, for this would be the strongest motivator for them to seek the same.[339]

Wesley was sure that you must either go forward or backwards in your life with God, for you cannot stand still. It was important, therefore, to keep up reading, meditation and daily prayer.[340] It was vital to "grow in grace every hour, the more the better. Use now all the grace you have; this is certainly right: but also now expect all the grace you want! This is the secret of heart religion– at the present moment to work and to believe. Here is Christ your Lord, the lover of your soul. Give yourself up to Him without delay; and, as you can,

---

[333] *Letters* (Telford), 5:138.

[334] *Letters* (Telford), 4:269.

[335] *Letters* (Telford), 5:46.

[336] Ibid., 9.

[337] Ibid., 108. Jane Hilton was an active correspondent with Wesley and she married William Barton (in 1769).

[338] Ibid., 77.

[339] Ibid., 6.

[340] *Letters* (Telford), 4:103.

without reserve."[341] Writing to Peggy Dale he advised her that "certainly you not only need not sin, but you need not doubt any more. ... But you can only return what He has given by continually receiving more."[342] He clarified for her that "although it is certain the kind of wandering thoughts which you mention are consistent with pure love, yet it is highly desirable to be delivered from them, because (as you observe) they hinder profitable thoughts." God can do this, either in a moment or by degrees as there is yet more of God to be experienced.[343] Since temptation would remain a fact of spiritual life, even for those perfected in love,[344] it was important to maintain confidence in God's grace by being open to "receive a thousand more blessings; believe more, love more: you cannot love enough. Beware of sins of omission."[345] Facing temptation was not a sign of losing your experience of grace: "Amidst a thousand temptations you may retain unspotted purity. Abide in Him by simple faith this moment! Live, walk in love! The Lord increase it in you a thousand-fold! Take out of His fullness grace upon grace."[346]

Cautions to Those Professing Christian Perfection

This became particularly important after the excesses of the Maxfield-Bell revival in London. To guide his people Wesley wrote *Cautions and Directions given to the Greatest Professors in the Methodist Societies* in 1762. This contained much general and practical advice on holy living, but was especially concerned with the danger of enthusiasm (expecting the end without the means), and ascribing all manner of experiences to the work of God–dreams, visions, voices, impressions, and revelations. To combat this, Wesley advised:

> Try all things by the written word, and let all bow before it. You are in danger of enthusiasm every hour, if you depart ever so little from Scripture; yea, or from the plain, literal meaning of any text, taken in connexion with the context. And so you are, if you despise or lightly esteem reason, knowledge, or human learning; every one of which is an excellent gift of God, and may serve the noblest purposes.[347]

The very desire to grow in grace could lead to enthusiasm, to seek something "beside new degrees of love to God and man." He emphasised that the promises relating to salvation given in Scripture are mainly fulfilled at either justification or entire sanctification. "It remains only to experience them in higher degrees" and this was especially true of love to God and neighbour,

---

[341] *Letters* (Telford), 6:65. See also *Letters* (Telford), 3:217; 4:181; 5:6, 33, 63.
[342] *Letters* (Telford), 4:305.
[343] Ibid., 307.
[344] *Letters* (Telford), 5:62.
[345] *Letters* (Telford), 4:181. See also *Letters* (Telford), 3:217.
[346] *Letters* (Telford), 4:319. See also *Letters* (Telford), 5:48.
[347] *Works* (Jackson), 11:430.

for "if you are looking for anything but more love, you are looking wide of the mark."[348] He also reminded the societies of the danger of antinomianism, and restated that all of the moral law was now found within the law of love; and as a consequence they ought not to despise the means of grace.[349]

Of particular importance were the many and varied discussions on the place of human infirmities and their relationship to sin. This seemed to cause more problems for Wesley and his followers than any other pastoral issue, and many of his letters were taken up with trying to bring clarity out of much confusion. As he reminded Mrs. Bennis,

> The essential part of Christian holiness is giving the heart wholly to God; and certainly we need not lose any degree of that light and love which at first attend this: it is our own infirmity if we do; it is not the will of the Lord concerning us. ... you only have to receive it by simple faith. Nevertheless you will still be encompassed with numberless infirmities; for you live in an house of clay, and therefore this corruptible body will more or less press down the soul, yet not so as to prevent your rejoicing evermore and having a witness that your heart is all His.[350]

A similar point was made to Elizabeth Hardy: "For want of better bodily organs, they sometimes inevitably think, speak, or act wrong. Yet I think they need the advocacy of Christ, even for these involuntary defects; although they do not imply a defect of love, but of understanding. However that be, I cannot doubt the fact. They are all love; yet they cannot walk as they desire."[351] He told Miss March that that "to carry perfection higher is to sap the foundation of it and destroy it from the face of the earth. ... you should have let go the substance–lest, by aiming at a perfection which we cannot have till hereafter, you should cast away that which now belongs to the children of God. This is love filling the heart."[352]

> Thus much is certain: they that love God with all their heart and all men as themselves are scripturally perfect. And surely such there are; otherwise the promise of God would be a mere mockery of human weakness. Hold fast this. But then remember on the other hand, you have this treasure in an earthern vessel; you dwell in a poor, shattered house of clay, which presses down the immortal spirit. Hence all your thoughts, words, and actions are so imperfect, so far from coming up to the standard (that law of love which, but for the corruptible body, your soul

---

[348] Ibid. He reminded them that 1 Cor. 13 describes the whole life of holiness until we reach heaven. See also *Letters* (Telford), 5:149.
[349] *Works* (Jackson), 11:430-31.
[350] *Letters* (Telford), 5:56.
[351] *Letters* (Telford), 4:167.
[352] Ibid., 251. This was a consequence of the faulty view held by Maxfield and Bell; see Ibid., 245.

would answer in all instances), that you may well say till you go to Him you love: 'Every moment, Lord, I need The merit of thy death.'[353]

He told Dorothy Furly that while sanctification was an instantaneous deliverance from all sin and an instantaneous power to cleave to God, it was not a power never to think a useless thought or speak a useless word. This was due to the fact that while in the body we are always liable to mistake.[354]

> I want you to be all love. This is the perfection I believe and teach. And this perfection is consistent with a thousand nervous disorders, which that high-strained perfection is not. Indeed, my judgement is that ... to overdo is to undo, and that to set perfection to high ... is the most effectual (because unsuspected) way of driving it out of the world.[355]

A similar letter was written to Mrs. Ryan on the realities of mistakes:

> Suppose you are saved from sin, it is certain that you are not saved from a possibility of mistake. On this side, therefore, Satan may assault you; you may be deceived either as to persons or things. You may think better or ... you may think worse of them than they deserve. And hence words or actions may spring which, if not sinful in you, are certainly wrong in themselves, and which will and must appear sinful to those who cannot read your heart.[356]

He doubted if any escaped some degree of prejudice and the cure for this was love alone "for we cannot be easily prejudiced against any whom we love till that love declines."[357] These letters and many others contained Wesley's intense and searching questions on his people's spiritual state in order to prevent them being led into error by their personal experience.[358] He warned them about being above instruction from others, disparaging their understanding and experience, as all of this led to the danger of enthusiasm and destroyed connexion.[359] Wesley continued to emphasise to his people that sin was "a voluntary transgression of a known law" and this was its "proper definition." "I think it is of all such sin as is imputed to our condemnation. And it is a definition which has passed uncensored in the church for at least fifteen

---

[353] Ibid., 208. See also Ibid., 13.

[354] Ibid., 188. Thomas Maxfield had claimed otherwise.

[355] Ibid.

[356] *Letters* (Telford), 3:242. See also *Letters* (Telford), 5:6. Sarah Ryan served as housekeeper of the New Room at Bristol and the Kingswood school, as well as managing a school for orphans in London.

[357] *Letters* (Telford), 4:317.

[358] For examples of these questions, see *Letters* (Telford), 3:240-41, 43-44; 4:3-5, 6-7, 164-65, 180-81, 184, 233, 40, 305-06, 07, 10; 5:33, 45, 50, 97, 113, 128, 152. They were particularly focused on those who testified to an experience of Christian perfection.

[359] *Letters* (Telford), 5:17-18.

hundred years."[360] To endlessly focus on these issues was to lose spiritual vitality. "All in the body are liable to mistakes, practical as well as speculative. Shall we call them sins or no? I answer again and again, call them what you please."[361] He told Samuel Furly that forty or fifty people he knew had a clear testimony to perfect love but who stated that they still needed Christ's atoning blood every moment, and they needed him as their Priest as much as King. Even if they could not explain it, none disagreed on it.[362] Wesley later wrote: "I believe that a truly sanctified person does involuntarily fall short in divers instances of the rule marked out in the 13th chapter to the Corinthians. And that on this account, they continually need their Advocate with the Father. And I never talked with one person who denied it."[363]

> Here is a plain fact. You may dispute, reason, cavil about it, just as long as you please. Meantime I know by all manner of proof that these are the happiest and the holiest people in the kingdom. ... And shall I cease to rejoice over these holy, happy men because they mistake in their judgement? If they do, I would to God you and I and all mankind were under the same mistake; provided we had the same faith, the same love, and the same inward and outward holiness.[364]

In the midst of all these claims and counter-claims, it was easy to lose confidence in the power of God's grace to keep the person in a relationship of perfect love. Wesley found many wrote to him concerning doubts and fears, wrong thoughts and negative feelings, but, as he wrote to Miss March, none of these "prove that there is sin in your heart or that you are not a sacrifice to love."[365] He mentioned about twenty persons in Bristol society who presently testify to salvation from sin and have the witness, but if they lose it there is nothing easier to deny than that they ever had it. There are at least four hundred in London with the same experience, but around half have now lost it and claim they never had it, "it is so ready a way of excusing themselves for throwing away the blessed gift of God."[366] He reminds her that "There are innumerable degrees, both in a justified and a sanctified state, more than it is possible for us to exactly define. I have always thought the lowest degree of the latter implies the having but one desire and one design."[367] It was important to read the

---

[360] *Letters* (Telford), 4:155.
[361] Ibid.
[362] Ibid., 185-86. See also Ibid., 13, 189-90, 191, 272.
[363] Ibid., 272. Wesley wrote that none in the London Society denied this. Even though he disliked some of their expressions and opinions, he admired their tempers and their holy, unblameable, useful lives and total dependence on Christ. The core experience was to be "unblameable in spotless love"; see *Letters* (Telford), 5:106.
[364] *Letters* (Telford), 4:186. See also Ibid., 189-90.
[365] Ibid., 310-11.
[366] Ibid., 313-14.
[367] *Letters* (Telford), 5:81.

testimonies of the dying saints and converse with them where possible.[368] He advised her to focus on love and the strength it brings: "At many times, indeed, we do not know how the power of the Highest suddenly overshadows us, while either the first or the pure love is shed abroad in our hearts. But at other times He confirms and increases that love in a gradual or almost insensible manner."[369] She was to continue in her walk with God "by simple faith and holy, humble love" and not be dissuaded by the arguments of others. He affirmed Mary Thornton, a friend of Miss March, had experienced "the pure love of God" and none should use her current trials to reason her out of it.[370] In a similar fashion, he wrote to Mrs. Moon: "There is no weakness either in our body or mind but Satan endeavours to avail himself of it. That kind of dullness or listlessness I take to be originally a pure effect of bodily constitution. As such it is not imputable to us in any degree unless we give way to it. So long as we diligently resist, it is no more blameable than sleepiness or weakness of body."[371]

Conclusion

It has been established that Wesley's picture of the fundamental nature of God and how he interacts with humanity did not greatly alter during this period. He continues to believe that God's essential nature is love and that all other aspects of his nature and character must flow from, and be in harmony with, this core affirmation. Wesley has demonstrated that this picture is biblical and can be found in the writings of the Church and modelled in the lives of its saints. It is this understanding that provides the framework for his theological method and theologising. If love and trust are central, then Christianity is essentially about the heart and not the mind, it is about passion and not performance, about purity of intention in a relationship and not intellectual comprehension of propositional truth as an academic exercise. This is not to say that the latter understanding has no place, but it is clearly subordinate to the former. A relationship of love cannot finally be conducted through a third party; it requires the actual presence together of the lover and the beloved. It is this intense conviction about God's love for us that brings Wesley to state that we must personally experience ("feel") that love before a lasting relationship is possible. The ministry of the Holy Spirit lies at the heart of the whole Wesleyan conception of salvation, since it is his ministry that enables the Christian to personally experience the love of God made available to us through Jesus Christ, to respond by grace and then to fully participate in the life of the Triune God and the community of faith. Post-Aldersgate, this perspective dominates

---

[368] Ibid., 95-96.
[369] Ibid., 135.
[370] Ibid., 148.
[371] Ibid., 69.

all of Wesley's writings. Clapper's argument for "heart religion" to be seen as Wesley's "orienting concern" is well-supported by Wesley's writings.

Wesley's developing theological method is in harmony with his understanding of the essential nature of Christianity as a relationship of love to be experienced (heart religion) and this emphasis places the living voice of the Holy Spirit to persons in community at the centre of his theological method. He was convinced that the Spirit can and does directly influence the hearts and minds of people, but if this is all he does it reduces Christianity to pure subjectivity. The difficulty is not with God's objective reality as a Person but with our subjective experience because it is distorted by human error in apprehending, understanding, describing and interpreting that reality due to the nature of present human existence. The Spirit, therefore, makes use of a number of 'means' in order to ensure a degree of objective witness to God's nature, character, purposes and their implications for human salvation. The primary 'means' the Spirit uses is Scripture, which is God's word written, and any direct impression of the Spirit must be in full harmony with this written word. Judgements concerning this harmony involves reason, the ethos of the community and the practical outcomes in personal and community life. In Wesley's theological method, it is the living voice of God through the Spirit that is absolutely indispensable and all other means are subordinate to this. There is really only one ultimate theological source and authority for Wesley– and that is God himself. All other elements must be understood and applied in ways that reflect this essential truth: the living presence of the Spirit must infuse the use of Scripture, reason, ethos and experience (both personal and community, past and present). This ensures that there is a place in theologising for each person's own experience of God reflected upon rationally, while being measured against the experiences and reasoned reflections of the community (past and present). These are in dynamic tension with the norm of Scripture as the primary means utilised by the Spirit to limit excessive subjectivism and error (Wesley's linking of the of Scripture as the only "rule" with the Spirit as the only "guide"). The crucial role of the community for Wesley is in originally creating and then maintaining, through the presence of the Spirit, an ethos that fundamentally shapes the process of theologising by providing the parameters and attitudes necessary to remain in harmony with that community and its interpretations and applications of Scripture. Here the emerging ethos of his own Methodist societies (and not simply the early church or the Church of England) is decisive. Scripture certainly plays a central and determinative role in Wesley's theological methodology, but it was his family, friends and church community that taught him to read the text soteriologically, to focus on the message as a whole rather than its parts, and to locate essential gospel truth by the analogy of faith rather than proof texts. It is equally important to note that this was not simply an historical or intellectual reading of the text, but an experimental one–it had to make a verifiable difference in life and practice as evidence of the validity of the interpretation and application.

Finding a conceptual model by which to explore and explicate Wesley's theological method has not been an easy task for the many scholars who have worked in this area. It is especially difficult to portray a dynamic model on paper. Any suitable model to be developed must take full account of the indispensable living presence of the Holy Spirit, who normally makes use of the means of grace, but is not absolutely bound to use any or all of them. This eliminates any purely mechanical model or static hierarchy amongst the elements. In the light of the research findings thus far, the model proposed is a living, biological, neural matrix. This is a living, dynamic, holistic, interconnected network of nodes, in which every element and their mutual relationships are essential for the whole to function in a healthy manner; however, the network can still function to some degree if one or more of the nodes are not utilised. The whole network is energised by the living presence of the Holy Spirit and without his presence it becomes dead and useless. The 'means', apart from the living presence of the Spirit, are simply sources and tools that can be manipulated by persons and communities for their own purposes. The critical elements (nodes) proposed for the matrix are Scripture, reason, community ethos and Christian experience (both personal and corporate). Scripture is the key node in the network and normally all the others *would* engage with it during theological reflection and *must* ultimately engage with it before any essential theological doctrines and/or their implications are articulated by the community of faith. The ministry of the Spirit apart from Scripture is dangerously subjective and open to distortion due to human sinfulness. Wesley's genius is found in the holistic picture that this model represents and this study contends that it is faithful to his actual theologising as we have access to it through his writings.

It is early in this period that Wesley makes the significant distinction between the substance and the circumstance of a doctrine. He understood the substance to be primarily anchored in Scripture, but the circumstance was to be determined by the experience of the Christian community located in time and space. At a theoretical level, the link between substance and circumstance may or may not be clear, but Wesley maintains a consistent viewpoint that the ability to conceptualise and articulate doctrinal truth is not the primary consideration – it is the heart experience of love that is critical. Wesley was convinced that the substance of his understanding of Christian perfection was scriptural and that his reading of the texts could be supported by other members of the Christian community, particularly those from the early church. This was undoubtedly a continuation of the position held in earlier years and illustrated particularly by his sermon on the circumcision of the heart. It is Wesley's understanding of the circumstance of Christian perfection that changes in this period. There are far fewer references to his own spiritual state during these years and an increasing focus on his pastoral leadership of the Methodist societies. Wesley's role as the spiritual guide of the people called Methodists enables him to preach, teach and counsel his followers directly and personally.

Importantly, it also gives him a forum in which to test his understanding of the substance of Christian perfection as he receives feedback from those he taught (their personal testimonies and written accounts), as well as being able to examine both their lives and their claims. The structures of his societies gave him a living laboratory in which to propose, test and evaluate his pastoral theology and here the wisdom and practical experience of his people are paramount, not doctrinal dissection and analysis. It is focused on heart experience and transformed lives rather than mental acuity and intellectual comprehension.

In his pastoral writings a number of vital affirmations emerge. Wesley continues to strongly maintain the intimate link between the living voice of the Spirit (the "guide") and the written word of Scripture (the "rule"). The Scripture must always be applied by the Spirit and so there is an emphasis on the Christian experience of the reader(s) rather than merely life experience in general. However, it was vital that his people listen to the Spirit and read the Bible within a Methodist framework; particularly the Methodist hermeneutical approach of working with the analogy of faith rather than seeking proof texts. Wesley keeps the emphasis in Christian perfection on love and the positive desire for its fullness, rather than the more negative focus on sin and the desire to be cleansed. The role of personal and community expectation and experience is very important. He constantly urges them to listen to Methodist preachers, participate in Methodist worship, and read Methodist works, with Wesley's own sermons and other writings being of critical importance. His people needed to have regular conversation with those who were either testifying to Christian perfection or diligently seeking it, for without community support and encouragement many would simply give up. There are constant references to personal testimony (both spoken and written), as well as the importance of the Conferences and other Methodist meetings. It is in this living laboratory that the circumstance of Christian perfection is worked through and the conditions needed to be as favourable as possible. He believes that to enter into disputes and argumentation over the nature and experience of Christian perfection will be completely counter-productive, as it tends to undermine the necessary trust in God's promises and faithfulness. This is why Wesley constantly urges his people not to read, hear or converse with those who would deny the Methodist understanding. The dialogue and debate with his critics was conducted at the level of doctrinal substance, but this type of conversation was not to be imported into his societies. This explains his many cautions against the misuse of reason. It was a fine tool in debate with his critics, but could easily undermine the "simple trust" (faith) so necessary if his people were to experience and maintain a relationship of perfect love. In the societies it was common sense and wisdom that were to be in evidence, not philosophical argument. As in every relationship of love, the acids of doubt, discouragement and criticism were fatal, hence the strategic role of the societies to provide an atmosphere (ethos) of encouragement and support.

It appears that there is a change in theological method when you move from Wesley's consideration of the substance of Christian perfection to its circumstance. Material on the substance is primarily found in his sermons, the *Notes*, and several smaller treatises, where Scripture is paramount–both in formal quotations, inexact references and allusions. The language and imagery of the sermons are shaped by the Bible and they are rich with direct references to Scriptural texts. In this setting, reason is clearly a tool used to work with community ethos and Christian experience in interpreting the text. However, when we move to the pastoral advice given in his letters, the lack of direct or indirect reference to Scripture in comparison with the sermons and treatises is noticeable. He constantly urges them to read Methodist publications (largely his own), and these are rich in Scripture–but Scripture that has already been interpreted and applied by Wesley and other sympathetic writers. His people are rarely referred to the Bible text on its own, which surely indicates the vital importance of the perspective of the reading community and Wesley's determination that this be a Methodist community. It seems that in working with the circumstance of perfection, Wesley was very much inclined to use pastoral wisdom (reason plus Christian experience, both personal and community, present and past) as a key component of his theological method. In all cases, the work of the Spirit in the person and the community is paramount, but it does appear that the Spirit works primarily through different means as the type of theologising changes–from the academic and theoretical substantiation and defence of his doctrinal position, to the practical and experiential wisdom that guides the lives and relationships of the people called Methodists.

CHAPTER 5

Wesley as the Mature Leader of the Methodist Movement: The Years of Reflection and Consolidation, 1770 – 1791

From the study of Wesley's development as the leader of the Methodist movement, a number of issues relating to his theological methodology have been identified. In particular, there appears to be a difference in approach to theologising between his writings on the substance and the circumstance of Christian perfection. In this period of his life we engage with the mature leader of Methodism as he deals with the final major theological challenges to his spiritual vision of the God-human relationship and its practical implications. One of these emerges from outside Methodism (the Calvinist controversy) and the other from within it: is Christian perfection a theological provincialism or is it of the essence of Methodism as a movement? This chapter examines his formal and pastoral writings to see how he responds to these issues and their ramifications for his people. It seeks to verify that the major aspects of Wesley's spiritual vision concerning the God-human relationship remains consistent with his earlier periods, and that the model proposed for understanding his theological method is faithful to Wesley's doctrinal and pastoral writings. His understanding of the substance of Christian perfection is still essentially the same as his ground-breaking sermon, "The Circumcision of the Heart" in 1733. The critical change observed after 1740 was in his pastoral writings on the circumstance of Christian perfection, with an emphasis on Christian experience, community ethos and pastoral wisdom. An examination of the material from this final stage of his life and ministry will establish that this finding remains unchallenged in these decades.

The chapter begins with a brief review of his spiritual vision to show how it remains consistent with the perspective of the Oxford years. The elements of his theological method are then examined and any changes from the previous period are noted. As the Methodist movement has now been in existence for over thirty years and a new generation has grown up within its communities, Wesley has to deal with a number of new issues concerning the spiritual experience of his people. Attention is therefore given to his understanding of the substance of Christian perfection in the light of the concerns that have arisen from within and outside of Methodism. The final section explores his pastoral methodology as he deals with key aspects of the experiential and practical outcomes of the doctrine.

Wesley's Spiritual Vision: His Understanding of the Nature of God, Human Beings and their Relationship

There is no evidence of any significant change in Wesley's spiritual vision during these final years. He continued to believe that God was essentially a God of love and that Christianity was concerned with a personal experience of this love, which was then returned to God and neighbour. Wesley consistently defined the whole purpose of current human existence as preparation for eternity, enabled by God who saved "first from the guilt of sin, having redemption through his blood; then from the power, which shall have no more dominion over thee; and then from the root of it, into the whole image of God. And being restored both to the favour and image of God, thou shalt know, love, and serve him to all eternity."[1] To love God wholeheartedly "is the truest happiness, indeed the only true happiness which is to be found under the sun. So does all experience prove the justness of that reflection which was made long ago: 'Thou hast made us for thyself; and our heart cannot rest until it resteth in thee.'"[2]

The Divine-Human Synergy in Salvation

During these decades the disputes with the Calvinists served to emphasise the centrality of love for Wesley's whole conception of salvation, and love required freedom (liberty) for its existence. He believed that the Calvinists had confounded the work of God as Creator with his work as Governor of the creation "wherein he does not, cannot possibly, act according to his own mere sovereign will; but, as he has expressly told us, according to the invariable rules both of justice and mercy." Wesley argued that "all reward as well as all punishment, pre-supposes free agency; and whatever creature is incapable of choice, is incapable of either one or the other." Thus when God acted as Governor he no longer acted as "mere Sovereign." We are creatures who can either obey or disobey God, "so every individual may, after all that God has done, either improve his grace, or make it of none effect." Therefore all will be rewarded for what they chose and none will be punished for what could not be chosen.[3]

---

[1] *Works*, 4:26. See also Ibid., 37.

[2] *Works*, 3:189. The quotation is from Augustine and is common in Wesley; see for example *Works*, 3:35, 97; 4:64; *Letters* (Telford), 7:58. On Wesley's use of Augustine, see John C. English, "References to St. Augustine in the Works of John Wesley," *Asbury Theological Journal* 60, no. 2 (Fall, 2005).

[3] *Works* (Jackson), 10:362-63. See also *Works*, 23:55.

> For [God] created man in his own image: ... endued with understanding, with will, or affections, and liberty–without which neither his understanding nor his affections could have been of any use, neither would he have been capable either of vice or virtue. He could not be a moral agent, ... all the manifold wisdom of God (as well as all his power and goodness) is displayed in governing man as man; ... as an intelligent and free spirit, capable of choosing either good or evil. ... governing men so as not to destroy either their understanding, will, or liberty! He commands all things ... to assist man in attaining the end of his being, in working out his own salvation–so far as it can be done without compulsion, without overruling his liberty. ... to afford man every possible help, in order to his doing good and eschewing evil, which can be done without turning man into a machine; without making him incapable of virtue or vice, reward or punishment.[4]

In order to affirm both the reality of human sinfulness that would seem to preclude a free response to God, and the need for liberty if a relationship of love were to be genuine, Wesley stressed the role of prevenient grace in salvation.[5]

> ... salvation begins with what is usually termed ... 'preventing grace'; including the first wish to please God, the first dawn of light concerning his will, and the first slight, transient conviction of having sinned against him. All these imply some tendency toward life, some degree of salvation, the beginning of a deliverance from a blind, unfeeling heart, quite insensible of God and the things of God. Salvation is carried on by 'convincing grace', usually in Scripture termed 'repentance', which brings a larger measure of self-knowledge, and a farther deliverance from the heart of stone. Afterwards we experience the proper Christian salvation, ... [6]

He explained to Isaac Andrews: "Undoubtedly faith is *the work of God*; and yet it is *the duty of man* to believe. And every man may believe *if* he will, though not *when* he will. If he seek faith in the appointed way, sooner or later the power of God will be present, whereby (1) God works, and by *His* power (2)

---

[4] *Works*, 2:540-41. See also *Works*, 2:400-03, 17, 37-50, 71-84, 88-89, 529, 53; 4:24; *Works* (Jackson), 10:361-63, 457-80; *Letters* (Telford), 5:211-12; 6:263, 287. For a practical application of his belief, see *Thoughts upon Slavery* in *Works* (Jackson), 11:59-79. For an examination of the relationship of liberty, understanding, affections and will, see Jerry L. Walls, "'As the Waters Cover the Sea': John Wesley on the Problem of Evil," *Faith and Philosophy* 13, no. 4 (1996); Granville C. Henry, "John Wesley's Doctrine of Free Will," *London Quarterly and Holborn Review* 185 (July 1960).

[5] *Works*, 3:199-209. See also *Works*, 4:4. For an example of how prevenient grace works in a person's life, see "On Conscience" in Ibid., 480-90.

[6] *Works*, 3:203-04. If God did not work first, salvation would be impossible. His conclusion was: "For, first, God works; therefore you *can* work. Secondly, God works; therefore you *must* work." See Ibid., 206. See also Ibid., 385-97, 432; *Works* (Jackson), 8:322-23; *Letters* (Telford), 5:263.

man believes."[7] Wesley went so far as to say "perfect love and Christian liberty are the very same thing; and those two expressions are equally proper, being equally scriptural. ... And what is Christian liberty but another word for holiness?"[8] He quoted with approval Augustine's dictum that "he that made us *without ourselves* will not save us *without ourselves*."[9]

> [God] did not take away your understanding, but enlightened and strengthened it. He did not destroy any of your affections; rather they were more vigorous than before. Least of all did he take away your liberty, your power of choosing good or evil; he did not force you; but being assisted by his grace you, like Mary, chose the better part. Just so has he assisted ... many thousands in a nation, without depriving any of them of that liberty which is essential to a moral agent.[10]

Wesley conceded that there may be rare cases where God worked for a time irresistibly in a person's life but even then they must make the final decision about their salvation. He was convinced that since God provided grace freely for all to seek his way, no one will go to hell for eternity but those who choose to do so; it would not be by God's absolute decree.[11] He was equally sure that all that is good in human beings was produced solely by the power of God, even when "God has now thoroughly cleansed our heart, and scattered the last remains of sin" we still remain unable to do good unless every moment we are endued with power from God.[12]

Wesley's Theological Methodology:
Its Sources, Tools and Their Interrelationship

Albert Outler identified this period as "a second major phase in Wesley's development as a 'folk theologian'."[13] In these decades "... he is intent upon an updating of his message in the light of unfolding cultural changes in an age of transition."[14] He had to deal with the debate between Calvinists and Wesleyans over predestination and antinomianism,[15] as well increasing pressure to separate

---

[7] *Letters* (Telford), 7:202. He explained: "In order of thinking God's working goes first; but not in order of time. Believing is the act of the human mind, strengthened by the power of God." See pp. 202-03. See also Ibid., 362.
[8] *Letters* (Telford), 5:203.
[9] *Works*, 2:490.
[10] Ibid., 489.
[11] Ibid., 366-68. See also *Works*, 23:355; *Works* (Jackson), 10:360; *Letters* (Telford), 6:239-40.
[12] *Works*, 3:53. See also *Works* (Jackson), 8:285; 13:337-38.
[13] *Works*, 2:353.
[14] Ibid., 351.
[15] Ibid., 349. For background on the development of the Calvinist dispute, see Ibid., 325-29. The emergence of *The Arminian Magazine* in 1778 to uphold "universal redemption" over against "particular redemption" is very important. See his

from the Church of England.[16] These issues set the parameters within which his theological method needs to be considered in these years.

"The true, the scriptural, experimental religion" of the heart

Wesley continued to maintain his conviction that the true definition of religion was "not this or that opinion, or system of opinions, be they ever so true, ever so scriptural. ... [It is] walking in the love of God and man."[17] When he wrote to his nephew Samuel Wesley on the definition of religion, he said, "I do not mean external religion, but the religion of the heart; the religion which Kempis, Pascal, Fénelon enjoyed: that life of God in the soul of man, the walking with God and having fellowship with the Father and the Son."[18] He sustained his belief that Christianity was primarily about a relationship in love rather than doctrinal correctness centred in rational comprehension. This can be illustrated by his only sermon specifically focused on the doctrine of the Trinity, which he regarded as an essential doctrine. He emphasised that it was belief in the fact of the Trinity that was critical, not any particular explanation of it.[19] "The Bible barely requires you to believe such *facts*, not the manner of them. Now the mystery does not lie in the *fact*, but altogether in the *manner*. ... But would it not be absurd in me to deny the fact because I do not understand the manner? That is, to reject *what God has revealed* because I do not comprehend *what he has not revealed*?"[20] In other words, it is the fact that is the object of our faith, not the manner, and we did not need to be able to understand this in order for belief to exist. Doctrinal "opinions" were not concerned with the essential "facts" of the faith and thus could not be the benchmark in deciding whether a person was or was not a Christian.

> ... it is certain that opinion is not religion: no, not right opinion, assent to one or to ten thousand truths. ... right opinion is as distant from religion as the east is from the west. Persons may be quite right in their opinions, and yet have no religion at all. And on the other hand persons may be truly religious who hold many wrong opinions. Can anyone possibly doubt of this while there are Romanists in the world? For who can deny, not only that many of them formerly have been truly religious (as à Kempis, Gregory Lopez, and the Marquis de Renty), but that many of them even at this day are real, inward Christians? And yet what an heap of

---

introductions in John Wesley, *The Arminian Magazine: Consisting of Extracts and Original Treatises on Universal Redemption*, vol. 1 (London: R. Hawes, 1778); John Wesley, *The Arminian Magazine: Consisting of Extracts and Original Treatises on Universal Redemption*, vol. 2 (London: J. Fry, 1779), iv-vi.

[16] See *Works*, 9:538.
[17] *Works*, 4:57. See also *Works*, 4:66-67; 23:38, 125.
[18] *Letters* (Telford), 8:218. See also *Works*, 2:483; *Letters* (Telford), 8:79.
[19] *Works*, 2:376-77. See also Ibid., 426-27; *Letters* (Telford), 5:270; 6:213.
[20] *Works*, 2:383-84.

erroneous opinions do they hold, delivered by tradition from their fathers! Nay, who can doubt of it while there are Calvinists in the world–asserters of absolute predestination? For who will dare to affirm that none of these are truly religious men? ... but many of them are now real Christians, loving God and all mankind. ...

Hence we cannot but infer that there are ten thousand mistakes which may consist with real religion; with regard to which every candid, considerate man will think and let think. But there are some truths more important than others. ... there are some which it nearly concerns us to know, as having a close connection with vital religion.[21]

When Wesley preached the funeral sermon for George Whitefield,[22] a staunch Calvinist and upholder of the very doctrines he so strongly opposed, he commended Whitefield for upholding "the grand scriptural doctrines," while admitting they disagreed over doctrines of "a less essential nature," and these clearly included the much disputed "opinions" over predestination and election, with their corollary of antinomianism.[23] Wesley commended all to "think and

---

[21] *Works*, 2:374-76. Wesley himself was content with the statements found in the Athanasian Creed; see p. 378-79. For an example of his views on the impact of Calvinism on spiritual life, see *Letters* (Telford), 5:282. See also his letter to his nephew Charles Wesley on the occasion of his younger brother becoming a Roman Catholic in *Letters* (Telford), 7:216-17, 30-31. His views on Roman Catholicism were expressed in *Works* (Jackson), 10:140-58, 173-75, 509-11. He based his rejection of their claims on the teaching of Scripture and his reading of "antiquity."

[22] George Whitefield (1717-1770) was a member of the Holy Club at Oxford, a close friend of the Wesleys and an outstanding evangelical preacher. Their relationship was strained after 1739 due to Whitefield's Calvinistic beliefs. For a thorough examination of their relationship, see James L. Schwenk, *Catholic Spirit: Wesley, Whitefield, and the Quest for Evangelical Unity in Eighteenth-Century British Methodism* (Lanham, MD: Scarecrow Press, 2008).

[23] A full examination of this critical debate is beyond the scope of this book. The historical background may be found in Rack, *Reasonable Enthusiast*, 197-202, 450-61; Albert Brown-Lawson, *John Wesley and the Anglican Evangelicals of the Eighteenth Century: A Study in Cooperation and Separation with Special Reference to the Calvinistic Controversies* (Durham, Eng: Pentland Press, 1994). Critical explorations of various aspects of the controversy may be found in Allan Coppedge, *John Wesley in Theological Debate* (Wilmore, KY: Wesley Heritage Press, 1987); Timothy L. Smith, "George Whitefield and Wesleyan Perfectionism," *WTJ* 19, no. 1 (Spring, 1984); Luke L. Keefer, "Characteristics of Wesley's Arminianism," *WTJ* 22, no. 1 (Spring, 1987); Timothy L. Smith, *Whitefield and Wesley on the New Birth* (Grand Rapids, MI: Francis Asbury Press, 1986); Herbert Boyd McGonigle, *Sufficient Saving Grace: John Wesley's Evangelical Arminianism* (Carlisle: Paternoster Press, 2001). Wesley's primary objection to the Calvinist doctrine of the absolute decrees was that they undercut the whole Scriptural picture of God as love. See for example his letter on this to Samuel Sparrow in *Letters* (Telford), 6:60-62. See also Ibid., 224; Tyson and Schlenther, 47-176. For an assessment of the common ground between the two camps, see Richard E. Brantley, "The Common Ground of Wesley and Edwards," *Harvard Theological Review*

let think" on these while holding fast to the "essentials." These he defined as giving God the glory for whatever good is found in persons, Christ's death/resurrection as the sole meritorious cause of all we do or enjoy, justification by faith, the new birth, and the indwelling of the Spirit.[24] Wesley particularly emphasised the presence of the Spirit in the person's life for "without this the purity of our doctrines would only increase our condemnation."[25] Even though Wesley himself strongly upheld the need of doctrinal orthodoxy on the "essentials," he continued to believe that this was not a crucial requirement for a person to experience God's salvation. In one of the last sermons he wrote, Wesley commented on some who said that no matter the change in people's hearts or lives, it was vital for them to have a clear doctrinal understanding of the "capital doctrines":

> I believe the merciful God regards the lives and tempers of men more than their ideas. I believe he respects the goodness of the heart rather than the clearness of the head; and that if the heart of a man be filled (by the grace of God, and the power of his Spirit) with the humble, gentle, patient love of God and man, God will not cast him into everlasting fire prepared for the devil and his angels because his ideas are not clear, or because his conceptions are confused. Without holiness, I own, no man shall see the Lord; but I dare not add, or clear ideas.[26]

He affirmed that a "catholic love" and a "catholic spirit" were the qualities that should be demonstrated by every Christian.[27] When defending against personal attacks "those who plead the cause of the God of love, are to imitate Him they serve; and however provoked, to use no other weapons than those of truth and love, of Scripture and reason."[28]

83, no. 3 (1990); Geoffrey Wainwright, *Geoffrey Wainwright on Wesley and Calvin* (Melbourne: Uniting Church Press, 1987); Robert Doyle Smith, "John Wesley and Jonathan Edwards on Religious Experience: A Comparative Analysis," *WTJ* 25, no. 1 (Spring, 1990).

[24] *Works*, 2:341-43. See Outler's introduction for important background material on their relationship and doctrinal disputes, pp. 325-29. See also Wesley's letters to the Countess of Huntingdon in *Letters* (Telford), 5:258-60, 274-75.

[25] Ibid., 343. Note again the emphasis on specifically Christian experience through the presence of the Spirit.

[26] *Works*, 4:175. The "capital doctrines" were identified as "the fall of man, justification by faith, and of the atonement made by the death of Christ, and of his righteousness transferred to them." For other lists of essential doctrines in this period, see *Letters* (Telford), 5:231, 327-28; 6:28.

[27] *Works*, 2:344. For an example, see his warm letter to James Hutton in *Letters* (Telford), 5:294 and the *Journal* entry in *Works*, 22:303. See also *Letters* (Telford), 6:226, 276.

[28] *Works* (Jackson), 10:413. Wesley himself did not always observe this; see Outler's n. 86 on his rather strong and personal condemnation of Augustus Toplady in *Works*, 22:474.

> ... the kingdom of God is not opinions (how right soever they be), but righteousness and peace and joy in the Holy Ghost. ... Shall we for opinions destroy the work of God, or give up love, the very badge of our profession? Nay, by this shall men know that we belong to the Lover of Souls, to Him who loved us and gave Himself for us.[29]

The Personal Encounter with God: The Holy Spirit and the Scriptures

In these last two decades of his life, Wesley continued to believe that every important truth relating to our salvation was revealed "in the oracles of God."[30] In a sermon reflecting on the rise and development of the Methodist movement, he emphasised that

> From the very beginning, from the time that four young men united together, each of them was *homo unius libri*–a man of one book. *God taught them* [emphasis mine] all to make his 'Word a lantern unto their feet, and a light in all their paths.' They had one, and only one rule of judgment with regard to all their tempers, words, and actions, namely, the oracles of God. They were one and all determined to be *Bible-Christians.* ... And indeed unto this day it is their constant endeavour to think and speak as the oracles of God.[31]

He appealed for his Methodists to consider this question: "Hath not the whole word of God been delivered to you, and without any mixture of error? Were not the fundamental doctrines both of free, full, present justification delivered to you, as well as sanctification, both gradual and instantaneous? Was not every branch both of inward and outward holiness clearly opened and earnestly applied?"[32] It was this belief that gave him the confidence that he had correctly understood the nature of religion:

> According to these [the oracles of God] it lies in one single point: it is neither more nor less than love–it is love which 'is the fulfilling of the law', 'the end of the commandment'. Religion is the love of God and our neighbour . ... This love, ruling the whole life, animating all our tempers and passions, directing all our thoughts, words, and actions, is 'pure religion and undefiled'.[33]

---

[29] *Letters* (Telford), 5:339. See also *Works*, 22:316; *Works* (Jackson), 13:264-67; *Letters* (Telford), 7:333; Tyson and Schlenther, 105, 113.

[30] *Works*, 3:31. See, for example, his refusal to speculate on angels and demons since there is minimal revelation concerning them in the Scriptures; *Works*, 2:474; 3:4-29; 4:7. Likewise he refused to speculate on the nature of Hades and heaven since Scripture is largely silent; see *Works*, 4:191-99; *Letters* (Telford), 5:221; 6:298; 7:82.

[31] *Works*, 3:504. See also *Works* 3:496; 4:145-46; *Works* (Jackson), 13:258-61.

[32] *Works*, 3:516.

[33] Ibid., 189. See also *Works*, 2:462-63, 70; 3:22, 99, 117.

The nature of true religion was fully outlined in 1 Cor. 13, "And to him who attentively considers the whole tenor both of the Old and New Testament it will be equally plain that works springing from this love are the highest part of the religion therein revealed."[34] Methodism "... is the religion of the Bible . ... So that whoever allows the Scripture to be the Word of God must allow this to be true religion."[35] He continued his rejection of mysticism primarily because it was unscriptural: "... it is not only quite unconnected with Scripture, but quite inconsistent with it. It strikes at the very foundation of Scripture. If this stands, the Bible must fall."[36] Wesley admitted that while the early Methodists were influenced by other people's doctrinal understanding, the basic direction was set by the Scriptures. "On Scripture and common sense I build all my principles. Just so far as it agrees with these I regard human authority."[37] He continued to acknowledge the input of the Anglican Homilies on their understanding of justification by faith, but "they were never clearly convinced that we are justified by faith alone till they carefully consulted these, and compared them with the Sacred Writings, particularly St. Paul's Epistle to the Romans."[38] Likewise, they learned much from the Roman Catholics on the doctrine of sanctification, "But it has pleased God to give the Methodists a full and clear knowledge of each, and the wide difference between them."[39] Wesley failed to realise that his understanding was in fact shaped by his reading community; a person from another reading community could look at these same texts and not find the same corroboration.

Wesley remained confident that a sound interpretation could only arise from first grasping the whole picture of salvation revealed in Scripture, rather than beginning with isolated proof texts which could easily be manipulated to prove almost any doctrinal or practical point.[40] For example, when considering the nature of "real religion," he reminded his people that "it runs through the Bible from the beginning to the end, in one connected chain. And the agreement of every part of it with every other is properly the analogy of faith."[41] He commented in another sermon: "How small a number will you find that have any conception of the analogy of faith! Of the connected chain of Scripture truths, and their relation to each other. Namely, the natural corruption of man, justification by faith, the new birth, inward and outward holiness."[42] In line

---

[34] *Works*, 3:405. See also Ibid., 292-307.
[35] *Works*, 3:585-86. See also *Letters* (Telford), 6:123.
[36] *Works* (Jackson), 13:436. See also *Works*, 22:217, 383.
[37] *Letters* (Telford), 6:49.
[38] *Works*, 3:505.
[39] Ibid., 506-07.
[40] For insightful comment on this issue, see Gutenson, "Theological Method for a Man of One Book," 54-61. For a thorough discussion of Wesley's understanding of inspiration and infallibility, see Jones, *Wesley's Use of Scripture*, especially 129-59.
[41] *Works*, 2:483.
[42] *Works*, 4:89. See also *Works*, 2:501.

with his earlier convictions, Wesley continued to emphasise that "God taught them" the value of the Scripture [43] and this underscores the continued reliance on the ministry of the Spirit and specifically Christian experience. When some of his followers found difficulties arising when they tried to compare their spiritual experience with their understanding of a particular text, Wesley warned them of the dangers of interpreting a text isolated from the overall tenor of Scripture. For example, when Hannah Ball sought help on interpreting Rev. 3:12 because it had produced doubts as to her own experience, he wrote:

> From what has lately occurred you may learn a good lesson–not to build your faith on a single text of Scripture, and much less on a particular sense of it. Whether this text be interpreted in one or the other way, the work of God in your soul is the same. Beware, therefore, of supposing that you are mistaken in the substance of your experience because you may be mistaken with regard to the meaning of a particular scripture. Pray; and observe that *God Himself may, and frequently does, apply a scripture to the heart* (either in justifying or sanctifying a soul) *in what is not its direct meaning* (emphasis mine).[44]

Wesley was convinced that a genuine heart experience of God need not be tightly linked to a correct interpretation of the text, since God has full authority over the text and can apply it through the Spirit as he chooses. This affirms that Scripture, while at the core of his theological methodology, could not be substituted for the direct work of the Spirit in the life.

The Personal Encounter with God: Reason and Experience

In the light of the rising influence of the Enlightenment and growing confidence in the powers of human reason, Wesley sought to explain the nature and critical role of reason for Methodist doctrine and practice.[45] He constantly warned both his supporters and his critics about the dangers of either undervaluing or overvaluing reason; in the latter case usually because they "do not receive the Scriptures as the oracles of God."[46] In a letter to Joseph Benson he wrote, "You will observe that it is dangerous on such subjects to depart from Scripture either as to language or sentiment. I believe that most of the controversies which have disturbed the Church have arisen from people's wanting to be wise above what is written, not contented with what God has plainly revealed there." He urged him not to forget this by "metaphysical

---

[43] *Works*, 3:504.
[44] *Letters* (Telford), 5:328. Hannah Ball was an important member of the High Wycombe society and a frequent correspondent with Wesley.
[45] *Works*, 3:588-89. He includes extensive quotations from both of his *Appeals*; see pp. 586-88. He also wrote approvingly of John Locke's *Essay Concerning Human Understanding;* see *Works*, 2:589; 22:313-14.
[46] *Works*, 2:588. See also Ibid.,568-86; *Letters* (Telford), 5:228.

disquisition" on things not revealed, nor to reason on such things, but to simply believe what was revealed in the Scriptures.[47] Wesley specifically rejected the teachings of Rousseau, Voltaire and David Hume who sought "to establish a religion which should stand on its own foundation, independent on [sic] any revelation whatever, yea, not supposing even the being of a God."[48] He commented: "how little information do we receive from unassisted reason" and so we need revelation to provide that indispensable support.[49] With the fresh outbreak of the Calvinist controversy in 1770, Wesley commented to Joseph Benson that very little is done in the world by clear reason: "Passion and prejudice govern the world, only under the name of reason. It is our part, by religion and reason joined, to counteract them all we can."[50] However, he recognised that to focus on reason, logic and argumentation was to lose the debate. It seems Wesley acknowledged that Calvinism was the more logical doctrinal system, and in writing to Charles Wesley, he declared that "just here we must stop reasoning or turn Calvinists. This is the very strength of their cause."[51] He told Richard Conyers, an evangelical Anglican vicar, that if the Calvinists and the Arminians were to be reconciled, then God must first change the hearts of the Calvinists.[52]

As in his earlier writings, he insisted that although faith "is always consistent with reason, yet reason cannot produce faith in the scriptural sense of the word."[53] Nor can it produce hope, the love of God or neighbour, virtue or happiness.[54] With this essential proviso, Wesley reiterated that reason was very useful, "both with regard to the foundation of [religion], and the superstructure. The foundation of true religion stands upon the oracles of God" and it is reason that enables us to understand and explain them to ourselves and to others.[55] "Is it not reason (*assisted by the Holy Ghost*) [emphasis mine] which enables us to understand what the Holy Scriptures declare concerning the being and attributes of God?" Reason also helps us to understand how God works in salvation as the Spirit opens and enlightens "the eyes of our understanding."[56] In a letter to Elizabeth Ritchie he noted that we should be guided by reason as far as it can go, but in many cases it was of little or no help and here believers

---

[47] *Letters* (Telford), 8:89. See also Ibid., 192. Benson was a close associate of Wesley on his travels in his later years, a very active and influential circuit preacher and an early editor of Wesley's works.

[48] *Works*, 4:68-69. Wesley's estimation of David Hume is also seen in *Works*, 22:321, 411-12.

[49] *Works*, 3:400. See also Ibid., 54.

[50] *Letters* (Telford), 5:203. See also Ibid., 217.

[51] *Letters* (Telford), 6:152-53.

[52] *Works*, 23:43.

[53] *Works*, 2:593.

[54] Ibid., 595-99.

[55] Ibid., 591-92.

[56] Ibid., 592. See also Ibid., 506.

needed the ministry of the Holy Spirit.[57] Wesley remained convinced that spiritual things could not be understood without the ministry of the Spirit.[58] He was willing to affirm the new philosophical and scientific developments of his century up to the point that they clashed with Scripture.[59] Thus he rejected the romantic and rationalist view of the unaided perfectibility of human nature by strongly maintaining a belief in the universality of original sin.[60] He was convinced that human experience refuted the whole notion of perfectibility apart from God's grace.[61] Commenting on the education of children, Wesley wrote that "Scripture, reason, and experience jointly testify that, inasmuch as the corruption of nature is earlier than our instructions can be, we should take all pains and care to counteract this corruption as early as possible. The bias of nature is set the wrong way." Education within the context of grace was designed to set it right.[62]

Given the dangers of faulty reasoning and the consequent faulty interpretation of Scripture, it was necessary to utilise Christian experience to confirm the correct interpretation. It was "by experience, the strongest of all arguments, you have been once and again convinced that salvation from inbred sin is received by simple faith, and by plain consequence in a moment; although it is certain there is a gradual work both preceding and following."[63] As pointed out earlier, Wesley believed that the essential definition of religion was to actually experience the love of God and neighbour; this would enable people to experience the happiness for which God had created them. He wrote to his nephew Charles Wesley and affirmed that "Scripture and reason tell you now, what experience will confirm if it pleases God to prolong your life–that He made your heart for Himself, and it cannot rest till it rests in Him."[64] He warned that human experience and emotion must always be checked by the plain declarations of Scripture. He rejected many of the teachings of the Roman Catholic mystics because "each of them makes his own experience the standard

---

[57] *Letters* (Telford), 7:319. He admitted to her that he was generally guided "by reason and by Scripture" rather than the impression of the Spirit. Elizabeth Ritchie was a close friend of Wesley in his latter years and a frequent correspondent; she helped nurse him during the final year of his life.

[58] *Works*, 2:388.

[59] See *Works* (Jackson), 9:509-14. He was quite positive about the philosophy of John Locke because he had a fear of God and a reverence for the Bible; see *Works* (Jackson), 13:455-70.

[60] See *Works*, 4:149-60. See also *Works*, 4:162-67, 69-76; 22:356-57; *Letters* (Telford), 5:327.

[61] *Works*., 4:157.

[62] *Works* (Jackson), 13:476.

[63] *Letters* (Telford), 7:129. See also *Works*, 3:224-25. Wesley was sure that a right interpretation of Scripture and sound experience went together; see for example *Letters* (Telford), 5:252.

[64] *Letters* (Telford), 7:81.

of religion."⁶⁵ Writing about Madame Guyon, Wesley noted that "the grand source of all her mistakes was this, the not being guided by the written word. She did not take the Scripture for the rule of her actions; at most it was but the secondary rule" with impressions being primary.⁶⁶ He commented that when translating Moravian hymns, he had "selected those which I judged to be most scriptural, and most suitable to sound experience."⁶⁷ While there was nothing wrong with passion in prayer and devotion, it was easy for Christians to allow their emotions to exceed what he felt were "the bounds of reason, and led them into a manner of speaking not authorized by the oracles of God. And surely these are the true standard, both of our affections and our language."⁶⁸

The Methodist Ethos

Wesley generally had a very low opinion of Christianity in the Eastern churches, and thought that the Western churches were more knowledgeable and had "more scriptural and more rational modes of worship."⁶⁹ However, this did not mean that he believed there was a golden age of the church–even prior to

---

⁶⁵ *Letters* (Telford), 6:44.

⁶⁶ *Works* (Jackson), 14:277. He made a similar point regarding another mystic in *Works*, 22:458.

⁶⁷ *Works*, 4:101.

⁶⁸ Ibid., 105.

⁶⁹ *Works*, 2:487. On Wesley and the debates regarding the influence of Eastern Christianity, see S. T. Kimbrough Jr., ed., *Orthodox and Wesleyan Spirituality* (Crestwood, NY: St. Vladimir's Seminary Press, 2002); Kimbrough, *Orthodox and Wesleyan Scriptural Understanding*; Kenneth J. Collins, "The Promise of John Wesley's Theology for the 21st Century: A Dialogical Exchange," *Asbury Theological Journal* 59, no. 1 & 2 (Spring-Fall, 2004): 172-73; John G. Merritt, "'Dialogue' within a Tradition: John Wesley and Gregory of Nyssa Discuss Christian Perfection," *WTJ* 22, no. 2 (Fall, 1987); A. M. Allchin, "The Epworth-Canterbury-Constantinople Axis," *WTJ* 26, no. 1 (Spring, 1991); K. Steve McCormick, "Theosis in Chrysostom and Wesley: An Eastern Paradigm on Faith and Love," *WTJ* 26, no. 1 (Spring, 1991); Troy W. Martin, "John Wesley's Exegetical Orientation: East or West?," *WTJ* 26, no. 1 (Spring, 1991); David Bundy, "Christian Virtue: John Wesley and the Alexandrian Tradition," *WTJ* 26, no. 1 (Spring, 1991); Michael J. Christensen, "Theosis and Sanctification: John Wesley's Reformulation of a Patristic Doctrine," *WTJ* 31, no. 2 (Fall, 1996); Randy L. Maddox, "Prelude to a Dialogue: A Response to Kenneth Collins," *WTJ* 35, no. 1 (Spring, 2000); Kenneth J. Collins, "John Wesley's Critical Appropriation of Tradition in His Practical Theology," *WTJ* 35, no. 2 (Fall, 2000); Seung-An Im, "John Wesley's Theological Anthropology: A Dialectic Tension between the Latin Western Patristic Tradition (Augustine) and the Greek Eastern Patristic Tradition (Gregory of Nyssa)" (PhD thesis, Drew University, 1994); Rob King, "The Spirit-Filled Life: Eastern Patristic Spirit-Christology for Contemporary Wesleyan Faith Practice," *WTJ* 38, no. 2 (Fall, 2003); David Bundy, "Visions of Sanctification: Themes of Orthodoxy in the Methodist, Holiness, and Pentecostal Traditions," *WTJ* 39, no. 1 (Spring, 2004).

the Constantinian period: "I regard no authorities but those of the Ante-Nicene Fathers; nor any of them in opposition to Scripture."[70] In these last two decades of his life, Wesley wrote a number of reviews and summaries of God's dealings with the Methodists that emphasised their orthodoxy and adherence to the Scriptures, antiquity and particularly the Church of England. For example, in his sermon, "On Laying the Foundation of the New Chapel," he defined Methodism as "the old religion, the religion of the Bible, the religion of the primitive church, the religion of the Church of England."[71] This was because Methodism had focused on love as the essence of true religion and "this is the religion of the primitive church, of the whole church in the purest ages."[72]

> And this is the religion of the Church of England, as appears from all her authentic records, from the uniform tenor of her liturgy, and from numberless passages in her Homilies. The scriptural primitive religion of love, which is now reviving throughout the three kingdoms, is to be found in her morning and evening service, and in her daily as well as occasional prayers; and the whole of it is beautifully summed up in that one, comprehensive petition, 'Cleanse the thoughts of our hearts by the inspiration of thy Holy Spirit, that we may perfectly love thee, and worthily magnify thy holy name.'[73]

He was equally sure that "whoever follows the direction of our excellent Church, in the interpretation of the Holy Scriptures, by keeping close to that sense of them which the Catholic Fathers and ancient Bishops have delivered to succeeding generations" will come to correctly understand the true nature of Christian holiness.[74]

Wesley retained throughout his whole ministry the deep conviction of the value of both the early Church and the Church of England as theological sources, but what is now explicit is the addition of his own Methodist movement to this group.[75] He thought that "true religion" was greatly increased in his own century,[76] particularly amongst the Methodists whom he described as "a new phenomenon in the earth; a body of people who, being of no sect or

---

[70] *Letters* (Telford), 7:106.

[71] *Works*, 3:585. Note Outler's comments in his introduction on p. 577-79 where he says that Wesley was especially concerned here to stress his continued membership of the Church of England in the face of growing pressures for separation. See also *Works*, 22:312-13; 23:404; *Letters* (Telford), 7:28; 8:140, 145.

[72] *Works*, 3:586. See his standard listing of the writings of the church fathers on this page, including some from the fourth century. See also Works, 22:441.

[73] *Works*, 3:586. See also Ibid., 590-92. The same quotation is found in *Works* (Jackson), 10:450.

[74] *Works* (Jackson), 14:270-71.

[75] For a discussion of the important role of the societies in theologising, see John W. Wright, "Wesley's Theology as Methodist Practice: Toward the Postmodern Retrieval of the Wesleyan Tradition," *WTJ* 35, no. 2 (Fall, 2000).

[76] *Works*, 3:442-53. See also Ibid., 465-78.

party, are friends to all parties, and endeavour to forward all in heart religion, in the knowledge and love of God and man. ... receiving all that love God in every church as our brother, and sister, and mother." To be in union with them required "no unity in opinions, or in modes of worship."[77] He urged Mary Bishop to join a Methodist society because "we have but one point in view–to be *altogether Christians*, scriptural, rational Christians."[78] Wesley believed that the Methodists were "called to propagate Bible religion through the land–that is, faith working by love, holy tempers and holy lives."[79] More explicitly, he believed that "this doctrine ['full sanctification'] is the grand depositum which God has lodged with the people called Methodists; and for the sake of propagating this chiefly He appeared to have raised us up."[80]

He was convinced that the faith community played an essential role in promoting and maintaining holiness of heart and life. He strongly criticised Whitefield's ministry in North America where, in spite of his effective preaching, so many deserted the faith. Wesley believed this was due to the failure to form groups for mutual accountability and encouragement.[81] In these decades he emphasised the vital role of Methodism itself in propagating and sustaining the message of Christian perfection. It had become obvious that the continuance of his message and movement could not simply depend upon his extensive written sermons, tracts and other published materials. The life and ministry of each local society was crucial; particularly the preachers and the doctrinal clarity and persuasiveness of their sermons on Christian perfection. His letters to the preachers were filled with exhortations to remain faithful to the task of consistently proclaiming Christian perfection in spite of opposition

---

[77] *Works*, 4:82-83.

[78] *Letters* (Telford), 5:154. May Bishop was a frequent correspondent; she was responsible for running two schools in the Bath area at various times.

[79] *Letters* (Telford), 6:291.

[80] *Letters* (Telford), 8:238. See also John Wesley, *Minutes of Several Conversations, between the Rev. John Wesley, A.M. And the Preachers in Connection with Him. Containing the Form of Discipline Established among the Preachers and People in the Methodist Societies* (London: G. Whitfield, 1797), 1. Wesley's *A Short History of the People Called Methodists* is instructive for tracing the growing number of testimonies to Christian perfection, especially during the holiness revival of 1760-63; see *Works*, 9:426-503. See also *Works*, 24:121; *Works* (Jackson), 10:455-56.

[81] *Works*, 3:595-99. See also *Works* (Jackson), 13:259-60; *Letters* (Telford), 5:344; 8:158, 73, 84, 246. For an account of Wesley's own discipleship structures, see D. Michael Henderson, *John Wesley's Class Meeting: A Model for Making Disciples* (Nappanee, IN: Evangel Publishing House, 1997); Albin, "'Inwardly Persuaded': Religion of the Heart in Early British Methodism," in *"Heart Religion"*; David Lowes Watson, *The Early Methodist Class Meeting: Its Origins and Significance* (Nashville, TN: Discipleship Resources, 1985).

from within and without the Methodist movement.[82] The lay members of the societies were to be equally active in promoting Christian perfection, and Wesley was glad to record their experience as he heard about it by correspondence or through his own visitation.[83] This was also the period when he published the definitive collection of hymns for his people as an essential element of their spiritual formation and the promotion of Christian perfection. In the preface he made the point that it was large enough

> ... to contain all the important truths of our most holy religion, whether speculative or practical; yea, to illustrate them all, and to prove them both by Scripture and reason. ... The hymns are ... carefully ranged under prayer heads, according to the experience of real Christians. So that this book is in effect a little body of experimental and practical divinity.
> ... In what other publication of the kind have you so distinct and full an account of scriptural Christianity?[84]

Wesley continued to stress the need of pastoral care and discipline within the societies to minimise spiritual loss amongst his followers. To neglect the band and society meetings would lead to a deterioration in spiritual life.[85] There was always a danger of replacing a dependency on the work of the Spirit with a mechanical application of their general rules.[86] This made it important to consult with those experienced in the ways of God over such questions,[87] as this was an "appointed means which it generally pleases God to bless."[88] The lives of the members of the societies were significant as models for seekers to follow and as sources of spiritual experience and encouragement.[89] Methodists needed to improve their understanding of the doctrine and practice of Christian perfection as much as possible in order to be of help to others and to minimise difficulties in these areas. Wesley told them that this "can no otherwise be done than by reading authors of various kinds as well as by thinking and

---

[82] See for example *Letters* (Telford), 6:111, 224, 226, 240, 376; 7:92, 98-99, 206, 352. See also *Works* (Jackson), 8:326.

[83] See for example *Letters* (Telford), 5:315; 6:37, 38; 7:98, 176, 193, 226-27; 9:518-21. Wesley continued to record testimonies in his *Journal* accounts for this period; see for example *Works*, 22:233-34, 36, 72, 76, 82, 345-46, 49-50, 75, 423, 32-35, 41, 44, 60, 62, 69; 23:6, 10, 24, 48, 130, 35, 37, 40, 65, 69, 87, 91, 204, 13, 34, 38, 45, 69, 317, 23, 37, 49, 55, 58, 75, 405, 15; 24:9, 11, 13, 33, 89, 128, 33, 69.

[84] *A Collection of Hymns for the Use of the People Called Methodists* (1780) in *Works*, 7:73-74. The structure of the hymnal laid out Wesley's mature understanding of the *ordo salutis*; see the contents (pp. 77-78) and the first section of the introduction to the volume (pp. 1-22).

[85] *Letters* (Telford), 8:246.

[86] *Letters* (Telford), 5:344. See also *Letters* (Telford), 6:263; 7:224.

[87] *Letters* (Telford), 5:278; 6:58, 126, 127, 178, 239.

[88] Ibid., 237.

[89] See for example *Letters* (Telford), 5:261-62, 290; 7:167.

conversation."⁹⁰ This highlighted the value of reading and subsequent Christian conversation amongst the members of the societies. There was a danger that his people would read the wrong material or things that were less than helpful for their spiritual journey and so he encouraged them to read Methodist publications particularly as they were easy to comprehend and follow.⁹¹

The "Substance" of Christian Perfection: Wesley's Doctrinal Understanding

In his introduction to the sermon "On Perfection" (Dec, 1784), Outler noted that holy living and its goal, perfection, was Wesley's most consistent theme over his whole ministry. The crucial doctrinal issues he had to continually clarify were: defining perfection in terms of the love of God and neighbour; defining sin as deliberate; to carefully nuance and emphasise the instantaneous and entire aspects of his doctrine of sanctification.⁹² Wesley continued the strong Christocentric focus in his understanding of the doctrine of holiness.⁹³ He told Robert Hopkins, a well-regarded circuit preacher, that God's greatest blessing was "Christ in a pure and sinless heart, reigning the Lord of every motion there."⁹⁴ In writing to Joseph Benson, Wesley affirmed, "... Christ does not give light to the soul separate from, but in and with, Himself. ... our perfection is not like that of a tree, which flourishes by the sap derived from its own root; but like that of a branch, which, united to the vine, bears fruit, but severed from it is 'dried up and withered.'"⁹⁵ It is as we enter into a relationship with Christ "that happiness begins – happiness real, solid, substantial. Then it is that heaven is opened in the soul, that the proper, heavenly state commences, while the love of God, as loving us, is shed abroad in the heart, instantly producing love to all mankind.⁹⁶ As we hold fast our faith in Christ, we are to

---

⁹⁰ *Letters* (Telford), 6:129-30. See also *Letters* (Telford), 8:247 and John Wesley, *Minutes of Several Conversations, between the Rev. John Wesley, A.M. And the Preachers in Connection with Him. From the Year 1744* (Leeds: Edward Baines, 1803), 33.
⁹¹ *Letters* (Telford), 6:125-26. See also Ibid., 201.
⁹² *Works*, 3:70-71. In Outler's opinion, the significant writings were: the sermons "The Circumcision of the Heart" (1733) and "Christian Perfection" (1741), the preface to the *Hymns and Sacred Poems* (1740), his letters of February 12 and March 5 1767, as well as the *Plain Account of Christian Perfection* in 1766. Wesley himself doubted if he could (in 1778) write a better sermon on Christian perfection than "The Circumcision of the Heart" and did not think he had significantly added to his own doctrinal understanding since; see *Works*, 23:105.
⁹³ *Works*, 3:89-102. See also Ibid., 103-14.
⁹⁴ *Letters* (Telford), 7:76.
⁹⁵ *Letters* (Telford), 5:204.
⁹⁶ *Works*, 3:96-97. The correlation of love, holiness and happiness continued throughout this period. See *Works*, 3:123, 92, 448; 4:57, 64-67; 22:290; 23:109; *Works* (Jackson),

"expect a continual growth in grace, in the loving knowledge of our Lord Jesus Christ. Expect that the power of the Highest shall suddenly overshadow you, that all sin may be destroyed, and nothing may remain in your heart but holiness unto the Lord. And this moment, and every moment, 'present yourselves a living sacrifice, holy, acceptable to God,' and 'glorify him with your body, and with your spirit, which are God's.'"[97]

Objections Considered

The objections raised by Wesley's critics in this period were essentially the same ones they had always raised. He continued to state that if Christian perfection was not promised in the Word of God, he would give it up. He reminded his detractors that all of God's commands are covered promises "For [God] cannot mock his helpless creatures, calling us to receive what he never intends to give."[98] In referring to Lk. 1:73-75, Wesley specially drew attention to the fact that the text promises "all the days of our life" and not simply at death.[99] In response to the objection that we cannot be saved from sin while in a sinful body, Wesley admitted that we cannot be free from mistakes, wrong judgments, wrong practice, wrong tempers or passions while in the body. He agreed that these were all violations of the Adamic law and thus sin under those conditions; however we are not now under Adamic law, but the law of love (Rom. 13:10) and here sin was defined as "a voluntary transgression of a known law." His critics argued that every transgression of God's law, whether voluntary or involuntary, was sin. They noted that St. John says, "All sin is a transgression of the law." Wesley responded, "True, but he does not say, 'All transgression of the law is sin.' This I deny: let him prove it that can."[100] Furthermore, "You say none is saved from sin in *your* sense of the word; but I do not admit of that sense, because the word is never so taken in Scripture. And you cannot deny the possibility of being saved from sin in *my* sense of the word. And this is the sense wherein the word 'sin' is over and over taken in Scripture."[101]

> Why should any man of reason and religion be either afraid of, or averse to, salvation from all sin? Is not sin the greatest evil on this side hell? ... does it not naturally follow that an entire deliverance from it is one of the greatest blessings on this side heaven? ... By sin I mean 'a voluntary transgression of a known law'.

11:463-65, 525; *Letters* (Telford), 5:174, 193, 201; 6:30-31, 149, 153; 7:72, 96, 131, 189, 190, 374; 8:9, 97, 128, 158, 258.

[97] *Works*, 3:102.

[98] Ibid., 76-77. Wesley listed such texts as Deut. 30:6; Matt. 19:19; 22:37; Heb. 10:16; Eph. 4:21, 23-24; 1 Thess. 5:23; Ps. 130:8; Matt. 1:21; Heb. 7:25; Ezek. 36:25-27.

[99] *Works*, 3:78.

[100] Ibid., 79.

[101] Ibid., 79.

... Do you then love sin, that you are so unwilling to part with it? Surely no. ... You rather wish to be totally delivered ... to have sin rooted out both of your life and your heart.

I have frequently observed, ... that the opposers of perfection are more vehement against it when it is placed in this view than in any other whatsoever. They will allow all you say of the love of God and man, of the mind which was in Christ, of the fruit of the spirit, of the image of God, of universal holiness, of entire self-dedication, of sanctification in spirit, soul, and body; ... All this they will allow, so we will allow sin, a little sin, to remain in us till death.[102]

Wesley rejected the notion that the body itself was sinful, as this is never asserted in Scripture and is in any case absurd "For no *body*, or matter of any kind, can be *sinful*: spirits alone are capable of sin. Pray in what part of the body should sin lodge? It cannot lodge in the skin, nor in the muscles, or nerves, or veins, or arteries; it cannot be in the bones any more than in the hair or nails. Only the soul can be the seat of sin."[103] The final objection claimed that there were no living witnesses to deliverance from sin. Wesley agreed that there were not many and there were also false witnesses. Some had now lost their experience but a group did remain who clearly testified to a settled experience: "if you keep to the account that is given above, and allow for the weakness of human understanding, you may see at this day undeniable instances of genuine, scriptural perfection."[104]

The Nature of Entire Sanctification Clarified

The relationship between entire sanctification and what Wesley meant by Christian perfection was often misunderstood, both by his critics and his supporters. In two significant sermons written in 1784 ("On Patience" and "On Perfection") Wesley sought to remove this confusion.[105] He noted that many had not spoken on this subject "according to the oracles of God," having taken entire sanctification as if it were entirely different from the initial sanctification wrought in justification. "But this is a great and dangerous mistake, and has a natural tendency to make us undervalue that glorious work of God which was wrought in us when we were justified. ... There is in that hour a general change from inward sinfulness to inward holiness. The love of the creature is changed into the love of the Creator, the love of the world into the love of God."[106] If this rich state of grace was true of justification, what more then was to be experienced in entire sanctification? To overly exalt the first work of grace was

---

[102] Ibid., 85.
[103] Ibid., 80.
[104] Ibid., 83.
[105] Ibid., 71-87, 170-79. The first sermon is actually focused on Christian perfection, defined in terms of the perfect love of God and neighbour.
[106] Ibid., 173-74.

to undervalue the subsequent one, while to undervalue the first left them in danger of claiming too much for entire sanctification. Wesley wrote that entire sanctification

> ... does not imply any new *kind* of holiness: ... From the moment we are justified till we give up our spirits to God, love is the fulfilling of the law–of the whole evangelical law, which took [the] place of the Adamic law ... Love is the sum of Christian sanctification: it is the one *kind* of holiness which is found, only in various *degrees*, in the believers who are distinguished by St. John into 'little children, young men, and fathers'. ... Everyone that is born of God, ... has the love of God in his heart, the love of his neighbour, ... But all of these are then in a low degree, in proportion to the degree of his faith. ... In the same proportion as he grows in faith, he grows in holiness: he increases in love, ... till it pleases God, after he is thoroughly convinced of inbred sin, of the total corruption of his nature, to take it all away, to purify his heart and cleanse him from all unrighteousness; ... Till this universal change was wrought in his soul, all his holiness was *mixed*. ... His love of God was frequently damped by the love of some creature; the love of his neighbour by evil surmising, ... His whole soul is now consistent with itself: there is no jarring string.[107]

Entire sanctification was thus the initial experience of the fullness of the love of God and neighbour and Christian perfection encompassed both the initial moment and the ever-deepening continuance of that relationship.

A second critical problem was how this experience of grace was to be realised–gradually or instantaneously? Wesley noted that there were many disputes about this "because the Scriptures are silent upon the subject; because the point is not determined–at least, not in express terms–in any part of the oracles of God."[108] He then gave the following account:

> Four or five and forty years ago ... two or three persons in London ... desired to give me an account of their experience. ... The next year two or three more persons at Bristol, and two or three in Kingswood, ... gave me exactly the same account of their experience. A few years after I desired all those in London who made the same profession to come to me all together at the Foundery, that I might be thoroughly satisfied. ... In the years 1759, 1760, 1761, and 1762, their numbers multiplied exceedingly, not only in London and Bristol, but in various parts of Ireland as well as England. Not trusting to the testimony of others, I carefully examined most of these myself; and in London alone I found six hundred and fifty-two members of our society who were exceeding clear in their experience, and of whose testimony I could see no reason to doubt. I believe no year has passed since that time wherein God has not wrought the same work in many others; ... And every one of these (after the most careful inquiry I have not found one exception either in Great Britain or Ireland) has declared that his deliverance from sin was *instantaneous*, ... Had half of these, or one-third, or one in twenty,

---

[107] Ibid., 174-76.
[108] Ibid., 176-77.

declared it was *gradually* wrought in *them*, I should have believed this with regard to *them*, and thought that *some* were gradually sanctified and some instantaneously. But as I have not found ... a single person speaking thus–as all who believe they are sanctified declare with one voice that the change was wrought in a moment–I cannot but believe that sanctification is commonly, if not always, an *instantaneous* work.[109]

As late as December 1789 he could write to Sarah Rutter (a member of the St. Neots society): "Gradual sanctification may increase from the time you was justified; but full deliverance from sin, I believe, is always instantaneous–at least I never yet knew an exception."[110] This was in harmony with the strong exhortation to his preachers found in *The Large Minutes*:

> Strongly and explicitly exhort all believers to "go on to perfection". ... You all agreed to defend it, meaning thereby ... salvation from all sin, by the love of God and man filling the heart. ... You are all agreed, we may be saved from all sin before death. The *substance* then is settled; but, as to the *circumstance*, is the change gradual or instantaneous? It is both the one and the other. From the moment we are justified, there may be a gradual sanctification, a growing in grace, a daily advance in the knowledge and love of God. And if sin cease before death, there must, in the nature of the thing be an instantaneous change; there must be a last moment wherein it does exist, and a first moment wherein it does not. ... Certainly we must insist on the gradual change; ... And are there not reasons why we should insist on the instantaneous also? If there be such a blessed change before death, should we not encourage all believers to expect it? ... because constant experience shows, the more earnestly they expect this, the more swiftly and steadily does the gradual work of God go on in their soul; ... Therefore whoever would advance the gradual change in believers should strongly insist on the instantaneous (emphasis mine).[111]

The experience itself was entered into by simple faith.[112] He freely admitted that human knowledge was always imperfect and he wondered why the manner and time of God bestowing "sanctifying grace" varied so widely: some received before they asked, some in a few days, others waited twenty, thirty or forty years, some just a few hours or minutes before death. Some retained it without interruption while others did not, even though they had no consciousness of having grieved the Spirit.[113] He reminded his followers that "there is an

---

[109] Ibid., 177-78. He affirmed essentially the same understanding in Ibid., 203-04. See also *A Short History of the People Called Methodists* in *Works*, 9:473-86; *Letters* (Telford), 7:96, 222, 267-68.

[110] *Letters* (Telford), 8:190.

[111] Wesley, *Minutes (1803)*, 48-49. This is also found in *Works* (Jackson), 8:328-29

[112] *Works*, 3:178-79. See also *Works*, 3:492-501, 21; 4:29-38, 49-59, 188-200; *Letters* (Telford), 7:267-68.

[113] *Works*, 2:584-85.

irreconcilable variability in the operations of the Holy Spirit on the souls of men" and so it was important to allow him to work as he pleased and not reason against him.[114]

The Nature of Christian Perfection Clarified

It was only after experiencing the moment of entire sanctification that Christians would

> ... then be *perfect*. The Apostle seems to mean by this expression, τέλειοι, ye shall be wholly delivered from every evil work, from every evil word, from every sinful thought; yea, from every evil desire, passion, temper, from all inbred corruption, from all remains of the carnal mind, from the whole body of sin: and ye shall be renewed in the spirit of your mind, in every right temper, after the image of him that created you, in righteousness and true holiness. Ye shall be entire, ὁλόκληροι. ... This seems to refer not so much to the kind as to the degree of holiness. As if he had said, 'Ye shall enjoy as high a degree of holiness as is consistent with your present state of pilgrimage.' ... so that loving him with all your heart (which is the sum of all perfection) you will 'rejoice evermore, pray without ceasing', and 'in everything give thanks'. ...[115]

Wesley confirmed to his people that the only perfection possible while in a corruptible body was to love God and neighbour with our whole being; "This is the sum of Christian perfection: it is all comprised in that one word, love."[116] Furthermore, "It was by a sense of the love of God shed abroad in his heart that every one of them was enabled to love God. Loving God, he loved his neighbour as himself, and had power to walk in all his commandments blameless."[117] Wesley was careful to clarify once more that he did not preach either angelic or adamic perfection.

> The highest perfection which man can attain while the soul dwells in the body does not exclude ignorance and error, and a thousand other infirmities. Now from wrong judgments wrong words and actions will often necessarily flow. ... Nor can I be freed from a liableness to such a mistake while I remain in a corruptible body. A thousand infirmities in consequence of this will attend my spirit till it returns to

---

[114] *Letters* (Telford), 7:298. See similar advice in *Letters* (Telford), 7:303-04; 8:110.
[115] *Works*, 3:179.
[116] Ibid., 74. Outler mentions in n. 19 that there are more than fifty summaries of "perfection" as love in Wesley's writings. Some of the key Scripture passages are Rom. 12:1; Gal. 5:22-23; Eph. 4:24; Phil. 2:5; Col. 3:10; I Thess. 5:23; 1 Pet. 1:15; 1 Pet. 2:5. See Ibid., 74-76. See also *Letters* (Telford), 6:335; 7:206-07.
[117] *Works*, 2:419. See also Ibid., 188.

God who gave it. And in numberless instances it comes short of doing the will of God as Adam did in paradise.[118]

We always need the merits of Christ's death "for innumerable violations of the Adamic as well as the angelic law. It is well therefore for us that we are not now under these, but under the law of love. 'Love is now the fulfilling of the law', which is given to fallen man. This is now, with respect to us, the perfect law. But even against this, through the present weakness of our understanding, we are continually liable to transgress. Therefore every man living needs the blood of atonement, or he could not stand before God."[119]

> Be not content with any religion which does not imply the destruction of all the works of the devil, that is, of all sin. We know weakness of understanding, and a thousand infirmities, will remain while this corruptible body remains. But sin need not remain: this is that work of the devil, ... which the Son of God was manifested to destroy in this present life. He is able, he is willing, to destroy it now in all that believe in him. ... Do not distrust his power or his love! Put his promise to the proof! He hath spoken: and is he not ready likewise to perform?[120]

His writings had regularly emphasised that "according to the degree of our love is the degree of our happiness."[121] While truth and love together were the essence of holiness, truth separated from love was nothing in God's sight.[122] Therefore, he admonished his people: "let *love* not visit you as a transient guest, but be the constant ruling temper of your soul."[123] He urged his Methodists: "Let truth and love possess your whole soul. Let them be the springs of all your affections, passions, tempers; the rule of all your thoughts. Let them inspire all your discourse; ... Let all your actions be wrought in love."[124] Wesley believed that "Christian revelation" had clearly demonstrated that "the love of God [was] the true foundation both of the love of our neighbour and all other virtues," and if the love of neighbour did not "spring from the love of God" it was no virtue at all.[125]

Wesley believed that "there have been from the beginning two orders of Christians," based on the strenuousness of their pursuit of Christian holiness.[126]

> From long experience and observation I am inclined to think that whoever finds redemption in the blood of Jesus, ... has then the choice of walking in the higher

---

[118] Works, 3:73. See also Works, 2:405-06, 74, 81-82; 3:159-62.
[119] Works, 3:73-74.
[120] Works, 2:483. See also Ibid., 410-12, 23-32.
[121] Works, 3:283.
[122] Ibid., 289.
[123] Ibid., 422.
[124] Ibid., 426.
[125] Ibid., 279-80. See also Ibid., 263-77, 306, 522-28.
[126] Ibid., 265.

or the lower path. I believe the Holy Spirit at that time sets before him the more excellent way, and incites him to walk therein, to choose the narrowest path in the narrow way, to aspire after the heights and depths of holiness, after the entire image of God. But if he does not accept this offer, he insensibly declines into the lower order of Christians.[127]

Wesley sought to encourage all to pursue the higher way, and then gave practical advice on spiritual disciplines to be followed for this to become a reality.[128] Of particular concern here were his repeated warnings about the danger of riches, since by these we were showing that we seek happiness in other than God.[129] He also warned of the danger of false and destructive zeal: "In a Christian believer love sits upon the throne, which is erected in the inmost soul; namely, love of God and man, which fills the whole heart, and reigns without a rival. ... This is that religion which our Lord has established upon earth, ever since the descent of the Holy Ghost on the day of Pentecost. This is the entire, connected system of Christianity."[130] So his Methodists were to be "most zealous of all for that which is the sum and perfection of religion–the *love* of God and man."[131] He reminded his people that when God has "enabled you to love him with all your heart and with all your soul, think not of resting there. That is impossible. You cannot stand still; you must either rise or fall." They were to be continually pressing forward as Paul had exhorted the Christians in Phil. 3:13-14.[132]

In one of his last sermons ("On the Wedding Garment", March 1790) Wesley returned to the theme of Christian perfection, and it marked the close of the theological explication that had begun with "The Circumcision of the Heart" in 1733.[133] He repeated that our salvation was finally due to the merits of Christ alone and then summarised what he had long understood by holiness as the love of God and neighbour, and this was possible only because of God's prior love for us.[134]

> ... the God of love is willing to save all the souls that he has made. This he has proclaimed to them in his Word, together with the terms of salvation revealed by the Son of his love, who gave his own life that they that believe in him might have everlasting life. And for these he has prepared a kingdom from the foundation of

---

[127] Ibid., 266.
[128] Ibid., 266-77.
[129] Ibid., 228-46. See also *Works*, 2:468, 560; 3:248-61, 519-28; 4:90-96, 123-25, 32-38, 78-86; 23:30; *Letters* (Telford), 5:201.
[130] *Works*, 3:313-14.
[131] Ibid., 319. See also Ibid., 321.
[132] Ibid., 501. For doctrinal reflection on this growth in love, see Mathew R. Schlimm, "The Puzzle of Perfection: Growth in John Wesley's Doctrine of Perfection," *WTJ* 38, no. 2 (Fall, 2003).
[133] *Works*, 4:139-48.
[134] Ibid., 144-47.

the world. But he will not force them to accept of it. He leaves them in the hands of their own counsel. He saith: ... Choose holiness by my grace, which is the way, the only way, to everlasting life. He cries aloud, Be holy, and be happy; happy in this world, and happy in the world to come.[135]

The "Circumstance" of Christian Perfection: Wesley's Pastoral Understanding

A number of significant events shaped much of Wesley's correspondence on Christian perfection during these final two decades of his life. The first was the inevitable reaction to the excesses of the Maxfield-Bell controversy during the holiness revival of the early 1760s.[136] Whilst this simply reinforced the negative evaluations of the Methodist movement amongst Wesley's detractors, it did not raise any new issues for theological debate among them. However, it did raise many questions amongst the Methodists themselves about the nature and experience of Christian perfection. Tensions also emerged between the theological expression of perfection found in the writings of Wesley and those of John Fletcher.[137] He had to deal with the implications of the changed attitude to Methodism in the nation as a whole due to its increasing acceptance and popularity. This was linked with concerns over the new generation of Methodists who had been raised within the movement and whose lifestyle was very different to that of Wesley himself and the first generation. The fresh outbreak of the Calvinist controversy in 1770 produced many questions concerning the relationship of grace and human response, the nature of sin and

---

[135] Ibid., 148.

[136] See chapter 4 of this book.

[137] For a detailed examination of this issue and the debates surrounding it, see Laurence W. Wood, *The Meaning of Pentecost in Early Methodism: Rediscovering John Fletcher as John Wesley's Vindicator and Designated Successor*, Pietist and Wesleyan Studies #15 (Lanham, MD: Scarecrow Press, 2002); David L. Cubie, "Perfection in Wesley and Fletcher: Inaugural or Teleological?," *WTJ* 11 (Spring, 1976); Timothy L. Smith, "How John Fletcher Became the Theologian of Wesleyan Perfectionism, 1770-1776," *WTJ* 15, no. 1 (Spring, 1980); Laurence W. Wood, "Pentecostal Sanctification in John Wesley and Early Methodism," *WTJ* 34, no. 1 (Spring, 1999); Laurence W. Wood, "Historiographical Criticisms of Randy Maddox's Response," *WTJ* 34, no. 2 (Fall, 1999); Randy L. Maddox, "Wesley's Understanding of Christian Perfection: In What Sense Pentecostal?," *WTJ* 34, no. 2 (Fall, 1999); Laurence W. Wood, *Pentecostal Grace* (Wilmore, KY: Francis Asbury Press, 1980); John L. Peters, *Christian Perfection and American Methodism* (Grand Rapids, MI: Francis Asbury Press, 1985). In fact, Fletcher died before Wesley and so the real debate between the two positions did not occur until the nineteenth century onwards. This debate may be traced in a number of articles in the *Wesleyan Theological Journal*, especially from 1970-80.

infirmities, and whether salvation could be lost and regained.[138] This dispute struck at the heart of Wesley's whole understanding of salvation, but in his approach he tried to emphasise the positive aspect of the Methodist message rather than the negative aspect of the Calvinist one.[139] This did not mean that he was willing to soften his criticisms of Calvinism and its implications for salvation. He wrote to Thomas Taylor, one of his circuit preachers, and urged him not to "preach against that unscriptural, blasphemous, mischievous doctrine [Calvinism] *constantly*–no, nor very *frequently*. But you ought *now* and *then* to bear a full, strong, express testimony against it; otherwise you are a sinner against God and your people and your own soul. I have done this too seldom, scarce once in fifty sermons: I ought to have done it one in fifteen or ten."[140] This was the whole point of publishing the *Arminian Magazine*, but even here it was not to rail against the Calvinists but to pursue what Wesley regarded as the Biblical pattern.[141] The letters and the lives recorded in it "contain the marrow of experimental and practical religion"; not to convince the Calvinists to change (which he felt they would not) but to preserve the Methodists.[142]

The Role of the Methodist Societies

Wesley believed that the Methodist movement was "only plain, scriptural religion, guarded by a few prudential regulations. The essence of it is holiness of heart and life; the circumstantials all point to this." However, if the "circumstantials" were despised, then the "essentials" would soon be lost and only rubbish would be left.[143] As we saw earlier, Wesley was aware that the continuance of his message and movement could not simply depend upon his extensive published materials; the life and ministry of his people, especially the preachers, was crucial. He knew that sermons on Christian perfection were not always gladly or regularly given by his preachers, and at every Conference they

---

[138] Wesley noted the rise of the controversy at the Bristol Conference of August 7-10, 1770; see *Works*, 22:243-44. Outler's n. 37 is especially important.

[139] *Letters* (Telford), 8:69. See also *Works* (Jackson), 10:358-61, 370-74; 11:492-96. For an earlier evaluation of the relationship of Arminianism and Calvinism, see the *Minutes* of 1744 in *Works* (Jackson), 8:284-85.

[140] *Letters* (Telford),6:295. See also *Letters* (Telford), 6:326, 331; 7:169; 8:95, 159, 256. Two of the more important responses to Calvinism by Wesley himself are found in *Works* (Jackson), 10:374-414, 415-46. See also Wesley, *Minutes (1803)*, 68, 101-02.

[141] See Wesley, *The Arminian Magazine: Consisting of Extracts and Original Treatises on Universal Redemption*, iii-viii. Within a few years Wesley had moved the focus to accounts of holy living; see John Wesley, *The Arminian Magazine, for the Year 1780*, vol. 3 (1780), iii-viii.

[142] *Letters* (Telford), 6:295. See also *Letters* (Telford), 7:138.

[143] *Works* (Jackson), 13:260. See his account of the decay of the society in Weardale in *Works*, 22:414.

were asked: "Are you going on to perfection? Do you expect to be perfected in love, in this life? Are you longing after it?"[144] In March 1772 he complained to Charles Wesley that "I find almost all our preachers in every circuit have done with Christian perfection. They say they believe it; but they never preach it, or not once in a quarter. What is to be done? Shall we let it drop, or make a point of it?"[145] Yet in May 1773 he felt able to declare: "In most parts of this kingdom there is such a thirst after holiness as I scarce ever knew before. Several here [Cork] in particular who enjoy it themselves are continually encouraging others to press after it. And two of our travelling preachers who for some years disbelieved it are now happy witnesses of it."[146] He wrote to members of the societies and asked about their preachers: "Does he preach Christian perfection clearly and explicitly?"[147] He reminded Mrs. Woodhouse (a key member of the Epworth society): "The great point is to conform to the Bible method of salvation–to have the mind which was in Christ, and walk as Christ walked. I hope all your three preachers insist upon this, which is the very essence of Christian perfection."[148] He commented on the circuit at Launceston in 1776:

> Here I found the plain reason why the work of God had gained no ground in this circuit all year. The preachers had given up the Methodist testimony. Either they did not speak of perfection at all (the peculiar doctrine committed to our trust), or they spoke of it only in general terms, without urging the believers to 'go on to perfection', and to expect it every moment. And wherever this is not earnestly done the work of God does not prosper.[149]

In the letters to the preachers themselves there is a continuing refrain regarding the content and frequency of their sermons on Christian perfection. The letter to Samuel Bardsley (a lay preacher on the Manchester circuit) in 1772 was typical: "Never be ashamed of the old Methodist doctrine. Press all believers to go on to perfection. Insist everywhere on the second blessing as receivable in a moment, and receivable now, by simple faith."[150] He reminded

---

[144] Wesley, *Minutes (1803)*, 14. They were also asked if they were reading the *Sermons*, the *New Testament Notes*, the *Plain Account* and the *Appeals*.
[145] *Letters* (Telford), 5:314.
[146] *Letters* (Telford), 6:25-26. See also *Letters* (Telford), 7:219, 77.
[147] *Letters* (Telford), 5:166. For other letters exhorting preachers and society leaders to encourage others to seek perfection, see *Letters* (Telford), 5:242, 254, 257, 261-62, 291, 306, 312; 6:97, 357, 359; 7:90, 153.
[148] *Letters* (Telford), 5:208.
[149] *Works*, 23:28. See also *Works*, 22:400, 60; 23:234, 304, 79, 92; *Letters* (Telford), 7:216, 259, 276, 283; 8:184.
[150] *Letters* (Telford), 5:315. See also *Letters* (Telford), 5:187, 290; 6:42, 65, 66, 79, 82, 87, 137, 191, 215, 238, 343, 378; 7:170, 178, 207, 209, 220, 239, 267-68, 314, 317, 321, 330; 8:111, 173, 175, 258 and Wesley, *The Arminian Magazine, for the Year 1780*, 207.

John Mason (a circuit preacher) that "If you press all the believers to go on to perfection and to expect deliverance from sin every moment, they will grow in grace. But if they ever lose that expectation, they will grow flat and cold."[151] The need to preach the message of perfection as soon as the person became a Christian was emphasised in the letter to Thomas Rankin in 1774:

> I have been lately thinking a good deal on one point, wherein perhaps we have all been wanting. We have not made it a rule, as soon as ever persons were justified, to remind them of going on to perfection. Whereas this is the very time preferable to all others. They have then the simplicity of little children, and they are fervent in spirit, ... But if we once suffer this fervour to subside, we shall find it hard enough to bring them again to this point.[152]

Doctrinally, the sermons were to stress that this was a definite, instantaneous work of grace subsequent to the new birth, receivable by simple faith alone and it was to be expected now. In a letter to Charles Wesley, he concluded:

> I find by long experience it comes exactly to the same point, to tell men they shall be saved from all sin when they die; or to tell them it may be a year hence, or a week hence, or any time but *now*. Our word does not profit, either as to justification or sanctification, unless we can bring them to expect the blessing *while we speak*.[153]

Wesley was insistent that his preachers were to proclaim the reality of Christian perfection continually, explicitly and insistently (preaching for a decision "now"). Thus his commendation of those like Isaac Brown (one of Wesley's favourite preachers) who "firmly believes this doctrine, that we are to be saved from all sin in this life."[154] On the other hand, those who spoke against Christian perfection were no longer to lead or preach.[155]

In the promotion of Christian perfection the laity were to be equally active. He advised one of his lay leaders: "Your own soul will be quickened if you earnestly exhort believers without fear or shame to press after *full* salvation as receivable *now*, and that by simple *faith*."[156] While this was to be pressed upon them as soon as possible, he advised Ann Bolton to look for clear signs of a spiritual hunger or else her exhortation may be premature:

---

[151] *Letters* (Telford), 6:66. See also *Letters* (Telford), 5:346-47; 6:190, 360; 7:106, 353.

[152] *Letters* (Telford), 6:103. See also Ibid., 138. Rankin was a Scot who served many circuits in England before being sent to America in 1773 and then returning to England in 1777, where he continued to serve as a preacher.

[153] *Letters* (Telford), 5:316. See also *Letters* (Telford), 5:276, 345, 48; 7:100.

[154] *Letters* (Telford), 7:102-03. See also *Works*, 23:270; *Letters* (Telford), 7:106, 107, 109, 119, 386.

[155] *Letters* (Telford), 8:188. See also Ibid., 255 and Wesley, *Minutes (1803)*, 146.

[156] *Letters* (Telford), 6:13. See also *Works*, 23:10; *Letters* (Telford), 6:59, 233.

Certainly till persons experience something of the second awakening, till they are feeling convinced of inbred sin so earnestly to groan for deliverance from it, we need not speak to them of *present* sanctification. We should first labour to work that conviction in them. When they feel it and hunger and thirst after full salvation, then is the time to show them it is nigh at hand, it may be received *just now* by simple faith.[157]

Wesley was convinced that "you can never speak too strongly or explicitly upon the head of Christian Perfection. If you speak only faintly and indirectly, none will be offended and none profited. But if you speak out, although some will probably be angry, yet others will soon find the power of God unto salvation."[158] These exhortations were not merely for the adult members, but also for the children. In writing to Jane Salkeld, schoolmistress at Weardale, he said: "Exhort all the little ones that believe to make haste and not delay the time of receiving the second blessing." He urged her to share her own testimony with them and to continue to press on in her own relationship with God.[159] In seeking Christian perfection, it was important that the lives of his people be models for others to follow. He told Mary Bishop that "Sister Jane's experience is clear and scriptural" and was a good model for her own spiritual experience.[160] He advised John Stretton that "the experience of Phoebe Bland is an admirable one, truly consistent both with Scripture and reason."[161] He pointed out that Gregory Lopez, Fénelon and several Methodist men and women were examples of "close, uninterrupted communion" with God, and should be a source of encouragement for others to follow.[162] Miss March was reminded that "it is certain no part of Christian history is so profitable as that which relates to great changes wrought in our souls: these, therefore, should be carefully noticed and treasured up for the encouragement of our brethren."[163] Personal experience was not only important for encouragement, it was also important in understanding and explaining how the experience of Christian perfection may be realised. He wrote to Hester Ann Roe:

> Mr. Fletcher shows (as does the *Plain Account of Christian Perfection*) that sanctification is plainly set forth in Scripture. But certainly before the *root* of sin is taken away believers may live above the *power* of it. Yet what a difference

---

[157] *Letters* (Telford), 6:144-45.

[158] Ibid., 74.

[159] *Letters* (Telford), 5:333. For another positive evaluation of the spiritual experience of children at Weardale (including Christian perfection), see *Works*, 22:328-29. See also *Works*, 22:329-37; 23:355, 58; *Letters* (Telford), 7:96.

[160] *Letters* (Telford), 5:290. See also *Letters* (Telford), 5:261-62; 7:167.

[161] *Letters* (Telford), 8:49. Stretton began the Methodist work in Canada in 1771.

[162] *Letters* (Telford), 5:283. See also *Letters* (Telford), 5:337-38; 6:8.

[163] *Letters* (Telford), 5:237.

between the *first* love and the *pure* love! You can explain this to Mr. Roe by your own experience. Let him follow on, and how soon may he attain it.[164]

Pastoral care was to be a priority within each society and Wesley informed Elizabeth Ritchie that "one admirable help toward conquering all is for believers to keep close together, to walk hand in hand, and provoke one another to love and to good works. And one means of retaining the pure love of God was the exhorting others to press earnestly after it."[165] He was glad that Mrs. Pawson had restored the select society as this was "an excellent means of recommending Christian perfection" and their ministry would be useful "to those that either already enjoy or are earnestly seeking perfect love."[166] Mary Bishop was told that all need advice and exhortation or else they would be in danger of falling away:

> It is to be expected that above one half of those who not only profess great things, but actually enjoy the great salvation, deliverance from inbred sin, will nevertheless sooner or later be moved from their steadfastness. Some of them, indeed, will recover what they had lost; others will die in their sins. The observing this should incite us to double watchfulness lest we should fall after their example.[167]

Freeborn Garrettson was told that "it is a very desirable thing that the children of God should communicate their experience to each other; and it is generally most profitable when they can do it face to face."[168] In all of these letters there is a stress on the role of pastoral wisdom and shared Christian experience. If there was no expectation of perfection, few would seek after it and there would be few, if any, testimonies to the experience. This underscores the vital importance of the Methodist ethos, where believers were taught to read and interpret the Scriptural text in the light of God's plan of salvation as understood by Wesley.

The conduct of the believers needed to be regulated and not simply left to personal freedom, as this opened the door to enthusiasm. On the other hand, Wesley recognised the danger of replacing a dependency on the work of the Spirit with a mechanical application of the Methodist general rules.[169] He

---

[164] *Letters* (Telford), 6:217. Hester Ann Roe was a frequent correspondent of Wesley's and was housekeeper in London at the time of his death.

[165] *Letters* (Telford), 6:94. See also *Letters* (Telford), 8:80, 156.

[166] *Letters* (Telford), 8:184. She was married to John Pawson, one of Wesley's most effective and influential preachers.

[167] *Letters* (Telford), 6:91.

[168] *Letters* (Telford), 7:276. See also *Letters* (Telford), 8:127. Garretson was born and raised in America and became one of the most significant Methodist preachers in Canada and America.

[169] *Letters* (Telford), 5:344. See also *Letters* (Telford), 6:263; 7:224.

reminded his people that "it is sinful to condemn anything which Scripture does not condemn," for there are many things that are a matter of personal conscience before God.[170] He wrote to Garrettson: "If I have plain Scripture or plain reason for doing a thing well. These are my rules, and my only rules. I regard not whether I had freedom or no. This is an unscriptural expression and a very fallacious rule. I wish to be in every point, great or small, a scriptural, rational Christian."[171] He noted that the Spirit led in three main ways: by applying relevant tests of Scripture, by suggesting reasons (Wesley identified this as his own experience) and by impressions; the latter were least desirable and it was often impossible to distinguish the divine from the diabolical.[172] Many of the members were concerned to distinguish between sin and temptation in a Christian's life, and this was clearly the work of the Spirit and not any general rule. Consulting with those experienced in the ways of God was an "appointed means which it generally pleases God to bless."[173] Similar advice was given with regard to distinguishing between right and wrong tempers in the Christian's life: "Truth and falsehood, and so right and wrong tempers, are often divided by an almost imperceptible line. It is the more difficult to distinguish right and wrong tempers or passions because in several instances the same motion of the blood and animal spirits will attend both one and the other. Therefore in many cases we cannot distinguish them but by the unction of the Holy One."[174] Here again there is a strong emphasis on the living authority of the Holy Spirit, to be discerned by the faith community in harmony with the Scriptures.

Wesley encouraged his people to read widely in order to enhance their understanding of Methodist doctrine and practice. He told them that this "can no otherwise be done than by reading authors of various kinds as well as by thinking and conversation. If we read nothing but the Bible, we should hear nothing but the Bible; and then what becomes of preaching?"[175] This emphasised the importance of reading and subsequent Christian conversation) amongst the members of the societies. He was aware that his people could read the wrong material or things that were less than helpful for their spiritual journey. For example, he warned Elizabeth Ritchie that while there were many excellent things in the writings of Madam Guyon, there were also many dangerous things. Unlike many of the mystic writers, Methodist works were easy to follow and she ought to stay with them because

---

[170] *Letters* (Telford), 8:125.

[171] Ibid., 112.

[172] Ibid., 154.

[173] *Letters* (Telford), 5:237.

[174] Ibid., 266.

[175] *Letters* (Telford), 6:129-30. See also *Letters* (Telford), 8:247 and Wesley, *Minutes (1803)*, 33.

... we know there is nothing deeper, there is nothing better in heaven or earth than love! There cannot be, unless there were something higher than the God of love! ... Here is the height, here is the depth, of Christian experience! 'God is love; and he that dwelleth in love dwelleth in God, and God in him.'[176]

A similar point was made to Ann Bolton when he advised her that reading some of the Catholic mystics was not helpful since they were not true to the Bible: "My dear friend, come not into their secret; keep in the plain, open Bible way. Aim at nothing higher, nothing deeper, than the religion described at large in our Lord's Sermon upon the Mount, and briefly summed up by St. Paul in the 13th chapter to the Corinthians. I long to have you more and more deeply penetrated by humble, gently, patient love."[177] Sorting this out was not easy without a great deal of experience, so he urged his people to keep to Methodist publications (including those Wesley had translated and/or edited), where they would find all that they needed, "speculative or practical."[178] The Methodist work on Christian perfection that he particularly encouraged both his preachers and his members to read was *A Plain Account of Christian Perfection*.[179] The sermons that he most often referred to were: "The Repentance of Believers,"[180] "The Scripture Way of Salvation,"[181] "Sin in Believers,"[182] and "The Spirit of Bondage and Adoption."[183]

The Nature of Christian Perfection

A number of crucial points in Wesley's understanding of Christian perfection were now being questioned by his followers: what was the exact nature of this perfection; was it subsequent to the new birth; was it a definite instantaneous work of grace; was it to be received by simple faith alone; was the witness of the Spirit constant and how was it to be distinguished from human emotions? Wesley strongly affirmed that "every doctrine must stand or fall by the Bible. If

---

[176] *Letters* (Telford), 6:136.

[177] *Letters* (Telford), 5:342. See also *Works* (Jackson), 14:275-78; *Letters* (Telford), 5:313, 47-48; 6:39, 43-44, 232-33; 7:129; 8:93.

[178] *Letters* (Telford), 6:125-26. See also Ibid., 201.

[179] See for example *Letters* (Telford), 5:229. Further recommendations to read the *Plain Account* are found in *Letters* (Telford), 5:215-16, 315, 318; 6:137, 217; 7:67, 98, 120. Wesley particularly emphasised its importance to answer those who say it is a "new doctrine," to respond to beliefs that it is of "works" and to uphold it is a work of grace accomplished in a "moment"; see *Letters* (Telford), 7:98. He also made note of his *Thoughts on Christian Perfection* in *Letters* (Telford), 6:113; 8:255 and *Farther Thoughts on Christian Perfection* in *Letters* (Telford), 5:318; 6:105.

[180] *Letters* (Telford), 5:213, 214, 325.

[181] *Letters* (Telford), 5:213, 276-77; 6:137.

[182] *Letters* (Telford), 5:214, 319-20.

[183] *Letters* (Telford), 5:228; 6:137.

the perfection I teach agrees with this, it will stand, in spite of all the enthusiasts in the world; if not, it cannot stand."[184] In writing to Lady Maxwell, he said, "If any one could show you by plain scripture and reason a more excellent way than that you have received, you certainly would do well to receive it; ... But I think it will not be easy for any one to show us either that Christ did not die for us all or that He is not willing as well as able to cleanse from all sin even in the present world."[185] He retained his strong conviction that the essence of perfection was to be found in love:

> But you have ... the whole of religion contracted to a point, in that word, '*Walk in love*, as Christ also loved us and gave Himself for us.' All is contained in humble, gentle, patient love. Is not this, so to speak, *a divine contrivance to assist the narrowness of our minds, the scantiness of our understanding*? [emphasis mine] Every right temper, and then all the right words and actions, naturally branch out of love. In effect, therefore, you want nothing but this–to be filled with the faith that worketh by love."[186]

Wesley continued to emphasise that the focus in Christian perfection is on love, the heart and relationships, and not doctrinal opinions. In this way, he believed that God accommodated his requirements to our intellectual limitations and in so doing made this experience available to all, not just an elite who can fully comprehend it doctrinally. He reminded Ann Loxdale, a member of the Shrewsbury Methodist society, to read frequently 1 Corinthians 13: "There is the true picture of Christian perfection! Let us copy after it with all our might." She was also to read regularly the *Plain Account* with its recurring stress on perfection as "humble, gentle, patient love."[187] Walter Churchey (a noteworthy Welsh Methodist layman and poet) was told: "Entire sanctification, or Christian perfection, is neither more nor less than pure love–love expelling sin and governing both the heart and life of a child of God. The Refiner's fire purges out all that is contrary to love, and that many times by a pleasing smart."[188] Here Wesley mentions both the positive (love expelling sin) and the negative (purging all that is contrary to love) side of entering into the experience. This is important to note, for Wesley was not consistent in his metaphors (though he did seem to have a preference for the positive side) and there are therefore ample grounds for his followers to utilise one metaphor over another, as well as to emphasise or nuance the elements of the doctrine and experience differently. In a letter to Joseph Benson in 1770 we discover the first intimations of the disagreement between Wesley and Fletcher over the

---

[184] Works (Jackson), 10:412.

[185] *Letters* (Telford), 5:226. Lady Maxwell was a Scot and a close friend and supporter of both George Whitefield and Wesley.

[186] Ibid., 299. See also Ibid., 341-42.

[187] *Letters* (Telford), 7:120. See also *Letters* (Telford), 8:123.

[188] *Letters* (Telford), 5:223. See also Ibid., 326.

name and nature of this perfection:

> This I term sanctification (which is both an instantaneous and a gradual work), or perfection, the being perfected in love, filled with love, which still admits of a thousand degrees. ... And you allow the whole thing which I contend for–an entire deliverance from sin, a recovery of the whole image of God, the loving God with all our heart, souls, and strength. And you believe God is able to give you this–yea, to give it you in an instant. ... And with all zeal and diligence confirm the brethren, (1) in holding fast that whereto they have attained–namely, the remission of all their sins by faith in a bleeding Lord; (2) in expecting a second change whereby they shall be saved from all sin and perfected in love.[189]

Wesley commented that "if they like to call this 'receiving the Holy Ghost,' they may: only the phrase in that sense is not scriptural and not quite proper; for they all 'received the Holy Ghost' when they were justified. ... O Joseph, keep close to the Bible both as to sentiment and expression!"[190] While Wesley undoubtedly supported Fletcher,[191] in a later letter he urged Benson to read and conform to the content of the *Minutes* and "The Spirit of Bondage and Adoption." He then commented: "Likewise think whether you can abstain from speaking of ... Mr. Fletcher's late discovery. The Methodists in general could not bear this. It would create huge debate and confusion."[192] In March 1775 he wrote to Fletcher:

> It seems our views of Christian Perfection are a little different, though not opposite. It is certain every babe in Christ has received the Holy Ghost, and the Spirit witnesses with his spirit that he is a child of God. But he has not obtained Christian perfection. Perhaps you have not considered St. John's threefold distinction of Christian believers: little children, young men and fathers. All of these had received the Holy Ghost; but only the fathers were perfected in love.[193]

THE RELATIONSHIP BETWEEN SIN AND INFIRMITIES

His people continued to struggle with the relationship between sin and human infirmities just as much as his critics, both in terms of defining their properties and in distinguishing between them. For the former we were clearly culpable and under condemnation; for the latter, there was no culpability and therefore no condemnation. To "set the state of perfection too high is the surest way to

---

[189] Ibid., 215.

[190] Ibid.

[191] See the warm approval of his writings, especially the *Checks to Antinomianism*, found in *Letters* (Telford), 6:123, 134, 137, 146, 175, 217, 239, 272. See also his glowing estimation of his life as a model of holiness in *Works* (Jackson), 11:273-365, especially pp. 364-65.

[192] *Letters* (Telford), 5:228.

[193] *Letters* (Telford), 6:146. See also Ibid., 221.

drive it out of the world,"[194] and to imply that perfection in love required a total freedom from mistakes or human infirmities was too set it too high. If infirmities are normal, what then was the difference between those testifying to perfection and those who did not? Wesley was certain that those perfected in love were not absolutely perfect: "it is sure you are a transgressor still–namely, of the perfect, Adamic law. But though it be true all sin is a transgression of this law, yet it is by no means true on the other hand (though we have so often taken it for granted) that all transgressions of this law are sin: no, not at all– only voluntary transgressions of it; none else are sins against the gospel law."[195]

> Nothing is sin, strictly speaking, but a voluntary transgression of a known law of God. Therefore every voluntary breach of the law of love is sin; and nothing else, if we speak properly. To strain the matter farther is only to make way for Calvinism. There may be ten thousand wandering thoughts and forgetful intervals without any breach of love, though not without transgressing the Adamic law. But Calvinists would fain confound these together. Let love fill your heart, and it is enough![196]

He reminded Mrs. Bennis that "you will find many things both in your heart and in your life contrary to the perfection of the Adamic law; but it does not follow that they are contrary to the law of love. Let this fill your heart, and it is enough."[197] The person's intention was a determining factor on whether a sin had been committed or not: "If useless words or thoughts spring from evil tempers, they are properly evil, otherwise not; but still they are contrary to the *Adamic law*: yet not to the law of love; therefore there is no condemnation for them, but they are a matter of humiliation before God."[198] He stated that "voluntary humility, calling every defect a sin, is not well-pleasing to God. Sin, properly speaking, is neither more nor less than 'a voluntary transgression of a known law of God.'"[199] Wesley reminded Philothea Briggs (another of his frequent correspondents) that the soul was in a corruptible body and she must not be unsettled by the consequences of this, as she had received a taste of both pardoning and pure love. He advised her to read both the *Farther Thoughts* and *Plain Account* for help on these matters.[200] Mrs. Marston, a member of the Worcester society, was told that an "abundance of deficiencies must remain as long as the soul remains in this house of clay. So long the corruptible body will more or less darken and press down the soul. But still your heart may be all

---

[194] *Letters* (Telford), 5:317. See also *Works* (Jackson), 14:261-64.
[195] *Letters* (Telford), 5:255.
[196] Ibid., 322.
[197] Ibid., 315.
[198] Ibid., 313.
[199] Ibid., 341.
[200] Ibid., 318.

love, and love is the fulfilling of our law."²⁰¹ Wesley was certain that while grace was given to make all things new in one sense, it did not normally mean that the natural temperament was effaced: "But generally the innocent natural temper does remain, only refined, softened, and cast into the mould of love."²⁰² Furthermore, "As long as we dwell in an house of clay it is liable to affect the mind; sometimes by dulling or darkening the understanding, and sometimes more directly by damping and depressing the soul and sinking it into distress and heaviness." In this state, doubt or fear naturally arose and Satan would further disturb us though he cannot pollute the heart God has cleansed.²⁰³ Wesley told Miss March that doubted if any human enjoyed unbroken right "tempers," even "in a soul that is filled with love."

> There is so close a connexion between right judgement and right tempers as well as right practice, that the latter cannot easily subsist without the former. Some wrong temper, at least in a small degree, almost necessarily follows from wrong judgement: I apprehend when many say, 'Sin must remain while the body remains,' this is what they mean, though they cannot make it out.²⁰⁴

Wesley commented on Elizabeth Harper's experience that very few attain a constant testimony to the love of God and neighbour, along with an uninterrupted calmness of mind unless they have found "a second change" in a moment.²⁰⁵ Likewise, a sense of want and weakness in trial was not a fault or a sin.²⁰⁶ The pastoral role of the preachers and members of the societies was critical in helping individual believers make these distinctions.

The Experience of Christian Perfection

Wesley made explicit in his pastoral advice that all Christians had a choice to make regarding the depth and richness of their relationship with God. He noted that there was a higher and a lower rank of Christian. While both of them may be in God's favour, "The latter avoid all known sin, do much good, use all the means of grace, but have little of the life of God in their souls and are much conformed to the world. The former make the Bible their whole rule, and their

---

²⁰¹ Ibid., 212-13.
²⁰² *Letters* (Telford), 6:45.
²⁰³ *Letters* (Telford), 5:267. See also *Letters* (Telford), 6:262, 281.
²⁰⁴ *Letters* (Telford), 5:192. Wesley defined "good tempers" as the love of God and neighbour, with the opposite being worldly-mindedness, malice, cruelty, revengefulness; see Ibid., 203-04.
²⁰⁵ *Works* (Jackson), 14:261-62. Elizabeth Harper was a member of the Redruth society in London and her journal was highly regarded by Wesley, who published extracts from it in 1772.
²⁰⁶ *Letters* (Telford), 5:200 See also *Letters* (Telford), 6:89.

sole aim is the will and image of God."[207] The critical concern here is the heart's desire for a deeper relationship with God–a matter of passion and relationship, not intellect and comprehension.

SEEKING THE EXPERIENCE OF PERFECT LOVE

When seeking Christian perfection it was important that the believer did not cast away their confidence in the work of God, even if remaining sin continued to vex them. For example, Wesley told Joseph Benson to read his sermons "Sin in Believers" and "The Repentance of Believers" as these would serve to remind him that there was deliverance from remaining sin and it was clearly promised by God in Ezek. 36:25 and Deut. 30:6.[208] The seeker had to keep the focus on God's prior love for us, rather than anything we initially seek to do: "If we were first to resign our will to God in order to be in favour with Him, our case would be desperate: nay, but you shall first be conscious of His favour, and then be resigned to Him."[209] Wesley believed that God normally brought a conviction of "inbred sin" before it was possible to be delivered from it.[210] He told Mary Bishop that she did not need to be convinced of every sin "in order to be renewed in love."[211] She was to keep praying for "faith and love" and she ought to focus on the love of God in Christ rather than her own sins. He advised her to pay no heed to Catholic teaching on "the darkness of faith" as it was "unscriptural" and he reminded her that "sometimes there is painful conviction of sin preparatory to full sanctification; sometimes a conviction that has far more pleasure than pain, being mixed with joyful expectation. Always there should be a gradual growth in grace, which *need* never be intermitted from the time we are justified."[212] He told her that Joseph Benson was in error if he claimed that a person was not a believer who had any sin remaining. The Wesleys had left the Moravians over this faulty perception and so he advised her to read the second *Journal* and "The Lord Our Righteousness" to gain a more correct understanding.[213] Misunderstandings also arose about the relationship of justification, initial sanctification and entire sanctification: "You seem a little inclined to that new opinion which lately sprung up among you– that we are (properly) sanctified when we are justified. You did not observe that this strikes at the root of perfection; it leaves no room for it at all. If we are never sanctified in any other sense than we are sanctified then, Christian perfection has no being."[214]

---

[207] *Letters* (Telford), 5:173.
[208] Ibid., 214. See also *Letters* (Telford), 5:319-20; 6:22, 281; 7:33.
[209] *Letters* (Telford), 7:66.
[210] See, for example, Ibid., 329.
[211] *Letters* (Telford), 5:191.
[212] Ibid., 210. See also *Letters* (Telford), 5:182; 6:75, 262, 279.
[213] *Letters* (Telford), 5:252.
[214] Ibid., 325. Wesley recommended reading the "The Repentance of Believers."

Wesley continued to stress the importance of seeking the experience of Christian perfection on the basis of "simple faith" and to expect it now.[215]

> And how soon may you be made a partaker of sanctification! And not only by a slow and insensible growth in grace, but by the power of the Highest overshadowing you in a moment, in the twinkling of an eye, so as to utterly abolish sin and to renew you in His whole image! If you are *simple of heart*, if you are willing to receive the heavenly gift, as a little child, *without reasoning*, why may you not receive it now (emphasis mine)?[216]

This passage highlights a matter that was becoming of increasing concern to Wesley. Many of his people were over-analysing their personal experience and this was having a negative impact on their spiritual progress. He wrote to Ann Bolton: "I do not advise you to *reason* whether you have faith or not, but simply to look up to Him that loves you for whatever you want."[217] Wesley urged her to keep away from "all unprofitable reasoning" and to keep "simple faith" for today. To help her, Wesley advised reading his sermons "The Repentance of Believers," "The Scripture Way of Salvation," Jenny Cooper's *Letters* and the *Plain Account*.[218] Similar advice was given to Miss March and Wesley was glad that she had ceased the "evil reasonings" that had so long hindered her: "Always remember the essence of Christian holiness is simplicity and purity; one design, one desire–entire devotion to God. But this admits of a thousand degrees and variations."[219] He emphasised to her that "the dealings of God with man are infinitely varied, and cannot be confined to any general rule; both in justification and sanctification. He often acts in a manner we cannot account for." [220] People were not simply to wait passively for this gift of faith and he advised Elizabeth Briggs (the sister of Philothea Briggs): "What you now want is to come boldly to the throne of grace, that the hunger and thirst after his full image which God has given you may be satisfied. Full salvation is nigh, even at the door. Only believe, and it is yours."[221] He counselled Miss March that the means of grace were important here, particularly reading, meditation and prayer.[222] Wesley reminded Mary Stokes, a member of the

---

[215] *Letters* (Telford), 5:193, 305, 337-38; 7:168, 322, 341.

[216] *Letters* (Telford), 7:293. He recommended reading "The Scripture Way of Salvation"; see *Letters* (Telford), 5:276-77.

[217] *Letters* (Telford), 5:151. See also Ibid., 171, 185-86.

[218] See Ibid., 213; 15-16.

[219] Ibid., 238. See also *Letters* (Telford), 6:113.

[220] *Letters* (Telford), 5:255.

[221] Ibid., 229. See also *Letters* (Telford), 6:17, 127-28. In a letter to John Fletcher, Wesley wrote, "I seldom find it profitable to converse with any who are not athirst for full salvation; and who are not big with earnest expectation of receiving it every moment." See Tyson and Schlenther, 162.

[222] *Letters* (Telford), 6:117. See also *Letters* (Telford), 7:162.

Bristol society, that God used every circumstance to foster holiness, and while affliction was one of them, it was not essential. She was to compare St. Paul with St. John–the former had suffered much more than latter, yet John was as holy as any other believer–so let God do his work.[223] Ann Loxdale was also told not to regard suffering as the regular way that God worked: "It is true that the usual method of our Lord is to purify us by joy in the Holy Ghost and a full consciousness of His love."[224]

Given the excesses of the London revival, Wesley expressed concern over people seeking spiritual experiences for their own sake:

> George Bell, William Green, and many others, then full of love, were favoured with extraordinary revelations and manifestations from God. But by this very thing Satan beguiled them from the simplicity that is in Christ. By insensible degrees they were led to value these extraordinary gifts more than the ordinary grace of God; and I could not convince them that a grain of humble love was better than all these gifts put together. ... Faith and hope are glorious gifts, and so is every ray of eternity let into the soul. But still these are but means; the end of all, and the greatest of all is love.[225]

He strongly urged his followers to seek nothing but love, to "aim at nothing higher than this."[226] He cautioned Ann Loxdale about her powerful experiences of God because they were so different to anyone else's: "I avoid, I am afraid of, whatever is peculiar, either in the experience or the language of anyone. I desire nothing, I will accept of nothing, but the common faith and common salvation; and I want you, my dear sister, to be only just such a common Christian as Jenny Cooper was." He urged her to read the *Plain Account* "and you may be assured there is no religion under heaven higher or deeper than that which is there described."[227] He reminded Samuel Mitchell, a circuit preacher in Ireland, that there is a real spiritual danger in seeking an experience higher than love: "Many in England have thought they attained to something higher than loving God with all their hearts. But this all came to nothing. It is a snare of the Devil."[228] In a letter to Hannah Ball, he reflected on the possibility of an awareness of each member of the Trinity in spiritual experience:

---

[223] *Letters* (Telford), 5:323. See also *Works* (Jackson), 14:277; *Letters* (Telford), 5:324; 6:20; 7:100-01; 8:158.

[224] *Letters* (Telford), 7:114. See also *Letters* (Telford), 8:4-5.

[225] *Letters* (Telford), 5:349. A similar analysis of the revival was given in *Letters* (Telford), 7:57.

[226] *Letters* (Telford), 6:33. See also Ibid., 230.

[227] *Letters* (Telford), 7:67. See also *Letters* (Telford), 7:127; 8:171; Wesley, *Minutes (1803)*, 49.

[228] *Letters* (Telford), 7:358. Wesley noted that the society at Chapel-en-le-Frith had been led into spiritual extravagance by not keeping the focus on love alone; see *Works*, 23:389.

> I have lately made diligent inquiry into the experience of many that are perfected in love. And I find a very few of them who have had a clear revelation of the several Persons in the ever-blessed Trinity. It therefore appears that this is by no means essential to Christian perfection. All that is necessarily implied therein is humble, gentle, patient love: love regulating all the tempers, and governing all the words and actions.[229]

He was insistent that this love had to include love of neighbour and not simply the love of God. "In the 13th of Corinthians you have the height and depth of genuine perfection; and it is observable St. Paul speaks all along of the love of our neighbour, flowing indeed from the love of God. Mr. De Renty is an excellent pattern of this."[230] To focus on the love of God to the exclusion of active love to neighbour actually weakened spiritual life.[231]

THE ASSURANCE OF PERFECT LOVE

Wesley continued to assert that God gave an assurance to all of the reality of their spiritual experience. While a consciousness of God's favour was not the condition of that favour,[232] he did expect that all would experience the witness of the Spirit. Wesley wrote: "A *babe* in Christ ... has the witness *sometimes*. A young man (in St. John's sense) has it continually. I believe one that is *perfected in love*, or *filled with the Holy Ghost*, may be properly termed a *father*. This we must press both babes and young men to aspire after–yea, to expect. And why not now?"[233] Writing to Thomas Tattershall, a circuit preacher, he noted: "I hope you still find a witness in yourself, not only of your acceptance, but of your salvation from inbred sin and of your loving God with all your heart. And you should constantly and explicitly exhort all believers to aspire after this, and encourage them to expect it *now*."[234] Philothea Briggs was told she "may always have an evidence both of God's love to you and of yours to Him. And at some times the former may be more clear, at other times the latter."[235] He was certain that the witness did not include a sense of eternal security: "It is true the full assurance of hope excludes all doubt of our final salvation; but it does not and cannot continue any longer than we walk closely

---

[229] *Letters* (Telford), 6:266. See also *Letters* (Telford), 6:222-23, 252-53, 270, 272, 392; 8:26-27, 201, 214, 248. Wesley commented to Lady Maxwell that he had found only a few within the Societies who could clearly testify to such a distinct experience of each member of the Trinity; "Formerly I thought this was the experience of all those that were perfected in love; but I am now clearly convinced that it is not"; see *Letters* (Telford), 7:392; 8:83.

[230] *Letters* (Telford), 5:268.

[231] *Letters* (Telford), 6:115.

[232] *Letters* (Telford), 7:61.

[233] *Letters* (Telford), 5:229.

[234] *Letters* (Telford), 7:178. See also *Letters* (Telford), 5:311; 6:283; 7:246.

[235] *Letters* (Telford), 5:240. See also Ibid., 241.

with God. And it does not include any assurance of our future behaviour; neither do I know any word in all the Bible which gives us any authority to look for a testimony of this kind."[236] Many were concerned over a lack of "feelings" in their Christian walk and Wesley shared the experience of his mother who did not "feel" as much as his father, yet did ten times more work. He advised that they work to do more and to pray that God would supply the feeling.[237] He warned his followers not to trust in their feelings but to base their confidence in God's Word; otherwise their trust would be in the feelings and not in Christ. "The promises are the most strengthening and comforting truths in all the oracles of God; particularly (to believers in Christ) the promises of full sanctification."[238] Likewise negative feelings were not in themselves an evidence of sin: "Yet distress is not sin; we may be grieved, and still resigned. And this is acceptable with God."[239] In writing to Mrs. Barton on the death of her child, Wesley reminded her that "rapturous joy, such as is frequently given in the beginning of justification or of entire sanctification, is a great blessing; but it seldom continues long before it subsides into calm, peaceful love."[240] He wrote to Mrs. Bennis that "a will steadily and uniformly devoted to God is essential to a state of sanctification, but not an uniformity of joy or peace or happy communion with God." These can rise and fall in degrees and are affected by the body or Satan. He advised her to read the sermon "Wandering Thoughts" and Elizabeth Harper's journal for help in this area.[241]

The exact nature of this witness remained a problem for many and there was always a danger of mistaking Satan's voice or one's own imagination for the voice of God. Wesley believed that no written rule would distinguish them– only the Spirit himself could do that.[242] He was confident that the genuine witness of the Spirit must always be accompanied by the evidence of transformed character–the fruits of the Spirit.[243] Wesley understood from experience that the witness of the Spirit could be lost but need not be. He wrote to Mrs. Bennis to say that "one who is now in the house with me has not lost that witness one moment for these ten years. Why should you lose it any more?"[244] He made the same point to Mary Stokes that she need lose "neither

---

[236] Ibid., 253.See also *Letters* (Telford), 5:280; 6:48, 323; 7:57-58.

[237] *Letters* (Telford), 6:18. Wesley continued to uphold that "feelings" (especially love, joy and peace) were a normal and natural part of being a Christian; it was Satan's device to destroy "the whole religion of the heart" by emphasising "naked faith" alone; see *Works*, 22:287, 406-07.

[238] *Letters* (Telford), 7:64. See also *Letters* (Telford), 8:190.

[239] *Letters* (Telford), 6:40. See also *Letters* (Telford), 7:377-78.

[240] *Letters* (Telford), 6:269. Wesley's notion of a Christian response to a child's death can be seen in *Letters* (Telford), 8:253.

[241] *Letters* (Telford), 6:68.

[242] *Letters* (Telford), 5:241.

[243] *Letters* (Telford), 7:18, 377.

[244] See for example *Letters* (Telford), 5:188, 286, 88.

the blessing itself nor the witness of it. Nay, rather you shall sink deeper and deeper into His love; you shall go on from faith to faith; and patience shall have its perfect work, until you are perfect and entire, wanting nothing."[245] One of the causes of losing the witness was "evil reasonings" and he warned "were you to substitute the deductions of reason for the witness of the Spirit you never would be established."[246]

MAINTAINING THE RELATIONSHIP OF PERFECT LOVE

Though Wesley once believed that those perfected in love could not fall, experience had now taught him otherwise.[247] He told Mrs. Barton that

> ... although many taste of that heavenly gift, ... yet so few, so exceeding few, retain it one year, hardly one in ten, nay one in thirty. Many hundreds in London were made partakers of it within sixteen or eighteen months; but I doubt whether twenty of them are now as holy and as happy as they were. And hence others had doubted whether God *intended that salvation* to be enjoyed long. That many *have* it for a season, that they allow, but are not satisfied that any *retain* it always. Shall not *you* for one? You will, if you watch and pray and continue hanging upon Him.[248]

In a further letter he emphasised: "... two things are certain: the one, that it is possible to lose even the pure love of God; the other, that it is not necessary, it is not unavoidable–it may be lost, but it may be kept. Accordingly we have some in every part of the kingdom who have never been moved from their steadfastness."[249] Wesley observed to Adam Clarke that "to retain the grace of God is much more than to gain it. Hardly one in three does this. And this should be strongly and explicitly urged upon those who have tasted of perfect love."[250] He told John King (an evangelical Anglican clergyman): "It requires a great deal of watchfulness to retain the perfect love of God; and one great means of retaining it is frankly to declare what God has given you, and earnestly to exhort all the believers you meet with to follow after full salvation."[251] The role of the Spirit in this matter was critical: "In order to be all devoted to the Lord, even those who are renewed in love still need the unction of the Holy One, to teach them in all circumstances the most excellent way, and

---

[245] Ibid., 294-95. See also *Letters* (Telford), 6:339.
[246] *Letters* (Telford), 7:377-78.
[247] *Works* (Jackson), 10:426. See also *Works*, 22:422.
[248] *Letters* (Telford), 5:185. See also *Letters* (Telford), 5:273; 6:241.
[249] *Letters* (Telford), 5:188-89. See also *Works*, 22:217, 375; 23:109, 25, 37, 65, 69, 204, 38, 69. 323; *Letters* (Telford), 7:96, 207; 8:190.
[250] *Letters* (Telford), 8:188. Adam Clarke was one of Wesley's most influential preachers and the author of a standard Methodist Bible commentary.
[251] *Letters* (Telford), 7:369. See also *Letters* (Telford), 8:14.

to enable them so to watch and pray that they may continually walk therein."[252] It was important that one who had experienced Christian perfection continue to increase in love for God, and to have deeper and deeper fellowship with him.[253]

> You do well strongly to insist that those who already enjoy it cannot possibly stand still. Unless they continue to watch and pray and aspire after higher degrees of holiness, I cannot conceive not only how they can go forward but how they can keep what they have already received. Certainly, therefore, this is a point much to be insisted on, both [in] public and private, that all who have tasted of the pure [love] of God should continually grow in grace, in the image of God, and in the knowledge of our Lord Jesus Christ.[254]

To this end, his letters often contained long lists of searching questions about the present spiritual experience of his followers. These questions usually centred on their deliverance from wrong tempers, their degree of assurance and their spiritual disciplines.[255] Wesley pointed out that spiritual growth may be clear and perceptible or no more so than the growth of a tree. The lack of perceptible growth was therefore not a sign that God was not working as long as the person kept their desire for God constant.[256] He reminded Mary Bosanquet (who would later marry John Fletcher) that "One great difference between the outward and inward work of God is, inward holiness is mostly instantaneous, given in a large degree at the moment when we are justified, or when we are sanctified or saved from inbred sin; but outward holiness is mostly gradual–wrought by little and little while we deny ourselves and take up our cross and work together with Him."[257] He noted that his brother Charles seemed to regard the length of a person's experience, whereas he tended to judge by the depth of it–especially in love. For example, he observed that Miss Johnson was "deep in grace" and lived like an angel here, yet there were some things in her character he did not like and these he imputed to "human frailty." The context seems to imply her stoicism, which once he admired but did so no longer as "I now see a Stoic and a Christian are different characters."[258]

The problem of excessive analysis of one's spiritual experience was equally evident in the life of those enjoying perfect love.[259] As with the earlier stages of the Christian life, a common cause of losing the experience was being reasoned

---

[252] *Letters* (Telford), 5:271.
[253] *Letters* (Telford), 5:149, 286, 288; 6:58, 191, 297, 319-20; 7:80, 103, 263; 8:4-5.
[254] *Letters* (Telford), 8:184. See also *Letters* (Telford), 5:189; 6:111, 230; 8:188.
[255] *Letters* (Telford), 5:152, 188, 300-01; 6:10, 15-16, 222-23, 225, 232, 266, 270; 7:19; 8:26-27, 85, 160, 181, 183.
[256] *Letters* (Telford), 5:331.
[257] *Letters* (Telford), 6:189-90.
[258] Ibid., 129. He particularly mentioned Clement of Alexandria as one whom he previously valued. See also Ibid., 139, 66.
[259] See for example *Letters* (Telford), 5:337; 6:57, 369, 382.

out of it.²⁶⁰ Commenting on the life of Phyllis (Philothea) Briggs, Wesley said: "She *did* taste of the pure love of God. But unprofitable reasonings stole away her strength. One would hope she is now recovering it."²⁶¹ This particularly applied to the experience of temptation and confusing human infirmities with sin. While in this life, temptation was a normal part of Christian experience and not an evidence of the loss of spiritual life.²⁶² He told Hannah Ball: "It is next to impossible to retain salvation from sin without having a clear witness of it, especially in time of temptation; they who then lose the witness commonly lose the blessing itself."²⁶³ He admitted that it was easy, under temptation, to confuse the normal human "tempers" with those that were sinful. He reminded them that the ministry of the Holy Spirit was essential here: "This is never more needful than with regard to anger; because there is an anger which is not sinful, a disgust at sin which is often attended with much commotion of the animal spirits: and I doubt whether we can well distinguish this from sinful anger but by that light from heaven."²⁶⁴ Likewise, he advised Mrs. Marston, "Undoubtedly as long as you are in the body you will come short of what you would be, and you will see more and more of your numberless defects and the imperfection of your best actions and tempers." But this need not hinder her spiritual life.²⁶⁵ The question of analysing the "tempers" also exercised Philothea Briggs, and Wesley wrote:

> One cannot be saved from evil tempers without being all devoted to God; neither can a soul be all devoted to God without being saved from sin: but it is often exceeding hard to judge of others, whether they are saved from all evil tempers, and whether they are all devoted to God or not; yea, it is hard to judge of ourselves–nay we cannot do it without the anointing of the Holy One given for that very purpose.²⁶⁶

In a letter to Miss March he said:

> You are a living witness of two great truths: the one, that there cannot be a lasting, steady enjoyment of pure love without the direct testimony of the Spirit concerning it, without God's Spirit shining on His own work; the other, that setting perfection too high is the ready way to drive it out of the world. A third thing you may learn from your own experience is that the heart of man contains

---

²⁶⁰ See for example *Letters* (Telford), 5:176, 254, 308; 7:17-18, 129; 8:88.
²⁶¹ *Letters* (Telford), 7:17-18.
²⁶² Ibid., 56.
²⁶³ Ibid., 93.
²⁶⁴ *Letters* (Telford), 5:243. See also Ibid., 256.
²⁶⁵ Ibid., 196.
²⁶⁶ *Letters* (Telford), 6:24. See also Ibid., 104.

things that one would think incompatible. Such are the tempers and sensations of those especially that are renewed in love.[267]

He urged her not to reason over this because the more we want God's work in us explained before we will accept it, the more we will wander spiritually.[268] He told Mrs. Bennis that she would always find in herself "unfitness" or else it was salvation by works. Those experiencing Christian perfection need not feel sinfulness any more, but they would always feel helplessness and so they must not doubt what God had done.[269] The core problem was "evil reasoning" which hindered both her holiness and happiness; she needed "true Christian simplicity." "Nothing is more clear, according to the plain Bible account, than sanctification, pure love reigning in the heart and life. And nothing is more plain than the necessity of this in order to feel happiness here and hereafter. Check all reasoning concerning these first principles, else you will exceedingly darken your soul."[270] Wesley defined simplicity as "that grace 'whereby the soul casts off all unnecessary reflections upon itself.'"[271] It was important to retain a simplicity and singleness of intention for the whole of life's spiritual journey.[272] On the other hand, Wesley was equally concerned that his followers not denigrate or abandon developing their understanding of Christian doctrine and experience. He believed that God did not want to destroy our desire for knowledge, but to regulate it.[273] In writing to Ann Bolton he said, "But I advise ... you to improve your understanding by every means. It is certain knowledge is an excellent gift of God *when under the guidance of love* [emphasis mine]."[274] Wesley remained concerned over people seeking an increase in knowledge for its own sake:

> I am less careful about your increase in knowledge any farther than it tends to love. There is a danger of your laying more stress on this than sound reason requires. Otherwise you would reap much profit from sermons, which do not improve your knowledge–which do not apply to the understanding so directly as to the heart. I feel more want of heat than light. *I value light; but it is nothing compared to love.* [emphasis mine] Aim at this, my dear friend, in all public exercises, and then you will seldom be disappointed. Then you will not stop on the threshold of perfection (I trust you do not now), but will press on to the mark,

---

[267] Ibid., 88.
[268] Ibid.
[269] *Letters* (Telford), 5:330-31.
[270] Ibid., 193-94. Similar warnings on "evil reasonings" or "unprofitable reasonings" are found in *Letters* (Telford), 6:6, 8, 243.
[271] *Letters* (Telford), 6:128. This was an unreferenced quotation from Fénelon.
[272] Ibid., 8. See also *Letters* (Telford), 7:74.
[273] *Letters* (Telford), 7:81.
[274] *Letters* (Telford), 6:15.

to the prize of the high calling of God in Christ Jesus, till you experimentally know all that love of God which passeth all (speculative) knowledge.[275]

This same concern was seen in a letter to Mary Bishop where he urged her to avoid certain kinds of reasoning. Wesley acknowledged the need to read and recommended Pascal's *Thoughts* (in the *Christian Library*) and the first two tracts in the *Preservative against Unsettled Notions in Religion*. She needed the continual help of God to understand aright and he reminded her that "the love, without which, St. Paul affirms, all we do profits us nothing, is that humble, meek, patient love of our neighbour, which supposes and flows from the love of God." A "degree of reasoning" was fine, if joined with humility and prayer; faith was much more important.[276] Wesley remains consistent here by keeping love as the core quality required and knowledge is of value to the degree that it is the servant of love and not the master. In a further letter, written after she had clearly experienced Christian perfection, he said, "He has given you a good understanding improved by experience and free conversation with many of His dearest children."[277]

RECOVERING THE RELATIONSHIP OF PERFECT LOVE

A vital question for Wesley's followers was whether the experience of Christian perfection could be recovered if it had been lost. He wrote to Mary Bosanquet: "The moment any are justified, they are babes in Christ, little children. When they have the abiding witness of pardon, they are young men .... It was not this, but much more, even salvation from inward sin, which above five hundred in London received. True, they did not (all or most of them) retain it; but they had it as surely as they had pardon. And you and they may receive it again."[278] On a visit to Whitby in 1783, Wesley noted:

> I met such a select society as I have not seen since I left London. They were about forty, of whom I did not find one who had not a clear witness of being saved from inbred sin. Several of them had lost it for a season, but could never rest till they had recovered it. And every one of them seemed now to walk in the full light of God's countenance.[279]

In a similar vein he wrote to Mrs. Bennis and noted that "many" all over England were in the same state she is; they were once "renewed in love" but after some time were moved from their steadfastness "yet several of these have within a few months recovered all they had lost, and some with increase, being far more established than ever they were before." This came by simple faith

---

[275] Ibid., 153. See also *Letters* (Telford), 6:335, 381; 8:88.
[276] *Letters* (Telford), 6:205-06. See also Ibid., 213.
[277] Ibid., 69-70.
[278] *Letters* (Telford), 5:175.
[279] *Works*, 23:317.

and by expecting it now.[280] The recovery of the experience would be instantaneous: "And you know it [perfect love] was given you in a moment. It was the same with Sally Ryan, with Nancy Bolton, and with all those whom I have known that are now enabled to pray without ceasing. To every one of them that blessing was given in an instant. So it will be given to *you* again."[281] An example of this was Miss Sparrow (a member of the London society): "From your whole account it appears beyond all reasonable doubt that you have tasted once and again of the pure love of God."[282]

Conclusion

In these final years Wesley continued to maintain the vision of the Christian life that he had held from his time at Oxford. He retained his conviction that God was to be understood essentially as a God of love who desired a loving relationship with all people; all other aspects of his nature, character and purpose are to be understood in relation to love. Furthermore, there is nothing in God's declarations or actions that would contradict the primacy of love. A love-based relationship could not exist without liberty and the power of contrary choice. In upholding the primacy of God's initiation of the relationship, Wesley remained steadfast in his opinion that grace, truly understood, enabled a genuine human response to God's invitation. Wesley was certain that his picture was both biblical and faithful to the early church and his Anglican heritage. Accordingly, he rejected the whole Calvinist conception of a Sovereign God who issues irresistible decrees to govern his creation. He considered this to be theologically unsound and fundamentally unfaithful to God's stated mission to seek the redemption of the whole race on the basis of his love and mercy alone. While he admitted individual texts could be read to support the Calvinist interpretation, he continued to argue for a holistic reading of Scripture (the analogy of faith). Wesley did not alter his belief that Christianity was primarily about the heart and not the mind, and he maintained that God's desire was for a relationship based in trust over doctrinal correctness centred in intellectual comprehension of propositional truth. The Calvinist controversy highlights his commitment to the religion of the heart as he continued to seek fellowship with Calvinists, even though he strongly opposed their doctrinal stance. However, he makes it clear in this period that it is not an option to wilfully ignore the place of theological reflection on the essentials of the faith as they have been stated by the early church.

The model that has been proposed for his theological method remains fruitful for this stage of his life and ministry. The elements of Scripture, reason, Christian experience and community ethos in a dynamic network energised by

---

[280] *Letters* (Telford), 5:190-91. See also *Letters* (Telford), 5:176; 6:237; 7:295; 8:134.
[281] *Letters* (Telford), 6:45.
[282] *Letters* (Telford), 5:308.

the Holy Spirit are still clearly referenced in his doctrinal and pastoral writings. While direct citations linking the work of the Spirit with Scripture are not as prominent as in the previous period of his life, there are now many more to the work of the Spirit utilising reason, Christian experience and community ethos, particularly in the letters. This is not surprising given the maturity of his movement, the rise of a new generation of Methodists, and the need to plan for its continuance after his death. These ensured that in these final decades of his life pastoral issues would continue to occupy his attention. Many areas of doctrine and practice are now settled and do not need to be revisited; this is particularly true of his spiritual vision and the intimate link between Scripture (the rule) and the Spirit (the guide). Scripture remains the critical means utilised by the Spirit in theologising, but God can apply the text to believers in ways other than the plain, logical reading of the text would suggest, making personal truth more important than propositional truth. There are constant references to Christian experience as an essential component of theological reflection and practice. Wesley continues to believe that Scripture, reason and Christian experience do not contradict each other when the ministry of the Spirit is actively sought by persons in community. What has become much clearer in this period is the indispensable role of the Methodist community itself, as it was shaped by the liturgy (sermons, hymns and testimonies especially), accountability structures, conferences and the reading of materials written or edited by Wesley. The continued health of Methodism is inextricably tied to the Spirit-formed ethos of its own community.

Matters of doctrinal substance concerning Christian perfection in this period are more focused on answering the questions raised by Methodists than engaging in continued debate with his critics from other theological traditions. He continues to defend his core conviction about humans now being under the covenant of grace and how this is perfectly compatible with the continuing presence of various infirmities caused by the limitations of bodily life since the fall. These infirmities are involuntary and do not carry culpability; sin is still to be defined as the voluntary violation of a known law of God and does involve culpability. With the maturing of his movement, it was important to clarify carefully the doctrinal distinction between entire sanctification and Christian perfection. His conclusion is that entire sanctification is the initial point of entry into Christian perfection but it is not the end of the spiritual journey; the pure love of God and neighbour can be enjoyed in a deeper and deeper level of relationship. His preferred understanding of perfection emphasises the positive aspect of the believer passionately seeking after God; the subsequent infilling of love expels all that is contrary to its full expression in character and life. There is a place for, and he does refer to, the more negative picture of purification and being cleansed from sin to enable the infilling of love, but does not regard it as normative. Wesley continues to emphasise that this whole experience is by grace alone and faith alone, and therefore the actual entry into the experience is instantaneous. This is witnessed to by the Spirit of God and without it, continuing in the relationship of perfect love is very difficult; however, the intensity of the witness does vary.

The focus of his writings is now on pastoral issues (the circumstance of perfection) rather than defending his doctrinal comprehension (the substance of perfection). There is an unmistakable emphasis on the vital importance of the Methodists themselves to keep the teaching and practice of holiness alive. The life and ministry of both preachers and laity is the best proof of his theological understanding. It was critical that his people to improve their grasp of Methodist doctrine and practice if this was to carry over to another generation and there is an explicit urging of them to read Methodist publications to help in this process. While Wesley did not elevate doctrine over heart experience, he argued that heart experience would not long survive without a clear biblical and doctrinal foundation. In his own case, this foundation had been prior to the heart experience, but for the new generation of Methodists so dependent on lay leaders and local preachers (who were not formally educated in divinity) it was vital that their experience be formed by a sound theological understanding. With many decades now having passed since Wesley had first encountered clear testimonies to Christian perfection, he had to emphasise points of caution in retaining the experience and then how to recover the relationship were it to be lost. Once again, Wesley rarely quoted passages of Scripture in his pastoral letters but he now explicitly advises his people to read his writings and these contain a plethora of Scripture quotations and allusions. This confirms that it is not simply the actual texts of Scripture that matter, but the way you read them. This emphasised the vital importance of the Methodist ethos and the "analogy of faith" to give the reading perspective. Wesley continues to warn of the danger of overvaluing or undervaluing reason and there are abundant warnings about trying to rationally analyse their Christian experience at the expense of a sustained trusting relationship. He cautions them about focusing on "evil reasonings" that undermine a loving relationship with God by creating doubt. The context of these warnings seems to indicate his concern is over an intellectualism divorced from a heart relationship. He certainly valued reading and the gaining of appropriate knowledge, but the kind of reading was critical because of the dangers posed by the intellectual background of the Enlightenment and its rising confidence in rationalism and logic. This was a major issue for many of his Methodists, since Calvinism seemed a much more logical and rational system. In these circumstances, Wesley continued to argue for a warm heart over a cold mind, passion over logic, and relationship over intellect. He affirms that knowledge and understanding are good, but they must be in the context of love and relationship. It is God himself who has made love the primary quality in a relationship with him rather than intellectual comprehension. This is in harmony with the Methodist conviction that God wants everyone to be in a right relationship with him, and love can be experienced and reciprocated by all, whereas intellectual comprehension cannot. This agrees with Wesley's conviction that Christian perfection can be experienced by everyone, including children. Through it all Wesley retains a strong emphasis on the role of the Spirit in personal relationship and discipleship. He makes it clear that there is no substitute for Christian experience within the community of faith as the source of genuinely Christian wisdom and discernment, for both doctrinal and practical issues. The role of Christian experience in challenging and confirming the interpretation and application of the Scriptures is of vital importance. Wesley avoids mere subjectivism by constantly tying Christian experience to the ethos of the community (both current and historical), which is itself shaped by their rational reflection on the Scriptures. The editing of his own works during this period to reflect his mature understanding confirms this process was a key part of his theological method in pastoral practice.

CHAPTER 6

Conclusion

This study has sought to discover John Wesley's approach to theology and whether he had a distinctive theological method that could be used today by his successors. In particular, the research has focused on his pastoral practice as the spiritual guide for the people called Methodists. His understanding of the doctrine of Christian perfection has been used to illustrate his theological method and to discover if there were any significant variations between the methodology he followed in formulating doctrine and its application in pastoral ministry. The research has supported the current consensus amongst Methodist scholars that John Wesley is to be regarded primarily as a pastoral theologian. His own writings demonstrate his lack of interest in "speculative divinity" and his deliberate preference for "practical divinity." Abraham's description of Wesley as a spiritual guide for his people is supported by Wesley's own account of his ministry and the pastoral nature of the majority of his writings. However, it would be a mistake to conclude that Wesley was unskilled in the formulation of doctrine or in academic theological debate. From the varied material dealing with the doctrine of Christian perfection and those areas of theological reflection immediately associated with it, a clear and consistent theology with a sustained evangelical Protestant focus emerges. His own stated interest is a pastoral theology that begins with, and then reflects upon, the reality of the Christian's encounter with the living God in Jesus Christ through the personal ministry of the Holy Spirit.

Wesley's Theological Perspective:
God and Humans Characterised by Love and Relationships

From the very beginning of his Oxford years Wesley had visualised God's essential nature as love; a love displayed amongst the Persons of the Triune Godhead and to all creation. God's desire for loving relationships then defines and shapes the expression of all the other divine attributes. Human beings, who are made in God's image, are to be understood primarily in terms of love and relationships, both with God and neighbour. The divine-human interaction is, therefore, to be defined by love and relationship and not by an intellectual comprehension of doctrine. Nor is it to be expressed by conformity to divine laws imposed by a Sovereign God, through a series of decrees that are isolated from mercy and justice. In harmony with this conception, he consistently declared that the whole of the law and commandments can be summed up by the call to love God supremely and the neighbour as oneself. Furthermore, this requirement was also a promise, for God does not ask anything of us that we cannot implement by his grace. This divine-human relationship requires that human beings are genuinely free and capable of the power of contrary choice. Wesley believed this was guaranteed by God's establishment of a covenant of grace to replace the covenant of works that had existed prior to the Fall. He acknowledged that life in body is now subject to the ravages of sin, both personal and corporate. However, God lovingly changed the covenant with us from works to grace to deal with this reality, and it is God's grace alone which enables us to meet the new demands. Under this covenant, sin is defined as a deliberate violation of the law of love, making it voluntary, intentional and culpable. This means that infirmities, errors, mistakes, and misjudgements, that are obvious violations of the original covenant of works with Adam, do not violate the covenant of grace as long as there is confession, repentance and gracious remediation. Under these conditions, all involuntary shortcomings that would earn condemnation under the covenant of works are now graciously covered by the atonement. This makes a relationship of perfect love defined by purity of intention, singleness of purpose and a heart's passion for God possible under the present conditions of bodily existence, but not perfect performance or conformity to a standard of conduct defined by impersonal law and sovereign decrees. Salvation is thus centred on a whole-hearted passion for God rather than perfect conformity to rules and regulations. Wesley believed this was biblical, clearly supported by antiquity, the Church of England and modelled in the lives of numerous 'saints' and the people called Methodists.

"The true, the scriptural, experimental religion" of the Heart

Many in the eighteenth century viewed Christianity as an intellectual system, centred on systematic theology; belief was then an intellectual quality involving the comprehension and application of propositional truth. This was certainly congenial to the developing Enlightenment approach to the study of religion and was popular with many Calvinists. Wesley believed that Calvinism erred by focusing on God's sovereignty, with the consequent emphasis on rules, regulations and perfect compliance. While Wesley was influenced by these developments, he clearly rejected their main thrust in order to embrace Christianity as a personal encounter with God, a relationship based on trust, centred in the heart, and with an affinity for personal knowledge rather than abstract truth. In the light of the analysis of Smith and Harrison, Wesley seems to retain a pre-modern understanding of religion.

In the light of this, Wesley contended for a gracious acceptance of diverse views on matters of theological opinion, provided that one's personal life and relationships were characterised by the transforming power of God's love. He seemed to be content to accept the essentials of the faith as they were expressed by the classical creeds of the early church and his own Anglican heritage. In the final decades of his ministry he does admit the need for these essentials to be understood to some degree in order to prevent heart religion becoming a fixation on feelings, lacking any anchoring in the classical theological affirmations of faith. He explicitly acknowledged the role of the theological teaching of the early Church, as well as the sixteenth and seventeenth century Anglican formularies expressed in its homilies, articles and liturgy. He felt this gave a firm foundation from which to read, interpret and apply the classical consensus of the faith to his own day.

Wesley's Theological Methodology: God and the Grace

Wesley initially seemed to uphold the emerging Enlightenment view that defined belief in terms of intellectual comprehension and faith as assent to propositional truth. His own spiritual journey led him to question this approach and he returned to the earlier view of belief in the context of personal encounter and relationship, with faith defined primarily in terms of trust. During 1738 he personally experienced the critical difference between defining Christianity in intellectual and behavioural terms and the experimental reality of a personal relationship with God through the presence of the Holy Spirit. This brings a new perspective to the whole process of theologising, centring on love and relationship rather than propositional truth and behavioural conformity to rules and regulations. It makes the heart and not the head the primary locus of God's gracious working; in this understanding, technical information is no substitute for actual lived experience. This retains a focus on the personal and community experience of the Christian faith rather than the emerging objectification to be found in so much scholarship of the modern period. The latter approach clearly favours the philosophical approach of formal systematic theology, with its inevitable dissection, analysis and resulting reductionism. Wesley as a pastoral theologian had a lucid and holistic vision of the nature of God and human beings, as well as the essential qualities of the relationship between them; it was this that set the framework for his theological methodology.

In examining the recent scholarly literature on Wesley studies, it is apparent that the most common method of approaching Wesley as a theologian has been by dissection and analysis, looking at aspects and themes of his work in some detail before trying to organise the material around some integrating concept that would tie the diverse findings together in a coherent system. The reductionist approach has led into a series of entrenched positions from which it is now very difficult to move. The elements identified in Wesley's methodology are not new and each element has been examined before (often in great detail) by other scholars. The component parts are not unique to Methodism and are found to some degree in all Christian traditions. However, while you may identify correctly the parts and their nature by dissection, in the process you lose the dynamic wholeness that characterised Wesley's theological method in pastoral practice.

The Living Voice of God: The Work of the Holy Spirit

During the period from 1725 to 1738 there is development in Wesley's understanding of the role of the Holy Spirit in the life of a Christian and in the community of faith. He comes to affirm that it is the presence of God himself through the Spirit that is critical for the relationship to be experimentally real, and God has the ability to communicate directly with all persons through the Spirit. It is the Spirit himself who challenges all theological opinions and practices, approves and confirms experientially that the understanding and application are within the framework of an authentic heart experience of God. The Spirit is free to do this directly with the person or via the use of 'means' and this is the key to Wesley's whole theological enterprise. This is the critical step that is missing from much current scholarship. There are plenty of references to the work of the Spirit in Wesley's use of the sources, doctrinal formulations and practical ministry, but none of them explicitly identify his primary role. From the sources consulted, only Leroy Howe and Lycurgus Starkey make the point that it is God himself who is the primary source of faith and understanding, but this is not explicitly developed in relation to Wesley's theological method. Wesley initially identified these means as Scripture, reason, antiquity, the Church of England and experience. It is the Spirit's use of these means of grace that enables Christians within their community of faith to avoid both enthusiasm (the absence of means) and rationalism (unaided human effort). In this evangelical understanding, the person/community doing the reading, interpretation and application of Scripture is never autonomous: it is always the role of the living Spirit to raise up 'prophets' to give fresh visions, new perspectives, and new insights; to recapture, renew, or refresh the soteriological beliefs and practices settled between the apostolic times and the early Fathers. There are no 'new' doctrines to be discovered, only re-statements and fresh applications.

The Written Voice of God: The Scriptures

As a Protestant, Wesley strongly upheld the primacy of Scripture for all theological reflection and practice. He was well aware that the Bible must not only be read, but it must be interpreted and then applied. These points are generally not denied by theologians, but how the Scripture functions authoritatively for Wesley is much more problematic; William J. Abraham and Joel B. Green have raised concerns that are echoed by many others. Appealing to the Bible as a source of propositional truth did not bring resolution to theological debates because Wesley's opponents made the same truth claims based on their understanding of the text. While seeing the Scripture as a means of grace does not answer every question raised by current scholarship, it does affirm that the Bible does occupy a privileged place in Wesley's estimation. As the Word of God written, the Bible is in full harmony with the living voice of God through the presence of the Holy Spirit. This study agrees with Scott J. Jones and many others that, for Wesley, the Scriptures have a soteriological focus and contain all that is necessary for both faith and practice. The Bible sets the boundaries for what is and what is not acceptable in a relationship with God, since the whole content faithfully portrays God's nature, character and purpose. Biblical truth was not to be found by isolating selected proof texts; it had to be read holistically (the analogy of faith) in the light of its intentions to initiate and develop a relationship of love. The central message of the Scripture was to be read in terms of love, trust and relationship, not propositions, assent and doctrinal systems.

The Personal Encounter with God: Reason

Given the central role of the Bible as a means of grace, it still had to be read, understood and applied in the life of the believer and the community of faith. Jones has demonstrated that Wesley linked Scripture with reason more often than with any of the other means. Given his historical setting with its increasing conviction that reason alone was the dominant source in theologising, Wesley had to avoid both overvaluing and undervaluing it. His early spiritual journey shows a greater confidence in the powers of reason but he soon came to realise its limitations; this study argues that he came to value reason more as common sense and pastoral wisdom. Randy L. Maddox and Rebekah L. Miles both agree that it made a wonderful tool when illuminated by the work of the Spirit, both personally and corporately, but without this it was inadequate as a source or authority in theologising. In Wesley's later years there are constant warnings about allowing an overemphasis on rationalism and logic to create intellectual doubts about God's revelation and way of working, thus undermining trust and harming the relationship.

The Ethos of the Faith Community

Wesley's life and ministry demonstrates the central importance of the community of faith in theologising, even if 'tradition' is a poor term to describe it. From the beginning Wesley makes explicit reference to the early church and his own Anglican heritage (almost exclusively in its sixteenth and seventeenth century forms), as well as a number of 'saints' from other periods of church history. As the Methodist movement developed Wesley overtly included it as an essential faith community for his people, and explicit references to antiquity and the Church of England decline. He believed that Christians could not afford to ignore the theological essentials established on a firm scriptural foundation by the early Fathers, and the Church of England, but if the message and experience of Christian perfection was to be kept alive, then the Methodist community itself was critical to this task. The major works by Thorsen and Jones do not adequately treat this development and only the writings of Angela Shier-Jones really make reference to its critical importance, though not in an exhaustive treatment.

The Personal Encounter with God: Christian Experience

Wesley always had an insatiable desire for an empirical and verifiable experience of God; a definite Christian experience and not simply general life experience. He constantly valued the contribution of Scripture, reason and ethos for his own life and ministry, but he was soon convinced that if Christianity is essentially about a loving relationship with God, then it must involve an inward experience and not just mental assent or outward behaviour. The events surrounding Wesley's attendance at the Aldersgate meeting brought to him the experiential evidence of the Spirit's presence that he had long been seeking. His theoretical convictions about the nature of the God-believer relationship now became an experiential assurance through the living presence of the Spirit. For the rest of his ministry, Wesley insisted on the indispensable necessity of the living voice of the Spirit to persons in community. There is no real dispute about any of this by the scholars studied, though it is the British Methodist theologian Clive Marsh who draws our attention to the crucial difference between life experience and specifically Christian experience through the presence of the Spirit.

Wesley's Theological Methodology: Developing an Effective Model

The Wesleyan Quadrilateral as a Model: Its Conception and Utility

Outler's contention that Scripture, reason and experience are core components in Wesley's theological methodology is strongly supported from Wesley's own extensive writings. The term 'tradition' only occurs in a negative context when referring to Roman Catholicism, but Wesley does clearly refer to antiquity and the Church of England, with an occasional reference to people and writings from other periods and church backgrounds. After 1740 there are frequent references to Methodism itself, especially post 1770. While it can be argued that tradition is not the best term to use, there is a sense in which it could have value as a shorthand reference to the heritage of the church as a source for theologising. This study has argued that a better term to use is ethos. The critical question debated amongst many Wesleyan scholars is whether Wesley's theological method is best summarised using Outler's term (the 'Quadrilateral') and whether in this form it is as clear, sophisticated and useful as Outler and a number of other scholars believe. The tendency is to arrange the elements in a hierarchy, normally with Scripture as the most important element and the others are then related to it in various schemes. Arguments then centre on the intellectual adequacy of the conception of the components parts and their rational links. The work of the Spirit, when mentioned at all, is then identified with one or more of the elements in the structure. The model suffers from being a static conception and is usually reduced to a mechanical diagram with fixed reference points. This provides plenty of material for scholarly debate, but as Abraham rightly points out, it makes it virtually useless for determining doctrine or practice in any authoritative way.

The Dynamic Neural Network as a Model: Its Conception and Utility

Wesley's understanding of Christianity is undoubtedly centred on love and relationships and his theological methodology is faithful to this vision. Love and relationships, by their very nature, cannot be reduced to intellectual comprehension, a system of ideas and mechanical formulae. Propositional statements and theological terminology are finally inadequate before the profound element of mystery involved in the God-human relationship, even though the actual experience of love can be strongly affirmed. The classical Christian confessions view the divine Trinity as Persons in an eternal relationship of love who exercise various functions and roles within that mutual relationship. Wesley's theological method has similar characteristics and it has been argued that this can be better captured by the model of a dynamic neural network, energised by the living presence of the Spirit. In this network there are mutually interlinked critical nodes, which are identified as Scripture, reason, community ethos and Christian experience, and these are continually energised by the living presence of the Spirit, making it a dynamic system. Current scholarly analysis is rather like the dissection of a living organism; you can separate out the parts, analyse, compare, evaluate and even put them back together again; you can then describe your understanding of how they work together. But no matter how perfectly you do this, dissection inevitably destroys the actual 'life' of the organism and a living creature is more than the sum of its parts put back together. I believe this is the critical limitation of the quadrilateral as a model. As currently envisaged it lacks 'life'–the immediate reality of the presence of the Spirit simultaneously energising and being the living link between the elements of the whole network.

Wesley sees God alone as the single and sole authority and source for all theologising. He is then free to use all, some or no means at all in communicating through the Holy Spirit his love, desire, invitation to and nurturing of a mutual relationship with persons and communities; Wesley makes this point explicitly. Arguments over the primacy of Scripture, reason, experience or tradition are pointless, as none of the means can substitute for, or be equal to, the authority of God himself. Wesley firmly believes that God normally uses the various means of grace, but they have no merit in themselves; there is only instrumental value as they are energised by the presence of the Spirit in the life of the believer and the faith community. To focus on the means is to lose the life and reduce his theological methodology to a mechanical system to be dissected, comprehended, analysed, evaluated, and manipulated by human beings. Amongst the means of grace, the Scripture (the soteriological "rule") plays a central and normally indispensable role, as it is in full harmony with the living voice of the Spirit (the "guide"). It is this dynamic, living system that defines the Methodist ethos and its approach to theologising. This energised, dynamic interlinking and interweaving of the means and our own lives points to Wesley's understanding of pastoral theology being akin to an immersion experience in which the means and the persons are simultaneously 'bathed' in the Spirit. It must be acknowledged that dissection and analysis have a place even in this model as it is important in order to increase our knowledge of how God works in persons and communities, but this must never become a substitute for the living system.

Wesley's Theological Method in Pastoral Practice
The "Substance" of Christian Perfection

Wesley had come to believe that the doctrine of Christian perfection was clearly scriptural, rational and true to the teaching of the early church, his own Anglican heritage and the writings of many Christians from other times and backgrounds. His doctrinal understanding is relatively consistent from 1733 onwards, with the publication of "The Circumcision of the Heart." Wesley's own key works that deal with doctrinal substance are found in his sermons, treatises, *Notes*, and edited works. In his own works Scripture is paramount and this is evidenced by the copious direct quotations, extensive strings of texts, references which are substantially accurate but not utilising the exact wording of the text, allusions, biblical imagery and language. The substance of the doctrine is anchored and tested in Scripture, as it has been understood and applied within the Methodist community of faith, using reason, community ethos and Christian experience. The latter is the essential confirmatory element that the theological reflection is true to God's nature and purposes. Wesley believed the Spirit was at work in both the persons and the community doing the reading and interpretation, as well as in the original writers whose material was consulted.

The "Circumstance" of Christian Perfection

Wesley maintained that it is not the ability to comprehend a doctrine that is critical, but the heart experience of love. Entering into, maintaining and recovering the heart experience was initially studied by the use of reason, the ethos of the community and the written testimonies of past saints. The critical change comes because of his own personal spiritual journey and the developing pastoral leadership of the Methodists. His leadership of the Methodist movement provided him with a regular ministry of preaching and teaching to his people in a group setting, as well as the opportunity of examining them regarding the outcome of his ministry in their lives. Methodist societies, classes and bands became a living laboratory to propose, test, evaluate, and restate doctrinal and practical understandings and applications. In this setting, pastoral wisdom and practical experience were paramount, not academic analysis of the biblical text or systematic theology. Guidance in matters relating to Christian experience depended heavily on the work and ministry of the Spirit. He worked through the lives of his people, Methodist sermons, hymns, prayers, conferences, books, tracts, letters, and conversations. Wesley's own direct pastoral ministry was carried out in person as well as by letter and then recorded in his diaries, journals and extensive correspondence. The focal point in this material is clearly pastoral wisdom, common sense, the ethos of the Methodist community, and Christian experience (his own and that of others). He frequently refers to the direct work of the Spirit in their lives and through the means of grace, and he makes particular note of the value of personal testimony, Christian conversation and conference. He refers people most commonly to his own written materials for extended help, but direct quotations or references to Scripture are not common in the letters themselves. This is because it was important that his people read, interpreted and applied the text in a Methodist framework, and this was best done in through material that Wesley (and other trusted writers) had prepared.

Conclusions

John Wesley is to be identified as a pastoral or practical theologian. The perspective from which he approached the task of theologising comes from his conviction that the essential nature of God is love and that all other facets of his nature, character and purposes are in harmony with this. Human beings are created in the image of God, and the interrelationship between God and his creation is characterised by a relationship of love. It is for this reason that Wesley can define the essential nature of Christianity as "the true, the scriptural, experimental religion" of the heart. God's plan of salvation has to do with the restoration of a relationship of love based on trust, rather than the intellectual command of doctrines and conformity to rules and regulations. This makes personal and community transformation the critical test of correct theological reflection, formulation, and application.

Wesley's writings undoubtedly make reference to Scripture, reason, experience, Christian antiquity, and the Church of England (these latter two being summarised as 'tradition' by Outler and others). Outler's coining of the term the 'Wesleyan quadrilateral' therefore has some validity and its usefulness has been demonstrated by many scholars from the Methodist tradition. It has not gone unchallenged and with the rise of postmodern thought its limitations are increasingly apparent. Most solutions offered thus far have been to try and rehabilitate the model or to scrap it altogether. This study contends that a new model can be developed that is based on the significant work done by Outler and others, but is faithful to the current postmodern setting with its emphasis on personal knowledge and community.

It has demonstrated that there is a failure on the part of much modern scholarship to consider Wesley's stated perspective as the base from which to construct a model of his theological method. The critical observation to be made is Wesley's insistence that God is a God of love, and that the whole goal of salvation is to restore human beings to an enjoyment of that love in a relationship with God himself and with other persons. Such love by its very nature must be experienced, it must be "felt." For Wesley, this was the key role of the Holy Spirit and his writings are filled with references to the witness of the Spirit and his work in people and communities. Furthermore, a loving relationship cannot finally be reduced to propositional statements in documents, carried out by third parties or limited to theoretical comprehension. As an evangelical, Wesley was convinced that God entered into a personal relationship with his people through the ministry of the Holy Spirit and therefore was perfectly capable of communicating with his people directly. In Wesley's estimation, this made God himself the one and only source of relational (theological) truth. Wesley also clearly believed that this direct experience of God was liable to be perceived wrongly and misunderstood due to the present realities of human existence blighted by personal sin and its consequences. This liability did not mean that God could not or would not work directly in a person's life, but a God of love could not leave his people in such a predicament.

Wesley's unique insight was to realise that God had made full provision to help humanity at this very point of need. The Holy Spirit could not only work directly in the human heart, he could also utilise indirect means of grace as instruments to convey God's personal communication. These means of grace are identified by Wesley as Scripture, reason, the community (Methodist) ethos and Christian experience. Each element only has value when the Spirit uses them; personal and community access to the Spirit's use of the means comes by faith (trust) alone. The model proposed to picture this is a dynamic, neural network in which the four elements are intimately intertwined and all are energised by the presence of the Spirit. The model is a holistic one, with the Spirit using the elements in whatever sequence and priority he deems best for the situation. Wesley believed that the Spirit would normally always use Scripture as the norm for understanding and living out our relationship of love with God and neighbour, with the other elements assisting in the process of interpretation and application. But he did not allow the means to replace the direct work of the Spirit and without his presence they were simply tools used by people and communities for their own purposes. This freedom of the Spirit allows him to use the network and the elements as he chooses to suit the particular situation or person and it is never ours to command.

There is always going to be an element of mystery in our experience of God as a Christian Methodist community, since the relationship with him is finally beyond the limits of human comprehension and language. God as a Person in his relationships and communication focuses upon personal and not propositional truth. Love is the essence of the relationship and it is centred on the heart; therefore we should not expect or focus upon precision, exactitude, and rational systems. In such a setting, the character of those involved in the communication is of prime importance, rather than their ability to construct and convey a logical intellectual system. Pastoral theology is primarily concerned with fostering a relationship and assisting the transformation of character, both personal and community, rather than constructing rational doctrinal systems. Consequently, Wesley's categorisation of the doctrinal substance and the experiential circumstance of a doctrine is critical in his pastoral methodology.

The key task of the pastoral theologian is to discern the voice of the Spirit in the midst of the means and people he uses; the critical evaluative tool is the wisdom to discern whether love and relationships are being promoted or hindered. This allows for and, in fact, expects there to be dynamic, shifting roles in theologising amongst the elements as the Spirit makes use of them. Wesley believes that all of them are finally in harmony with the living voice of the Spirit, and dissonance indicates that we have not yet heard the Spirit fully and/or faithfully. The Spirit begins with the current reality of our people in our time and setting; through his direct presence or utilising one or other of the means he challenges our present theological understanding or application of the Christian faith and by the same process seeks to bring about an increasing depth of faithful relationship with God and neighbour. Just like the environment in which we live, it passes unnoticed until a change gets our attention; so his people immersed in this Methodist ethos and Christian experience would take it for granted until 'upset' by the work of the Spirit in their lives and community. This would lead to an examination of the situation under the guidance of the Spirit and he would normally use the means of grace to do so–Scripture in particular. After reflection, involving pastoral wisdom and discernment (both personal and community), a new understanding or application would be posited and then tested in practice amongst the people. If the relationship with God and neighbour deepened as a result, then in time this became the new environment until a further challenge arose.

Bibliography

Primary Sources

Baker, Frank, ed. *A Union Catalogue of the Publications of John and Charles Wesley.* Durham, NC: The Divinity School, Duke University, 1966.

Browne, Peter. *The Procedure, Extent, and Limits of Human Understanding.* London: Innys, 1729.

Heitzenrater, Richard P., ed. *Diary of an Oxford Methodist: Benjamin Ingham, 1733-1734.* Durham, NC: Duke University Press, 1985.

Wesley, Charles. *The Journal of the Rev. Charles Wesley, M.A.* 2 vols., ed. Thomas Jackson. London: John Mason, 1849. Reprint, Kansas City: Beacon Hill Press of Kansas City, 1980.

Wesley, John. *The Arminian Magazine: Consisting of Extracts and Original Treatises on Universal Redemption.* Vol. 1. London: R. Hawes, 1778.

_____. *The Arminian Magazine: Consisting of Extracts and Original Treatises on Universal Redemption.* Vol. 2. London: J. Fry, 1779.

_____. *The Arminian Magazine, for the Year 1780.* Vol. 3, 1780.

_____. *The Arminian Magazine, for the Year 1781.* Vol. 4, 1781.

_____. *The Arminian Magazine, for the Year 1782.* Vol. 5, 1782.

_____. *John Wesley's Sunday Service of the Methodists in North America with Other Occasional Services.* London, 1784. Reprint, With an Introduction by James F. White, The United Methodist Publishing House and the United Methodist Board of Higher Education and Ministry, 1984.

_____. *Minutes of Several Conversations, between the Rev. John Wesley, A.M. And the Preachers in Connection with Him. Containing the Form of Discipline Established among the Preachers and People in the Methodist Societies.* London: G. Whitfield, 1797.

_____. *Minutes of Several Conversations, between the Rev. John Wesley, A.M. And the Preachers in Connection with Him. From the Year 1744.* Leeds: Edward Baines, 1803.

_____. *Minutes of Several Conversations, between the Rev. John Wesley, M.A. And Others. From the Year 1744, to the Year 1789.* London: Thomas Cordeaux, 1817.

_____, ed. *A Christian Library Consisting of Extracts and Abridgments of the Choicest Pieces of Practical Divinity Which Have Been Published in the English Tongue.* London: Thomas Cordeaux, 1819. Reprint, First published in 1750 in 50 vols.

_____. *A Compendium of Natural Philosophy, Being a Survey of the Wisdom of God in the Creation.* 3 vols. New edition. Revised, corrected and adapted to the present state of science by Robert Mudie ed. London: Thomas Tegg & Son, 1836.

_____. *The Works of John Wesley.* 14 vols., 3rd ed., ed. Thomas Jackson. London: Wesleyan Methodist Book Room, 1872. Reprint, Kansas City, MO: Beacon Hill Press of Kansas City, 1979.

_____. *The Journal of the Rev. John Wesley.* 9 vols., ed. Nehemiah Curnock. London: Epworth Press, 1909-16.

_____. *The Letters of the Rev. John Wesley.* 8 vols., ed. John Telford. London: Epworth Press, 1931.

_____. *John Wesley.* ed. Albert C. Outler. A Library of Protestant Thought. New York: Oxford University Press, 1964.

_____. *The Bicentennial Edition of the Works of John Wesley.* 35 vols. projected, ed.-in-Chief, Frank Baker. Nashville, TN: Abingdon Press, 1984-. vols. 7, 11, 25, and 26 of this edition originally appeared as the *Oxford Edition of the Works of John Wesley.* [Oxford: Clarendon, 1975-1983].

_____. *Sermons and Hymns of John Wesley.* Abingdon Press, 1999. Accessed CD-ROM.

_____. *The Works of John Wesley: The Bicentennial Edition.* Abingdon Press, 2005. Accessed CD-ROM.

_____. *Explanatory Notes Upon the New Testament.* London: Wesleyan Methodist Book Room, n.d.

Wesley, John, and Charles Wesley. *John and Charles Wesley: Selected Writings and Hymns.* The Classics of Western Spirituality, ed. Frank Whaling. New York: Paulist Press, 1981.

Wesley, Samuel. *The Pious Communicant Rightly Prepared; or, a Discourse Concerning the Blessed Sacrament: ... To Which Is Added, a Short Discourse of Baptism: With a Letter Concerning the Religious Societies.* London: Charles Harper, 1700.

Wesley, Susanna. *Susanna Wesley: The Complete Writings.* ed. Charles Wallace Jr. New York: Oxford University Press, 1997.

Secondary Sources

Abraham, William J. "Response: The Perils of a Wesleyan Systematic Theologian." *WTJ* 17, no. 1 (Spring, 1982): 23-29.

_____. "The Wesleyan Quadrilateral." In *Wesleyan Theology Today: A Bicentennial Theological Consultation,* ed. Theodore H. Runyon, 119-26. Nashville, TN: Kingswood Books, 1985.

_____. *The Logic of Evangelism.* Grand Rapids, MI: Wm. B. Eerdmans, 1989.

_____. "The Revitalization of United Methodist Doctrine and the Renewal of Evangelism." In *Theology and Evangelism in the Wesleyan Heritage,* ed. James C. Logan, 35-50. Nashville, TN: Abingdon Press, 1994.

_____. *Waking from Doctrinal Amnesia: The Healing of Doctrine in the United Methodist Church.* Nashville, TN: Abingdon Press, 1995.

_____. "On How to Dismantle the Wesleyan Quadrilateral: A Study in the Thought of Albert C. Knudson." *WTJ* 20, no. 1 (Spring, 1985): 34-44.

_____. *Canon and Criterion in Christian Theology: From the Fathers to Feminism.* Oxford: Oxford University Press, 1998.

_____. "Keeping up with Jones on John Wesley's Conception and Use of Scripture." *WTJ* 33, no. 1 (Spring, 1998): 5-13.

_____. *Saving Souls in the Twenty First Century: A Missiological Midrash on John*

Wesley. Sheffield, ENG: Cliff College Publishing, 2003.

---. *The Logic of Renewal*. Grand Rapids, MI: Wm. B. Eerdmans, 2003.

---. "The End of Wesleyan Theology." *WTJ* 40, no. 1 (Spring, 2005): 7-25.

---. "What's Right and What's Wrong with the Quadrilateral?" Unpublished private paper from personal correspondence with Dr. Abraham, n.d.

Ackley, Heather Ann. "A Constructive Wesleyan Theological Proposal: Redemption and Sanctification of Human Gender and Sexuality." *Asbury Theological Journal* 59, no. 1 & 2 (Spring-Fall, 2004): 191-205.

Albin, Thomas R. "'Inwardly Persuaded': Religion of the Heart in Early British Methodism." In *"Heart Religion" in the Methodist Tradition and Related Movements*, ed. Richard B. Steele, 33-66. Lanham, MD: Scarecrow Press, 2001.

Allchin, A. M. "The Epworth-Canterbury-Constantinople Axis." *WTJ* 26, no. 1 (Spring, 1991): 23-37.

Anderson, Gerald H. "The Challenge of the Ecumenical Movement to Methodism." *Asbury Seminarian* 14, no. 2 (1960): 21-31.

Armstrong, Anthony. *The Church of England, the Methodists and Society 1700-1850*. London: University of London Press, 1973.

Atkinson, Nigel. *Richard Hooker and the Authority of Scripture, Tradition and Reason: Reformed Theologian of the Church of England?* Carlisle: Paternoster Press, 1997.

Baker, Frank. "John Wesley's Churchmanship." *London Quarterly and Holborn Review* 185 (July 1960): 210-15.

---. "John Wesley's Churchmanship (II)." *London Quarterly and Holborn Review* 185 (October 1960): 269-74.

---. "Wesley's Puritan Ancestry." *London Quarterly and Holborn Review* 187 (July 1962): 180-86.

---. *John Wesley and the Church of England*. London: Epworth Press, 1970.

---. "Unfolding John Wesley: A Survey of Twenty Years' Studies in Wesley's Thought." *Quarterly Review* 1, no. 1 (1980): 44-58.

---. "Susanna Wesley: Puritan, Parent, Pastor, Protagonist, Pattern." In *Dig or Die*, ed. James S. Udy and Eric G. Clancy, 77-88. Sydney: World Methodist Historical Society Australasian Section, 1981.

---. "Practical Divinity-John Wesley's Doctrinal Agenda for Methodism." *WTJ* 22, no. 1 (Spring, 1987): 7-15.

Banks, Stanley. "Our Wesleyan Heritage: Christian Perfection." *Asbury Seminarian* 14, no. 2 (1960): 33-51.

Bassett, Paul M., and William M. Greathouse. *Exploring Christian Holiness: The Historical Development*. Vol. 2 Exploring Christian Holiness. Kansas City, MO: Beacon Hill Press of Kansas City, 1985.

Bassett, Paul M. "The Holiness Movement and the Protestant Principle." *WTJ* 18, no. 1 (Spring, 1983): 7-29.

---, ed. *Holiness Teaching-New Testament Times to Wesley*. Edited by A. F. Harper. Vol. 1, Great Holiness Classics. Kansas City, MO: Beacon Hill Press of Kansas City, 1997.

Bebbington, D. W. *Evangelicalism in Modern Britain: A History from the 1730s to the 1980s*. London: Unwin Hyman, 1989.

Bennett, David. "How Arminian Was John Wesley?" *Evangelical Quarterly* 72, no. 3 (2000): 237-48.

Berger, Teresa. *Theology in Hymns?: A Study of the Relationship of Doxology and

Theology According to A Collection of Hymns for the Use of the People Called Methodists (1780). Translated by Timothy E. Kimbrough. Nashville, TN: Kingswood Books, 1995.

Bett, Henry. *The Spirit of Methodism*. London: Epworth Press, 1937.

Bevins, Winfield H. "Pneumatology in John Wesley's Theological Method." *Asbury Theological Journal* 58, no. 2 (Fall, 2003): 101-13.

──────. "The Historical Development of Wesley's Doctrine of the Spirit." *Wesleyan Theological Journal* 41, no. 2 (Fall, 2006): 161-181.

Blankenship, Paul F. "The Significance of John Wesley's Abridgement of the Thirty-Nine Articles as Seen from His Deletions." *Methodist History* 2, no. 3 (1964): 35-47.

Blevins, Dean G. "The Grace: Toward a Wesleyan Praxis of Spiritual Formation." *WTJ* 32, no. 1 (Spring, 1997): 69-84.

Borgen, Ole E. *John Wesley on the Sacraments: A Definitive Study of John Wesley's Theology of Worship*. Nashville, TN: Abingdon Press, 1972. Reprint, Grand Rapids, MI: Zondervan, 1985.

──────. "No End without the Means : John Wesley and the Sacraments." *Asbury Theological Journal* 46, no. 1 (1991): 63-85.

Bounds, Christopher T. "What is the Range of Current Teaching on Sanctification and What Ought a Wesleyan to Believe on this Doctrine?" *The Asbury Journal* 62, no. 2 (Fall 2007): 3353.

Brantley, Richard E. *Locke, Wesley, and the Method of English Romanticism*. Gainesville, FL: University of Florida, 1984.

──────. "The Common Ground of Wesley and Edwards." *Harvard Theological Review* 83, no. 3 (1990): 271-303.

Brendlinger, Irv A. "Transformative Dimensions within Wesley's Understanding of Christian Perfection." *Asbury Theological Journal* 59, no. 1 & 2 (Spring-Fall, 2004): 117-26.

Brown, Earl Kent. "Feminist Theology and the Women of Mr. Wesley's Methodism." In *Wesleyan Theology Today: A Bicentennial Theological Consultation*, ed. Theodore H. Runyon, 143-50. Nashville, TN: Kingswood Books, 1985.

Brown, Dale W. "The Wesleyan Revival from a Pietist Perspective." *WTJ* 24 (1989): 7-17.

Brown-Lawson, Albert. *John Wesley and the Anglican Evangelicals of the Eighteenth Century: A Study in Cooperation and Separation with Special Reference to the Calvinistic Controversies*. Durham, Eng: Pentland Press, 1994.

Bryant, Barry E. "John Wesley's Doctrine of Sin." PhD thesis, King's College, University of London, 1992.

Bundy, David. "Christian Virtue: John Wesley and the Alexandrian Tradition." *WTJ* 26, no. 1 (Spring, 1991): 139-63.

──────. "Visions of Sanctification: Themes of Orthodoxy in the Methodist, Holiness, and Pentecostal Traditions." *WTJ* 39, no. 1 (Spring, 2004): 104-36.

Burdon, Adrian. *Authority and Order: John Wesley and his Preachers*. Aldershot, ENG: Ashgate Publishing, 2005.

Burtner, Robert W., and Robert E. Chiles, eds. *A Compend of Wesley's Theology*. New York: Abingdon Press, 1954.

Butler, David. *Methodists and Papists: John Wesley and the Catholic Church in the Eighteenth Century*. London: Darton, Longman and Todd, 1995.

Callen, Barry L., and Richard P. Thompson, eds. *Reading the Bible in Wesleyan Ways:*

Some Constructive Proposals. Kansas City, MO: Beacon Hill Press of Kansas City, 2004.

Callen, Barry L. *Discerning the Divine: God in Christian Theology*. Louisville, KY: Westminster John Knox Press, 2004.

Campbell, Ted A. "John Wesley and Conyers Middleton on Divine Intervention in History." *Church History* 55, no. 1 (1986): 39-49.

_____. *John Wesley and Christian Antiquity: Religious Vision and Cultural Change*. Nashville, TN: Kingswood Books, 1991.

_____. "The 'Wesleyan Quadrilateral': The Story of a Modern Methodist Myth." In *Doctrine and Theology in the United Methodist Church*, ed. Thomas A. Langford, 154-61. Nashville, TN: Kingswood Books, 1991.

_____. "Scripture as an Authority in Relation to Other Authorities: A Wesleyan Evangelical Perspective." *Quarterly Review* 11, no. 3 (1991): 33-40.

_____. "Wesley's Use of the Church Fathers." *Asbury Theological Journal* 50-51, no. 2-1 (1995-1996): 57-70.

_____. "The Interpretative Role of Tradition." In *Wesley and the Quadrilateral: Renewing the Conversation*, ed. W. Stephen Gunter, Scott J. Jones, Ted A. Campbell, Rebekah L. Miles and Randy L. Maddox, 63-75. Nashville, TN: Abingdon Press, 1997.

_____. *Methodist Doctrine: The Essentials*. Nashville, TN: Abingdon Press, 1999.

_____. "The Shape of Wesleyan Thought: The Question of John Wesley's 'Essential' Christian Doctrines." *Asbury Theological Journal* 59:1 & 2 (Spring/Fall 2004): 27-48.

_____. "Scripture and Tradition in the Wesleyan Tradition." In *Orthodox and Wesleyan Scriptural Understanding and Practice*, 159-69. Edited by S.T. Kimbrough, Jr. Crestwood, NY: St Vladimir's Seminary Press, 2005.

Cannon, William R. *The Theology of John Wesley, with Special Reference to the Doctrine of Justification*. New York: Abingdon Press, 1946.

_____. "Perfection." *London Quarterly and Holborn Review* 184 (July 1959): 213-17.

Cell, George Croft. *The Rediscovery of John Wesley*. New York: Henry Holt & Company, 1935. Reprint, Lanham, MD: University Press of America, 1983.

Chapman, David M. *In Search of the Catholic Spirit: Methodists and Roman Catholics in Dialogue*. Peterborough, ENG: Epworth Press, 2004.

Chilcote, Paul W., ed. *The Wesleyan Tradition: A Paradigm for Renewal*. Nashville, TN: Abingdon Press, 2002.

Cho, John Chongnahm. "Adam's Fall and God's Grace : John Wesley's Theological Anthropology." *Evangelical Review of Theology* 10, no. 3 (1986): 202-13.

Christensen, Michael J. "Theosis and Sanctification: John Wesley's Reformulation of a Patristic Doctrine." *WTJ* 31, no. 2 (Fall, 1996): 71-94.

Church, The United Methodist. *The Book of Discipline of the United Methodist Church - 2000*. United Methodist Communications, 2004. Accessed. Available from http://umc.org/ interior.asp?ptid=1&mid=519.

Clapper, Gregory S. "'True Religion' and the Affections: A Study of John Wesley's Abridgement of Jonathan Edwards' Treatise on Religious Affections." *WTJ* 19:2 (Fall 1984): 77-89.

_____. *John Wesley on Religious Affections: His Views on Experience and Emotion and Their Role in the Christian Life and Theology*. Metuchen, NJ: Scarecrow Press,

1989.

———. "*Orthokardia*: The Practical Theology of John Wesley's Heart Religion." *Quarterly Review* 10, no. 1 (1990): 49-66.

———. "John Wesley's "Heart Religion" and the Righteousness of Christ." *Methodist History* 35, no. 3 (1997): 148-56.

———. "Wesley's 'Main Doctrines' and Spiritual Formation and Teaching in the Wesleyan Tradition." *WTJ* 39, no. 2 (Fall, 2004): 97-121.

Clark, J. C. D. *English Society, 1660-1832: Religion, Ideology and Politics During the Ancien Regime*. 2nd ed. Cambridge: Cambridge University Press, 2000.

Clarke, Adam. *Memoirs of the Wesley Family: Collected Principally from Original Documents*. Vol. II. 2 vols. London: William Tegg, 1860.

Clutterbuck, Richard. "Our Doctrines." *Epworth Review* 24, no. 3 (1997): 21-33.

———. "Theology as Interaction: Ecumenism and the World Church." In *Unmasking Methodist Theology*, ed. Clive Marsh, Brian Beck, Angela Shier-Jones and Helen Wareing, 59-69. London: Continuum, 2004.

Cobb, Jr., John B. *Grace & Responsibility: A Wesleyan Theology for Today*. Nashville, TN: Abingdon Press, 1995.

Collins, Kenneth J. "A Hermeneutical Model for the Wesleyan *Ordo Salutis*." *WTJ* 19, no. 2 (Fall, 1984): 23-37.

———. "Twentieth-Century Interpretations of John Wesley's Aldersgate Experience: Coherence or Confusion?" *WTJ* 24 (1989): 18-31.

———. "Other Thoughts on Aldersgate: Has the Conversionist Paradigm Collapsed?" *Methodist History* 30, no. 1 (1991): 10-25.

———. "A Reply to Randy Maddox." *Methodist History* 31, no. 1 (1992): 51-54.

———. "John Wesley's Critical Appropriation of Early German Pietism." *WTJ* 27, no. 1 & 2 (Spring-Fall, 1992): 57-92.

———. *A Faithful Witness: John Wesley's Homiletical Theology*. Wilmore, KY: Wesley Heritage Press, 1993.

———. "The Motif of Real Christianity in the Writings of John Wesley." *Asbury Theological Journal* 49, no. 1 (1994): 49-62.

———. "The Soteriological Orientation of John Wesley's Ministry to the Poor." *Asbury Theological Journal* 50, no. 1 (1995): 75-91.

———. "Real Christianity as Integrating Theme in Wesley's Soteriology: The Critique of a Modern Myth." *Asbury Theological Journal* 51, no. 2 (1996): 15-43.

———. *The Scripture Way of Salvation: The Heart of John Wesley's Theology*. Nashville, TN: Abingdon Press, 1997.

———. "A Reconfiguration of Power: The Basic Trajectory in John Wesley's Practical Theology." *WTJ* 33, no. 1 (Spring, 1998): 164-84.

———. "Why the Holiness Movement Is Dead." *Asbury Theological Journal* 54, no. 2 (1999): 27-35.

———. *A Real Christian: The Life of John Wesley*. Nashville, TN: Abingdon Press, 1999.

———. "Recent Trends in Wesley Studies and Wesleyan/Holiness Scholarship." *WTJ* 35, no. 1 (Spring, 2000): 67-86.

———. "John Wesley's Critical Appropriation of Tradition in His Practical Theology." *WTJ* 35, no. 2 (Fall, 2000): 69-90.

———. *John Wesley: A Theological Journey*. Nashville, TN: Abingdon Press, 2003.

———. "The Promise of John Wesley's Theology for the 21st Century: A Dialogical

Exchange." *Asbury Theological Journal* 59, no. 1 & 2 (Spring-Fall, 2004): 171-80.
———. *Wesley Bibliography*. Asbury Theological Seminary, 2005. Accessed October 7 2005. Available from http://www.ats.wilmore.ky.us/news/wesley.htm.
———. *The Theology of John Wesley: Holy Love and the Shape of Grace*. Nashville, TN: Abingdon Press, 2007.
Coppedge, Allan. "John Wesley and the Issue of Authority in Theological Pluralism." *WTJ* 19, no. 2 (Fall, 1984): 62-76.
———. *John Wesley in Theological Debate*. Wilmore, KY: Wesley Heritage Press, 1987.
Cox, Leo George. *John Wesley's Concept of Perfection*. Kansas City, MO: Beacon Hill Press of Kansas City, 1964.
Cragg, Gerald R. *The Church and the Age of Reason, 1648-1789*. Harmondsworth, ENG: Penguin Books, 1970.
Cubie, David L. "Perfection in Wesley and Fletcher: Inaugural or Teleological?" *WTJ* 11 (Spring, 1976): 22-37.
———. "Wesley's Theology of Love." *WTJ* 20, no. 1 (Spring, 1985): 122-54.
———. "Placing Aldersgate in John Wesley's Order of Salvation." *WTJ* 24 (1989): 32-53.
Cushman, Robert E. "Orthodoxy and Wesley's Experimental Divinity." *Quarterly Review* 8, no. 2 (1988): 71-89.
———. *John Wesley's Experimental Divinity: Studies in Methodist Doctrinal Standards*. Nashville, TN: Abingdon Press, 1989.
Davies, Rupert E. *Methodism*. London: Penguin, 1963.
Dawes, Stephen. "The Primacy of Scripture and the Methodist Quadrilateral." The Methodist Sacramental Fellowship, January 1998.
———. "The Spirituality of 'Scriptural Holiness'." *Epworth Review* 30, no. 2 (2003): 51-57.
———. "Revelation in Methodist Practice and Belief." In *Unmasking Methodist Theology*, ed. Clive Marsh, Brian Beck, Angela Shier-Jones and Helen Wareing, 109-17. London: Continuum, 2004.
Dean, Jonathan. "'Mystics and Pharisees': Methodist Identity in an Ecumenical Age." *Epworth Review* 34, no. 4 (October 2007): 6-22.
Dorr, Donal J. "Wesley's Teaching on the Nature of Holiness." *London Quarterly and Holborn Review* 190 (July 1965): 234-39.
Dunning, H. Ray. "Perspective for a Wesleyan Systematic Theology." In *Wesleyan Theology Today: A Bicentennial Theological Consultation*, ed. Theodore H. Runyon, 51-55. Nashville, TN: Kingswood Books, 1985.
———. *Grace, Faith, and Holiness: A Wesleyan Systematic Theology*. Kansas City, MO: Beacon Hill Press of Kansas City, 1988.
Eayrs, George. *John Wesley, Christian Philosopher and Church Founder*. London: Epworth Press, 1926.
English, John C. "John Wesley's Indebtedness to John Norris." *Church History* 60, no. 1 (1991): 55-69.
———. "References to St. Augustine in the Works of John Wesley." *Asbury Theological Journal* 600, no. 2 (Fall, 2005): 5-24.
Felleman, Laura Bartels. "John Wesley and the 'Servant of God'." WTJ 41, no. 2 (Fall, 2006): 72-86.
Ferguson, Duncan S. "John Wesley on Scripture: The Hermeneutics of Pietism."

Methodist History 22, no. 4 (1984): 234-45.
Ferrel, Lowell O. "John Wesley and the Enthusiasts." *WTJ* 23, no. 1 & 2 (Spring-Fall, 1988): 180-87.
Fitchett, W. H. *Wesley and His Century: A Study in Spiritual Forces*. London: John Murray, 1925.
Flemming, Dean. "The Third Horizon: A Wesleyan Contribution to the Contextualization Debate." *WTJ* 30, no. 2 (Fall, 1995): 139-63.
Foster, Durwood. "Wesleyan Theology: Heritage and Task." In *Wesleyan Theology Today: A Bicentennial Theological Consultation*, ed. Theodore H. Runyon, 31-37. Nashville, TN: Kingswood Books, 1985.
Franklin, Patrick S. "John Wesley in Conversation with the Emerging Church." *The Asbury Journal* 63, no. 1 (Spring 2008): 75-93.
Fraser, M. Robert. "Strains in the Understandings of Christian Perfection in Early British Methodism." PhD thesis, Vanderbilt University, 1988.
Frost, Francis. "The Three Loves: A Theology of the Wesley Brothers." *Epworth Review* 24, no. 3 (1997): 86-116.
Glasson, Francis. "Wesley's New Testament Reconsidered." *Epworth Review* 10, no. 2 (1983): 28-34.
Glasson, Barbara. "Stories and Storytelling: The Use of Narrative within Methodism." In *Unmasking Methodist Theology*, ed. Clive Marsh, Brian Beck, Angela Shier-Jones and Helen Wareing, 99-108. London: Continuum, 2004.
Goodwin, Charles H. *The Methodist Pentecost: The Wesleyan Holiness Revival 1758-1763* Merlin Methodist Monograph Number 4. Ilkeston: Moorley's Bookshop, 1996.
_____. "Setting Perfection Too High: John Wesley's Changing Attitudes toward the 'London Blessing'." *Methodist History* 36, no. 2 (1998): 86-96.
_____. "Methodist Pentecost: The Wesleyan/Holiness Revival of 1758-1763." *WTJ* 33, no. 1 (Spring, 1998): 58-91.
Greathouse, William M. *John Wesley's Theology of Christian Perfection* Occasional Paper No. 4 of the Wesley Fellowship. Ilkeston: The Wesley Fellowship, 1989.
Green, V. H. H. *The Young Mr. Wesley: A Study of John Wesley and Oxford*. London: Wyvern Books, 1963.
_____. *John Wesley*. London: Thomas Nelson & Sons, 1964.
Green, Joel B. "Reading the Bible as Wesleyans." *WTJ* 33, no. 2 (Fall, 1998): 116-29.
_____. "Scripture in the Church: Reconstructing the Authority of Scripture for Christian Formation and Mission." In *The Wesleyan Tradition: A Paradigm for Renewal*, ed. Paul W. Chilcote, 38-51. Nashville, TN: Abingdon Press, 2002.
_____. "Contribute or Capitulate? Wesleyans, Pentecostals and Reading the Bible in a Post-Colonial Mode." *WTJ* 39, no. 1 (Spring, 2004): 74-90.
Griffin, Eric Richard. "Practical Catholicism: John Wesley's Theology of Bishops Reconsidered." *Churchman* 112, no. 4 (1998): 324-38.
Gunter, W. Stephen. *The Limits of 'Love Divine': John Wesley's Response to Antinomianism and Enthusiasm*. Nashville, TN: Kingswood Books, 1989.
_____. "Personal and Spiritual Knowledge: Kindred Spirits in Polanyian and Wesleyan Epistemology." *WTJ* 35, no. 1 (Spring, 2000): 130-48.
Gunter, W. Stephen, Scott J. Jones, Ted A. Campbell, Rebekah L. Miles, and Randy L. Maddox. *Wesley and the Quadrilateral: Renewing the Conversation*. Nashville, TN: Abingdon Press, 1997.
Gutenson, Chuck. "Theological Method for a Man of One Book." *Asbury Theological*

Journal 59:1 & 2 (Spring/Fall, 2004): 49-61.

Haas, John W., Jr. "John Wesley's Views on Science and Christianity: An Examination of the Charge of Antiscience." *Church History* 63, no. 2 (1994): 378-92.

Harper, Steve. "John Wesley: Spiritual Guide." *WTJ* 20, no. 2 (Fall, 1985): 91-96.

_____. "Wesley's Sermons as Spiritual Formation Documents." *Methodist History* 26, no. 3 (1988): 131-38.

Harrison, Peter. *'Religion' and the Religions in the English Enlightenment*. Cambridge: Cambridge University Press, 1990.

_____. *The Bible, Protestantism, and the Rise of Natural Science*. Cambridge: Cambridge University Press, 1998.

Heitzenrater, Richard P. *The Elusive Mr. Wesley: John Wesley His Own Biographer*. Vol. 1. 2 vols. Nashville, TN: Abingdon Press, 1984.

_____. *The Elusive Mr. Wesley: John Wesley as Seen by Contemporaries and Biographers*. Vol. 2. 2 vols. Nashville, TN: Abingdon Press, 1984.

_____. *Mirror and Memory: Reflections in Early Methodism*. Nashville, TN: Kingswood Books, 1989.

_____. "Great Expectations: Aldersgate and the Evidences of Genuine Christianity." In *Aldersgate Reconsidered*, ed. Randy L. Maddox, 49-91. Nashville, TN: Abingdon Press, 1990.

_____. *Wesley and the People Called Methodists*. Nashville, TN: Abingdon Press, 1995.

_____. "John Wesley's Principles and Practice of Preaching." *Methodist History* 37, no. 2 (1999): 89-106.

Henderson, D. Michael. *John Wesley's Class Meeting: A Model for Making Disciples*. Nappanee, IN: Evangel Publishing House, 1997.

Henry, Granville C. "John Wesley's Doctrine of Free Will." *London Quarterly and Holborn Review* 185 (July 1960): 200-04.

Hildebrandt, Franz. *From Luther to Wesley*. London: Lutterworth Press, 1951.

Hindley, J. Clifford. "Philosophy of Enthusiasm: A Study in the Origins of "Experimental Theology"." *London Quarterly and Holborn Review* 182 (April 1957): 99-109.

_____. "Philosophy of Enthusiasm: A Study in the Origins of "Experimental Theology" (II)." *London Quarterly and Holborn Review* 182 (July 1957): 199-210.

Horst, Mark L. "Experimenting with Christian Wholeness: Method in Wesley's Theology." *Quarterly Review* 7, no. 2 (1987): 11-23.

Howcroft, Kenneth G. "Reason, Interpretation and Postmodernism: Is There a Methodist Way of Reading the Bible?" *Epworth Review* 25, no. 3 (1998): 28-41.

Howe, Leroy T. "United Methodism in Search of Theology." In *Doctrine and Theology in the United Methodist Church*, ed. Thomas A. Langford, 52-63. Nashville, TN: Kingswood Books, 1991.

Hughes, H. Maldwyn. *Wesley and Whitefield*. London: Charles H. Kelly, n.d.

Hynson, Leon O. "The Wesleyan Quadrilateral in the American Holiness Tradition." *WTJ* 20, no. 1 (Spring, 1985): 19-33.

_____. "The Right of Private Judgement." *Asbury Theological Journal* 60, no. 1 (Spring, 2005): 89-104.

_____. *Through Faith to Understanding: Wesleyan Essays on Vital Christianity*. Lexington, KY: Emeth Press, 2005.

Im, Seung-An. "John Wesley's Theological Anthropology: A Dialectic Tension between the Latin Western Patristic Tradition (Augustine) and the Greek Eastern Patristic Tradition (Gregory of Nyssa)." PhD thesis, Drew University, 1994.

Jennings, Theodore W. "John Wesley *against* Aldersgate." *Quarterly Review* 8, no. 3 (1988): 3-22.

———. "The Meaning of Discipleship in Wesley and the New Testament." *Quarterly Review* 13, no. 1 (1993): 3-20.

Johnson, W. Stanley. "Christian Perfection as Love for God." *WTJ* 18, no. 1 (Spring, 1983): 50-60.

Jones, Bernard E. "Reason and Religion Joined: The Place of Reason in Wesley's Thought." *London Quarterly and Holborn Review* 189 (April 1964): 110-13.

Jones, Margaret. "Some Eighteenth Century Methodist Theology: The Arminian/ Methodist Magazine." *Epworth Review* 27, no. 1 (2000): 8-19.

Jones, Scott J. *John Wesley's Conception and Use of Scripture*. Nashville, TN: Kingswood Books, 1995.

Keefer, Luke L. "Characteristics of Wesley's Arminianism." *WTJ* 22, no. 1 (Spring, 1987): 87-99.

Khoo, Lorna Lock-Nah. *Wesleyan Eucharistic Spirituality*. Adelaide: ATF Press, 2005.

Kimbrough Jr., S. T., ed. *Orthodox and Wesleyan Spirituality*. Crestwood, NY: St. Vladimir's Seminary Press, 2002.

———, ed. *Orthodox and Wesleyan Scriptural Understanding and Practice*. Crestwood, NY: St. Vladimir's Seminary Press, 2005.

King, Rob. "The Spirit-Filled Life: Eastern Patristic Spirit-Christology for Contemporary Wesleyan Faith Practice." *WTJ* 38, no. 2 (Fall, 2003): 103-23.

Kisker, Scott Thomas. "Justified but Unregenerate? The Relationship of Assurance to Justification and Regeneration in the Thought of John Wesley." *WTJ* 28, no. 1 & 2 (Spring-Fall, 1993): 44-58.

———. *Foundation for Revival: Anthony Horneck, the Religious Societies, and the Construction of an Anglican Pietism*. Lanham, MD: Scarecrow Press, 2008.

Kissack, Reginald. "John Wesley's Concept of the Church." *Asbury Seminarian* 14, no. 2 (1960): 7-20.

Knight III, Henry H. *The Presence of God in the Christian Life: John Wesley and the Grace*. Lanham, MD: Scarecrow Press, 1992.

———. "The Role of Faith and the Grace in the Heart Religion of John Wesley." In *"Heart Religion" in the Methodist Tradition and Related Movements*, ed. Richard B. Steele, 273-90. Lanham, MD: Scarecrow Press, 2001.

Knox, Ronald A. *Enthusiasm: A Chapter in the History of Religion with Special Reference to the XVII and XVIII Centuries*. Oxford: Clarendon Press, 1950.

Kurowski, Mark T. "The First Step toward Grace: John Wesley's Use of the Spiritual Homilies of Macarius the Great." *Methodist History* 36, no. 2 (1998): 113-24.

Lacy, H. Edward. "Authority in John Wesley." *London Quarterly and Holborn Review* 189 (April 1964): 114-19.

Lampe, G. W. H. "Authority in Bible, Church and Reason." *London Quarterly and Holborn Review* 182 (October 1958): 252-56.

Langford, Thomas A. *Practical Divinity: Theology in the Wesleyan Tradition*. Nashville, TN: Abingdon Press, 1983.

———. "Constructive Theology in the Wesleyan Tradition." In *Wesleyan Theology Today: A Bicentennial Theological Consultation*, ed. Theodore H. Runyon, 56-61. Nashville, TN: Kingswood Books, 1985.

_____. "Is There Such a Thing as Wesleyan Theology?" *Epworth Review* 15, no. 2 (1988): 67-78.

_____. "Introduction: A Wesleyan/Methodist Theological Tradition." In *Doctrine and Theology in the United Methodist Church*, ed. Thomas A. Langford, 9-16. Nashville, TN: Kingswood Books, 1991.

_____. "The United Methodist Quadrilateral: A Theological Task." In *Doctrine and Theology in the United Methodist Church*, ed. Thomas A. Langford, 232-44. Nashville, TN: Kingswood Books, 1991.

_____, ed. *Doctrine and Theology in the United Methodist Church*. Nashville, TN: Kingswood Books, 1991.

Lawson, John. "Saving Faith as Wesley Saw It." *Christianity Today* 8, no. 4 (1964): 3-4.

Lindström, Harald. *Wesley and Sanctification: A Study in the Doctrine of Salvation*. Wilmore, KY: Francis Asbury Press, 1980. Reprint, New York: Abingdon Press, 1946.

Lodahl, Michael. "Theology on the Rough Road to Emmaus: Questioning the Quadrilateral." In *It's All About Grace: Wesleyan Essays in Honor of Herbert L. Prince*, 17-24. Edited by Samuel M. Powell. San Diego, CA: Point Loma Press, 2004.

Lowery, Kevin Twain. *Salvaging Wesley's Agenda: A New Paradigm for Wesleyan Virtue Ethics*. Eugene, OR: Pickwick Publications, 2008.

Macquiban, Timothy S. A. "Dialogue with the Wesleys: Remembering Origins." In *Unmasking Methodist Theology*, ed. Clive Marsh, Brian Beck, Angela Shier-Jones and Helen Wareing, 17-28. London: Continuum, 2004.

Maddox, Randy L. "Responsible Grace: The Systematic Nature of Wesley's Theology Reconsidered." *Quarterly Review* 6, no. 1 (1986): 24-34.

_____. "John Wesley: Practical Theologian?" *WTJ* 23, no. 1-2 (Spring-Fall, 1988): 122-47.

_____. "John Wesley and Eastern Orthodoxy: Influences, Convergences and Differences." *Asbury Theological Journal* 45, no. 2 (1990): 29-53.

_____, ed. *Aldersgate Reconsidered*. Nashville, TN: Kingswood Books, 1990.

_____. "Opinion, Religion and "Catholic Spirit": John Wesley on Theological Integrity." *Asbury Theological Journal* 47, no. 1 (1992): 63-87.

_____. "Continuing the Conversation." *Methodist History* 30, no. 4 (1992): 235-41.

_____. "Wesleyan Resources for a Contemporary Theology of the Poor." *Asbury Theological Journal* 49, no. 1 (1994): 35-47.

_____. *Responsible Grace: John Wesley's Practical Theology*. Nashville, TN: Kingswood Books, 1994.

_____. "Reading Wesley as a Theologian." *WTJ* 30, no. 1 (Spring, 1995): 7-54.

_____. "Holiness of Heart and Life: Lessons from North American Methodism." *Asbury Theological Journal* 50-51, no. 2-1 (1995-1996): 151-72.

_____. "The Enriching Role of Experience." In *Wesley and the Quadrilateral: Renewing the Conversation*, ed. W. Stephen Gunter, Scott J. Jones, Ted A. Campbell, Rebekah L. Miles and Randy L. Maddox, 108-12. Nashville, TN: Abingdon Press, 1997.

_____, ed. *Rethinking Wesley's Theology for Contemporary Methodism*. Nashville, TN: Kingswood Books, 1998.

_____. "Reclaiming an Inheritance: Wesley as Theologian in the History of Methodist Theology." In *Rethinking Wesley's Theology for Contemporary*

Methodism, ed. Randy L. Maddox, 213-26. Nashville, TN: Abingdon Press, 1998.

———. "Reconnecting the Means to the End: A Wesleyan Prescription for the Holiness Movement." *WTJ* 33, no. 2 (Fall, 1998): 29-66.

———. "Respected Founder/Neglected Guide: The Role of Wesley in American Methodist Theology." *Methodist History* 37, no. 2 (1999): 71-88.

———. "Wesley's Understanding of Christian Perfection: In What Sense Pentecostal?" *WTJ* 34, no. 2 (Fall, 1999): 78-110.

———. "Prelude to a Dialogue: A Response to Kenneth Collins." *WTJ* 35, no. 1 (Spring, 2000): 87-98.

———. "A Change of Affections: The Development, Dynamics, and Dethronement of John Wesley's Heart Religion." In *"Heart Religion" in the Methodist Tradition and Related Movements*, ed. Richard B. Steele, 3-31. Lanham, MD: Scarecrow Press, 2001.

———. "Vital Orthodoxy: A Wesleyan Dynamic for 21st Century Christianity." *Methodist History* 42, no. 1 (2003): 3-19.

———. "'Celebrating the Whole Wesley': A Legacy for Contemporary Wesleyans." *Methodist History* 43, no. 2 (January 2005): 74-89.

Marsh, Clive, Brian Beck, Angela Shier-Jones and Helen Wareing, eds. *Unmasking Methodist Theology*. London: Continuum, 2004.

Marsh, Clive. "Appealing to 'Experience': What Does It Mean?" In *Unmasking Methodist Theology*, ed. Clive Marsh, Brian Beck, Angela Shier-Jones and Helen Wareing, 118-30. London: Continuum, 2004.

Martin, Troy W. "John Wesley's Exegetical Orientation: East or West?" *WTJ* 26, no. 1 (Spring, 1991): 104-38.

Matthews, Rex D. "'With the Eyes of Faith': Spiritual Experience and the Knowledge of God in the Theology of John Wesley." In *Wesleyan Theology Today: A Bicentennial Theological Consultation*, ed. Theodore H. Runyon, 406-15. Nashville, TN: Kingswood Books, 1985.

McAdoo, Henry R. *The Spirit of Anglicanism: A Survey of Anglican Theological Method in the Seventeenth Century*. New York: Charles Scribner's Sons, 1965.

McConnell, Francis J. *John Wesley*. New York: Abingdon Press, 1939.

McCormick, K. Steve. "Theosis in Chrysostom and Wesley: An Eastern Paradigm on Faith and Love." *WTJ* 26, no. 1 (Spring, 1991): 38-103.

McEwen, Gilbert D. *The Oracle of the Coffee House: John Dunton's Athenian Mercury*. San Marino, CA: The Huntington Library, 1972.

McGonigle, Herbert Boyd. *John Wesley and the Moravians*. Ilkeston: The Wesley Fellowship, 1993.

———. *Sufficient Saving Grace: John Wesley's Evangelical Arminianism*. Carlisle: Paternoster Press, 2001.

McGrath, Alister E. *Iustitia Dei: A History of the Christian Doctrine of Justification*. Vol. II, *From 1500 to the Present Day*. 2 vols. Cambridge: Cambridge University Press, 1986.

———. *The Foundations of Dialogue in Science and Religion*. Oxford: Blackwell Publishers, 1998.

Meadows, Philip R. "'Candidates for Heaven': Wesleyan Resources for a Theology of Religions." *WTJ* 35, no. 1 (Spring, 2000): 99-129.

———. "Wesleyan Theology in a Technological Age." WTJ 41, no. 1 (Spring, 2006): 18-40.

Meeks, M. Douglas, ed. *The Future of Methodist Theological Traditions*. Nashville, TN: Abingdon Press, 1985.

———, ed. *Trinity, Community, and Power: Mapping Trajectories in Wesleyan Theology*. Nashville, TN: Kingswood Books, 2000.

Mercer, Jerry L. "Toward a Wesleyan Understanding of Christian Experience." *WTJ* 20, no. 1 (Spring, 1985): 78-93.

Merritt, John G. "'Dialogue' within a Tradition: John Wesley and Gregory of Nyssa Discuss Christian Perfection." *WTJ* 22, no. 2 (Fall, 1987): 92-116.

Miles, Rebekah L. "The Instrumental Role of Reason." In *Wesley and the Quadrilateral: Renewing the Conversation*, ed. W. Stephen Gunter, Scott J. Jones, Ted A. Campbell, Rebekah L. Miles and Randy L. Maddox, 77-106. Nashville, TN: Abingdon Press, 1997.

———. "'The Arts of Holy Living': Holiness and the Grace." *Quarterly Review* 25, no. 2 (Summer, 2005): 141-57.

Miller, Richard A. "Scriptural Authority and Christian Perfection: John Wesley and the Anglican Tradition." PhD thesis, Drew University, 1991.

Mills, W. Douglas. "Robert Earl Cushman and a Study of Predestination in the Wesleyan Tradition." *Methodist History* 38, no. 1 (1999): 3-13.

Monk, Robert C. *John Wesley: His Puritan Heritage*. Nashville, TN: Abingdon Press, 1966.

Nausner, Helmut. "Some Notes on Christian Perfection." *Quarterly Review* 3, no. 1 (1983): 71-82.

Newton, John A. *Susanna Wesley and the Puritan Tradition in Methodism*. London: Epworth Press, 1968.

———. "The Ecumenical Wesley." *Ecumenical Review* 24 (1972): 160-75.

Niles, Lori Haynes. "Toward a Wesleyan Theology of Failure." *WTJ* 43, no. 1 (Spring, 2008): 120-132.

Noble, Tom A. "Endnote: Reflections on Holiness." Unpublished paper from the Guatemala Nazarene Theology Conference, April 2002,

O'Malley, J. Steven. "Recovering the Vision of Holiness: Wesley's Epistemic Basis." *Asbury Theological Journal* 41, no. 1 (1986): 3-17.

———. "Pietistic Influence on John Wesley: Wesley and Gerhard Tersteegen." *WTJ* 31, no. 2 (Fall, 1996): 48-70.

Oden, Thomas C. *Systematic Theology: The Living God*. Vol. 1. San Francisco: HarperCollins, 1987.

———. *Doctrinal Standards in the Wesleyan Tradition*. Grand Rapids, MI: Francis Asbury Press, 1988.

———. *John Wesley's Scriptural Christianity: A Plain Exposition of His Teaching on Christian Doctrine*. Grand Rapids, MI: Zondervan, 1994.

Ogden, Schubert M. "Doctrinal Standards in the United Methodist Church." In *Doctrine and Theology in the United Methodist Church*, ed. Thomas A. Langford, 39-51. Nashville, TN: Kingswood Books, 1991.

Ogletree, Thomas W. "In Quest of a Common Faith: The Theological Task of United Methodists." *Quarterly Review* 8, no. 1 (1988): 43-53.

Olson, Roger E. "The World Its Parish: Wesleyan Theology in the Postmodern Global Village." *Asbury Theological Journal* 59:1 & 2 (Spring/Fall, 2004): 17-25.

Ott, Philip W. "Medicine as Metaphor: John Wesley on Therapy of the Soul." *Methodist History* 33, no. 3 (1995): 178-91.

Outler, Albert C. "John Wesley as Theologian-Then and Now." *Methodist History* 12, no. 4 (1974): 63-82.
_____. *Theology in the Wesleyan Spirit*. Nashville, TN: Discipleship Resources, 1975.
_____. "The Place of Wesley in the Christian Tradition." In *The Place of Wesley in the Christian Tradition: Essays Delivered at Drew University in Celebration of the Commencement of the Publication of the Oxford Edition of the Works of John Wesley*, ed. Kenneth E. Rowe. Metuchen, NJ: Scarecrow Press, 1976.
_____. "A New Future for Wesley Studies: An Agenda for 'Phase III'." In *The Future of the Methodist Theological Traditions*, ed. M. Douglas Meeks, 34-52. Nashville, TN: Abingdon Press, 1985.
_____. "The Wesleyan Quadrilateral-in John Wesley." *WTJ* 20, no. 1 (Spring 1985): 7-18.
_____. "A Focus on the Holy Spirit: Spirit and Spirituality in John Wesley." *Quarterly Review* 8, no. 2 (1988): 3-18.
_____. "Introduction to the Report of the 1968-72 Theological Study Commission." In *Doctrine and Theology in the United Methodist Church*, ed. Thomas A. Langford, 20-25. Nashville, TN: Kingswood Books, 1991.
_____. "The Wesleyan Quadrilateral-in John Wesley." In *Doctrine and Theology in the United Methodist Church*, ed. Thomas A. Langford, 75-88. Nashville, TN: Kingswood Books, 1991.
_____. "Towards a Re-Appraisal of John Wesley as a Theologian." In *The Wesleyan Theological Heritage: Essays of Albert C. Outler*, ed. Thomas C. Oden and Leicester R. Longden, 39-54. Grand Rapids, MI: Zondervan, 1991.
_____. "John Wesley's Interests in the Early Fathers of the Church." In *The Wesleyan Theological Heritage: Essays of Albert C. Outler*, ed. Thomas C. Oden and Leicester R. Longden, 97-110. Grand Rapids, MI: Zondervan, 1991.
_____. "John Wesley: Folk Theologian." In *The Wesleyan Theological Heritage: Essays of Albert C. Outler*, ed. Thomas C. Oden and Leicester R. Longden, 111-24. Grand Rapids, MI: Zondervan, 1991.
Parris, John R. *John Wesley's Doctrine of the Sacraments*. London: Epworth Press, 1963.
Peckham, Colin N. *John Wesley's Understanding of Human Infirmities*. Ilkeston: The Wesley Fellowship, 1997.
Peters, John L. *Christian Perfection & American Methodism*: Pierce & Washabaugh, 1956. Reprint, Francis Asbury Press, 1985.
Piette, Maximin. *John Wesley in the Evolution of Protestantism*. Translated by J. B. Howard. London: Sheed & Ward, 1937.
Podmore, Colin. *The Moravian Church in England, 1728-1760*. Oxford: Clarendon Press, 1998.
Porter, Roy. *The Creation of the Modern World: The Untold Story of the British Enlightenment*. New York: W. W. Norton & Company, 2000.
Rack, Henry D. "John Wesley as Theologian." *Epworth Review* 27, no. 1 (2000): 43-47.
_____. *Reasonable Enthusiast: John Wesley and the Rise of Methodism*. 3rd ed. London: Epworth Press, 2002.
Rattenbury, J. Ernest. *Wesley's Legacy to the World: Six Studies in the Permanent Values of the Evangelical Revival*. London: Epworth Press, 1928.
_____. *The Conversion of the Wesleys: A Case Study*. London: Epworth Press, 1938.

Reed, Rodney L. "Calvin, Calvinism, and Wesley : The Doctrine of Assurance in Historical Perspective." *Methodist History* 32, no. 1 (1993): 31-43.

Renshaw, John R. "The Atonement in the Theology of John and Charles Wesley." ThD thesis, Boston University, 1965.

Richey, Russell E., Dennis M. Campbell and William B. Lawrence. *Marks of Methodism: Theology in Ecclesial Practice*. Nashville, TN: Abingdon Press, 2005.

Rieger, Joerg, and John J. Vincent, eds. *Methodist and Radical: Rejuvenating a Tradition*. Nashville, TN: Kingswood Books, 2003.

Rivers, Isabel. *Reason, Grace, and Sentiment: A Study of the Language of Religion and Ethics in England 1660-1780*. Vol. 1, *Whichcote to Wesley*. Cambridge: Cambridge University Press, 1991.

Rogal, Samuel J. *A Biographical Dictionary of 18th Century Methodism*. 10 vols. Lampeter: Edwin Mellon Press, 1997-1999.

Rogers, Charles A. "The Concept of Prevenient Grace in the Theology of John Wesley." PhD thesis, Duke University, 1967.

Rowe, G. Stringer. "Mrs. Wesley's Conference with Her Daughter. An Original Essay by Mrs. Susannah Wesley." *Proceedings of the Wesley Historical Society* 1, no. 3 (1896-97): 34.

Rowe, Kenneth E., ed. *The Place of Wesley in the Christian Tradition*. Metuchen, NJ: Scarecrow Press, 1976.

Runyon, Theodore H., ed. *Wesleyan Theology Today: A Bicentennial Theological Consultation*. Nashville, TN: Kingswood Books, 1985.

_____. "Introduction." In *Wesleyan Theology Today: A Bicentennial Theological Consultation*, ed. Theodore H. Runyon, 1-4. Nashville, TN: Kingswood Books, 1985.

_____. *The New Creation: John Wesley's Theology Today*. Nashville, TN: Abingdon Press, 1998.

Rupp, Gordon. *Religion in England, 1688-1791*. Oxford: Clarendon Press, 1986.

Schlimm, Mathew R. "The Puzzle of Perfection: Growth in John Wesley's Doctrine of Perfection." *WTJ* 38, no. 2 (Fall, 2003): 124-42.

Schwenk, James L. *Catholic Spirit: Wesley, Whitefield, and the Quest for Evangelical Unity in Eighteenth-Century British Methodism*. Lanham, MD: Scarecrow Press, 2008.

Schmidt, Martin. *John Wesley: A Theological Biography*. Translated by Norman P. Goldhawk. Vol. I: 17th June 1703 - 24th May 1738. Nashville, TN: Abingdon Press, 1972.

_____. *John Wesley: A Theological Biography*. Translated by Norman P. Goldhawk. Vol. II.1: John Wesley's Life Mission. New York: Abingdon Press, 1972.

_____. *John Wesley: A Theological Biography*. Translated by Dennis Inman. Vol. II.2: John Wesley's Life Mission. London: Epworth Press, 1973.

_____. "Wesley's Place in Church History." In *The Place of Wesley in the Christian Tradition: Essays Delivered at Drew University in Celebration of the Commencement of the Publication of the Oxford Edition of the Works of John Wesley*, ed. Kenneth E. Rowe. Metuchen, NJ: Scarecrow Press, 1976.

Shelton, R. Larry. "John Wesley's Approach to Scripture in Historical Perspective." *WTJ* 16, no. 1 (Spring 1981): 23-50.

_____. "The Trajectory of Wesleyan Theology." *WTJ* 21, no. 1 & 2 (Spring-Fall, 1986): 160-76.

Shier-Jones, Angela. "Conferring as Theological Model." In *Unmasking Methodist*

Theology, ed. Clive Marsh, Brian Beck, Angela Shier-Jones and Helen Wareing, 82-94. London: Continuum, 2004.

———. *A Work in Progress: Methodists Doing Theology*. Peterborough, ENG: Epworth Press, 2005.

Shontz, William H. "Anglican Influence on John Wesley's Soteriology." *WTJ* 32, no. 1 (Spring, 1997): 33-52.

Smith, Wilfred Cantwell. *The Meaning and End of Religion*. New York: The New American Library, 1964.

———. *Belief and History*. Charlottesville: University Press of Virginia, 1977.

———. *Faith and Belief*. Princeton: Princeton University Press, 1979.

Smith, Harmon L. "Wesley's Doctrine of Justification: Beginning and Process." *London Quarterly and Holborn Review* 189 (April 1964): 120-28.

Smith, Robert Doyle. "John Wesley and Jonathan Edwards on Religious Experience: A Comparative Analysis." *WTJ* 25, no. 1 (Spring, 1990): 130-46.

Smith, Timothy L. "How John Fletcher Became the Theologian of Wesleyan Perfectionism, 1770-1776." *WTJ* 15, no. 1 (Spring, 1980): 68-87.

———. "George Whitefield and Wesleyan Perfectionism." *WTJ* 19, no. 1 (Spring, 1984): 63-85.

———. "John Wesley and the Wholeness of Scripture." *Interpretation* 39, no. 3 (1985): 246-62.

———. *Whitefield and Wesley on the New Birth*. Grand Rapids, MI: Francis Asbury Press, 1986.

———. "John Wesley and the Second Blessing." *WTJ* 21, no. 1 & 2 (Spring-Fall, 1986): 137-59.

Snyder, Howard A. "The Church as Holy and Charismatic." *Evangelical Review of Theology* 6, no. 2 (1982): 172-201.

———. "John Wesley and Macarius the Egyptian." *Asbury Theological Journal* 45, no. 2 (1990): 55-60.

———. "The Babylonian Captivity of Wesleyan Theology." *WTJ* 39, no. 1 (Spring, 2004): 7-34.

Stacey, John, ed. *John Wesley: Contemporary Perspectives*. London: Epworth Press, 1988.

Stamm, Mark W. *Let Every Soul Be Jesus' Guest: A Theology of the Open Table*. Nashville, TN: Abingdon Press, 2006.

Stanley, John E. "A Theology of Urban Ministry, Supported by the Wesleyan Quadrilateral." *WTJ* 38, no. 1 (Spring, 2003): 138-59.

Staples, Rob L. "Sanctification and Selfhood: A Phenomenological Analysis of the Wesleyan Message." *WTJ* 7, no. 1 (Spring 1972): 3-16.

———. "The Present Frontiers of Wesleyan Theology." *WTJ* 12 (Spring, 1977): 5-15.

———. "Wesleyan Perspectives on the Doctrine of the Holy Spirit." In *The Spirit and the New Age: An Inquiry into the Holy Spirit and Last Things from a Biblical Theological Perspective*, ed. Alex R. G. Deasley and R. Larry Shelton, 199-236. Anderson, IN: Warner Press, 1986.

———. "John Wesley's Doctrine of the Holy Spirit." *WTJ* 21, no. 1 & 2 (Spring-Fall, 1986): 91-115.

Starkey, Jr., Lycurgus M. *The Work of the Holy Spirit: A Study in Wesleyan Theology*. Nashville, TN: Abingdon Press, 1962.

Steele, Richard B. *"Gracious Affection" and "True Virtue" According to Jonathan Edwards and John Wesley*. Metuchen, NJ: Scarecrow Press, 1994.

_____. "Introduction." In *"Heart Religion" in the Methodist Tradition and Related Movements*, ed. Richard B. Steele, xix-xlv. Lanham, MD: Scarecrow Press, 2001.

Stevenson, George J. *Memorials of the Wesley Family*. London: Partridge & Co., 1876.

Stoeffler, F. Ernest. "The Wesleyan Concept of Religious Certainty: Its Pre-History and Significance." *London Quarterly and Holborn Review* 189 (April 1964): 128-39.

Stone, Bryan P. "Wesleyan Theology, Scriptural Authority, and Homosexuality." *WTJ* 30, no. 2 (Fall, 1995): 108-38.

Strawson, William. "Wesley's Doctrine of the Last Things." *London Quarterly and Holborn Review* 184 (July 1959): 240-49.

Thomas, James S. "How Theology Emerges from Polity." In *Wesleyan Theology Today: A Bicentennial Theological Consultation*, ed. Theodore H. Runyon, 14-19. Nashville, TN: Kingswood Books, 1985.

Thomas, Howe Octavius. "John Wesley's Awareness and Application of the Method of Distinguishing between Theological Essentials and Theological Opinions." *Methodist History* 26, no. 2 (1988): 84-97.

_____. "John Wesley's Understanding of Theological Distinction between "Essentials" and "Opinions"." *Methodist History* 33, no. 3 (1995): 139-48.

_____. "Whenceforth Wesley: John Wesley's Theology from Then to Now." *Methodist History* 43, no. 4 (July, 2005): 258-72.

Thompson, Edgar W. "Episcopacy: John Wesley's View." *London Quarterly and Holborn Review* 181 (April 1956): 113-17.

_____. *Wesley: Apostolic Man: Some Reflections on Wesley's Consecration of Dr. Thomas Coke*. London: Epworth Press, 1957.

Thompson, Richard P. "John Wesley's Concept of Inspiration and Literary-Critical Approaches to Scripture." *WTJ* 34, no. 1 (Spring, 1999): 151-76.

Thorsen, Donald A. "Experimental Method in the Practical Theology of John Wesley." *WTJ* 24 (1989): 117-41.

_____. *The Wesleyan Quadrilateral: Scripture, Tradition, Reason & Experience as a Model of Evangelical Theology*. Grand Rapids, MI: Francis Asbury Press, 1990.

_____. "The Future of Biblical Studies in the Wesleyan Tradition: A Theological Perspective." *WTJ* 30, no. 2 (Fall, 1995): 182-202.

_____. "*Sola Scriptura* and the Wesleyan Quadrilateral." *WTJ* 41, no. 1 (Fall, 2006): 7-27.

Towlson, Clifford W. *Moravian and Methodist: Relationships and Influences in the Eighteenth Century*. London: Epworth Press, 1957.

Tracy, Wesley D. "John Wesley, Spiritual Director: Spiritual Guidance in John Wesley's Letters." *WTJ* 23, no. 1 & 2 (Spring-Fall, 1988): 148-62.

Tripp, David H. "'Observe the Gradation!' John Wesley's Notes on the New Testament." *Quarterly Review* 10, no. 2 (1990): 49-64.

Turner, John Munsey. "Methodism: An Apologia." *Epworth Review* 15, no. 2 (1988): 18-25.

_____. *John Wesley: The Evangelical Revival and the Rise of Methodism in England*. London: Epworth Press, 2002.

Tuttle Jr., Robert G. *John Wesley: His Life and Theology*. Grand Rapids, MI: Zondervan, 1978.

_____. *Mysticism in the Wesleyan Tradition*. Grand Rapids, MI: Zondervan, 1989.

Tyerman, Luke. *The Life and Times of the Rev. Samuel Wesley, M.A.* London: Simpkin, Marshall & Co., 1866.

Tyson, John R. "John Wesley and William Law: A Reappraisal." *WTJ* 17, no. 2 (Fall, 1982): 58-78.

_____. "Essential Doctrines and Real Religion: Theological Method in Wesley's *Sermons on Several Occasions*." *WTJ* 23, no. 1 & 2 (Spring-Fall, 1988): 163-79.

_____. "Sin, Self and Society: John Wesley's Hamartiology Reconsidered." *Asbury Theological Journal* 44, no. 2 (1989): 77-89.

_____. *Assist Me to Proclaim: The Life and Hymns of Charles Wesley*. Grand Rapids, MI: Wm. B. Eerdmans, 2007.

Tyson, John R. with Boyd S. Schlenther. *In the Midst of Early Methodism: Lady Huntingdon and Her Correspondence*. Lanham, MD: Scarecrow Press, 2006.

United Methodist Church. *The Book of Discipline of the United Methodist Church*. Nashville, TN: United Methodist Publishing House, 1972.

_____. *The Book of Discipline of the United Methodist Church – 2000*. United Methodist Communications, 2004. http://umc.org/interior.asp?ptid=1&mid=519 (accessed).

Vickers, Jason E. "Charles Wesley's Doctrine of the Holy Spirit: A Vital Resource for the Renewal of Methodism Today." *Asbury Theological Journal* 61, no. 1 (Spring, 2006): 47-60.

Wainwright, Geoffrey. *Geoffrey Wainwright on Wesley and Calvin*. Melbourne: Uniting Church Press, 1987.

_____. "John Wesley's Trinitarian Hermeneutics." *WTJ* 36, no. 1 (Spring, 2001): 7-30.

Wall, Robert W. "Toward a Wesleyan Hermeneutic of Scripture." *WTJ* 30, no. 2 (Fall, 1995): 50-67.

Walls, Jerry L. "What Is Theological Pluralism." *Quarterly Review* 5, no. 3 (1985): 44-62.

_____. "'As the Waters Cover the Sea': John Wesley on the Problem of Evil." *Faith and Philosophy* 13, no. 4 (1996): 534-62.

Watson, Philip S. "Wesley and Luther on Christian Perfection." *Ecumenical Review* 15, no. 3 (1963): 291-302.

Watson, David Lowes. *The Early Methodist Class Meeting: Its Origins and Significance*. Nashville, TN: Discipleship Resources, 1985.

_____. "The 'Much-Controverted Point of Justification by Faith' and the Shaping of Wesley's Evangelistic Message." *WTJ* 21, no. 1 & 2 (Spring-Fall, 1986): 7-23.

Wellings, Martin and Andrew Wood. "Facets of Formation: Theology through Training." In *Unmasking Methodist Theology*, ed. Clive Marsh, Brian Beck, Angela Shier-Jones and Helen Wareing, 70-81. London: Continuum, 2004.

Whidden, Woodrow W. "Wesley on Imputation: A Truly Reckoned Reality or Antinomian Polemical Wreckage?" *Asbury Theological Journal* 52, no. 2 (1997): 63-70.

Wilder, Franklin. *Father of the Wesleys*. New York: Exposition Press, 1971.

Wilkinson, David. "The Activity of God in Methodist Perspective." In *Unmasking Methodist Theology*, ed. Clive Marsh, Brian Beck, Angela Shier-Jones and Helen Wareing, 142-54. London: Continuum, 2004.

Wilkinson, Alan. "Authority in Religion and Science." *London Quarterly and Holborn Review* 192 (January 1967): 35-42.

Williams, Colin W. *John Wesley's Theology Today: A Study of the Wesleyan Tradition in the Light of Current Theological Dialogue.* Nashville, TN: Abingdon Press, 1960.

Witherington III, Ben. "*Praeparatio Evangelii*: The Theological Roots of Wesley's View of Evangelism." In *Theology and Evangelism in the Wesleyan Heritage*, ed. James C. Logan, 51-80. Nashville, TN: Abingdon Press, 1994.

Wolfteich, Claire. "A Difficult Love: Mother as Spiritual Guide in the Writing of Susanna Wesley." *Methodist History* 38, no. 1 (1999): 53-62.

Wood, A. Harold. *The Aldersgate Experience of John Wesley*. Melbourne: Uniting Church Press, 1988.

Wood, A. Skevington. "Lessons from Wesley's Experience." *Christianity Today* 7 (April 1963): 4-6.

_____. *The Burning Heart: John Wesley, Evangelist.* London: Paternoster Press, 1967.

_____. "The Eighteenth Century Methodist Revival Reconsidered." *Evangelical Quarterly* 53, no. 3 (1981): 130-48.

_____. *Love Excluding Sin: Wesley's Doctrine of Sanctification* Wesley Fellowship Occasional Paper #1. Derbys, England: Moorley's Bookshop, 1986.

Wood, Charles. "Wesleyan Constructive Theology." In *Wesleyan Theology Today: A Bicentennial Theological Consultation*, ed. Theodore H. Runyon, 47-50. Nashville, TN: Kingswood Books, 1985.

Wood, Laurence W. "Wesley's Epistemology." *WTJ* 10, no. 1 (Spring 1975): 48-59.

_____. *Pentecostal Grace*. Wilmore, KY: Francis Asbury Press, 1980.

_____. "The Attainment of Christian Perfection as a Wesleyan/Holiness Re-Interpretation of the Anglican Rite of Confirmation." *Asbury Theological Journal* 50-51, no. 2-1 (1995-1996): 173-95.

_____. "Pentecostal Sanctification in John Wesley and Early Methodism." *WTJ* 34, no. 1 (Spring, 1999): 24-63.

_____. "Historiographical Criticisms of Randy Maddox's Response." *WTJ* 34, no. 2 (Fall, 1999): 111-35.

_____. *The Meaning of Pentecost in Early Methodism: Rediscovering John Fletcher as John Wesley's Vindicator and Designated Successor* Pietist and Wesleyan Studies #15. Lanham, MD: Scarecrow Press, 2002.

World Methodist Council. "Wesleyan Essentials of Christian Faith." World Methodist Council, 1996. http://www.worldmethodistcouncil.org/index .php?option=com_ content&task=view&id=22&Itemid=9 (accessed).

Wright, John W. "Wesley's Theology as Methodist Practice: Toward the Postmodern Retrieval of the Wesleyan Tradition." *WTJ* 35, no. 2 (Fall, 2000): 7-31.

Wynkoop, Mildred Bangs. "A Hermeneutical Approach to John Wesley." *WTJ* 6, no. 1 (Spring 1971): 13-22.

_____. *A Theology of Love: The Dynamic of Wesleyanism*. Kansas City, MO: Beacon Hill Press of Kansas City, 1972.

_____. "John Wesley-Mentor or Guru?" *WTJ* 10 (Spring 1975): 5-14.

Yang, Jung. "The Doctrine of God in the Theology of John Wesley." PhD thesis, University of Aberdeen, 2003.

Yrigoyen, Jr., Charles. *John Wesley: Holiness of Heart and Life*. Nashville, TN: Abingdon Press, 1996.

Index

"A good Christian", 49, 54, 58, 64, 69
"Analogy of faith, The", 77, 106, 132, 134, 156, 158, 168, 206, 208, 214
A Farther Appeal to Men of Reason and Religion, 91, 109, 114
à Kempis, Thomas, 47, 54, 98
A Plain Account of Christian Perfection, 121, 191
Abraham, William J., 7, 9, 10, 11, 12, 23, 24, 25, 33, 34, 40, 213
Accountability, 48, 116, 118, 174, 207
Accountable discipleship, 9
Adamic law, 177, 179, 194
Adamic perfection. *See* Perfection (Adamic)
Affections, 34, 50, 55, 56, 58, 95, 101, 102, 121, 123, 131, 135, 162, 163, 172, 182
Aldersgate, 37, 49, 58, 64, 65, 68, 69, 71, 72, 75, 80, 81, 84, 86, 87, 88, 101, 155, 215, 226, 227, 229, 230, 231, 239
An Earnest Appeal to Men of Reason and Religion, 109
Anderson, Gerald H., 21
Andrews, Isaac, 162
Angelic law, 182
Anglican, 9, 17, 31, 37, 73, 76, 84, 88, 94, 107, 116, 132, 168, 170, 201, 206, 212, 214, 217, 224, 230, 233, 236, 239
Anglicanism, 14, 30, 42, 47, 71, 73, 74, 79, 84, 85, 105, 106, 165, 232
Antinomian, 238
Antinomianism, 98, 123, 152, 163, 165
Antiquity (Christian), 9, 11, 17, 22, 23, 225
Apostolic Church, 61, 63, 70, 78, 82
Arminian, 46, 54, 57, 66, 131, 147, 163, 185, 186, 221, 223, 230
Arminianism, 49
Arminian Magazine, 164, 185
Assent, 41, 43, 53, 59, 60, 63, 64, 66, 69, 71, 75, 76, 77, 81, 86, 96, 110, 164, 212, 214
Assurance (personal, inward, felt), 19, 20, 46, 48, 53, 63, 65, 69, 70, 71, 72, 73, 74, 75, 77, 82, 84, 85, 87, 109, 112, 129, 130, 148, 199, 200, 202, 215
Atkinson, Nigel, 9, 47, 223
Atonement, 66, 119, 136, 137, 166, 182, 211
Augustine, 161, 163, 172, 227, 230
Backslide, 148
Baker, Frank, 7
Ball, Hannah, 169, 198, 203
Baptism, 34, 46, 49, 54, 58
Bardsley, Samuel, 186
Belief, 2, 26, 28, 29, 40, 41, 42, 50, 55, 66, 75, 79, 86, 100, 106, 115, 133, 134, 141, 145, 162, 164, 167, 171, 206, 211, 212
Bell, George, 121, 198
Bennis, Elizabeth (Mrs), 148
Benson, Joseph, 169, 170, 176, 192, 196
Bevins, Winfield H., 18, 101
Bible, 12, 14, 15, 22, 28, 41, 48, 55, 74, 76, 78, 81, 87, 93, 104, 105, 106, 108, 110, 111, 114, 116, 132, 133, 158, 159, 164, 167, 168, 171, 173, 174, 186, 190, 191, 193, 195, 200, 201, 204, 213, 214, 224, 228, 229, 230
Bishop, Mary, 174, 188, 189, 196, 205
Bland, Phoebe, 188
Böhler, Peter, 64, 65, 80, 81, 82, 83, 84
Bolton, Ann, 144, 187, 191, 197, 204
Bolton, Nancy, 206
Book of Common Prayer, 31
Book of Discipline, 10, 12, 36, 225, 238
Bosanquet, Mary, 202, 205
Briggs, Elizabeth, 197
Briggs, Philothea, 194, 197, 199, 203
Bristol, 85, 142, 153, 154, 179, 185, 198
Brown, Isaac, 187
Browne, Peter, 16, 77
Bryant, Barry E., 8, 22
Calvinist, 52, 57, 75, 86, 105, 120, 133, 141, 147, 160, 163, 165, 170, 184, 206
Calvinism, 54, 165, 170, 185, 194, 208, 211, 235

Cambridge Platonism, 16
Campbell, Ted A., 10, 11, 12, 17, 27, 99, 225, 228, 231, 233
Cannon, William R., 6, 43
Capital doctrines, 166
Catholic love, 166
Catholic spirit, 99, 166
Cautions and Directions given to the Greatest Professors in the Methodist Societies, 151
Charity, 56, 60, 62
Christain experience, 207
Christian character, 31, 49
Christian community, 5, 20, 25, 30, 68, 85, 115, 130, 157
Christian experience, 4, 9, 18, 19, 23, 44, 45, 55, 70, 81, 83, 88, 90, 98, 102, 103, 109, 112, 114, 132, 140, 157, 158, 159, 160, 166, 169, 171, 189, 191, 203, 206, 207, 208, 209, 215, 216, 217, 218, 219, 220
Christian fellowship, 97
Christian Library, 31, 94, 97, 98, 105, 117, 205, 221
Christian life, 3, 5, 7, 20, 29, 31, 36, 45, 46, 49, 53, 62, 78, 82, 100, 107, 111, 119, 124, 202, 206
Christian ministry, 3
Christian perfection, 2, 3, 4, 5, 14, 32, 37, 38, 45, 50, 58, 60, 61, 68, 75, 86, 90, 91, 108, 110, 113, 115, 117, 118, 120, 121, 122, 123, 127, 128, 132, 133, 135, 138, 139, 140, 142, 144, 146, 147, 148, 149, 153, 157, 158, 159, 160, 174, 175, 176, 177, 178, 179, 181, 183, 184, 185, 186, 187, 188, 189, 191, 192, 193, 196, 197, 199, 202, 204, 205, 207, 208, 210, 215, 217
Christian practice, 13, 30, 32, 49, 55, 76, 77, 79, 89
Christlike, 86, 133
Church, 1, 2, 7, 16, 17, 19, 20, 27, 28, 33, 34, 39, 40, 43, 47, 49, 54, 60, 70, 78, 79, 83, 85, 94, 116, 117, 122, 133, 137, 153, 156, 157, 172, 173, 174, 206, 212, 214, 215, 217
Church (primitive), 44, 56, 70, 116, 117, 173
Church of England, 2, 9, 15, 17, 22, 27, 32, 35, 36, 37, 40, 42, 43, 44, 47, 54, 68, 74, 83, 84, 88, 98, 105, 115, 116, 117, 122, 126, 133, 156, 164, 173, 211, 213, 214, 215, 218, 223
Churchey, Walter, 192
Circumcision of the Heart, 86, 118, 138, 142, 176
Clark, J. C. D., 15, 38, 39
Clarke, Adam, 44, 201
Cleanse (heart), 55, 117, 142, 173, 179, 192
Coates, Alexander, 141
Commandments, 39, 55, 60, 78, 123, 125, 143, 181, 211
Common sense, 115, 158, 168, 214, 218
Community, 2, 18, 24, 30, 32, 35, 38, 39, 40, 48, 64, 72, 73, 74, 77, 79, 80, 81, 83, 84, 85, 89, 90, 93, 94, 98, 99, 101, 103, 104, 106, 111, 112, 115, 116, 117, 133, 155, 156, 157, 158, 159, 168, 174, 190, 207, 209, 212, 213, 214, 215, 217, 218, 219, 220
Community ethos, 90, 132, 156, 157, 159, 160, 206, 207, 209, 216, 217, 218, 219
Conference, 3, 23, 31, 44, 112, 116, 121, 126, 137, 139, 141, 145, 185, 207, 218, 233, 235
Conscience, 9, 24, 42, 46, 87, 99, 106, 112, 129, 130, 132, 190
Consensus, 9, 22, 33, 35, 36, 78, 79, 100, 103, 210, 212
Consensus (theological), 5
Conversation (Christian), 8, 15, 31, 32, 73, 80, 81, 121, 124, 145, 158, 174, 176, 190, 205, 218, 221, 225, 228, 231, 233
Conyers, Richard, 170, 225
Cooper, Jenny, 197, 198
Correspondence (John Wesley), 12, 45, 53, 56, 57, 76, 79, 101, 104, 105, 106, 108, 122, 140, 141, 145, 175, 184, 218, 223
Corruptible body, 152, 181, 182, 194
Covenant, 69, 70, 86, 91, 118, 124, 135, 136, 144, 207, 211
Covenant of grace, 86, 91, 118, 124, 136, 207, 211
Covenant of works, 86, 91, 118, 124, 135, 211
Covered promise, 107, 177
Cure (of sin), 51, 52, 91, 127, 131, 153
Cushman, Robert E., 22

General index 243

Dale, Peggy, 147, 148, 151
David, Christian, 73
Dawes, Stephen, 23, 25, 46, 116
De Renty, Marquis, 57, 164
Death (dying), 1, 4, 5, 46, 51, 61, 62, 64, 66, 71, 114, 119, 122, 126, 128, 135, 137, 139, 140, 141, 142, 145, 153, 166, 177, 178, 180, 182, 189, 200, 207
Deliverance (full), 61, 121, 126, 127, 137, 149, 153, 162, 177, 178, 179, 180, 187, 188, 189, 193, 196, 202
Depravity, 45, 46
Depression (religous, 'heaviness'), 131, 132, 148
Desire, 44, 48, 51, 63, 66, 71, 87, 88, 93, 97, 105, 107, 116, 123, 145, 151, 152, 154, 158, 181, 196, 197, 198, 202, 204, 206, 210, 215, 216
Diary (John Wesley), 47, 79
Direct witness (Spirit), 46, 88, 130, 148
Discipleship, 8, 108, 117, 174, 209
Dissent, 40, 73, 117
Divine attributes, 54, 210
Doctrinal standard(s), 8, 9, 10, 11, 12, 22, 24, 227, 233
Doctrinal systems, 89, 214, 220
Doctrine, 2, 3, 4, 5, 6, 8, 9, 14, 17, 18, 20, 21, 27, 30, 33, 35, 37, 46, 49, 51, 53, 58, 60, 64, 67, 73, 74, 75, 76, 79, 81, 84, 85, 86, 88, 90, 95, 96, 99, 100, 102, 104, 105, 106, 110, 111, 112, 114, 116, 117, 118, 121, 132, 133, 134, 139, 142, 150, 157, 161, 164, 165, 168, 169, 174, 175, 176, 185, 186, 187, 190, 191, 192, 204, 207, 208, 210, 216, 217, 220
Dodd, William, 108, 132
Duty, 55, 57, 135, 145, 162
Dynamic neural network, 216
Early Christianity, 16
Eastern church, 172
Education, 20, 39, 45, 79, 83, 95, 171
Eighteenth century, 2, 3, 15, 37, 38, 39, 42, 43, 57, 86, 89, 211
Election, 52, 54, 105, 165
Empirical, 47, 77, 86, 215
Empirical method, 77
Enlightenment, 2, 15, 23, 24, 38, 39, 41, 75, 169, 208, 211, 212, 229, 234

Enthusiasm, 15, 16, 18, 19, 20, 62, 72, 89, 94, 102, 104, 111, 130, 151, 153, 189, 213
Entire sanctification, 19, 113, 126, 128, 138, 145, 151, 178, 179, 181, 196, 200, 207
Epistemology, 24, 25
Epworth, 6, 14, 22, 23, 24, 27, 29, 32, 34, 38, 43, 44, 46, 64, 80, 98, 172, 186, 222, 223, 224, 225, 226, 227, 228, 229, 230, 231, 233, 234, 235, 236, 237
Essentials (doctrinal), 43, 49, 79, 166, 185, 206, 212, 214
Established (church), 4, 5, 11, 16, 18, 35, 37, 40, 48, 52, 58, 74, 91, 123, 124, 136, 155, 183, 201, 205, 214
Ethos (community). *See* Community ethos
Evangelical, 6, 10, 14, 27, 29, 34, 38, 42, 77, 165, 223, 225, 232, 234, 235, 236, 237, 239
Evangelicalism, 39, 40, 223
Evidence, 6, 8, 9, 19, 21, 24, 26, 38, 41, 44, 46, 47, 51, 59, 68, 69, 72, 74, 75, 77, 82, 83, 84, 86, 87, 91, 92, 101, 112, 113, 119, 125, 128, 129, 148, 156, 158, 161, 199, 200, 203, 215
Evil, 40, 55, 63, 102, 119, 122, 123, 126, 149, 162, 163, 177, 179, 181, 194, 197, 201, 203, 204, 208
Experience, 1, 2, 4, 5, 9, 10, 11, 12, 13, 15, 16, 17, 18, 19, 20, 21, 22, 23, 24, 25, 26, 27, 28, 29, 30, 32, 33, 36, 37, 47, 48, 49, 56, 58, 59, 60, 61, 62, 64, 65, 68, 69, 70, 71, 72, 73, 74, 77, 78, 79, 80, 81, 82, 83, 84, 87, 88, 89, 90, 91, 94, 96, 97, 98, 100, 101, 102, 103, 107, 108, 110, 111, 112, 113, 114, 115, 117, 119, 120, 121, 123, 125, 126, 128, 129, 130, 132, 134, 137, 138, 140, 141, 143, 144, 145, 146, 148, 149, 150, 151, 153, 154, 155, 156, 157, 158, 160, 161, 162, 166, 169, 171, 172, 175, 178, 179, 180, 182, 184, 187, 188, 189, 190, 191, 192, 195, 197, 198, 199, 200, 201, 202, 203, 204, 205, 206, 207, 208, 212, 213, 215, 216, 217, 218, 219, 220
Experience (personal), 19, 21, 32, 49, 54, 61, 73, 81, 83, 84, 87, 88, 89, 101, 126, 153, 161, 188, 197
Experimental, 20, 45, 61, 93, 94, 156, 164, 175, 185, 211, 212, 218

Experimental method, 18, 19, 20, 30, 47, 237
Explanatory Notes on the New Testament, 31, 222
Explanatory Notes on the Old Testament, 31
Faith, 9, 12, 13, 14, 18, 19, 20, 25, 29, 30, 32, 34, 39, 40, 41, 42, 43, 44, 45, 46, 48, 49, 50, 55, 58, 59, 60, 61, 62, 63, 64, 65, 66, 67, 68, 69, 71, 72, 73, 74, 75, 76, 77, 78, 80, 81, 82, 83, 84, 85, 86, 87, 88, 89, 91, 92, 93, 94, 95, 98, 100, 101, 102, 103, 104, 105, 106, 108, 109, 110, 112, 115, 121, 122, 123, 124, 125, 126, 127, 128, 131, 136, 137, 139, 140, 144, 146, 147, 149, 150, 151, 152, 154, 155, 157, 158, 162, 164, 166, 168, 169, 170, 171, 174, 176, 179, 180, 186, 187, 188, 190, 191, 193, 196, 197, 198, 200, 201, 205, 206, 207, 209, 212, 213, 214, 217, 219, 220
Faith working by love, 56, 68, 93, 100, 123, 136, 174, 192
Farther Thoughts on Christian Perfection, 120, 142, 191
Feeling(s), 63, 71, 102, 111, 126, 129, 130, 154, 188, 200, 212
Fénelon, Francois, 57, 164, 188, 204
Fetter Lane Society, 84
Flesh, 58, 133
Fletcher, John, 35, 143, 147, 184, 188, 192, 193, 197, 202, 227, 236, 239
Foard, Ann, 145, 149
Folk theologian, 1, 34, 163
Forensic language, 51
Forgiveness, 51, 59, 65, 73, 82, 124
Foster, Durwood, 28, 228
Foundery, The, 85, 121, 179
Frailty (human), 131, 202
Free agency, 161
Free grace, 66, 67, 81, 92
Free will, 53
Fruits of the Spirit, 101, 129, 200
Furly, Dorothy, 142, 146, 153
Furly, Samuel, 107, 142, 143, 145, 154
Garrettson, Freeborn, 189
General Conference, 8, 10, 11
General Rules, 108

Georgia, 37, 48, 53, 58, 61, 63, 64, 70, 78, 87
Germany, 72, 74, 84, 147
God, 4, 6, 9, 13, 18, 19, 20, 24, 25, 26, 29, 30, 32, 33, 34, 35, 39, 41, 42, 43, 45, 46, 48, 50, 51, 52, 53, 54, 55, 56, 57, 58, 59, 60, 61, 62, 63, 64, 65, 66, 67, 68, 69, 70, 71, 72, 73, 75, 76, 77, 78, 79, 81, 82, 83, 86, 87, 88, 89, 91, 92, 93, 95, 96, 97, 98, 99, 100, 101, 102, 103, 104, 105, 106, 107, 108, 109, 110, 111, 112, 113, 114, 118, 119, 120, 121, 122, 123, 124, 125, 126, 127, 128, 129, 130, 131, 132, 133, 134, 135, 136, 137, 139, 140, 142, 143, 144, 145, 146, 147, 148, 149, 150, 151, 152, 153, 154, 156, 158, 160, 161, 162, 163, 164, 165, 166, 167, 168, 169, 170, 171, 173, 174, 175, 176, 177, 178, 179, 180, 181, 182, 183, 185, 186, 188, 189, 190, 191, 192, 193, 194, 195, 196, 197, 198, 199, 200, 201, 202, 203, 204, 205, 206, 207, 208, 210, 211, 212, 213, 214, 215, 216, 217, 219, 220, 221, 225, 227, 230, 232, 233, 238, 239
God (will of), 46, 65, 66, 69, 110, 119, 128, 138, 182
God of love, 37, 161, 166, 183, 191, 206, 219
God-human relationships, 37
Good works, 46, 50, 55, 63, 64, 67, 68, 69, 78, 130, 189
Gospel, 7, 32, 34, 35, 48, 66, 67, 68, 70, 71, 116, 127, 138, 156, 194
Grace, 53, 54, 56, 59, 60, 61, 62, 63, 65, 66, 67, 68, 70, 72, 78, 85, 91, 98, 102, 103, 107, 110, 111, 113, 120, 122, 124, 125, 126, 127, 132, 134, 137, 142, 143, 145, 147, 148, 150, 151, 152, 154, 155, 157, 161, 162, 163, 166, 171, 177, 178, 179, 180, 184, 187, 191, 195, 196, 197, 198, 201, 202, 204, 206, 207, 211, 212, 213, 214, 216, 217, 218, 219, 220, 224, 230, 233
Gradual sanctification, 180
Gradual work (grace), 121, 126, 139, 140, 144, 171, 180, 193
Green, Joel B., 11, 22, 28, 213
Green, V. H. H., 6, 42
Gregory S. Clapper, 34
Guideline, 10, 12, 13, 22, 24, 25, 28, 31,

General index

114, 129
Guilt, 51, 119, 161
Gutenson, Chuck, 14
Guyon, Madam, 190
Happy, 51, 56, 62, 92, 143, 154, 184, 186, 200, 201
    Happiness, 39, 50, 51, 52, 55, 56, 60, 68, 81, 82, 86, 87, 92, 101, 124, 132, 161, 170, 171, 176, 182, 183, 204
Hardy, Elizabeth, 142, 146, 148, 152
Harper, Elizabeth, 195, 200
Harrison, Peter, 40, 41
Heart (clean), 113
Heart experience, 88, 98
Heart religion, 4, 95, 96, 97, 150, 156, 174, 212
Heaviness through Manifold Temptations (sermon), 131
Heitzenrater, Richard P., 35, 38, 47, 48, 49, 57, 74, 77, 79, 80, 85, 86, 99, 121, 221, 229
Hermeneutics, 14, 22, 227, 238
    Hermeneutical, 14, 33, 75, 106, 107, 132, 138, 158
Herrnhut, 73, 84
Holiness, 14, 32, 34, 46, 47, 50, 53, 54, 55, 56, 58, 59, 60, 62, 67, 68, 81, 82, 85, 86, 87, 91, 92, 100, 101, 108, 120, 122, 124, 127, 128, 131, 133, 136, 138, 139, 152, 154, 163, 166, 167, 168, 173, 174, 176, 177, 178, 179, 181, 182, 183, 184, 185, 186, 193, 197, 198, 202, 204, 208
Holy, 8, 14, 45, 46, 47, 49, 51, 55, 56, 62, 66, 68, 72, 76, 77, 79, 80, 86, 91, 92, 96, 98, 99, 116, 117, 120, 125, 128, 144, 151, 154, 155, 173, 174, 175, 176, 177, 184, 185, 198, 201
Holy Ghost, 59, 61, 63, 72, 73, 100, 101, 106, 131, 132, 142, 167, 170, 183, 193, 198, 199
Holy living, 8, 45, 46, 47, 49, 62, 76, 79, 80, 86, 151, 176, 185
Holy Spirit, 4, 9, 16, 18, 21, 36, 46, 52, 55, 61, 62, 64, 66, 71, 88, 89, 90, 98, 101, 103, 104, 106, 109, 110, 117, 119, 122, 128, 147, 155, 156, 157, 167, 171, 173, 181, 183, 190, 203, 207, 210, 212, 213, 214, 216, 219, 234, 236, 238
Holy Writ, 104, 107

Homilies, 27, 31, 48, 54, 63, 117, 168, 173, 230
Hooley, Ann, 145
Hope, 1, 4, 48, 60, 61, 62, 63, 65, 67, 69, 70, 84, 131, 143, 147, 170, 186, 198, 199, 203
Hopkins, Robert, 176
Horst, Mark L., 32
Howcroft, Kenneth G., 22
Howe, Leroy T., 11, 25, 213
Hughes, H. Maldwyn, 29
Human freedom, 51
Human infirmities, 152, 193, 194, 203
Human weakness, 152
Hymns and Sacred Poems, 108, 113, 142, 176
Ignorance, 96, 107, 120, 122, 131, 133, 181
Image of God, 50, 51, 52, 53, 57, 92, 144, 161, 178, 196, 202, 218
Incarnation, 94
Infirmities, 66, 119, 120, 122, 133, 135, 136, 152, 181, 182, 185, 194, 207, 211
Infirmity, 87, 119, 144, 152
Initial sanctification, 91, 113, 114, 178, 196
Instantaneous sanctification, 140
Instantaneous work (grace), 82, 180, 187, 191
Intellectual assent, 55, 88, 125
Intellectual comprehension, 4, 52, 64, 71, 81, 88, 94, 134, 155, 158, 206, 208, 210, 212, 216
Intention, 87, 93
Intention (perfect, pure), 2, 11, 47, 54, 57, 62, 69, 70, 87, 101, 133, 144, 155, 194, 204, 211
Intuition (spiritual), 102, 104, 112
Inward holiness, 54, 178, 202
Jones, Bernard E., 21
Jones, Scott J., 11, 13, 22, 34, 214, 225, 228, 231, 233
Journal (John Wesley), 3, 31, 93, 218
Joy, 61, 62, 65, 68, 71, 72, 74, 100, 101, 112, 130, 131, 143, 146, 167, 198, 200
Justice (God's), 52, 54
Justification, 6, 43, 46, 72, 100, 225, 230, 232, 236, 238
Justification by faith, 72, 100, 106, 166, 168, 238

Justify, 46, 65, 169
King, John, 201
Kissack, Reginald, 21
Lacy, H. Edward, 21, 230
Langford, Thomas A., 6, 10, 11, 15, 22, 23, 24, 27, 28, 29, 31, 34, 101, 115, 225, 229, 230, 231, 233, 234
Law (God's), 70, 177
Law (of love), 125, 143, 144, 152, 177, 182, 194, 211
Law, William, 47, 83, 98, 238
Lee, Jenny, 149
Letters (John Wesley), 3, 31, 45, 47, 48, 78, 79, 80, 83, 99, 108, 116, 139, 140, 145, 152, 153, 159, 166, 174, 176, 185, 186, 189, 202, 207, 208, 218
Liberty, 51, 54, 150, 161, 162, 163, 206
Life experience, 18, 79, 85
Lindström, Harald, 6, 118, 231
Living voice (of the Spirit), 101, 213
Living witnesses, 48, 70, 72, 82, 83, 84, 85, 94, 140, 178
Locke, John, 16, 41, 47, 169, 171, 224
London, 6, 8, 14, 15, 19, 21, 29, 32, 34, 38, 39, 42, 43, 44, 53, 64, 71, 74, 77, 80, 81, 83, 85, 94, 98, 99, 105, 113, 120, 133, 140, 141, 145, 151, 153, 154, 162, 164, 174, 179, 189, 195, 198, 201, 205, 206, 221, 222, 223, 224, 225, 226, 227, 228, 229, 230, 231, 232, 233, 234, 235, 236, 237, 238, 239
London revival, 120, 145, 198
Lopez, Gregory, 164, 188
Lord's Supper (Communion), 46, 67, 68, 113
Love, 4, 35, 41, 44, 45, 46, 50, 51, 52, 53, 54, 55, 56, 57, 58, 59, 60, 61, 62, 63, 66, 69, 71, 73, 74, 78, 79, 84, 86, 87, 88, 91, 92, 94, 95, 96, 97, 98, 99, 101, 103, 105, 106, 109, 111, 112, 113, 114, 115, 117, 118, 119, 120, 121, 122, 123, 124, 125, 126, 127, 128, 130, 131, 132, 133, 134, 135, 136, 137, 138, 139, 141, 142, 143, 144, 145, 146, 148, 149, 150, 151, 152, 153, 154, 155, 156, 157, 158, 161, 162, 163, 164, 165, 166, 167, 168, 170, 171, 173, 174, 176, 178, 179, 180, 181, 182, 183, 186, 189, 191, 192, 193, 194, 195, 196, 198, 199, 200, 201, 202, 203, 204, 205, 206, 207, 208, 210, 211, 212, 214, 216, 217, 218, 219, 220
Love excluding sin, 121, 122
Love expelling sin, 192
Love filling the heart, 138, 152, 180
Loxdale, Ann, 192, 198
Lutheran(s), 78
Maddox, Randy L., 6, 8, 10, 12, 14, 15, 16, 17, 18, 19, 20, 21, 24, 26, 27, 30, 31, 32, 33, 34, 51, 56, 64, 80, 86, 95, 96, 97, 99, 101, 122, 123, 128, 172, 184, 214, 225, 226, 228, 229, 231, 232, 233, 239
March, Miss J. C., 110, 143, 145, 149, 152, 154, 155, 188, 195, 197, 203
Marsh, Clive, 18, 19, 23, 81, 88, 215, 226, 227, 228, 231, 232, 236, 238
Marston, Mrs, 194, 203
Mason, John, 83, 187, 221
Maxfield, Thomas, 121, 139, 151, 152, 153, 184
Maxfield-Bell controversy, 184
Maxwell, Lady, 192, 199
McEwen, Gilbert D., 45, 232
Means (of grace), 50, 56, 61, 62, 63, 65, 67, 70, 78, 85, 91, 95, 102, 103, 122, 127, 134, 152, 157, 195, 197, 213, 214, 216, 217, 218, 219, 220
Medicine, 51, 96
Mental assent, 9, 215
Mercy (God's), 52, 53, 54, 57, 59, 75, 105, 124, 125, 138, 161, 206, 211
Merit (human), 67, 125, 216
Method, 1, 4, 5, 9, 14, 18, 26, 28, 30, 32, 36, 45, 46, 47, 48, 52, 59, 76, 80, 93, 99, 103, 132, 156, 168, 186, 198, 212, 224, 229, 237
Methodical, 32, 33, 45, 47
Methodist, 6, 7, 10, 11, 12, 14, 15, 19, 22, 23, 24, 25, 27, 28, 29, 31, 32, 34, 42, 44, 73, 74, 80, 81, 85, 93, 95, 99, 101, 107, 116, 117, 120, 121, 139, 141, 142, 144, 147, 148, 172, 173, 174, 188, 189, 201
Methodism, 6, 11, 12, 18, 21, 27, 28, 29, 34, 38, 42, 44, 48, 72, 95, 97, 98, 100, 116, 165, 174, 184
Methodist Conference (es), 117
Methodist publications (importance of), 159, 176, 191, 208
Methodist society(-ies), 3, 18, 37, 64, 74, 80, 151, 156, 157, 185, 218, 221

General index

Miles, Rebekah L., 15, 16, 56, 214, 225, 228, 231, 233
Mind (carnal), 126, 181
Minutes of Conversations Between the Rev. Mr. Wesley and Others, 8
Mistakes, 98, 107, 122, 135, 136, 153, 154, 165, 172, 177, 194, 211
Mitchell, Samuel, 198
Modern worldview, 86
Moon, Emma, 150
Moral duty, 44, 45
Moravians, 58, 61, 64, 67, 70, 73, 74, 80, 84, 87, 99, 113, 196, 232
Motives, 45, 67
Mystical, 28, 45, 58, 94
Mystics, 46, 57, 69, 78, 98, 171, 191
Natural man, 52
Natural religion, 41, 42
Natural senses, 16
Nature (of God), 2, 4, 30, 37, 49, 50, 53, 90, 91, 95, 109, 155, 161, 212, 218
Nature (of humans), 69, 87, 171
Nelson, Robert, 6, 43, 69, 228
New birth, 73, 82, 84, 91, 100, 102, 107, 128, 129, 166, 168, 187, 191
Newton, John A., 22, 44, 45, 99, 132, 233
Nonconformity, 40
Nonjurors, 43, 56, 70, 78
On Laying the Foundation of the New Chapel (sermon), 173
On Patience (sermon), 178
On Perfection (sermon), 176, 178
On the Wedding Garment (sermon), 183
Opinions (doctrinal), 29, 97, 101, 192
Oracles of God, 44, 94, 96, 108, 109, 116, 132, 149, 167, 169, 170, 172, 178, 179, 200
Ordo salutis, 85, 91, 175
Original sin, 51, 66, 91, 100, 106, 107, 171
Original Sin (Sermon), 11, 21, 91, 100
Orthodoxy, 9, 71, 96, 122, 166, 173
Our Lord's Sermon on the Mount, 138, 191
Outler, Albert C., 1, 2, 3, 5, 7, 8, 9, 10, 11, 14, 15, 18, 22, 24, 25, 26, 29, 32, 36, 58, 64, 79, 91, 92, 93, 97, 100, 106, 115, 118, 119, 120, 126, 129, 163, 166, 173, 176, 181, 185, 215, 218, 219, 222, 234

Outward means, 103
Oxford, 6, 7, 15, 16, 17, 25, 37, 40, 42, 44, 48, 49, 53, 58, 63, 68, 75, 76, 77, 79, 80, 86, 96, 106, 160, 165, 206, 210, 221, 222, 228, 230, 232, 234, 235
Oxford University, 7, 17, 25, 44, 106, 222
Passion, 56, 102, 167, 177, 182, 190
Pastoral advice, 3, 144, 150, 159, 195
Pastoral care, 175
Pastoral ministry, 1, 2, 33, 36, 38, 49, 70, 210, 218
Pastoral practice, 1, 2, 3, 5, 37, 90, 141, 209, 210, 213
Pastoral theologian, 3, 4, 5, 30, 35, 37, 210, 212, 220
Pastoral theology, 8, 158, 210, 217
Pastoral writings, 3, 158, 160, 207
Peace, 61, 62, 63, 71, 72, 73, 74, 100, 101, 112, 130, 131, 132, 143, 146, 167, 200
Perfect, 52, 53, 55, 57, 58, 60, 62, 66, 69, 87, 108, 114, 118, 119, 120, 123, 124, 130, 134, 135, 137, 138, 141, 142, 143, 146, 149, 152, 154, 158, 163, 178, 181, 182, 189, 194, 201, 202, 206, 208, 211
Perfect love, 52
Perfection, 2, 4, 21, 37, 52, 53, 58, 60, 61, 69, 86, 87, 91, 108, 113, 114, 115, 117, 118, 120, 121, 122, 128, 132, 133, 134, 136, 137, 138, 139, 140, 141, 142, 143, 147, 148, 149, 150, 152, 153, 157, 158, 159, 160, 174, 175, 176, 178, 180, 181, 183, 184, 186, 187, 188, 189, 191, 192, 193, 194, 196, 199, 203, 204, 207, 208, 210
Perfection (Adamic), 50, 181
Performance, 46, 57, 63, 69, 70, 71, 87, 91, 118, 123, 155, 211
Perseverance, 75, 105
Personal choice, 46
Personal commitment, 46
Personal salvation, 39, 44, 70
Personal transformation, 61, 129
Personal trust, 43, 59, 125
Personhood, 51
Piety, 17, 42, 43, 46, 47, 49, 94, 116, 143
Porter, Roy, 15, 38, 39, 40, 77, 234
Postmodern, 1, 2, 218, 219
Postmodernism, 29

Power of choice, 54, 86
Practical Christianity, 19, 29
Practical divinity, 31
Practical theology, 29, 31, 49
Preachers (Methodist), 8, 35, 60, 121, 140, 141, 147, 158, 174, 180, 185, 186, 187, 189, 191, 195, 201, 208
Preaching, 21, 48, 64, 67, 71, 95, 108, 139, 140, 146, 174, 187, 190, 218
Predestination, 52, 53, 75, 86, 104, 105, 113, 163, 165
Prevenience, 9
Prevenient grace, 22, 26, 52, 162, 235
Primitive church. *See* Church (primitive)
Promises (of God), 145
Proof texts, 76, 134, 142, 156, 158, 168, 214
Propitiation, 59
Propositional, 41, 216, 219
Propositional truth, 4, 41, 54, 55, 59, 76, 81, 86, 88, 89, 107, 155, 206, 207, 211, 212, 213, 220
Propositions, 41, 76, 77, 94, 97, 214
Protestant, 1, 7, 26, 41, 51, 74, 89, 106, 210, 213, 222, 223
   Protestantism, 6, 29, 30, 39, 41, 78, 229, 234
Providence, 40, 50
Puritan, 20, 29, 44, 45, 46, 94, 223, 233
Rack, Henry D., 6, 38, 43, 44, 45, 48, 85, 99, 121, 165, 234
Rankin, Thomas, 187
Rationalism, 39, 76, 208, 213, 214
Reading community, 79, 159, 168
Real religion, 165, 168
Reason, 1, 2, 4, 5, 8, 9, 10, 11, 12, 13, 15, 16, 17, 18, 20, 21, 22, 23, 24, 25, 26, 27, 28, 32, 33, 36, 37, 39, 41, 42, 43, 45, 46, 47, 50, 53, 56, 68, 75, 76, 78, 80, 81, 83, 86, 88, 89, 90, 102, 103, 104, 105, 106, 109, 110, 111, 115, 116, 117, 126, 129, 130, 132, 135, 138, 142, 144, 147, 148, 149, 151, 154, 155, 156, 157, 158, 159, 166, 169, 170, 171, 172, 175, 177, 179, 181, 186, 188, 190, 192, 197, 201, 204, 206, 207, 208, 213, 214, 215, 216, 217, 218, 219
Reasonable, 44, 75, 76, 107, 109, 110, 206
Reconciled, 59, 63, 66, 170

Reconciliation, 82
Redemption, 59, 65, 100, 140, 161, 163, 182, 206
Reformed churches, 117
Regeneration, 117, 120
Relational truth, 41, 89
Relationship, 4, 13, 15, 20, 23, 28, 29, 30, 32, 35, 37, 39, 40, 41, 43, 45, 49, 51, 52, 53, 54, 55, 57, 58, 59, 60, 64, 65, 70, 71, 75, 77, 79, 80, 81, 83, 84, 86, 87, 88, 90, 91, 92, 93, 94, 95, 96, 97, 98, 101, 105, 106, 111, 115, 118, 123, 124, 125, 126, 127, 131, 136, 138, 139, 141, 143, 146, 149, 152, 154, 155, 156, 157, 158, 159, 160, 162, 164, 165, 166, 176, 178, 179, 184, 185, 188, 192, 193, 195, 196, 206, 207, 208, 209, 210, 211, 212, 213, 214, 215, 216, 218, 219, 220
Religion, 19, 20, 39, 40, 41, 43, 51, 52, 61, 68, 72, 78, 79, 86, 90, 91, 92, 93, 94, 95, 96, 100, 102, 109, 111, 117, 122, 130, 138, 164, 165, 167, 168, 170, 171, 172, 173, 174, 175, 177, 182, 183, 185, 191, 192, 198, 200, 206, 211, 218
Renshaw, John R., 19, 21, 22, 29, 235
Repentance, 50, 100, 120, 125, 126, 129, 162, 211
Responsibility (human), 105
Revelation, 14, 15, 20, 24, 41, 43, 45, 47, 59, 60, 75, 76, 80, 89, 167, 170, 182, 199, 214
Righteous, 55, 59
   Righteousness, 57, 59, 65, 67, 68, 72, 91, 92, 98, 100, 123, 127, 166, 167, 181
Ritchie, Elizabeth, 170, 171, 189, 190
Rivers, Isabel, 15, 18, 19, 20, 31, 235
Roe, Hester Ann, 188, 189
Rogers, Charles, 22, 26, 235
Roman Catholic, 17, 115, 117, 165, 171
   Roman Catholicism, 17, 42, 98, 118, 165, 215
Rules and Exercises of Holy Dying, 54
Rules and Exercises of Holy Living, 54
Rutter, Sarah, 180
Ryan, Sarah, 153
Sacred writings, 58, 168
Salkeld, Jane, 188
Salvation, 4, 14, 18, 41, 43, 46, 48, 49, 50, 52, 53, 54, 56, 57, 59, 60, 61, 64, 65, 66,

General index 249

67, 68, 71, 73, 74, 78, 81, 82, 83, 85, 86, 87, 91, 95, 96, 97, 99, 100, 101, 102, 105, 106, 107, 109, 113, 114, 117, 122, 123, 131, 138, 141, 145, 147, 151, 154, 155, 156, 161, 162, 163, 166, 167, 168, 170, 171, 177, 180, 183, 185, 186, 187, 188, 189, 197, 198, 199, 201, 203, 204, 205, 218, 219

Salvation by faith, 66

Sanctification, 6, 34, 65, 100, 110, 124, 125, 130, 131, 138, 141, 147, 148, 153, 167, 168, 174, 176, 178, 179, 180, 187, 188, 192, 193, 196, 197, 200, 204

Saved from (all) sin, 66, 113, 120, 136, 141, 147, 150, 153, 177, 203

Schmidt, Martin, 14, 15, 29, 31, 235

Science, 40, 43, 45, 76, 77, 98, 221

Scientific method, 47, 77, 86

Scriptural Authority, 14, 15, 16, 17, 18, 19, 23, 28, 42, 43, 233, 237

Scriptural Christianity, 95, 175

Scriptural language, 108

Scripture, 1, 2, 4, 5, 9, 10, 11, 12, 13, 14, 15, 16, 17, 18, 19, 20, 21, 22, 23, 24, 25, 26, 27, 28, 32, 33, 36, 37, 39, 42, 44, 46, 47, 48, 50, 51, 54, 59, 68, 72, 74, 75, 76, 78, 80, 81, 82, 83, 84, 85, 87, 88, 89, 90, 91, 93, 94, 96, 97, 100, 103, 104, 105, 106, 107, 108, 110, 111, 112, 113, 115, 116, 117, 118, 119, 120, 121, 125, 126, 127, 129, 130, 132, 133, 134, 137, 142, 143, 148, 149, 151, 156, 157, 159, 162, 165, 166, 167, 168, 169, 171, 173, 175, 177, 178, 181, 188, 190, 197, 206, 208, 213, 214, 215, 216, 217, 218, 219, 220, 222, 223, 225, 227, 228, 230, 235, 236, 237, 238

Searching the Scriptures, 103, 111

Second (time), 126

Second awakening, 126, 188

Second blessing, 126, 186, 188

Self-discipline, 55, 56, 60, 70

Self-examination, 46

Senses (physical), 102, 129

Senses (spiritual), 16, 18, 19, 77, 89, 102, 110

Sermons on Several Occasions, 93, 238

Shier-Jones, Angela, 19, 23, 24, 116, 215, 226, 227, 228, 231, 232, 235, 236, 238

Sin, 8, 15, 19, 22, 25, 29, 30, 46, 48, 49, 51, 52, 54, 57, 58, 59, 61, 63, 65, 66, 71, 72, 73, 75, 82, 86, 87, 91, 110, 112, 113, 114, 117, 118, 119, 120, 121, 122, 123, 125, 126, 127, 128, 131, 134, 135, 136, 137, 142, 143, 146, 147, 149, 151, 152, 153, 154, 158, 161, 163, 177, 178, 179, 180, 181, 182, 184, 187, 188, 190, 192, 193, 194, 195, 196, 197, 200, 203, 207, 211, 219, 224, 238, 239

Sin (commission), 131, 135, 143

Sin (condemnation), 87, 118, 119, 120, 136, 143, 144, 153, 166, 190, 193, 194

Sin (culpable), 87, 118, 135, 144, 193, 207, 211

Sin (deliberate), 57, 110, 176, 211

Sin (inbred), 126, 144, 171, 179, 188, 189, 196, 199, 202, 205

Sin (inward), 126, 178, 205

Sin (omission), 119, 131, 135, 136, 143, 151

Sin (outward), 73, 91, 119

Sin (remaining), 73, 113, 126, 127, 134, 196

Sin (voluntary), 57, 87, 118, 153, 177, 194, 207, 211

Sin (wilful), 57, 61, 66, 118, 119, 136

Sin as disease, 51, 52, 60, 91, 119, 127

Sin as leprosy, 51, 126

Sin in Believers (sermon), 119, 120, 134, 191, 196

Sinless perfection, 108, 133, 136, 139

Sinner, 46, 59, 125, 185

Small group(s), 48

Smith, John, 106

Smith, Wilfred Cantwell, 40, 236

Snyder, Howard, 22, 236

Social religion (Christianity as), 92

Societies (Methodist). *See* Methodist society (-ies)

Sola fide, 14, 54

Sola gratia, 54

Sola scriptura, 10, 13, 14, 15, 18, 25, 27, 28, 29, 237

Soteriology, 30, 58, 73, 93, 106, 122, 226, 236

Sources (theological), 1, 2, 3, 4, 11, 12, 13, 14, 15, 16, 17, 18, 21, 22, 24, 27, 28, 33,

36, 38, 41, 43, 74, 77, 78, 90, 93, 102, 115, 130, 156, 157, 163, 173, 175, 213, 221, 222

Sovereignty of God, 104, 105, 211

Spangenberg, August, 70

Sparrow, Miss, 206

Speculative divinity, 9, 210

Spirit (as guide), 59

Spirit (human), 61, 69, 70

Spiritual formation, 4, 8, 175

Spiritual guide, 33, 34, 35, 88, 157, 210

Spiritual journey, 3, 4, 32, 37, 49, 52, 71, 77, 90, 126, 150, 176, 190, 204, 207, 212, 214, 217

Spiritual senses. *See* Senses (spiritual)

Spiritual vision (Wesley's), 4, 90, 91, 160, 161, 207

Starkey, Jr., Lycurgus M., 18, 21, 101, 103, 213, 236

State of grace, 48, 85, 136, 137, 149, 178

Stillness, 67, 85, 99

Stoeffler, F. Ernest, 21, 237

Stokes, Mary, 197, 200

Stretton, John, 188

Substance (doctrinal), 4, 30, 51, 90, 95, 114, 115, 122, 152, 157, 158, 159, 160, 169, 180, 207, 208, 217, 220

Systematic theology, 5, 30, 211, 212, 218

Tattershall, Thomas, 199

Taylor, Jeremy, 47, 54, 68

Taylor, Thomas, 185

Tempers (heart), 55, 78, 95, 101, 102, 119, 139, 154, 166, 167, 174, 177, 182, 190, 194, 195, 199, 202, 203, 204

Temptation, 119, 131, 133, 144, 151, 190, 203

Testimony, 23, 24, 44, 69, 73, 75, 76, 79, 81, 82, 83, 89, 101, 104, 111, 112, 128, 129, 130, 134, 138, 141, 148, 154, 158, 179, 185, 186, 188, 195, 200, 203, 218

The Christian's Pattern (Imitatio Christi), 61

The Circumcision of the Heart (sermon), 58, 60, 69, 132, 157, 160, 183, 217

The Doctrine of Justification according to the Church of England, 8

The Fall, 45, 51, 69, 211

The Fathers, 25, 43, 79, 88, 222

The Great Duty of Frequenting the Christian Sacrifice, 69

The Large Minutes, 114, 180

The law and the testimony, 81, 84

The living voice of God, 101, 156, 214

The Lord Our Righteousness (sermon), 196

The mind of Christ, 54

The Model Deed, 8

The Nature of Enthusiasm (sermon), 130

The people called Methodists, 38, 110, 113, 139, 174, 175, 180, 224, 229

The Principles of a Methodist, 133

The Principles of a Methodist Farther Explained, 100

The Repentance of Believers (sermon), 119, 120, 123, 134, 191, 196, 197

The Righteousness of Faith (sermon), 91

The Scripture Way of Salvation (sermon), 91, 191, 197, 226

The Spirit of Bondage and Adoption (sermon), 191, 193

The true, the scriptural, experimental religion, 93, 94, 164, 211, 218

The way to heaven, 93

The Wilderness State (sermon), 131

The Witness of Our Own Spirit (sermon), 129

The Witness of the Spirit (sermon), 130

Theological guidelines, 12

Theological method, 1, 2, 3, 4, 5, 9, 10, 17, 18, 23, 27, 28, 35, 36, 37, 47, 49, 75, 76, 77, 78, 79, 83, 87, 88, 90, 103, 118, 141, 155, 156, 157, 159, 160, 164, 206, 209, 210, 213, 215, 216, 217, 219, 224, 228, 232, 238

    Theological methodology, 2, 3, 4, 5, 8, 13, 16, 31, 37, 49, 74, 77, 90, 93, 97, 156, 160, 163, 169, 212, 215, 216, 217

Theological opinion(s), 6, 9, 211, 213

Theological reflection, 12, 13, 80, 85, 88, 90, 157, 206, 207, 210, 213, 217, 218

Theology of Love, 30, 97, 114, 118, 227, 239

Thirty-Nine Articles, 76, 224

Thornton, Mary, 155

Thorsen, Donald A., 10, 13, 14, 15, 16, 17, 18, 19, 20, 23, 25, 27, 28, 29, 30, 36,

General index 251

110, 215, 237
Thoughts on Christian Perfection, 120, 142, 191
Tools (theological), 4, 74, 93, 130, 157, 163, 219
Tradition, 1, 2, 4, 5, 9, 10, 11, 12, 13, 15, 16, 17, 18, 19, 20, 21, 22, 23, 24, 25, 26, 27, 28, 32, 33, 36, 39, 42, 43, 45, 46, 47, 60, 88, 89, 103, 115, 116, 135, 165, 207, 212, 214, 215, 216, 218
Transformed life, 85, 112
Transgressions (involuntary), 118
Transgressions (voluntary), 194
Trinitarian, 50, 238
Trinity, 50, 96, 164, 198, 199, 216, 233
True religion, 42, 52, 56, 57, 95, 101, 168, 170, 173, 225
Trust, 4, 41, 54, 59, 63, 64, 65, 66, 68, 71, 81, 86, 87, 91, 105, 118, 126, 149, 155, 158, 186, 200, 204, 206, 211, 212, 214, 218, 219
Trusting faith, 9
Tucker, Josiah, 133
Understanding, 2, 3, 4, 5, 10, 13, 15, 16, 18, 21, 23, 24, 25, 27, 29, 32, 33, 34, 37, 38, 41, 44, 45, 46, 48, 49, 50, 53, 54, 55, 56, 57, 58, 59, 60, 61, 64, 65, 69, 71, 73, 74, 76, 77, 79, 81, 82, 83, 85, 86, 87, 88, 90, 91, 93, 94, 95, 96, 97, 99, 100, 102, 106, 108, 109, 112, 114, 115, 116, 117, 118, 119, 120, 121, 122, 123, 124, 126, 130, 132, 135, 138, 140, 141, 144, 146, 152, 153, 155, 156, 157, 158, 160, 162, 163, 166, 168, 169, 170, 175, 176, 178, 180, 182, 185, 188, 190, 191, 192, 195, 196, 204, 205, 207, 208, 209, 210, 211, 212, 213, 216, 217, 219, 220
United Methodist Church, 5, 6, 8, 10, 11, 12, 36, 222, 225, 229, 231, 233, 234, 238
Unscriptural, 111, 120, 132, 134, 168, 185, 190, 196
Victory (over sin), 65, 66, 118, 126
Virtue, 17, 39, 51, 54, 56, 58, 60, 61, 69, 75, 162, 170, 182
Wandering thoughts, 120, 151, 194
Wandering Thoughts (sermon), 8, 120, 200
Wesley, Charles, 18, 19, 34, 83, 121, 139, 165, 170, 186, 187, 221, 222, 235, 238
Wesley, Charles (nephew), 171

Wesley, Samuel, 43, 44, 74, 238
Wesley, Samuel (nephew), 164
Wesley, Susanna, 44, 45, 222, 223, 233, 239
Wesleyan Quadrilateral, 1, 2, 3, 5, 8, 9, 10, 11, 12, 13, 14, 15, 16, 17, 18, 21, 22, 23, 24, 26, 27, 28, 35, 110, 215, 218, 222, 225, 229, 234, 236, 237
Whitefield, George, 53, 133, 165, 192, 236
Wilderness state (wandering), 149
Will (divine), 32, 46, 65, 66, 69, 109, 110, 119, 120, 123, 128, 138, 161, 162, 182
Will (human), 45, 46, 52, 55, 61, 66, 77, 86, 87, 136, 196
Williams, Colin, 6, 21
Wisdom (pastoral), 108, 159, 160, 189, 214, 218, 220
Wisdom (practical), 77
Witness (indirect), 112
Witness (living). *See* Living witnesses
Witness (written), 12, 94
Witness of the Spirit, 63, 65, 70, 72, 82, 111, 112, 113, 114, 129, 131, 191, 199, 200, 201, 219
Wood, Laurence W., 16
Works (good). *See* Good works
Works of mercy, 46, 143
Works of piety, 46, 143
Written voice of God, 104, 213
Written word (of Scripture), 158
Wynkoop, Mildred Bangs, 30, 33, 97, 114, 118, 239

Studies in Evangelical History and Thought
(All titles uniform with this volume)
Dates in bold are of projected publication.
Condensed details are given for volumes published before 2004.

Andrew Atherstone
Oxford's Protestant Spy
The Controversial Career of Charles Golightly
Charles Golightly (1807–85) was a notorious Protestant polemicist. His life was dedicated to resisting the spread of ritualism and liberalism within the Church of England and the University of Oxford. For half a century he led many memorable campaigns, such as building a martyrs' memorial and attempting to close a theological college. John Henry Newman, Samuel Wilberforce and Benjamin Jowett were among his adversaries. This is the first study of Golightly's controversial career.
Andrew Atherstone is an Anglican minister and has worked for churches in Islington, Reading and Oxfordshire, UK.
2007 / 978-1-84227-364-7 / xvi + 334pp

John Brencher
Martyn Lloyd-Jones (1899–1981) and Twentieth-Century Evangelicalism
'An evaluation of perhaps the greatest British preacher of the twentieth century', David Bebbington.
2002 / 978-1-84227-051-6 / xvi + 268pp

Donald A. Bullen
A Man of One Book?
John Wesley's Interpretation and Use of the Bible
John Wesley claimed to be 'a man of one book'—the Bible. He was clear in his mind what the Bible meant and taught. Donald Bullen carefully explores the biblical hermeneutic of John Wesley. Using the insights of reader-response criticism we may comprehend better Wesley's understanding and interpretation of the Bible. The so-called 'Quadrilateral', rooted in American Methodism, gives further insight into Wesley's use of tradition, experience, reason, scripture and their inter-relation.
Donald A. Bullen is a Methodist Minister in Liverpool, UK.
2007 / 978-1-84227-513-9 / xxx + 230pp

Jonathan D. Burnham
A Story of Conflict
The Controversial Relationship between Benjamin Wills Newton and John Nelson Darby
Burnham explores the controversial relationship between the two principal leaders of the early Brethren movement. In many ways Newton and Darby were products of their times, and this study of their relationship provides insight not only into the dynamics of early Brethrenism, but also into the progress of nineteenth-century English and Irish evangelicalism.
Jonathan D. Burnham is the University Professor of Church Leadership, Palm Beach Atlantic University and Senior Pastor, Boca Raton Community Church, Florida, USA.
2004 / 978-1-84227-191-9 / xxiv + 268pp

Robert W. Caldwell III
Communion in the Spirit
The Holy Spirit as the Bond of Union in the Theology of Jonathan Edwards
This study explores the central connection Edwards drew between his doctrines of religious experience and the Trinity: the person and work of the Holy Spirit. Edwards envisioned the Spirit's inter-trinitarian work as the affectionate bond of union between the Father and the Son, a work which, he argued, is reduplicated in a finite way in the work of redemption. Salvation is ultimately all about being drawn in love into the trinitarian life of the Godhead. Dr Caldwell takes us through the major regions of Edwards' theology—his trinitarianism, his doctrine of the end for which God created the world, his christology, and his doctrines of justification, sanctification and glorification—to demonstrate the centrality of the Holy Spirit throughout his theology.

Robert W. Caldwell III is Assistant Professor of American Church History, Southwestern Baptist Theological Seminary, Fort Worth, Texas, USA.

2006 / 978-1-84227-422-4 / xvi + 212pp

Richard Carwardine
Transatlantic Revivalism
Popular Evangelicalism in Britain and America, 1790–1865
The focus of this classic text is on British and American evangelicals during the late-eighteenth century to the mid-nineteenth century, examining the effect of aggressive conversion techniques used by American evangelicals upon the revival movement.

Richard Carwardine is Rhodes Professor of American History, St Catherine's College, University of Oxford, UK.

2006 [1978] / 978-1-84227-373-9 / xviii + 250pp

James M. Collins
Exorcism and Deliverance Ministry in the Twentieth Century
An Analysis of the Practice and Theology of Exorcism in Modern Western Christianity
This study seeks to demonstrate that exorcism/deliverance ministry is an innately enthusiastic practice utilising Knox's classic study of Christian enthusiasm. The twentieth century is an ideal arena for such a study since it frames a complete lifecycle for this rite from its infancy during the early decades, through its heyday in the 1970s and 80s on to creeping routinisation by the end of the century. The study provides the foundation for future investigation of the manner in which enthusiastic experience is presented for apologetic purposes, the relationship between exorcism/deliverance ministry and millenarianism and the practice of this rite within non-Western churches.

James M. Collins is Pastor of Redhill Baptist Church, UK.

2009 / 978-1-84227-626-6 / xviii + 236

J.N. Ian Dickson
Beyond Religious Discourse
Sermons, Preaching and Evangelical Protestants in Nineteenth-Century Irish Society
Drawing extensively on primary sources, this pioneer work in modern religious history explores the training of preachers, the construction of sermons and how Irish evangelicalism and the wider movement in Great Britain and the United States shaped the preaching event. Evangelical preaching and politics, sectarianism, denominations, education, class, social reform, gender, and revival are examined to advance the argument that evangelical sermons and preaching went significantly beyond religious discourse. The result is a book for those with interests in Irish history, culture and belief, popular religion and society, evangelicalism, preaching and communication.

J.N. Ian Dickson is Senior Lecturer and Director of Postgraduate Studies at Belfast Bible College, Northern Ireland, UK.

2007 / 978-1-84227-217-6 / xx + 296pp

Neil T.R. Dickson
Brethren in Scotland 1838–2000
A Social Study of an Evangelical Movement
'A pioneering and noteworthy book', Mark A. Noll.
2003 / 978-1-84227-113-1 / xxviii + 510pp

Neil T.R. Dickson and Tim Grass (eds)
The Growth of the Brethren Movement
National and International Experiences
The essays in this book have been contributed in honour of Dr H.H. Rowdon, a teacher of several generations of students at the London Bible College (now London School of Theology) and a historian of the Brethren movement. The book includes reflections on the historiography of the Brethren, but it is their character and growth which form the principal focus.
Neil T.R. Dickson is the Convenor of the Brethren Archivists and Historians Network.
Tim Grass is a Fellow of the Royal Historical Society and Associate Tutor in Church History at Spurgeon's College, London.
2006 / 978-1-84227-427-9 / xiv + 272pp

Daniel W. Draney
When Streams Diverge
The Origins of Protestant Fundamentalism in Los Angeles
The importance of this study is that it examines the complex political and religious currents influencing the modern world. It focuses on the emergence of Protestant fundamentalism in Los Angeles, beginning with late nineteenth-century trends towards religious radicalism and culminating in the splitting of radical and moderate fundamentalist groups at the Bible Institute of Los Angeles in the late 1920s. Highlighted in this study are the complex tensions between mainline Protestants and an emerging sectarian trend among those who would become militant fundamentalists, which continues to shape Protestant religion today.
Daniel W. Draney is Adjunct Instructor in the field of American Religious History at Fuller Theological Seminary, Pasadena, California, USA.
2008 / 978-1-84227-523-8 / xvi + 266pp

James M. Gordon,
James Denney (1856–1917)
An Intellectual and Contextual Biography
James Denney is now best known for his *The Death of Christ*, considered a standard treatment of objective atonement understood in substitutionary terms. However there is a breadth and depth to Denney's thought, a richness and passion in his theological work, an attractive integrity and spiritual immediacy in his writing, that resists any reducing of his legacy to that of being an apologist for one aspect of Christian doctrine. This is the first major study of Denney to use the large corpus of Denney's unpublished theological papers and sermons held in New College, Edinburgh. These, together with Denney's published work, and wider biographical research, form the basis for this intellectual and contextual biography of one of Scotland's most attractive and forceful theological personalities.
James M. Gordon is Principal of the Scottish Baptist College, at the University of Paisley, Scotland, UK.
2006 / 978-1-84227-399-9 / xviii + 286pp

Tim Grass
The Lord's Watchman
Edward Irving
The theology of Edward Irving has been rediscovered in recent decades, and his contributions to our understanding of the person and work of Christ and the work of the Holy Spirit have excited considerable interest among both academics and leaders of the charismatic movement. But what made him tick? Based on extensive research and the use of newly-discovered family letters, this biography portrays Irving as first and foremost a pastor, formed by his upbringing in southern Scotland. Not only was he arguably one of the first modern charismatics, but he was also one of the last Scottish Covenanters.

Tim Grass is a Fellow of the Royal Historical Society and Associate Tutor in Church History at Spurgeon's College, London, UK.

2009 / 978-1-84227-426-2 / approx. 390pp

Crawford Gribben and Timothy C.F. Stunt (eds)
Prisoners of Hope?
Aspects of Evangelical Millennialism in Britain and Ireland, 1800–1880
This volume of essays offers a comprehensive account of the impact of evangelical millennialism in nineteenth-century Britain and Ireland.

Crawford Gribben is Senior Lecturer in Early Modern Print Culture, Long Room Hub, Trinity College, Dublin, Ireland.

Timothy C.F. Stunt has taught in England, Switzerland and the USA.

2004 / 978-1-84227-224-4 / xiv + 208pp

Mathew Guest
Evangelical Identity and Contemporary Culture
A Congregational Study in Innovation
In response to the decline of church attendance in the twentieth century the evangelical movement has, since the 1960s, sought a more profound engagement with its cultural context in an attempt to be more relevant. This volume explores how evangelical congregations have appropriated the values and media of contemporary culture in the propagation of a Christian message, and explores how this process has reconfigured the parameters of evangelical identity. It builds on an ethnographic study of St Michael-le-Belfrey church in York, a recognized leader in charismatic renewal, mission and evangelical innovation since the 1960s, exploring how a persistent tradition of cultural engagement may generate growth, while at the same time bringing about significant changes in the structure and function of the evangelical congregation, and in the social construction of Christian identity itself.

Mathew Guest is Lecturer in Theology and Society, University of Durham, UK.

2007 / 978-1-84227-440-8 / xxvi + 264pp

Khim Harris
Evangelicals and Education
Evangelical Anglicans and Middle-Class Education in Nineteenth-Century England
This groundbreaking study investigates the history of English public schools founded by nineteenth-century Evangelicals. It documents the rise of middle-class education and Evangelical societies such as the influential Church Association, and includes a useful biographical survey of prominent Evangelicals of the period.

Khim Harris was previously a Lecturer at the University of Western Australia, and is now the Manager of Education at Perth Zoo, Western Australia.

2004 / 978-1-84227-250-3 / xviii + 422pp

James Heard
Inside Alpha
Explorations in Evangelism
From small beginnings in the early 1970s, Alpha has grown to become a global success. Churches from across the denominational spectrum have enthusiastically seized upon the course, seeing it as the remedy for declining church attendance. Heard explores such claims through richly grounded qualitative research on six Alpha courses. He assesses Alpha's primary aim of converting non-churchgoers and its longer-term goal of spiritual maturity, and questions whether the Alpha programme is as successful as it claims at uniting evangelism and discipleship, mission and spiritual formation.
James Heard is Curate of All Saints, Fulham, London, UK.
2010 / 978-1-84227-672-3 / approx. 300pp

Mark Hopkins
Nonconformity's Romantic Generation
Evangelical and Liberal Theologies in Victorian England
A study of the theological development of key leaders of the Baptist and Congregational denominations at their period of greatest influence, including C.H. Spurgeon and R.W. Dale, and of the controversies in which those among them who embraced and rejected the liberal transformation of their evangelical heritage opposed each other.
Mark Hopkins lectures at the Theological College of Northern Nigeria in Bukuru.
2004 / 978-1-84227-150-6 / xvi + 284pp

Don Horrocks
Laws of the Spiritual Order
Innovation and Reconstruction in the Soteriology of Thomas Erskine of Linlathen
Horrocks argues that Thomas Erskine's unique historical and theological significance as a soteriological innovator has been neglected. This timely reassessment reveals Erskine as a creative, radical theologian of central and enduring importance in Scottish nineteenth-century theology, perhaps equivalent to that of S.T. Coleridge in England.
Don Horrocks is Public Affairs Manager for the Evangelical Alliance and a Research Associate, London School of Theology, UK.
2004 / 978-1-84227-192-6 / xx + 362pp

Kenneth S. Jeffrey
When the Lord Walked the Land
The 1858–62 Revival in the North East of Scotland
'A milestone in the study of religious movements', David Bebbington.
2002 / 978-1-84227-057-8 / xxiv + 304pp

William K. Kay
Apostolic Networks in the United Kingdom
Apostolic networks link congregations together through personal relationships. They centre around apostolic figures who have the ability to mobilise resources, make rapid decisions and utilise charismatic gifts. Networks of churches organised in this way can respond to postmodernity and cultural innovation. This book takes the story of the emergence of apostolic networks in Britain from the visionary work of Arthur Wallis through the charismatic renewal into the full-fledged Restoration Movement of the 1980s. It covers the events of the 1990s, including the Toronto Blessing, and contains fresh information based upon interviews with leading figures and new survey data, as well as re-analysis of historical documents.
William K. Kay is Director of the Centre for Pentecostal and Charismatic Studies at the University of Wales, Bangor, UK.
2007 / 978- 1-84227-409-5 / xxii + 378pp

John Kenneth Lander
Itinerant Temples
Tent Methodism, 1814–1832
'Takes us to the heart of sociological and ecclesiastical questions about Methodist identity', T.S.A. Macquiban.
2003 / 978-1-84227-151-3 / xx + 268pp

Donald M. Lewis
Lighten Their Darkness
The Evangelical Mission to Working-Class London, 1828–1860
'A splendid work', Sheridan Gilley.
2001 [1986] / 978-1-84227-074-5 / xviii + 372pp

R. Todd Mangum
The Dispensational–Covenantal Rift
The Fissuring of American Evangelical Theology from 1936 to 1944
This study explores how the fight between dispensationalists and covenant theologians started and how sociological factors were largely responsible for enflaming it. Surprisingly, most of the original protagonists on both sides were Presbyterians, and soteriology, rather than eschatology, was the original bone of contention between them. Understanding how the feud began may hold the key for rapprochement today.
R. Todd Mangum is Associate Professor of Theology, Biblical Theological Seminary, Hatfield, Pennsylvania, USA.
2007 / 978-1-84227-365-4 / xvi + 320pp

David B. McEwan
Wesley as a Pastoral Theologian
Theological Methodology in John Wesley's Doctrine of Christian Perfection
In this book, Wesley's theological methodology is uncovered from the perspective of his holistic vision of the God–human relationship being centred in love and defined by the qualities of trust and passion, rather than an intellectual comprehension of propositional truths about God. Accordingly, pastoral theology is much more important than academic, systematic theology for Christian experience and spiritual formation. In his theological method Scripture, reason, community ethos and Christian experience are utilised in an interconnected dynamic network, energised by the presence of the Holy Spirit. God is clearly the sole theological authority and the elements of the system are the means he uses for communication with his people. This interconnected system is explored through an investigation of the doctrine and practice of Christian perfection as Wesley offered pastoral guidance to the people called Methodists. This is a valuable contribution to the current interest in pastoral theology and theological methodology.
David B. McEwan is Academic Dean and Lecturer in Theology at Nazarene Theological College, Brisbane, Australia
2010 / 978-1-84227-621-1 / approx. 260pp

Patricia Meldrum
Conscience and Compromise
Forgotten Evangelicals of Nineteenth-Century Scotland
The book explores the history of Evangelical Episcopalians in nineteenth-century Scotland. Doctrinal differences with the Scottish Episcopal Church, particularly concerning evangelism, eucharistic and baptismal thought, are studied in detail against the background of the social history of this important group of churchmen.
Patricia Meldrum has worked for the Medical Research Council, Cambridge, and taught biology at the Cambridgeshire College of Arts and Technology, UK.
2006 / 978-1-84227-421-7 /xxiv + 416pp

Herbert McGonigle
'Sufficient Saving Grace'
John Wesley's Evangelical Arminianism
'A distinguished contribution to Wesley studies', Henry D. Rack.
2001 / 978-1-84227-045-5 / xvi + 350pp

Lisa S. Nolland
A Victorian Feminist Christian
Josephine Butler, the Prostitutes and God
Josephine Butler was an unlikely candidate for taking up the cause of prostitutes. This book explores the particular mix of perspectives and experiences that came together to envision and empower her remarkable achievements. It highlights the vital role of her spirituality and the tragic loss of her daughter.
Lisa S. Nolland is chaplain at an inner-city secondary school in Bristol and gained her doctorate at the University of Bristol, UK.
2004 / 978-1-84227-225-1 / xxiv + 328pp

Don J. Payne
The Theology of the Christian Life in J.I. Packer's Thought
Theological Anthropology, Theological Method, and the Doctrine of Sanctification
J.I. Packer has wielded widespread influence on evangelicalism for more than three decades. This study pursues a nuanced understanding of Packer's theology of sanctification by tracing the development of his thought, showing how he reflects a particular version of Reformed theology, and examining the unique influence of theological anthropology and theological method on this area of his theology.
Don J. Payne is Associate Dean and Assistant Professor of Theology and Ministry at Denver Seminary, Denver, Colorado, USA.
2006 / 978-1-84227-397-5 / xx + 322pp

Ian M. Randall
Evangelical Experiences
A Study in the Spirituality of English Evangelicalism 1918–1939
'A quite exceptional piece of work', Harold Rowdon.
1999 / 978-0-85364-919-9 / xii + 310pp

Ian M. Randall
Spirituality and Social Change
The Contribution of F.B. Meyer (1847–1929)
'A wide-ranging, perceptive, sympathetically critical study', Clyde Binfield.
2003 / 978-1-84227-195-7 / xx + 184pp

Dyfed Wyn Roberts (ed.)
Revival, Renewal, and the Holy Spirit
The revival of 1904–05 had a profound effect not only on Wales, but also on many other nations. This volume of academic papers from the centenary conference in 2004 explores the local and international impact of the revival as well as previous eighteenth- and nineteenth-century Welsh revivals. Contributors include David Bebbington and Mark A. Noll.
Dyfed Wyn Roberts is a Minister of Emmanuel Church, Anglesey, Wales, UK.
2009 / 978-1-84227-374-6 / xx + 286pp

James Robinson
Pentecostal Origins
Early Pentecostalism in Ireland in the Context of the British Isles
Harvey Cox describes Pentecostalism as 'the fascinating spiritual child of our time' that has the potential, at the global scale, to contribute to the 'reshaping of religion in the twenty-first century'. This study grounds such sentiments by examining at the local scale the origin, development and nature of Pentecostalism in Ireland in its first twenty years. Illustrative, in a paradigmatic way, of how Pentecostalism became established within one region of the British Isles, it sets the story within the wider context of formative influences emanating from America, Europe and, in particular, other parts of the British Isles. As a synoptic regional study in Pentecostal history it is the first survey of its kind.

James Robinson is a retired teacher whose doctorate, on which this study is based, was completed at Union Theological College, Belfast, Northern Ireland, UK.
2005 / 978-1-84227-329-6 / xxviii + 378pp

Geoffrey Robson
Dark Satanic Mills?
Religion and Irreligion in Birmingham and the Black Country
'A formidable research achievement', David Hempton.
2002 / 978-1-84227-102-5 / xiv + 294pp

Doreen Rosman
Evangelicals and Culture
In this seminal work, evangelicals' attitudes to music, art, literature and academic study are examined in the period 1790 to 1833.

Doreen Rosman lectured in the School of History, University of Kent, 1974–2001.
2009 / 978-1-84227-576-4 / approx. 250pp

Nigel Scotland
Apostles of the Spirit and Fire
American Revivalists and Victorian Britain
This is a book about American revivalist religion and the ways in which it impacted British Christianity in nineteenth-century England. The term 'revivalist' seems to have first been used in the period after the 'Second Great Awakening' in the United States. It designated those individuals and churches who sought to manufacture or create revival by human endeavour rather than, as in former times, pray and wait for a sovereign move of God's Spirit. Revivalism had a number of marked features which are charted in detail in chapter 1. It was inevitably characterised by emotion, excitement and religious exercises. Particular attention has been given to ways in which the different American revivalists understood revival and the methods by which they sought to achieve it. The book includes a focus on one or two female revivalists whose work has tended to be overlooked in some studies.

Nigel Scotland is a Tutor at Trinity College, Bristol, and an Honorary Research Fellow at the University of Gloucestershire, UK.
2009 / 978-1-84227-366-1 / xxii + 242pp

Roger Shuff
Searching for the True Church
Brethren and Evangelicals in Mid-Twentieth-Century England
Shuff holds that the influence of the Brethren movement on wider evangelical life in England in the twentieth century is often underrated. The peak of their strength occurred when evangelicalism was at it lowest ebb, immediately before World War II. They then moved into decline as evangelicalism regained ground in the post war period. Accompanying this downward trend has been a sharp accentuation of the contrast between Brethren congregations who engage constructively with the non-Brethren scene and the isolationist group commonly referred to as 'Exclusive Brethren'.
Roger Shuff is Pastor of Westerham Evangelical Congregational Church, UK.
2005 / 978-1-84227-254-1 / xviii+ 296pp

Mark Smith (ed.)
British Evangelical Identities Past and Present
Volume 1. Aspects of the History and Sociology of Evangelicalism in Britain and Ireland
Evangelical Christianity has been characterised by a remarkable degree of dynamism and diversity. This volume explores that diversity by investigating the interaction of evangelicalism with national and denominational identities, race and gender, and its expression in spirituality and culture from the evangelical revivals of the eighteenth century to evangelical churches and movements of the present. A second volume will investigate similar issues in relation to evangelical interactions with the Bible and theology.
Mark Smith is University Lecturer in Local and Social History, University of Oxford, UK.
2008 / 978-1-84227-390-6 / xvi + 280pp

James H.S. Steven
Worship in the Spirit
Charismatic Worship in the Church of England
'A pioneering volume', David Martin.
2002 / 978-1-84227-103-2 / xvi + 238pp

Peter K. Stevenson
God in Our Nature
The Incarnational Theology of John McLeod Campbell
This radical reassessment of Campbell's thought arises from a comprehensive study of his preaching and theology. Previous accounts have overlooked both his sermons and his Christology. This study examines the distinctive christology evident in his sermons and shows that it sheds new light on Campbell's much debated views about atonement.
Peter K. Stevenson is Director of Training, Spurgeon's College, London, UK.
2004 / 978-1-84227-218-3 / xxiv + 458pp

Kenneth J. Stewart
Restoring the Reformation
British Evangelicals and the Francophone Réveil 1816–1849
Stewart traces British missionary initiative in post-Revolutionary Francophone Europe from the genesis of the London Missionary Society, the visits of Robert Haldane and Henry Drummond, and the founding of the Continental Society. While British Evangelicals aimed at the reviving of a foreign Protestant cause of momentous legend, they received unforeseen reciprocating emphases from the Continent which forced self-reflection on Evangelicalism's own relationship to the Reformation.
Kenneth J. Stewart is Professor of Theological Studies, Covenant College, Lookout Mountain, Georgia, USA.
2006 / 978-1-84227-392-0 / xvi + 282pp

Rob Warner
Reinventing English Evangelicalism, 1966–2001
A Theological and Sociological Study
Grounded in empirical data and interviews with many senior evangelicals, this study explores the trends within evangelicalism in the latter twentieth century and develops new insights into the increasing diversity, conflicting identities and relative durability of the evangelical tradition. As such, this book provides a detailed theological analysis and a constructive sociological critique for anyone wanting a fuller understanding of the social and religious significance and the evolutionary dynamics of this influential and diversifying religious tradition.
Rob Warner is Lecturer in Sociology of Religion and Practical Theology, University of Wales, Lampeter, UK.
2007 / 978-1-84227-570-2 / xx + 284pp

Martin Wellings
Evangelicals Embattled
Responses of Evangelicals in the Church of England to Ritualism, Darwinism and Theological Liberalism 1890–1930
'Wellings' important book…fills a large hole in the history of modern Anglicanism', John Walsh.
2003 / 978-1-84227-049-3 / xviii + 352pp

James Whisenant
A Fragile Unity
Anti-Ritualism and the Division of Anglican Evangelicalism in the Nineteenth Century
'Enables the reader to emerge with a genuine understanding of the issues', Dale A. Johnson.
2003 / 978-1-84227-105-6 / xvi + 530pp

Paul Richard Wilkinson
For Zion's Sake
Christian Zionism and the Role of John Nelson Darby
This groundbreaking book debunks decades of misrepresentation of Christian Zionism and questionable theology, exploding the myth that J.N. Darby stole the doctrine of the pre-tribulation Rapture from his contemporaries. By revealing the truth behind the man and his message, Paul Wilkinson vindicates Darby and spotlights the imminent return of the Lord Jesus Christ as the centre piece of his theology.
Paul Richard Wilkinson is Assistant Minister at Hazel Grove Full Gospel Church, Stockport, Cheshire, UK.
2007 / 978-1-84227-569-6 / xxii + 308pp

Linda Wilson
Constrained by Zeal
Female Spirituality amongst Nonconformists 1825–1875
'A significant contribution to current debates on women and religion', Sue Morgan.
2000 / 978-0-85364-972-4 / xvi + 294pp

New and unscheduled titles:

Cary Balzer
John Wesley's Developing Soteriology and the Influence of The Caroline Divines
978-1-84227-522-1 / approx. 300pp

Grayson Carter
Anglican Evangelicals
Protestant Secessions from the Via Media, c.1800–1850

This study examines, within a chronological framework, the major themes and personalities which influenced the outbreak of a number of Evangelical clerical and lay secessions from the Church of England and Ireland during the first half of the nineteenth century. Though the number of secessions was relatively small—between a hundred and two hundred of the 'Gospel' clergy abandoned the Church during this period—their influence was considerable, especially in highlighting in embarrassing fashion the tensions between the evangelical conversionist imperative and the principles of a national religious establishment. Moreover, through much of this period there remained, just beneath the surface, the potential threat of a large Evangelical disruption similar to that which occurred in Scotland in 1843. Consequently, these secessions provoked great consternation within the Church and within Evangelicalism itself, they contributed to the outbreak of millennial speculation following the 'constitutional revolution' of 1828–32, they led to the formation of several new denominations, and they sparked off a major Church–State crisis over the legal right of a clergyman to secede and begin a new ministry within Protestant Dissent.

[2001] / 978-1-84227-401-9 / xvi + 470pp

James M. Gordon
Evangelical Spirituality
From the Wesleys to John Stott (Revised Edition)

Through a series of penetrating studies, contrasting the experiences and emphases of contemporary figures, Evangelical spirituality is placed in a living historical and cultural context. The variety of figures include the Wesleys, Edwards, Whitefield, Simeon, Hannah More, Spurgeon, Forsyth and Stott. In the process the study reveals the recurring hallmarks and enriching variety, the changing continuities and openness to growth and development that have characterized Evangelical spiritual tradition. This completely revised edition includes a new essay reflecting on contemporary developments, continuing change, and increasing variety in the expressions of Evangelical spirituality. In addition the core chapters have been revised, and referenced literature completely updated to take into account a growing field of academic study and wider interest.

2nd edn / 978-1-84227-361-2 / approx. 300pp

Joseph P. Gouverneur
The Third Wave
A Case Study of Romantic Narratives within Late Twentieth Century Charismatic Evangelicalism
978-1-84227-514-6 / approx. 300pp

Stephen R. Holmes (ed.)
British Evangelical Identities
Volume 2. Theology and Biblical Studies
978-1-84227-391-3 / approx. 300pp

Hugh Osgood
African Neo-Pentecostal Churches and British Evangelicalism 1985–2005
978-1-84227-633-4 / approx. 300pp

Mark S. Sweetnam
Each Waking Band
Studies in Dispensational Spirituality 1800–2000
Dispensationalism emerged from the ferment of prophetic speculation that stirred the evangelical world at the start of the nineteenth century. From these origins it spread to become one of the most widely diffused and culturally significant modes of biblical interpretation. In spite of its importance, scholarly engagements with dispensationalism have been limited. This volume provides a number of new studies by leading scholars of dispensationalism, which examine the nature of dispensationalist spirituality and dispensationalism's impact as a 'lived theology'.
978-1-84227-529-0 / approx. 300pp

D. Allen Tennison
Logic of the Spirit
The Shape of Pneumatology in the Pentecostal Movement in the United States 1901–1930
978-1-84227-673-0 / approx. 300pp

Barbara Waddington
The Letters, Diary and Journal of Edward Irving
978-1-84227-577-1 / approx. 300pp

Tim Walsh
'To Meet and Satisfy and a Very Hungry People'
The Origins and Fortunes of English Pentecostalism 1907–1925
978-1-84227-624-2 / approx. 300pp

Haddon Willmer
Evangelicalism 1785–1835: An Essay (1962) and Reflections (2004)
Awarded the Hulsean Prize in the University of Cambridge in 1962, this interpretation of a classic period of English Evangelicalism, by a young church historian, is now supplemented by reflections on Evangelicalism from the vantage point of a retired Professor of Theology.
978-1-84227-219-0 / approx. 300pp

www.ingramcontent.com/pod-product-compliance
Lightning Source LLC
Chambersburg PA
CBHW061436300426
44114CB00014B/1708